£1-20

C000121335

SOLUTIONS
FOR WRITERS

NOVELS

The Husband
The Magician
Living Room
The Childkeeper
Other People
The Resort
The Touch of Treason
A Deniable Man
The Best Revenge

PLAYS

Napoleon (The Illegitimist)
(New York and California, 1953)

A Shadow of My Enemy
(National Theater, Washington D.C.
and Broadway, 1957)

NONFICTION

A Feast for Lawyers

SOL STEIN

SOLUTIONS FOR WRITERS

Practical Craft Techniques
for Fiction and Non-fiction

SOUVENIR PRESS

First published in the USA by
St Martin's Press, New York
under the title *Stein on Writing*

First British edition published 1998 by
Souvenir Press Ltd,
43 Great Russell Street, London WC1B 3PA

ISBN 0 285 63441 0 (casebound)
ISBN 0 285 63444 5 (paperback)

Printed and bound by WBC, Bridgend, Mid Glam.

For Liz,

who knows better,

with love

Acknowledgments

I am grateful for the experienced advice on this book, as on many of my other books, from Patricia Day and Elizabeth Day Stein. My editors at St. Martin's Press, Tom McCormack and Marian Lizzi, provided me with both encouragement and thoughtful suggestions, as did Loretta Hudson.

For their insights, I am indebted beyond easy measure to the writers famous, infamous, and not-yet-known, as well as the teachers, readers, and students with whom I shared a life of editorial work and joy, and from whom I learned much of what is between these covers.

Contents

Preface   *ix*

Part I: The Essentials

CHAPTER *1*   The Writer's Job May Be Different Than You Think   *3*
CHAPTER *2*   Come Right In: First Sentences, First Paragraphs   *15*
CHAPTER *3*   Welcome to the Twentieth Century   *42*

Part II: Fiction

CHAPTER *4*   Competing with God: Making Fascinating People   *49*
CHAPTER *5*   Markers: The Key to Swift Characterization   *74*
CHAPTER *6*   Thwarting Desire: The Basics of Plotting   *82*
CHAPTER *7*   The Actors Studio Method for Developing
Drama in Plots   *90*
CHAPTER *8*   The Crucible: A Key to Successful Plotting   *94*
CHAPTER *9*   Suspense: Keeping the Reader Reading   *97*
CHAPTER *10*   The Adrenaline Pump: Creating Tension   *105*
CHAPTER *11*   The Secrets of Good Dialogue   *110*
CHAPTER *12*   How to Show Instead of Tell   *122*
CHAPTER *13*   Choosing a Point of View   *129*
CHAPTER *14*   Flashbacks: How to Bring Background into
the Foreground   *143*
CHAPTER *15*   The Keys to Credibility   *152*
CHAPTER *16*   The Secret Snapshot Technique: Reaching For
Hidden Treasure   *156*
CHAPTER *17*   How to Use All Six of Your Senses   *160*
CHAPTER *18*   Love Scenes   *167*
CHAPTER *19*   Creating the Envelope   *186*

Part III: Fiction and Nonfiction

CHAPTER *20*   Amphetamines for Speeding Up Pace   *193*
CHAPTER *21*   Liposuctioning Flab   *197*

Contents

CHAPTER 22   Tapping Your Originality   209
CHAPTER 23   The Door to Your Book: Titles That Attract   212

Part IV: Nonfiction

CHAPTER 24   Using the Techniques of Fiction to
             Enhance Nonfiction   223
CHAPTER 25   Conflict, Suspense, and Tension in Nonfiction   232
CHAPTER 26   Quoting What They Say   240
CHAPTER 27   Guts: The Decisive Ingredient   242

Part V: Literary Values in Fiction and Nonfiction

CHAPTER 28   Commercial? Popular? Literary?   249
CHAPTER 29   Particularity   254
CHAPTER 30   Similes and Metaphors   264
CHAPTER 31   Increasing the Effect on the Reader
             through Resonance   268

Part VI: Revision

CHAPTER 32   Triage: A Better Way of Revising Fiction   277
CHAPTER 33   Reprieve: Revising Nonfiction   290

Part VII: Where to Get Help

CHAPTER 34   Where to Get Help   297
             For British Readers   302
CHAPTER 35   A Final Word   305

A Glossary of Terms Used by Writers and Editors   307

Preface

Some years ago I addressed the Southern California Chapter of the National Writers Club on a day when a rowboat might have been more appropriate than a car for getting to the meeting. The torrential rain seemed determined to widen the Pacific Ocean at the expense of a state that was once described to me as "mostly desert." I managed the few hundred feet between the parking lot and the hotel without drowning. Once inside, I expected to find the meeting room deserted. Instead I happily discovered a full house, eighty-eight professional nonfiction writers and journalists come to hear me talk about fiction. I asked these weather-proof stalwarts, "How many of you want to write the Great American Novel?" and eighty-eight hands shot up.

If there are writers in America who do not have several hundred pages of a would-be novel in a drawer or at least in mind, I have not met them. Conversely, every novelist I've known has occasion to write nonfiction. For those writers who, at least initially, want to read only about fiction or nonfiction, I offer a road map to this book.

The Contents page provides an overview of the main subjects covered. Part I, "The Essentials," is for all writers. Part II concerns the craft of fiction. Eavesdropping by nonfiction writers is permitted. Part III deals with subjects of interest to all writers. Part IV deals mainly with the application of fictional techniques for the enhancement of nonfiction. Part V, "Literary Values," deals with upscale writing, both fiction and nonfiction. Part VI, "Revision," has separate chapters for fiction and nonfiction. Part VII contains a chapter on where to get help, a final word, and a glossary of terms used by writers and editors.

The reader will find that I frequently use examples from writers I have known or worked with because their material is familiar to me. From time to time I also quote from my own work, allegedly for copyright reasons and convenience, but perhaps also to underscore that I practice what I teach. If I quote often from the *New York Times*, it is convenience as well as merit that guides me; it is the newspaper I read every day. The *Times* has also been in the vanguard of publications using the techniques of fiction to enhance journalism.

Preface

Women usually outnumber men among my students, readers, and friends, and I trust they will forgive me for using a male pronoun to stand for both genders. Saying "he or she" repeatedly is a distraction to both writer and reader.

I once went to a convention in Seattle, and three people gave me gifts of an umbrella for the trip. It didn't rain. I hope this book has a few surprises for you.

Sol Stein
Scarborough, New York
May 1995

I

The Essentials

1

The Writer's Job May Be Different Than You Think

This is not a book of theory. It is a book of usable solutions—how to fix writing that is flawed, how to improve writing that is good, how to create interesting writing in the first place.

For thirty-six years I worked one-on-one with writers who had contract deadlines. My primary interest was to provide them with the techniques for solving editorial problems and improving their work in time to meet their deadlines. I could not provide writers with new genes, an ear, or talent. What I passed on was the craft other writers had developed to get their manuscripts in shape for publication.

As an editor and publisher, I frequently heard that an editor's job was to help the writer realize his intentions. That is true except for the fact that many writers have inappropriate intentions. The four most common I've heard are "I am expressing myself"; "I have something to say"; "I want to be loved by readers"; and "I need money." Those are all occasional outcomes of the correct intention, which is to provide the reader with an experience that is superior to the experiences the reader encounters in everyday life. If the reader is also rewarded with insights, it is not always the result of the writer's wisdom but of the writer's ability to create the conditions that enable pleasure to edify.

The writer comes to the editor bearing his talent, experience, and hope for his manuscript. The editor provides distance, experience with other writers, and the tools of craft that are efficient substitutes for trial and error. I have had the good fortune to work with some of the most successful writers of our time. They had much to teach me. What they taught and what they may have learned is in this book.

As a young writer brimming with hope and arrogance, I was subjected, luckily, to the wisdom and tyranny of several extraordinary teachers of writing: Wilmer Stone, Theodore Goodman, Jacques Barzun, Lionel Trilling, and Thornton Wilder. I would like to convey the most important thing I learned from each.

Wilmer Stone was faculty advisor to *The Magpie*, the literary magazine of DeWitt Clinton High School in the Bronx, New York, then one of the best-known public secondary schools in the United States. In those remarkable days, DeWitt Clinton served not only its neighborhood but qualified students from anywhere else in the vastness of New York City. One of them was James Baldwin, who, each school day, took the long subway ride from Harlem in Manhattan to DeWitt Clinton at the topmost part of the Bronx. Out of our adolescent camaraderie came his most extraordinary book, *Notes of a Native Son*, which he much later would claim I compelled him to publish.

Each Friday afternoon at three, while other students decamped for their homes, the lights were on in the *Magpie* tower high above the rectangle of the school. There Wilmer Stone met with Richard Avedon, then a poet, who became one of the most famous photographers in the world, the editor Emile Capouya, Jimmy Baldwin, myself, and a few others whose names hide behind the scrim of time. What went on in that tower was excruciatingly painful. Wilmer Stone read our stories to us in a monotone as if he were reading from the pages of a phone directory. What we learned with each stab of pain was that the words themselves and not the inflections supplied by the reader had to carry the emotion of the story.

Today I still hear the metronome of Wilmer Stone's voice, and counsel my students to have their drafts read to them by the friend who has the least talent for acting and is capable of reading words as if they had no meaning.

My family was depression-poor, and the only college I could try for was one whose expense would be as close to zero as possible. In those days the College of the City of New York, better known as CCNY, took in the top fifteen percent of New York City high school graduates, whose only expense would be secondhand books and subway fare. There Theodore Goodman's reputation was such that all who had a craving to write gravitated toward his classes. To teach short story writing, he had us read James Joyce's "The Dead" over and over. It was from this practice that I learned the value of dissecting a piece of writing repeatedly until it surrendered its secrets.

The most important thing I took away from Teddy Goodman came about at the beginning of the one private conference each student was entitled to. I was by then a head taller than Goodman, but he was Napoleon to us all. He glared at me and said, "Look how you're dressed."

I looked down and could see only what I had seen in the mirror that morning, the suit and shirt and tie that was customary for students at the time.

"Your suit is blue," he said. "Your shirt is blue, your tie is blue. That's what's wrong with your writing."

When my ordeal was over I slunk away from Goodman's cubicle to rethink the sameness of my writing and to learn the value of variety. It took some time for me to learn the other lesson, that a writer, shy or not, needs a tough skin, for no matter how advanced one's experience and career, expert criticism cuts to the quick, and one learns to endure and to perfect, if for no other reason than to challenge the pain-maker.

The master's seminar I attended at Columbia University was with William York Tindall, who continued Goodman's process of closely examining a single piece of work to teach us how to read other works. That seminar created an appetite for what was then quite possibly the best-known doctoral seminar in America, led in discordant concert by two extraordinary men, Jacques Barzun and Lionel Trilling, both of whom left their marks in writing as well as teaching.

The official title of the seminar was "Backgrounds in Contemporary Thought and Culture." Its true subject was "So you think you know how to write? Let's see." It was a tough course to get into. Thirty-five were selected, and only eight students survived the academic year. Each week we had to read a designated book and write a piece about it. The piece would come under as close a scrutiny as any editor ever gave a work.

A cocky Sol Stein thought he would trick his advisors and submitted a typed version of an article of his that had already been published as the lead piece in an academic journal. Barzun and Trilling skewered my prose with almost as much comment in the margins as I had on the page. What had been acceptable to the magazine was not acceptable to their higher standard. What I learned from my destroyed work were the two simple objectives of all prose writing, to be clear and to be precise. Precision and clarity became my watchwords, my guides to self-correction, and my most prized editing tools, especially six or seven years later when I was editing the work of both Barzun and Trilling for the *Mid-Century* magazine.

I was a playwright long before I became a novelist. In 1952, a year before I saw my first play on stage, I was granted back-to-back playwriting fellowships at Yaddo, the artists' colony in Saratoga Springs, New York, and the McDowell Colony in Peterborough, New Hampshire. To my astonishment, my employer, the U.S. State Department, granted me leave for both. At Yaddo, I occupied what was known as the Carson McCullers cottage, though the vibrations came not from the spirit of Carson McCullers but from two thousand bees whose colony was embedded in the hollow wall. On arriving at McDowell, I was given an even greater surprise for a young playwright. Though most of the people there were composers and painters, there was one other playwright, Thornton Wilder. What a mind-walloping opportunity: one of the most accomplished American playwrights of the century and a neophyte working on his first play in the same environment!

Thornton Wilder taught me two things. First, the necessity of sitting through bad plays, to witness coughing and squirming in the audience, to have ears up like a rabbit to catch what didn't work, to observe how little tolerance an audience has for a mishap, ten seconds of boredom breaking an hour-long spell. I was soon to take advantage of the New Dramatists Committee, an organization that enabled me to see free of charge some sixty plays in less than two years. I learned more from the painfully bad than from the few remarkable plays that kept me enthralled. Today, I urge my students once they have begun to master craft, to read a few chapters of John Grisham's *The Firm*, or some other transient bestseller, to see what they can learn from the mistakes of writers who don't heed the precise meanings of the words they use. They also learn to read the work of literary prize-winners to detect the rare uncaught error in craft. What they are doing is perfecting their editorial eye and their self-editing talent, learning to read as a writer.

Wilder taught me something else. He took me to watch a country square dance from an unoccupied balcony in a recreation hall, and pointed out things that writers are supposed to see. The New Hampshire folk came to dances in families—mothers, fathers, and adolescent children. As we watched from the balcony, Wilder pointed out the barely noticeable sexual interplay between fathers and daughters and mothers and sons as they danced the evening away. In the fifties, a dull age in which so much was forbidden, Wilder taught me that what a writer deals with is the unspoken, what people see or sense in silence. It is our job, in nonfiction as well as fiction, to juxtapose words that reveal what previously may have been blinked, and provide insights obscured by convention and shame.

*   *   *

The century I have inhabited has not seen the abandonment of war and violence. It has not solved the problem of poverty, nor has it improved human nature. However, we can credit the century with producing the public realization that sex has to be good for both partners. That is also the key to writing both fiction and nonfiction. It has to be a good experience for both partners, the writer and the reader, and it is a source of distress to me to observe how frequently writers ignore the pleasure of their partners.

The pleasures of writer and reader are interwoven. The seasoned writer of both nonfiction and fiction, confident in his craft, derives increasing pleasure from his work. The reader in the hands of a writer who has mastered his craft enjoys a richer experience.

When I ask a group of professional writers to state the essential difference between nonfiction and fiction, most are unable to do so. And when they try, an audience of one hundred will provide answers so disparate as to seem to come from a hundred different planets rather than common experience. Let us state the difference in the simplest way.

Nonfiction conveys information.

Fiction evokes emotion.

Because the intended results are so different, the mind-sets required for writing fiction and nonfiction are different. In fiction, when information obtrudes the experience of the story pauses. Raw information comes across as an interruption, the author filling in. The fiction writer must avoid anything that distracts from the experience even momentarily. A failure to understand this difference between nonfiction and fiction is a major reason for the rejection of novels.

Though the ostensible purpose of nonfiction is the conveyance of information, if that information is in a raw state, the writing seems pedestrian, black-and-white facts in a colorful world. The reader, soon bored, yearns for the images, anecdotes, characterization, and writerly precision that make informational writing come alive on the page. That is where the techniques of fiction can be so helpful to the nonfiction writer.

Over many years I have observed that the failure of story writers is often attributable to an incontrovertible fact. We are all writers from an early age. Most of what we write is nonfiction—essays for school, letters to friends, memoranda to colleagues—in which we are trying to pass on information. We are raised with a traditional nonfiction mind-set. Even when we write love letters, we are trying to communicate how we feel and not necessarily trying to evoke an emotion in the recipient, though that might be better suited to our purpose.

In previous centuries, when letter writing was more often than today a form of personal art, letters had more of an emotional effect on readers, even those to whom the writing was not addressed, as we know from reading some of the great correspondence that has been collected in books.

The lifelong habit of writing traditional nonfiction, passing on information, is curable through attention to the fiction writer's primary job, which is creating *an emotional experience for the reader*. The novelist is like the conductor of an orchestra, his back to the audience, his face invisible, summoning the experience of music for the people he cannot see. The writer as conductor also gets to compose the music and play all of the instruments, a task less formidable than it seems. What it requires is the conscious practice of providing an extraordinary experience for the reader, who should be oblivious to the fact that he is seeing words on paper.

A second matter insinuates itself between the writer and success. All of us, in our daily speech to others, are not only trying to communicate information but to get something off our minds and into the consciousness of the listeners. When we write, we put down on paper what we think, know, or believe we know and pay little attention to the effect on the reader. That is discourteous in life and unsuccessful in writing.

We practice our craft to service the reader, not our psyches. The material we deal with may come from our observation and insight. As writers we don't expel the result as raw material, we transmute it to provide what the reader most wants, an experience different from and richer than what he daily abides in life. As E. L. Doctorow once put it, "Good writing is supposed to evoke sensation in the reader, not the fact that it's raining, but the feeling of being rained upon."

The good news is that the nonfiction mind-set has been changing. In recent years, ambitious journalists and writers of nonfiction books have increasingly adopted some of the techniques of fiction to enhance the readers' experience of their writing. In journalism, the change has been revolutionary. In the early part of the twentieth century, journalists were taught to provide readers with the who, what, when, where, and why of their stories in the first paragraph. The result was the reader read the first paragraph and, sated, moved on to the first paragraph of the next story. How frustrating it must have been for journalists writing pieces of ten or fifteen or twenty paragraphs, finding readers skipping away after the first. Today, the best of good journalists are arousing their readers' curiosity in the first paragraph and seducing them into the rest of the story. A news story has become a story that contains the news.

In television, where new programs are frequent and often short-lived, one exemplar of broadcast journalism that has lasted more than a quarter of a century is *60 Minutes*, which weekly holds an audience of tens of millions. Its creator, Don Hewitt, tells us, "TV is good not when you see it or hear it but when you feel it." Though it deals in fact, *60 Minutes*, like fiction, is concerned with evoking the emotions of its audience.

Don Hewitt's creation thrives on the revelation of character. Its interviewers peel layers of camouflage to reveal matters that its subjects would rather conceal, it uncovers cover-ups, it causes people to speak of things that are revelatory, incriminating, or painful. The segments often bring out the dark side of human nature, which at times excites its audience's interest in the opposite, justice and goodwill. It does, in other words, what creative writing aspires to.

It should not be surprising that *60 Minutes* has had imitators that do not imitate well, programs of scandal and gossip laden with sentimentality and cloaked in melodrama. An unfortunate amount of so-called transient fiction does the same thing.

Though the new nonfiction uses some of the techniques of fiction, important differences exist. Nonfiction stems from fact, and all attempts to evoke emotion in its readership cannot—or at least should not—take leave from its roots. It can make us feel what happened, but dares not invent what happened. Nonfiction can describe effectively what people do and thereby move us, but it cannot invent those actions. Nonfiction can report what people say, but it cannot guess what they were thinking. To help us understand the essential difference between nonfiction and fiction, let's look at an example:

TRADITIONAL NONFICTION: New York City has more than 1,400 homeless people.

BETTER NONFICTION: The man who has laid claim to the bench on the corner of 88th Street and Park Avenue is one of New York City's 1,400 homeless people.

FICTION: His skin the color of rust, the man sits on his park bench next to his bag of belongings, staring at the brightly lit windows in the apartments across the street, at the strange race of people who still have hope.

In the transition from plain fact to fiction, we lose statistics and focus on the individual character. The writer, having invented the character, can convey what the character thinks.

To orient us, consider for a moment the relationship between the writer, the book, and the reader. The writer, of course, writes the book. The book then acts on the reader's mind and emotions, unseen by the writer. In fact when the writer finishes his work, he can vanish from the earth and his book will continue to affect the reader's mind and emotions. The writer becomes dispensable. The work must do the job.

Can a novelist or story writer work on the reader's emotions consciously while writing a first draft? Not easily, except through long practice and prowess. But the less experienced writer can *plan* the reader's adventure before he writes each scene, and in revising that scene after a respite away from it, with the steel gaze of an editor he can see how the reader's experience might be improved.

What of the nonfiction writer who sees himself solely as the communicator of fact, who is offended by the idea of working on the emotions of his audience? We sometimes speak of academic writing, of courtroom transcripts, of material that does not compel our attention or elicit a strong desire to continue reading, as *dry*. What we mean by "dry" is that it does not enable us to see as we read, it does not move us, and, most important, it does not stimulate our intellect with insight, its ostensible purpose. The writers of thousands of academic articles and books each year, of hundreds of thousands of legal papers and millions of business memoranda, are discourteous to their readers and fail in their purpose. They do not understand the power of language or the techniques for its use.

Isn't there something distasteful in evoking the emotions of an audience? Some of the great villains of our age have been spellbinders, working the public's emotions. In old newsreels we see Hitler in the Nuremberg stadium or Mussolini on his balcony building frenzy in an audience that has abdicated sense for sensation. But we are moved by heroes as well, often as a result of war: Lincoln, Churchill, Roosevelt. Their effect lies in the language they are cloaked in. Let us consider for a moment the most admired of the three. The historian Shelby Foote reminds us, "Lincoln was highly intelligent. Almost everything he did was calculated for effect." That statement is one no writer should ever forget. "Almost everything he did was calculated for effect."

We like to think of ourselves as moved to action by facts and reason, yet we shrink from politicians who may have got their facts right but who bore us with language that is flat, cliché-ridden, robbed of effectiveness by their unimaginative prose. They want us to agree; what we feel is utter boredom. Researchers, scientists, academicians marshal their facts to a higher standard, but with their neglect of the emotive power of language they often speak only to each other, their parochial words dropping like sand on a private desert.

Despite our alleged reverence for fact, the truth is that our adrenaline rises most in response to effective expression. When a writer or speaker understands the electricity of fresh simile and metaphor, his choice of words empowers our feelings, his language compels our attention, acceptance, and action. When Shakespeare speaks, when Lincoln orates, we are moved not by information but by the excellence of their diction. Alone in a living room, our book lit by a chair-side lamp, we are enraptured by what is said because of the author's choice of words and their order on the page. The best of good writing will entice us into subjects and knowledge we would have declared were of no interest to us until we were seduced by the language they were dressed in.

This book encompasses both modes of writing, fiction and nonfiction. The practitioners of each have differing attitudes. In my experience, most novelists and short story writers are eager to improve their craft, even after they have been published many times. Nonfiction writers who do not have to create living characters are sometimes complacent about a craft in which publication comes easier and is paid for with greater regularity. This book may inspire some nonfiction writers to reach for treasure on a higher shelf.

Fiction and nonfiction both can benefit from the writer's imagination as well as his memory. For the story writer, witnessing—or remembering—incidents in life must be more than an act of reporting. It is the taking-off point not of what happened, but of what might have happened. That is what enables some fiction to provide us with an experience that we characterize as extraordinary.

Reporting in nonfiction can be accurate, like a photograph taken merely to record. The best of nonfiction, however, sets what it sees in a framework, what has happened elsewhere or in the past. As the recorded events march before us, a scrim lifts to convey another dimension, the highlighting focuses our attention, sight becomes insight, reporting becomes art. The evidence is in this book.

For the writer who intends to master his craft, I have a small-craft warning.

Imagine yourself as a youngster standing beside a bicycle for the first time. You watched someone riding this two-wheeled vehicle in a straight line. You may have wondered how the rider kept his balance, why the bicycle didn't tip over. At your side is an experienced bicyclist who tells you how it's done. You learn that by holding the handlebars steady and pedaling fast the bicycle moves forward without tipping. You are told that by steering gently with the handlebars, turning the front wheel in the direction you want to go, you can manipulate the vehicle elegantly, avoiding pedestrians and other obstacles, as long as you keep pedaling. If you stop pedaling or even slow too much, the bicycle will become unstable, wobbly, and your control of it will loosen until the bicycle will sway to one side and start to fall. You learn that to halt you have to press the hand brakes just so and be prepared to lower a leg for stability as you come to a stop.

Those are the essentials of cycling, but it doesn't mean you can ride a bicycle. What you need is practice. You learn to coordinate your movements. You discover how rapidly you have to rotate the pedals in order to keep the bicycle moving, and how to redirect the handlebars gradually to turn a corner. Only with repetition do you find out how to slow down and stop without tipping over. Once you master riding, what you have learned will stay with you for the rest of your life. You may abandon the bicycle for an automobile, then years later take it up for exercise and find that in moments you are rolling ahead, fully coordinated, your brain responding to what you learned in your practice sessions long ago.

It is the same with writing.

Except that writers provide themselves with a monumental obstacle to achieving skill. Ballet dancers practice technique. Pianists wear down their black and white keys with hours of daily practice. Actors rehearse, and rehearse again. Painters perfect still-life objects at various angles, practice obtaining the best perspectives, experiment with color and texture, do sketches in preparation for oil. By practice one learns to use what one has understood. Only writers, it seems, expect to achieve some level of mastery without practice.

Do all writers resist the techniques that will help them master their craft? No. Some, eager to get published, seize on the advice of anybody with an authoritative title or a persuasive personality. Others find excuses for not writing at the same time every day, balk at re-revising incessantly, or excuse themselves because their lives are beset by difficulties. I am deaf to that excuse because I worked with the most disadvantaged writer in history, Christy Brown, who had the use of his brain, the little toe on his left foot, and little else. When he was a seemingly helpless baby lying on the kitchen floor of a cottage in Ireland, his remarkable mother saw him reach out with his left foot and with his one good toe manage to pick up a crayon that one of his siblings had dropped. That was the beginning of a writer. Eventually someone at IBM made a special typewriter for Christy that enabled him to punch in a letter at a time with his one working toe. I published five of Christy Brown's books, one of which made the national bestseller lists. I urge you to see the video of a remarkable film called *My Left Foot*. It won an Oscar for Daniel Day-Lewis, who played Christy. The film may cure you of fishing for an excuse for not writing.

Once in California I had a letter from a nonfiction writer who wanted desperately to write fiction but wondered if at sixty she was too old to begin. I told her that Elia Kazan was fifty-seven when he started with fiction and that I had published four active octogenarians in a single year, the lexicographer Eric Partridge, J. B. Priestley, Hannah Tillich, and Bertram Wolfe. If you're a writer, you are never retired by someone else. You not only keep going, but the very act of writing helps keep you alive.

More than half a millennium ago, Chaucer, the great English writer of the Middle Ages, had this to say about the writer's work:

> The lyf so short, the craft so long to lerne,
> Th'assay so hard, so sharp the conquering.

Life is short, Chaucer is telling us, the craft takes long to learn, the work is hard, but ah, when it is right, the writer's triumph soars. Few among contemporary writers have expressed that pleasure as well as Kate Braverman did about finishing her remarkable short story "Tall Tales from the Mekong Delta":

> Writing is like hunting. There are brutally cold afternoons with nothing in sight, only the wind and your breaking heart. Then the moment when you bag something big. The entire process is beyond intoxicating. As soon as Lenny began speaking, I knew I had mainlined it. I felt like I was strapped in the cockpit with the stars in my face and the expanding universe on my back. In my opinion, that's the only way a writer should travel. When I finished "Tall Tales" I thought, this one is a keeper. This is a trophy brought back from the further realm, the kingdom of perpetual glistening night where we know ourselves absolutely. This one goes on the wall.

13

As you perfect your craft through practice, remember the joy of finally getting on a bicycle and riding to your destination without giving a second thought to the technique that now comes naturally. Experience the pleasure of getting the right word, the right phrase, the right sentence, the right paragraph, and finally the ecstasy of creating a keeper for your wall.

2

Come Right In:
First Sentences, First Paragraphs

Elia Kazan, brilliant director of stage and screen as well as a late-blooming novelist, told me that audiences give a film seven minutes. If the viewer is not intrigued by character or incident within that time, the film and its viewer are at odds. The viewer came for an experience. The film is disappointing him.

Today's impatient readers give a novelist fewer than seven minutes. Some years ago I was involved in an informal study of the behavior of lunch-hour browsers in mid-Manhattan bookstores. In the fiction section, the most common pattern was for the browser to read the front flap of the book's jacket and then go to page one. No browser went beyond page three before either taking the book to the cashier or putting the book down and picking up another to sample.

Thereafter, whenever an author told me that his novel really got going on page ten or twenty or thirty, I had to pass on the news that his book in all likelihood was doomed unless he could revise it so that the first three pages aroused the reader's interest enough to quarantine him from distraction for the several hours the book demanded from him.

Readers have not grown more patient since that bit of research was conducted. Today, first sentences and first paragraphs of any writing are increasingly important for arousing the restless reader.

Arousal is nature's stimulus for the propagation of the human race. The unaroused male of the species is as useless for that purpose as a worm. Arousal can happen sooner or later, but it must happen.

Similarly arousal is an author's stimulus for the reader. Without early arousal, the reader does not yet trust that he will enjoy the experience that the writer has prepared. The ideal goals of an opening paragraph are:

1. To excite the reader's curiosity, preferably about a character or a relationship.
2. To introduce a setting.
3. To lend resonance to the story.

Long before I edited a couple of Budd Schulberg's books, he published his first novel, *What Makes Sammy Run?*, a book whose opening I like to quote from. *Sammy* was a huge bestseller in 1941. This is the way it starts:

> The first time I saw him he couldn't have been more than sixteen years old, a little ferret of a kid, sharp and quick. Sammy Glick. Used to run copy for me. Always ran. Always looked thirsty.

To prove that writers know what works even if they don't take advantage of their knowledge in their own writing, I ask my students to pick out the most important word in Schulberg's opening. See if you can't find it in the paragraph just quoted.

Most writers quickly come up with the correct answer: "ferret." It characterizes sixteen-year-old Sammy in a flash.

Next I ask for the second most important word in that paragraph. See if you can't detect it.

That may take a bit more time, but after a moment's thought a majority will zero in on "thirsty," an original way of saying Sammy was hungry, meaning ambitious.

The words "always ran" convey quickly that Sammy is a hustler.

That opening is an inspiring example of quick characterization and especially of a way to arouse the reader's interest because in a few words we sense a conflict brewing. The narrator knows Sammy is overly ambitious. The kid wants what? Everything!

Therein lies a clue. As readers, we are immediately interested in a character who wants something badly.

The fact that the narrator is Sammy's boss also piques the reader's curiosity. Will the narrator continue to put up with Sammy's drive? Will Sammy get fired? Will Sammy succeed, and if so at what and how will he do it? The story is off and running in the first paragraph. We want to know what will happen.

At the time that Schulberg wrote *What Makes Sammy Run?* he wasn't an old master. He was a young first novelist. If one understands the principles of intriguing the reader, one doesn't need decades of experience.

James T. Farrell, a friend who achieved fame for his novel *Studs Lonigan*, once gave me a copy of a collection of his short stories called *French Girls Are Vicious,* in which the title story contains an interesting example for writers. The narrator begins, "I don't like French girls. Perhaps it's because of my Puritan upbringing . . ."

We assume the speaker is a man. At the beginning of the second paragraph a surprise is waiting for us. The narrator is a woman! Our curiosity is aroused when a surprise unsettles our expectation.

It is astonishing how much the first words of a novel or story affect editors, reviewers, and readers. They are the trigger of curiosity, what writers have long called the "narrative hook." In addition, the early words suggest the kind of book one is reading.

Thornton Wilder, my early mentor in playwriting, also wrote novels, the most famous of which, *The Bridge of San Luis Rey*, starts this way:

> On Friday noon, July the twentieth, 1714, the finest bridge in all
> Peru broke and precipitated five travelers into the gulf below.

It's precise as to date and time and the number of people. But the key to arousing our interest is in the words "finest bridge." Bridges deteriorate. Many are hazardous. But this bridge that suddenly hurtled five people to their death was "the finest." We want to know what happened, and why.

Here's another:

> Yank Lucas fell asleep late one night and left the gas burning on the
> kitchen range.

We want to know more. That's the opening of John O'Hara's 1967 novel, *The Instrument*.

James Baldwin began his short story "Going to Meet the Man" with this unembellished way of interesting the reader:

> "What's the matter?" she asked.

Here's a quieter—yet intriguing—opening sentence by one of the century's grand masters, Graham Greene, from an early (1935) novel, *England Made Me*.

> She might have been waiting for her lover.

Maxine Hong Kingston kindled the reader's interest in *The Woman Warrior* with the kind of hook that almost always works:

> "You must not tell anyone," my mother said, "what I am about to tell you."

See how much Irwin Shaw accomplished in the first sentence of his story "The Eighty-Yard Run":

> The pass was high and wide and he jumped for it, feeling it slap flatly against his hands, as he shook his hips to throw off the half-back who was diving at him.

Anthony Burgess, in both his fiction and nonfiction, enjoyed shocking the reader into attention. The following attention-getter is the opening of his twenty-second novel, *Earthly Powers*:

> It was the afternoon of my eighty-first birthday, and I was in bed with my catamite when Ali announced the archbishop had come to see me.

That first sentence tells us the narrator is old, that he is in bed with some-one of the same sex, that this is a regular event in his life, and the event this day is being interrupted by a visit from an archbishop! That certainly piques the reader's curiosity about what kind of confrontation is about to happen.
    Another example:

> On the day he lost his right foot, Walter Van Brunt had been haunted, however haphazardly, by ghosts of the past.

Losing a foot is not an everyday occurrence. From the first sentence we know we are going to witness an important day in the life of Walter Van Brunt. Moreover, Van Brunt is haunted by "ghosts of the past." Who or what are they? The interjection—"however haphazardly"—conveys a touch of literary flavor. Would a commercial action-adventure author ever say "however haphazardly"?
    That's a lot to get from a first sentence. It's from a 1987 novel, *World's End*, by T. Coraghessan Boyle, who has been called "one of the most gifted writers of his generation."

Saul Bellow, winner of the Nobel Prize for Literature, most often uses characterization to attract a reader's attention. Here are the opening sentences of four of his novels:

> When it came to concealing his troubles, Tommy Wilhelm was not less capable than the next fellow.

> What made me take this trip to Africa?

> If I am out of my mind, it's all right with me, thought Moses Herzog.

> Shortly after dawn, or what would have been dawn in a normal sky, Mr. Artur Sammler with his bushy eye took in the books and papers of his West Side bedroom and suspected strongly that they were the wrong books, the wrong papers.

In order, the openings are from Bellow's first novel, *Seize the Day; Henderson the Rain King*, his most celebrated novel; *Herzog;* and *Mr. Sammler's Planet*. Note that all of Bellow's beginnings except *Henderson* seize the attention of the reader by characterization, which we get soon enough.

All right, you say, these are well-known writers, prize-winning writers, what about writers like me? Fair enough. Here are some first sentences from work by students of mine who have yet to publish:

> I wanted to strangle mother but I'd have to touch her to do it.

That's by Loretta Hudson. The narrator wants to perform an act that is taboo and punishable, but what causes the reaction of the reader is the countervailing force, the repugnance at having to touch the person you want to strangle. I have heard audiences gasp when that opening sentence is read to them.

The same student started a story with an entirely different hook in the first sentence:

> It would have been nice if the stork had dropped me down the right chimney.

That visual opening presents the narrator's problem—the wrong parents!—in an attention-grabbing way. How abstract the beginning would have sounded had the author started, "I was born to the wrong parents."

Here's one by another beginner:

> A telephone ringing in the middle of the night is not a welcome
> sound.

What should be clear by now is that writers with differing skills and
experiences have all tried to engage the reader's curiosity at the outset. There are questions you can ask yourself about your own first sentence:

- Does it convey an interesting personality or an action that we want
  to know more about?
- Can you make your first sentence more intriguing by introducing
  something unusual, something shocking perhaps, or something
  that will surprise the reader?

Your entire story or novel may depend on that first sentence arresting the
reader's attention. A terrific sentence on page two won't help if the
reader never gets there.

Is it absolutely essential for the first sentence to hook the reader? The
first sentence of the next example is a simple statement of the narrator's
name. The rest of the paragraph appears on the surface to be conventional, but is it? It's from the title story of John Cheever's short story
collection *The Housebreaker of Shady Hill.**

> My name is Johnny Hake. I'm thirty-six years old, stand five feet
> eleven in my socks, weigh one hundred and forty-two pounds
> stripped, and am, so to speak, naked at the moment and talking into
> the dark. I was conceived in the Hotel St. Regis, born in the Pres-
> byterian Hospital, raised on Sutton Place, christened and confirmed
> in St. Bartholomew's, and I drilled with the Knickerbocker Greys,
> played football and baseball in Central Park, learned to chin myself
> on the framework of East Side apartment-house canopies, and met
> my wife (Christina Lewis) at one of those big cotillions at the Wal-
> dorf. I served four years in the Navy, have four kids now, and live

* "The Housebreaker on Shady Hill" has always held a special interest for me because I've lived
in that house for more than thirty years. I hasten to add we are not the people in that house. The
house on Shady Hill is not the house Johnny Hake lives in. It is the house he steals from in the
story.

in a banlieue called Shady Hill. We have a nice house with a garden and a place outside for cooking meat, and on summer nights, sitting there with the kids and looking into the front of Christina's dress as she bends over to salt the steaks, or just gazing at the lights in Heaven, I am thrilled by more hardy and dangerous pursuits, and I guess this is what is meant by the pain and sweetness of life.

You can't be more direct than that. There's Johnny Hake encapsulating his life for the reader. Cheever, however, is a sly craftsman. In the first sentence his character lets drop that he is "naked at the moment and talking into the dark." Not the kind of thing you'd put into a résumé. A few more sentences and he's "looking into the front of Christina's dress as she bends over to salt the steaks." That's in the middle of a sentence, seemingly a throwaway, but in fact a hook for the reader. A craftsman like Cheever will season even the most conventional beginning with just enough that is unconventional to rouse the reader's curiosity.

John Fowles is one of the more accomplished novelists of this century. His career began in 1963 with the publication of a relatively simple novel called *The Collector*. If you haven't read it, I urge you to. Let's look at how he starts the book:

> When she was home from her boarding school I used to see her almost every day sometimes, because their house was right opposite the Town Hall Annex. She and her younger sister used to go in and out a lot, often with young men, which of course I didn't like.

The end of the second sentence is the first omen of what proves to be an exceptionally suspenseful book. Let's see how the first paragraph continues:

> When I had a free moment from the files and ledgers I stood by the window and used to look down over the road over the frosting and sometimes I'd see her. In the evening I marked it in my observations diary, at first with X, and then when I knew her name with M. I saw her several times outside too. I stood right behind her once in a queue at the public library down Crossfield Street. She didn't look once at me, but I watched the back of her head and her hair in a long pigtail. It was very pale, silky, like Burnet cocoons. All in

one pigtail coming down almost to her waist, sometimes in front, sometimes at the back. Sometimes she wore it up. Only once, before she came to be my guest here, did I have the privilege to see her with it loose and it took my breath away it was so beautiful, like a mermaid.

That first long paragraph introduces the two main characters, the narrator and his victim. Note the amount of concrete detail. I will reproduce that paragraph, highlighting the ominous phrases.

When she was home from her boarding school I used to see her almost every day sometimes, because their house was right opposite the Town Hall Annex. She and her younger sister used to go in and out a lot, often with young men, **which of course I didn't like**. When I had a free moment from the files and ledgers I stood by the window and used to look down over the road over the frosting and sometimes I'd see her. In the evening **I marked it in my observations diary, at first with X, and then when I knew her name with M**. I saw her several times outside too. I stood right behind once in a queue at the public library down Crossfield Street. She didn't look once at me, but I watched the back of her head and her hair in a long pigtail. It was very pale, silky, like Burnet cocoons. All in one pigtail coming down almost to her waist, sometimes in front, sometimes at the back. Sometimes she wore it up. Only once, **before she came to be my guest here**, did I have the privilege to see her with it loose and it took my breath away it was so beautiful, like a mermaid.

As readers, what do we take away from that first paragraph?

- The narrator didn't like "M" seeing other young men, though she didn't even know him!
- He kept an "observations diary." He found out her name.
- Once he stood right behind her. She didn't notice him, but he was studying her hair as if he were preparing to become her lover.
- And "she came to be my guest"? What she becomes is his prisoner!

An even more sly craftsman is Vladimir Nabokov. Here's the beginning of his most famous novel:

Lolita, light of my life, fire of my loins. My sin, my soul. Lo-lee-ta: the tip of the tongue taking a trip of three steps down the palate to tap, at three, on the teeth. Lo. Lee. Ta.

The second paragraph continues:

She was Lo, plain Lo, in the morning, standing four feet ten in one sock. She was Lola in slacks. She was Dolly at school. She was Dolores on the dotted line. But in my arms she was always Lolita.

That's ostensibly the first paragraph of Vladimir Nabokov's *Lolita*, which created a sensation when it was published in 1955. "Ostensibly" because we find there's a Foreword in front of the novel signed by one John Ray, Jr., Ph.D. Nabokov liked to have fun with his audience, and so in front of the book proper, he planted a mock Foreword supposedly written by a scholar. That Foreword is as intriguing as the beginning of the actual book. It describes the book as a confession, tells us the book's author died in prison, uses concrete specifics—a diagnosis, a date, a lawyer's name—and lets drop that the writer of the foreword was himself awarded a prize for a modest work in which "certain morbid states and perversions" were discussed. We might say that Nabokov began *Lolita* twice, and both beginnings, in different ways, were designed to excite the interest of the reader.

The opening paragraphs of *Lolita* proper—the announcing of the sounds of her name and the revelation that the protagonist is having an affair with a schoolgirl—pulls the reader in two ways: Scandalous subject matter and the immediate sense that here is a writer who plays with language artfully.

I thought it might be useful to follow a writer's thoughts as he developed a first paragraph. I am not psychic. The experience I tapped is my own. The lawyer George Thomassy appeared in my novels *The Magician, The Childkeeper*, and *Other People*. When it came time for him to appear again in *The Touch of Treason*, I wanted to start with Thomassy looking over a courtroom where he was to try a major case. My objectives for that beginning were the three that I suggested earlier:

- To lend resonance to the story.
- To convey Thomassy's personality to new readers and reintroduce him to those who'd encountered him before.
- To establish a courtroom setting.

In the end you died. There could be a courtroom like this, Thomassy thought; all the good wood bleached white, the judge deaf to objections because He owned the place. The law was His, the advocacy system finished.

If that's what it was going to be like, George Thomassy wanted to live forever, because here on earth, God willing or not, you could fight back.

The courtroom Thomassy is viewing is in his mind. He is imagining the "courtroom" of judgment day. The reader knows the judge is He, and He "owned the place. The law was His." It is apparent that Thomassy resents the authority of judges. Thomassy wants an arena where he can fight back. His most characteristic trait is to try to win under every circumstance, yet to continue to do so would be impossible; he would have to live forever.

That's a lot to cram into a few lines. I hoped the essence of my intent would come across, and that the reader, at minimum, would be anticipating the courtroom drama to come.

What can a newcomer do in a first paragraph? A lot. The following is the first paragraph of a novel by a student in my advanced fiction seminar who is writing about a painter:

Shoshana stormed through the silent apartment. Mason, you son of a bitch! Where are you? Instinct told her: Mason had fled. You gutless coward, she raged. Returning to her studio, Shoshana stabbed the brush she carried into a jar of turpentine. Just try to get in one hour's ego-affirming work of one's own. No way!

The writer, Anne Mudgett, is using action to characterize. She is also setting up conflict between the narrator and Mason, and involving the reader in Shoshana's emotional state.

We saw how James T. Farrell used surprise. In the example that follows, surprise is used by a student, Steve Talsky, whose work is yet to be published:

I am the way, the answer and the light, through me all things are possible.

He had written this once as a joke on the headboard of his bed.

The reader gets an impression of a character who is unusual and about whom one wants to know more. Not least, one has the sense that this author's work has resonance.

The value of a well-written opening is that it makes the reader ready to give himself to the writer's imagined people for the duration.

It should be clear by now that the unusual is a factor in arousing the reader's interest. And so is action and conflict. So many writers fight an uphill battle trying to interest their readers in matters that have no inherent conflict. The worst possible way to start a story is with something like "They were a wonderful couple. He loved her and she loved him. They never argued."

The result is instant boredom. Boredom is the greatest enemy of both reader and writer. Do we gaze with wonder at the nice, average, normal-looking people we pass in the street? Our attention is arrested by the seven-footer and the midget, the oldster with the mechanical waddle, the child who bounces as she walks. Recall how people react to the sound of metal crunching metal, announcing an accident. They hasten to see what happened. Highways get choked when drivers slow down to gawk at the remains of an collision. To the student of literature it should come as no surprise that news programs concentrate on bad news first, on events filled with conflict.

Beginning a book with an intriguing opening is the easy way to capture the reader. There are, however, more leisurely ways to seduce the reader, through omens.

You have heard people say, "I've got a feeling something is going to happen." How is that done? In *The Magician,* the opening pages convey the town of Ossining at the end of a month of intermittent snowfall. Boys in twos and threes with shovels are clearing neighbors' sidewalks. The third sentence has a slight omen:

> An occasional older man, impoverished or proud, could be seen daring death with a shovel in hand, clearing steps so that one could get in and out of the house, or using a small snowblower on a driveway in the hope of getting his wife to the supermarket and back before the next snow fell.

"Daring death" is an omen. And the rhythm of the words at the end of the sentence is designed to strengthen the ominous feeling in "the next snow fell."

The second paragraph also ends with the thump-thump-thump of monosyllabic words:

> It seemed impossible that spring might come, and that these humped gray masses would eventually vanish as water into the heel-hard ground.

I then lift the reader's spirit with a sight of "huge evergreens dusted with snow, and above them the bare webs of leafless silver maples reflecting sunlight." We see young children enjoying the snow. During a brief tour, we find out we are in the richest county of the United States, but the center of the village of Ossining has numerous empty storefronts. Nearby homes have been fled from. And another omen central to the book looms:

> The biggest drain on taxes was, of course, the schools, in which violence was not unknown.

And soon another:

> It was not an unusual town in a country on the decline after only two centuries.

In the next paragraph—still on page two—we find out that the most famous site in that village is Sing Sing prison, known throughout the world. And we, innocently it seems, then find ourselves watching the protagonist, a young man named Ed Japhet, practicing magic tricks in front of a large mirror in his parents' bedroom. Of course I could have started with that scene, but I preferred the gentle buildup of omens that something is wrong in the village where the action takes place, in the country, perhaps in the world. The reader's apprehension has been raised. Something is going to happen. And it does.

Sometimes a single omen can do the work of several if it starts the engine of the novel. A novel is like a car—it won't go anywhere until you turn on the engine. The "engine" of both fiction and nonfiction is the point at which the reader makes the decision *not to put the book down*. The engine should start in the first three pages, the closer to the top of page one the better.

Josiah Bunting, novelist and college president, had a penchant for finding the place where the engine turned on in other people's books. He read a novel of mine called *The Childkeeper* in manuscript and immediately pointed to the place where the engine started. It's here as an example of how even a slight omen can encourage the reader to keep reading.

In the first two pages we learn that Roger Maxwell, a banker content with wife and children, has just received a promotion that enables him to buy a new house for his family. Friends put him on to the best real estate agent in the vicinity of Chappaqua and Pleasantville, a man named Stickney.

On the phone, Stickney asks a few questions. Note how innocuous they seem:

> "Children?" asked Stickney.
> "Four," said Roger. "One's away at college, but we've got to keep a room for him."
> "Guests?"
> "Sometimes. Especially the children. They like to have their friends sleep over."

And so it goes for a few more lines, while Stickney flips through his cards listing houses that might be suitable. Then he says:

> "Could you come up Sunday, say at two?"
> "Of course."
> "You'll bring the children?"
> "Yes."
> Stickney was pleased. Children were part of his strategy.

That last sentence, according to Josiah Bunting, was when the engine turned on. As it happens, we soon learn that Stickney intends to sell Maxwell a house that's a haven for children. It has a huge two-story room with bunk beds made of canoes and a forest of stuffed animals. The novel, published in 1975, long before child abuse became a frontburner topic, was about its opposite, parent abuse. We see evidence of that in the most ordinary context, bit by bit, until the story explodes.

The only hint of the theme is in the epigraph that appears before page one. Epigraphs, please note, can be useful omens. I turned a saying of Oscar Wilde's on its head:

> Parents begin by loving their children; as they grow older they judge them; sometimes they forgive them.

It is a useful exercise for writers to spend time in their libraries at home or in public libraries, looking at the first few pages of the books that have pleased them most in order to find the exact place where the engine turns on, where the reader will not want to put the book down.

There are many ways to arouse the reader's interest at the start of a story or novel. A character can want something important, want it badly, and want it now. Or a likable character can be threatened. The reader who savors language can be aroused by the author's language, but that arousal won't last unless the reader also becomes involved in the life of a character who is quickly more interesting than most of the people who surround us in life.

If your aim is publication, your best bet is to start with a scene that the reader can see. Where do you start that scene? As close to its climax as is feasible if your aim is to involve the reader quickly.

Nonfiction

At the beginning of a piece of nonfiction, the goal of the writer is the same as that of a writer of fiction: to spark the reader's interest sufficiently to engage him in reading the rest. The principle applies to both transient and durable nonfiction.

Most writing for newspapers, for instance, is by its nature transient, usually written one day, read the next, and no longer available thereafter. Most writers of books, essays, and similar work hope that what they write will endure. These categories overlap. Much that appears in hardcovers isn't durable. And some writing for transient media has remained as part of the culture that is passed from generation to generation.

Though the work I have guided has been mainly durable in its intent, journalists and others hare persuaded me of their eagerness to make their transient copy livelier, stronger, and more enjoyable. The once "good, gray" *New York Times* is no longer gray but colorful.

An easy way to interest the reader at the outset is by the use of surprise. Here are two examples from the *Times* by Stephen Manes and Keith Brasher respectively:

> When it comes to shopping for a computer, the most important peripheral runs at 98.6 degrees Fahrenheit and is known as a friend.

> Here on a stony meadow in West Texas at the end of 10 miles of unpaved road through mesquite-covered, coyote-infested shrub

land, several hundred bearers of a strategic commodity of the
United States of America are gathered.

They are goats.

The trend toward such openings is resisted by some who think that lively
writing is somehow impure. For them I have an image that I convey to
my classes. Imagine a continuous line, with Life at one end, Death at the
other.

Life————————————————————————Boredom————Death

On that line boredom—a loss of experience—belongs close to death.
Successful writing immerses the reader in heightened experience—
emotional, intellectual, or both—more rewarding than the life around
him. Dull writing doesn't provide pleasure. And whatever information
and insight it contains will be available only to those who are prepared
to tolerate the task of mining dull prose.

For purists I would point out that much academic writing is counter-
educational because its dullness insulates its information from nearly
everybody. Geoffrey Cotterell is credited with saying, "In America only
the successful writer is important, in France all writers are important, in
England no writer is important, in Australia you have to explain what a
writer is." As this extravagant exaggeration entertains, it manages to
make its point much better than a straight-faced dissertation on the same
subject would.

If readers could talk back to writers (they sometimes do by not reading their work) they might say, "Would you knowingly go to a physician
who was weak in his craft? Would you attend a badly conducted concert
just because it was available? Would you bring your car for a tune-up to
a mechanic who thought fine-tuning was a waste of his time?" The
reader trusts the writer to do his best. If he does his second-best, he
shouldn't be surprised if his reader finds another writer to read.

During most of the thirty-six years in which I was a publisher of books,
I had the responsibility of seeing a hundred new titles reach the public
each year. The great majority were nonfiction; a few became standard
works. There is no reason why nonfiction—including journalism—
cannot be as interesting and enjoyable as fiction. Information sticks best
when it is crafted to touch the reader's emotions. The journalist or biographer or historian need not also be a novelist to use the devices of fiction
to have his work provide a more intense experience for his readers.

When the journalist crams who, what, when, where, and why into the first paragraph, how can he hold the reader's attention for the whole of what he has written? Naked facts are frequently not enough to invite a reader's attention to the rest of the story. It is their context—the writing, the container of the information—that illuminates facts for the reader and gives them significant meaning. Writers of nonfiction have the right—perhaps even the responsibility—to access the wonders of the writer's craft to make their work interesting and enjoyable.

It was once thought that responsible journalism in reporting the news required adherence to dry fact and that only columnists and feature writers could allow color, metaphor, and even exaggeration for effect into their writings. As an example of how untrue that is of today's journalism, I chose the following lead front-page story from the *New York Times* quite arbitrarily on a day when I was addressing this subject in public. Needless to say, there are worthy and interesting newspapers in quite a few cities from which examples could have been chosen. Here is the first paragraph under the byline of Calvin Sims:

> An 87-year-old water main ruptured outside of Grand Central Terminal just before the morning rush hour yesterday, unleashing a deluge that ruined a newly renovated subway station and plunged commuters into a snarl of flooded subway lines and pulverized asphalt. The 20-inch main, which runs east and west along 42d Street between Park and Lexington Avenue, broke at about 5:45 A.M. Water surged upward, heaving 42d Street into a small mountain range, then cascaded down staircases and ventilation grates like so many waterfalls, flooding the subway tracks below. The repair process was delayed for hours because the city's Environmental Protection Department misidentified the site of the rupture and mistakenly shut off the wrong main.

Note the colorful exaggeration that strays from strict fact. The street asphalt was not literally crushed into powder ("pulverized") but broken into slabs and pieces. And 42d Street did not literally become "a small mountain range," which my dictionary identifies as "a mass of land that rises to a great height, especially of over one thousand feet."

The reporter's use of exaggeration and metaphor apparently caused no qualms among his editors. Those opening sentences were meant to tempt the reader to read on.

On the same front page quoted above, there was a related story under a three-column headline plus a subhead:

A DAY THAT NEW YORK SHOULDA STOOD IN BED.
EXPRESSWAYS STALL, SUBWAYS STUMBLE AND BUSES STAGGER

That headline and subhead serve as the beginning, hooking the reader. As for the subhead, expressways don't stall, cars do; subways cannot stumble, nor can buses stagger. But all that colorful inaccuracy gets the idea across with a touch of humor and pulls the reader into a story in which buses "limped up and down avenues" and "Taxis crawled along at a speed somewhere between that of a turtle and a snail"—none of which was literally true. What counts is that the reader is entertained while reading about what happened, and none of the similes, metaphors, and exaggerations mislead a single reader one bit.

Exceptionally good first paragraphs buoy editors and prize-givers as well as readers. A terrific ending will never be experienced by readers put off by a poor beginning, which is why beginnings get so much emphasis here. What can the journalist writing news stories on the run do to hook the reader?

When John F. Burns of the *New York Times* won a Pulitzer Prize for his reporting in 1993, his paper reproduced the following paragraph as an example of his prize-winning style in his reporting from the former Yugoslavia:

> As the 155-millimeter howitzer shells whistled down on this crumbling city today, exploding into buildings all around, a disheveled stubble-bearded man in formal evening attire unfolded a plastic chair in the middle of Vase Miskina Street. He lifted his cello from its case and began playing Albinoni's Adagio.

Burns helps us see a besieged city by focusing on a single individual performing an eccentric and somehow beautiful act. Spotlighting an individual who is characterized, however briefly, is an excellent way of involving the reader's emotions.

Can it be done in the course of a reporter's harried work? John Burns wrote 163 articles in the former Yugoslavia in a little over nine months, 103 of them with Sarajevo datelines at a time when TV crews couldn't get into the city or get their film out of the city. If Burns could write so many articles in so short a period and still remember not just to report facts but to involve the reader's emotions by focusing on an individual, no journalist in a more comfortable environment has an excuse for not trying.

The workaday experience of reporting news, particularly local news, does not have the built-in drama of reporting from a war zone, but that doesn't prevent the use of the same techniques to hook readers into local news stories. Let's look at some examples and determine what makes them work:

> Yesterday morning Henry Sorbino walked into the K-Mart on Eleventh Street carrying an umbrella and walked out carrying an umbrella and someone else's purse.

What is the key ingredient that makes that opening sentence work? Did you note that repeating the word "umbrella" underscored Sorbino's walking out with someone else's purse? That technique—repetition for effect—increases the dramatic impact of what's being described.

Can you pick out the ingredient that makes the difference in the following lead?

> At exactly 10:19 A.M. yesterday, a grandmother's purse on a conveyor belt at Orange County airport set off an alarm that caused two security guards to rush to the scene.

Did you note the word "grandmother"? The reporter could have said her name, Alice Hackmeyer, instead, but it wouldn't have created the same contrast with the event as "grandmother" does.

Did you note also that the introduction of action—the security guards rushing to the scene—helped dramatize that first sentence?

Here's another easily adaptable technique. First the blah version:

> The Buschkowski family moved from a rented apartment into its own home for the first time today.

That doesn't sound like news. And it certainly doesn't sound interesting, though it is factually accurate. How might a first sentence excite the reader's curiosity?

> It took fourteen years for the Buschkowski family to move two blocks.

That lead turns on the engine of curiosity, the driving force that gets readers beyond the first sentences.

Here's another blah beginning of a kind that's found in hundreds of papers every day:

> Carl Gardhof was sentenced in Superior Court to eighteen months in jail this morning.

It sounds as if the reporter, bored with reporting endless routine cases, decided to bore his readers in turn. If he'd trained himself as an observer, he might have written the following:

> Carl Gardhof, his head held high as if he had done nothing wrong, was sentenced in Superior Court to eighteen months in jail this morning.

A visual element can almost always be introduced to perk up a lead. This one conveys the attitude of the person without the cliché of "maintaining his innocence." We haven't yet found out what Carl Gardhof did. It'd be nice if it was for something like this:

> Carl Gardhof, his head held high as if he had done nothing wrong, was sentenced in Superior Court to eighteen months in jail this morning for stealing a Bible.

But even if it was for punching a policeman, or a third offense of shoplifting, or whatever, that first sentence has it made because of the visual that starts it, which needn't be a head held high:

> Carl Gardhof, who had trouble keeping his eyes on the judge, was sentenced in Superior Court to six months in jail this morning for his fourth conviction of flashing in public.

Most reported offenses sound ordinary. A visual touch can make them seem out-of-the-ordinary and stimulate the reader to continue with the story.

If court reporting can be lifted out of dullness, think what technique can do for the reporting of routine social events:

> George Brucell was led into the meeting room by the chairman.

Again, blah.

> George Brucell, a tall man, had to duck his head as the chairman
> ushered him into the meeting room.

Head-ducking is not much of an action, but a reporter who is a keen observer of small detail would have the advantage of the novelist in
picturing Brucell and giving him an action, however small, like ducking
his head:

> George Brucell, a tall man, had to duck his head as the chairman
> ushered him into the meeting room to loud applause.

Better because of the introduction of sound.

The following are all from the *New York Times*. Note how they involve the reader by focusing on a person:

> Since learning last year that he had multiple sclerosis, Andy Torok
> has become less and less steady on his feet, and his worries have
> accumulated along with the hand prints on his apartment's white
> walls.

That story made page one. Its real subject was the suspension of auto
union talks because workers were loath to chip in for health care costs.
All the facts are in the body of the story, but the reader, hooked by a beginning that focuses on an individual, gathers the facts as he reads an
interesting piece.

In enhancing journalism with the techniques of fiction, caution is required. It's easy to overdo the attempt at analogy. One can feel the *New
York Times* reporter straining for effect in the following attempt to lure
the reader into the sometimes dull material of a House of Representa-
tives vote:

> Washington, Aug. 5 [1993]—If politics is theater, as the skeptics
> say, tonight was classic Hitchcock, with a very large dose of Frank
> Capra.
>
>   There on the House floor, Bill Clinton's budget package and his
> Presidency clung to credibility every bit like Eva Marie Saint in
> "North by Northwest," clinging to the face of Mount Rushmore.
> Mr. Clinton's Democratic supporters held a 216-to-214 margin.

Come Right In

The following *Times* story starts the right way:

> It is nearly 10 P.M. and the toll taker at the Triborough Bridge's
> Manhattan Plaza is near the end of her shift. Her routine is me-
> thodical, icily efficient. She glances out the window to see the kind
> and size of vehicle approaching. She then pushes a button to elec-
> tronically post the fare on a display screen.
>
> In a practiced movement, she reaches out for money. She hands
> back a token or change. She does this 300 times an hour, three sec-
> onds a car, an endless stream of stop-and-go.
>
> Such are the labors of one of life's invisible people, a toll taker
> for the Triborough Bridge and Tunnel Authority, which last year
> collected $653.6 million from 277 million vehicles. This particular
> transaction is recorded in grainy black-and-white images on a jerky
> surveillance video tape. The woman, who officials would not name,
> is about to become a statistic, one of 26 Bridge and Tunnel officers
> to be robbed at gunpoint this year, already three times the number
> in all 1992.
>
> A black car stops. A man in a ski mask thrusts a sawed-off shot-
> gun through his window. As quickly as the human mind can per-
> ceive and respond, the toll taker shoves a trayful of money into his
> hands. The car lurches into the darkness.

So far so good. The writer, Douglas Martin, has pulled you through
four paragraphs of a story about robberies at tollbooths by focusing on
an individual. But the hazard of overdoing it is there. The next paragraph
reads:

> The woman pivots to catch the license plate number. Then her head
> drops like a rock, her back heaves convulsively and she bites her
> lip. An armed sergeant is at her window in 10 seconds. The robber
> has not been caught.

That paragraph needs editing. The account turns melodramatic. The toll
taker's head drops like a cliché, her back "heaves convulsively"—and
unbelievably. She clichés her lip. And suddenly there is an armed sergeant at her window. Did she get the license plate? We'll never know.

Journalists seeking to pack as much information as possible into the
opening paragraph might usefully attend to the following by Natalie
Angier, from the science section of the *New York Times*:

As any serious migraine sufferer knows, an attack can bring pain without pity or horizon, a pain so stupendous that it obliterates work, family, thought, otherness. Yet for all its galactic sweep when it strikes, migraine is a mundane and commonplace ailment, afflicting about 12 percent of the population. It is a trait passed along from parent to offspring with the seeming ease of wispy hair or nearsightedness: three-quarters of all sufferers are thought to have an inherited predisposition to the disorder.

Note the use of metaphoric language, "pain without pity or horizon." How much stronger "horizon" is than "endless" would be. Note also "galactic sweep," an effective and original way of conveying degree. Contrast helps. In the same sentence as "galactic sweep" the ailment is characterized as "mundane and commonplace." ("Commonplace" alone would have served. See "One plus one equals one half," page 205.) Instead of just tossing "genetic predisposition" at the reader, Angier talks of "wispy hair or nearsightedness." It's a writerly paragraph that arouses our expectation not only of information but fine writing as well.

Here is a short list of reminders that can help if you're drafting a first paragraph in a hurry to meet a deadline: Does your first sentence trigger curiosity to make the reader want to continue? What will the reader *see* in that first sentence? Have you focused on an individual? Have you given us a visible characteristic of that individual? Have you portrayed the individual doing or saying something? Is there a startling or odd fact that will trap attention?

Let's see what some experienced writers of features, articles, and books have been doing with first sentences.

> Andy Warhol, draftsman of shoes, is dead, and the people viewing his remains are mostly wearing scuffed white sneakers.

Note the visual parallel. An obit or memorial piece doesn't have to be dull. That was Stuart Klawans, writing in *Grand Street*.
Jay McInerney knows how to make his opening sentence visual:

> A year after his death, the recurring image I associate with Raymond Carver is one of people leaning toward him, working very hard at the act of listening.

A novel comparison also makes a good hook:

> At the Academy Awards, the entrance to the Shrine Civil Auditorium is flanked by four giant Oscars quite, or so it seems to me, like sullen art deco Nazis.

The sentence might have been improved by omitting "or so it seems to me" but the comparison is startling and strong nevertheless. It was by Stanley Elkin for *Harper's* magazine. Here's another:

> I'm talking to my friend Kit Herman when I notice a barely perceptible spot on the left side of his face.

That's Randy Shilts in *Esquire* focusing on an ominous blemish.
  Here's a lead that might be a turn-off:

> The doctor told me that I had cancer of the prostate.

But Anatole Broyard was a brilliant as well as brave writer, and here's how he actually started his essay "Intoxicated by My Illness":

> So much of a writer's life consists of assumed suffering, rhetorical suffering, that I felt something like relief, even elation, when the doctor told me that I had cancer of the prostate.

He enhances the hard fact with contrast, resonance, and surprise. In death, life.
  Can you bring a fresh insight to your first sentence? Fiction writers are said to "reach down their throats" for truths that enable them to write from the inside. Can candor at the beginning help your article, perhaps something you would rather the world not know that you might keep secret if you were not a writer?
  Alternatively, can you mint a new description for a familiar object the way Stanley Elkin did when he saw the Academy Award statues as Art Deco Nazis?
  Let's look at some examples of first sentences from short nonfiction that has endured:

> Saints should always be judged guilty until they are proved innocent . . .

That's just the first half of the first sentence of George Orwell's essay "Reflections on Gandhi." We don't think of judging saints. And Orwell inverts the usual "innocent until proven guilty," producing two attention-getters in half a sentence.

Orwell, though best known for his novels *Animal Farm* and *1984,* was one of the best nonfiction writers of the century. No journalist, whether or not he covers political events, should miss reading Orwell's essay "Politics and the English Language."

Can good writing about natural history hook the reader at the start? Here's an example by Loren Eiseley:

> I have long been an admirer of the octopus.

Octopus? Admirer? That opening is both surprising and a touch amusing. One goes on reading, which is what first sentences are supposed to encourage.

A first sentence can be used to announce a theme dramatically. Witness the following by Robert Warshow from *Encounter* magazine:

> The two most successful creations of American movies are the gangster and the Westerner: men with guns.

To demonstrate the use of effective first sentences in longer nonfiction, I have selected first sentences from two autobiographies by authors I knew well:

> Many problems confront an autobiographer, and I am confident that I have not solved them.

> I see no reason why the reader should be interested in my private life.

Both examples entice with a slight surprise because they do the opposite of what we expect. Both seem to be disclaimers. Each is a cover-up for a fault. They both might be characterized as pseudo-candor, which can be as effective as candor. They are both interesting beginnings that invite us to go on.

The first is from Sidney Hook's *Out of Step: An Unquiet Life in the 20th Century.* The second is from Bertram D. Wolfe's *A Life in Two Centuries*, a book important enough to make the front page of *The New York Times Book Review.*

Let's move from first sentences in longer nonfiction to first paragraphs that invite the reader to continue:

> From all available evidence no black man had ever set foot in this tiny Swiss village before I came. I was told before arriving that I would probably be a "sight" for the village. I took this to mean that people of my complexion were rarely seen in Switzerland, and also that city people are always something of a "sight" outside of the city. It did not occur to me—possibly because I am an American— that there could be people anywhere who had never seen a Negro.

That first paragraph is by a then largely unknown writer named James Baldwin. The last sentence in the quoted paragraph could have been its first, an immediate hook, but if the author had done that, the paragraph would wind down instead of building toward a climax, which is more effective.

The subject of another first paragraph was the republication by Scribner's of Peter Fleming's first book, written right after an adventure when he was only twenty-four. A blah lead-in would have been:

> Peter Fleming was only twenty-four when he experienced and wrote his *Brazilian Adventure*.

Here's how it was done:

> Children, those energetic dervishes, are too busy testing themselves against the world to know the meaning of boredom for very long; high adventure waits for them in every breakable object. It is in adolescence that boredom, time without life, insinuates itself into each passing day. But the adolescent with a good mind and a university education to acquire may wait until he is 24 or more before life begins to pall. That is precisely the age at which Peter Fleming, in 1932, answered an advertisement.

The fact in the last sentence of the paragraph would normally have gone into the first sentence. It was put last for two reasons. It was given the job of thrusting the reader forward into the next paragraph. More important was the establishment of tone.

In my first reading of nonfiction I sometimes find that a good lead is buried elsewhere in the draft. Brought forward it can replace a less worthy beginning and help ensure that a reader will be turned on to reading the whole.

Thomas Henry Huxley was a nineteenth-century physician credited with popularizing Darwin's ideas and other scientific thought of his time. Popularizing? Try, if you can, this opening paragraph of his famous essay "The Method of Scientific Investigation":

> The method of scientific investigation is nothing but the expression of the necessary mode of working of the human mind. It is simply the mode at which all phenomena are reasoned about, rendered precise and exact. There is no more difference, but there is just the same kind of difference, between the mental operations of a man of science and those of an ordinary person as there is between the operations and methods of a baker or of a butcher weighing out his goods in common scales and the operations of a chemist in performing a difficult and complex analysis by means of his balance and finely graduated weights. It is not that the action of the scales in the one case and the balance in the other differ in the principles of their construction or manner of working, but the beam of one is set on an infinitely finer axis than the other and of course turns by the addition of a much smaller weight.

Huxley's essay, believe it or not, is used as a model in some twentieth-century textbooks. It is not, to put it mildly, a model of clarity, and it certainly isn't interesting to read. Let's look at someone else's treatment of the same material:

> Scientific investigation is a precise yet commonplace way of examining information. A baker or a butcher weighing out his goods and a chemist performing a difficult and complex analysis with finely graduated weights are doing the same kind of thinking.

The edited example contains fewer than one quarter the words yet gets the idea across. It is not the brevity that counts but the fact that the Huxley version is bloated with abstractions and is boring to read. Huxley may have done his work as a scientist but not as a writer. I would be willing to wager that any writer who has absorbed the material in this chapter could write an opening paragraph that's a lot more interesting than Huxley's.

Which leads me to an important point. The craft of creative writing is at least as complex as the craft of science. I have one student who is an aeronautical engineer and another who is an obstetrician, and I dare say both would admit that writing to a professional standard involves craft at least as complex as their occupations. You wouldn't want a layman walking into a hospital operating theater to deliver a child. Nor would you want a layman to design the next airplane you travel in. But writing? Can't everybody do it?

3

Welcome to the Twentieth Century

Imagine this: You are in a theater in the midst of a packed audience. The curtain goes up. The stage is set, but you don't see actors. You can hear them talking offstage, though the words are unclear. By the sound of their voices, the actors must be doing things. But what? It's all happening offstage!

The audience is restless. Everyone wants the actors to come onstage so that they can be seen. Such is the yearning of today's audiences for what we have come to call "immediate scenes," scenes that take place before the eye.

In the nineteenth century, novels and stories were filled with summations of offstage events, past or present, almost always told to the reader in summary form. These clumps of narrative summary are not experienced by today's readers with the immediacy and excitement of a witnessed event. With good reason. Even in societies that are not technologically advanced, a high proportion of the people born in the first half of this century experienced the phenomenon of moving pictures, which revolutionized entertainment even for the illiterate. In mid-century, the advent of television brought a visual medium into homes. Television and movies are full of immediate scenes, visible to the eye, ready to be experienced firsthand. This has influenced stories and novels more than we realize. Twentieth-century audiences now insist on seeing what they are reading. If you examine twentieth-century fiction, you'll find a dramatic increase in immediate scenes and a corresponding decrease in narrative summary. There has also been a decrease in descriptions of indoor and outdoor places that put the story on hold, making impatient twentieth-century readers start to skip.

* * *

Understanding the difference among the three main components of fiction—description, narrative summary, and immediate scene—can be of immense help to a writer of nonfiction also. The nonfiction writer who learns to use immediate scenes wherever he can will also find a dramatic improvement in the reception of his work. Nonfiction writers should pay close attention to the three forms of fiction—which I am about to define again—because the principles involved relate to their work as well.

Description is a depiction of a locale or person. The Latin root of the word "depiction," *pingere*, means "to picture" or to fashion a visual image.

Narrative summary is the recounting of what happens offstage, out of the reader's sight and hearing, a scene that is told rather than shown.

An **immediate scene** happens in front of the reader, is visible, and therefore filmable. That's an important test. If you can't film a scene, it is not immediate. Theater, a truly durable art, consists almost entirely of immediate scenes.

Just as every form of writing that is expected to be read with pleasure moves away from abstraction, every form of pleasurable writing benefits from conveying as much as possible before the eye, onstage rather than offstage.

John Cheever is a master of using description to do much more than describe. Witness the beginning of *Bullet Park,* which describes a railroad station in a manner that is also a depiction of the narrator's state of mind at the outset of the book:

> Paint me a small railroad station then, ten minutes before dark. Beyond the platform are the waters of the Wekonsett River, reflecting a somber afterglow. The architecture of the station is oddly informal, gloomy but unserious, and mostly resembles a pergola, cottage or summer house although this is a climate of harsh winters. The lamps along the platform burn with a nearly palpable plaintiveness. The setting seems in some way to be at the heart of the matter. We travel by plane, oftener than not, and yet the spirit of our country seem to have remained a country of railroads. You wake in a pullman bedroom at three a.m. in a city the name of which you do not know and may never discover . . .

Cheever's description is not static. It is part of the storytelling, and that is a key to description as it is used by our better writers: It has more than one function. For instance, in *The End of the Affair,* Graham Greene uses description of a room to characterize the person whose room it is:

> I had never been in his study before: I had always been Sarah's friend, and when I met Henry it was on Sarah's territory, her haphazard living-room where nothing matched, nothing was period or planned, where everything seemed to belong to that very week because nothing was ever allowed to remain as a token of past taste or past sentiment. Everything was used there; just as in Henry's study I now felt that very little had ever been used. I doubted whether the set of Gibbon had once been opened, and the set of Scott was only there because it had—probably—belonged to his father, like the bronze copy of the Discus Thrower. And yet he was happier in his unused room simply because it was his: if one possesses a thing securely, one need never use it.

Narrative summary, if written well and briefly, can transport the reader from one immediate scene to another, though this isn't always necessary. Fiction and reporting have now borrowed a film technique called "jump cutting," moving from one scene into the next with no transition for time to pass or locales to change. If the scenes must be linked, brief narrative summary can do the linking. How brief?

> Martin double-locked his door and went to work. In the office . . .

In the first part of the first sentence, we actually see Martin locking his door. That's immediate scene. "Went to work" is narrative summary. Just three words get us from one scene to the next.

Narrative summary, if kept short, can be useful in setting up an immediate scene:

> I am lying on the familiar couch, listening to the sound of Dr. Koch breathing, waiting for me to continue talking. I'd been telling him about the botched weekend, about Bill and Thomassy. I don't want to talk any more, to him or to anybody. Finally, I tell him I'm fed up, I don't want to be in therapy, I want to be back in life.
>
> "You do not stop living," he says, "when you take time to stop and think."

We can visualize the narrator on the psychiatrist's couch, listening to the doctor breathing. When the doctor speaks, we are back in the immediate scene.

If a narrator tells the reader that Herman sat at a lunch counter "drinking endless cups of coffee, waiting for Jill," that's narrative summary. The reader cannot see "endless cups" of anything. A summary of repetitive action does not create a clear image. It's easy enough to fix:

> As Herman sipped the last dregs of coffee, he looked up to see the counterman holding the pot ready to refresh his cup. When the steam stopped rising from the cup, he sipped again. As the counterman approached for the third time, Herman shook his head, and got up from the stool. He reached into his pocket for bills, and tossed two singles on the counter. Jill could go to hell.

The tiny bit of action keeps the author from intruding with a summary. The reader is able to feel something of what Herman feels when he is kept waiting.

Editors tell us that a primary reason for the rejection of novels is that they consist of far too much static description and narrative summary. Even a successful writer like P. D. James can tax a reader with an excess of description that does not move the story along:

> There is Miss James's insistence on describing absolutely everything. . . . so much of her scene-setting serves no other purpose than to create impenetrable atmosphere. For instance, pages are devoted to describing in loving detail the locale of a lunch that Dalgliesh eats with a friend . . . yet the story never returns there. . . . A character can't enter a room without being lost in its furnishings. A result is the loss of all sense of pace.

That public reprimand from the chief daily book critic of the *New York Times,* Christopher Lehmann-Haupt, appeared in a review of James's 1995 novel *Original Sin.* If an experienced writer like P. D. James can slip, why hazard the ice? My advice to writers yearning for publication is to minimize description, and be sure you don't stop the story while describing. You are a storyteller, not an interior decorator.

Though today's readers want immediate scenes as the primary source of their experience, editors still see too many manuscripts with a plethora of narrative summary as if written for nineteenth-century audiences. The news is that the authors of these manuscripts are writing for audiences that are dead. Readers today insist on seeing characters onstage.

That doesn't mean we can't enjoy the works of previous centuries. We can and do. But as creatures of our time, we often find the pace of earlier writing slow, the descriptions languid, and the recounting of offstage matters less involving than scenes before our eyes. Imitating nineteenth-century writing impedes the chances of publication.

I am not arguing for so-called action as it is abused in popular media. In fiction, action consists of what people do and say. Hemingway said it perfectly: "Never mistake motion for action." Adversarial dialogue is action. Combative words can excite readers' emotions more than swordplay. When characters speak, we see them as they talk, which means that dialogue is always in immediate scene. Stage plays are in immediate scene. So are films, and now, for the most part, novels.

To keep the reader reading, you want his involvement to be a continuous experience. The best reading experiences defy interruption. I think I am especially sensitive to glitches that interrupt the reader's experience because of my years as a playwright. In the theater, we instantly know if there is a loss of audience attention. Playgoers, if taken out of their experience even for a moment, cough and rustle in their seats. Writers of books don't have the advantage of seeing and hearing their audience's reaction. We have to train ourselves to detect and remove interruptions of the reader's experience. Static descriptions interrupt the story. So does a summary of what has happened offstage between scenes or elsewhere.

The ideal is not to break the reader's experience even for a few seconds. Which leads me to a common fault of the inexperienced writer. He is writing a scene that the reader can experience, but he feels the need to provide some information. Instead of finding a way to have the information come naturally out of the characters in the scene, he states the information baldly. The author's voice interrupts the scene.

When I speak to groups of writers, I sometimes hold up a large pane of glass. I ask the writers to imagine that the glass separates the writer from his readers. The readers are having their experience entirely on the other side of the glass. If they hear the author even for a phrase or two, it interrupts their experience. Information that seems to come from the author rather than a visible character is an intrusion from the other side of the glass. Writers are directors of what transpires on the other side of the glass. They are not one of the actors.

In sum, if you want to improve your chances of publication, keep your story visible on stage and yourself mum.

II

Fiction

4

Competing with God:
Making Fascinating People

Think of the novels you have loved most. Do you remember a character you lived with page after page, perhaps hoping the book would never end? What do you remember most clearly, the characters or the plot?

Now think of the movies you've seen that affected you the most. Do you remember the actors or the plot?

There's a book called *Characters Make Your Story* that you don't have to read because the title says it all: Characters make your story. If the people come alive, what they do becomes the story.

Writers of literary and much mainstream fiction usually begin by imagining a character. The same is true of the writers of the most popular mysteries centered around a character: Sherlock Holmes, Miss Marple, Hercule Poirot, or Kinsey Millhone. The characters engage us first and are remembered most. The plots of individual books are chapters in their lives.

Some writers of popular and transient fiction begin with a character, but a large percentage who write category books (e.g., adventure, spy, westerns, science fiction, romance novels) start with a plot, then populate it with characters. That method usually results in hackwork, at which some writers have become so skilled that they have made millions with stories that even their devoted readers acknowledge seem "made up."

Other writers can't help starting out with a theme that obsesses them. They imagine characters whose lives might involve the theme, or they work out a plot first. If their allegiance is to character, their theme-originated story has a better chance of survival.

During all the many years in which I was an editor and publisher, what did I hope for when I picked up a manuscript? I wanted to fall in love, to be swept up as quickly as possible into the life of a character so interesting that I couldn't bear to shut the manuscript in a desk overnight. It went home with me so that I could continue reading it.

We know what love is, we think of the other person at odd moments, we wonder where they are, what they are doing, we seem a bit crazy to the rest of the world. That's exactly the feeling I have about characters I fall in love with in books.

From those experiences I am convinced that *we need to know the people in the car before we see the car crash*. The events of a story do not affect our emotions in an important way unless we know the characters. Some books center on catastrophic events that don't move me at all. The characters in those books come across as stereotypes with names. If they are not alive, why should I care if their well-being is threatened?

Let's look at proof that characters come first:

> Harry jumped off the Brooklyn Bridge.

The typical reaction is "So what?" Who's Harry? Suppose we add just one word, a second name of someone you may remember, a popular singer and film star. With the addition of a second name, does your reaction to the sentence change?

> Harry Belafonte jumped off the Brooklyn Bridge.

Suddenly the sentence means something. If you remember the singer Harry Belafonte, you can visualize the character. Why did he jump? With no characterization beyond a name, because it's someone we know about, we begin to care. Of course this example has nothing to do with the real Harry Belafonte, whose name we have borrowed for this demonstration.

One of the devices used by successful thriller writers is to give a small role to a real person, usually a high officeholder. That's what Jack Higgins did in his breakthrough novel, *The Eagle Has Landed*, in which Winston Churchill makes a cameo appearance. Writers who use this technique do not attempt to characterize famous individuals in depth. A trace to jog memory is enough. Watch what happens in the following:

> Harry Truman was not a man to be governed by rules. When he was President, he used to take long walks each morning to destinations of his own choosing, trailed by Secret Service agents who sometimes had trouble keeping up with him. What few people

know is that once, when visiting New York, Harry Truman decided to stroll across the Brooklyn Bridge against the advice of his Secret Service escort—he never listened to them. Halfway across Truman saw another early-morning walker, an old man wearing a fedora pulled down almost to his eyes, trying to hoist himself up onto the railing. Truman, the most universally admired President of the last half century, realized instantly that the old man could have no other purpose than to jump.

We get interested in the action of a man about to jump off a bridge because we know the observer. What will Harry Truman do? The engine of the story has turned on. Our curiosity is involved. We want to know more.

When neighbors report gossip to us about people we know, we can be titillated or sometimes even moved. A writer cannot depend on "sometimes." His characterization must elicit emotion from a wide variety of readers without fail. How does he do it? He learns the art of characterization, adding details and depth until he has created a character whom we may know better than all but our closest friends.

Let's take it one step at a time. How does a writer characterize in simple ways?

What we do in life is lazy. We say the first thing that comes into our heads. Think of a ticket taker at a movie house. He sees people passing in a stream. He can only make quick generalizations. That man is tall, that woman is skinny. How does a writer deal with similar facts?

Frank is so tall, he entered the room as if he expected the lintel to hit him, conveying the image of a man with a perpetually stiff neck.

The man is not just tall, he is being characterized *through an action*.

What about the woman who was described as skinny? How does a writer deal with that fact?

She always stood sideways so people could see how thin she was.

Again, the writer is not just describing; he is characterizing *by an action*. We individualize by seeing characters doing things and saying things, not by the author telling us about them. Don't ever stop your story to characterize. Avoid telling the reader what your character is like. Let the reader see your characters talking and doing things.

Let's look at some examples of characterization by novelist Nanci Kincaid, in her talented first novel *Crossing Blood*:

> Once we looked in Patricia's window and saw her in her half-slip. . . . First she curled her eyelashes, holding a mirror in her hand. Then, out of the blue, she picked up a lipstick, smeared it on, and kissed the mirror. Kissed it. She made little kiss marks and looked them over real close, studying them. She was dead serious about it. Jimmy got mad and made us get down off the trash cans and stop looking. He swatted Donald to make the rest of us stop laughing at Patricia.

The same author will now introduce a character called Skippy. Kincaid doesn't tell us Skippy was brave; she lets the reader experience Skippy's bravery through an action:

> Skippy will pick up a snake as quick as he will a cat. He will let one crawl on his neck and down his arm, a black snake, until me and Roy go crazy watching him. More than once he let me and Roy hold one, which we did, but we had to practically quit breathing to do it.

Exaggeration is another technique for characterizing:

> Laverne weighed two tons naked.

Nobody believes for a second that Laverne weighed four thousand pounds. In speech we hear it said about an object that "it weighed a ton." We exaggerate constantly. It's a way of communicating quickly, and often effectively.

Comparison to a known quantity or quality is sometimes a useful form of exaggeration:

> Archie was Wilt Chamberlain tall.

> Bruce wafted me around that dance floor. If I'd shut my eyes, he could have been Fred Astaire.

Exaggeration can be especially useful when dealing with children. Here's Nanci Kincaid again:

The worst thing about George, though, worse than his nasty mouth full of missing and broken teeth, worse than his fleas and sore spots, was the fact that he was missing one eyeball. He had an empty hole in his head. You could poke your finger in there and he wouldn't even twitch.

Reproving someone who is late, a layman might write, "I've been waiting a long time for you." That doesn't characterize either the speaker or the latecomer. "I've been waiting forever for you" is an exaggeration— and also a cliché. It doesn't characterize. Here's how an experienced writer, Rita Mae Brown, did it in her novel *High Hearts*:

"Girl, my fingernails could grow an inch just waiting for you."

In *The Best Revenge* I needed to introduce a character who would prove to be influential, a tough lawyer named Bert Rivers, who is short and bald. If he was described as short and bald, that would be a movie-house ticket taker's description. Nick Manucci, in the company of his lawyer, Dino, sees his opponent's lawyer for the first time, and says:

"This distributor has a lawyer so short you wouldn't be able to see him if he sat behind a desk. And he's Yul Brynner bald. But when he shakes your hand you know this dude could squeeze an apple into apple juice. Every time Dino opens his mouth, this lawyer pisses into it."

That's not the author talking, it's a character talking, and therefore an acceptable exaggeration. It also characterizes the speaker.

Can you characterize more than one person at a time? Of course you can. You characterize the speaker as well as the person spoken about. A novice writing what first comes to mind might write, "My father is a pompous judge." That's telling the reader, not showing him. Here's the way it was done in the voice of a character named Jane Riller in *The Best Revenge*:

My father is still living, but less and less. Judge James Charles Endicott Jackson, his "appellations" as he called his full name, that tall, lean, hollow-cheeked man who had made such a religion of the law, preached from the head of our dining-room table each evening of my young life.

A character would not likely say, "My mother always gave in to my father." That's telling the reader. Here's how Jane Riller says it:

> When they stood next to their car at the bus station, for a moment I thought my mother was going to leave the Judge's side long enough to come forward and say a few words more than good-bye. But it was only the wind ruffling her dress, not a movement of her body that I saw. I admired her as one would a pioneer farm woman, someone who had lived a life no longer possible. What great and unacknowledged actresses the women of my mother's background were; to avoid shattering the fragile innocence of their spouses, some of them simulated not only their orgasms but their entire lives.

Jane's snapshot of her mother also characterizes Jane. It shows what she, as a young woman, rebelled against. She wanted to go out into the world where you could experience everything. Note that the paragraph starts with a visual image—the parents standing next to their car at the bus station—and ends with the character's conclusion. Had the order been reversed, the effect would be lessened. Also note that Jane is characterizing not only her mother but a whole class of people.

Can characterizing a whole class of people be done by a beginning writer? Here's another example from Nanci Kincaid's first novel to demonstrate that it doesn't take decades of experience to use the techniques that writers have developed over centuries:

> Migrant kids know they are white trash, so they never speak a single word the whole two weeks they come to school. The rich kids will not sit by them at lunch. They invite each other to birthday parties held at the swimming pools in their backyards. The rich daddies usually go into politics. They slowly get bald and fat and buy up everything for miles around. When the legislature is in session Tallahassee swarms with them. Mother says half of them have girlfriends put up at the Howard Johnson's.

Is it possible to characterize with a single word?

In a work in progress, I wanted to reintroduce two characters who've been in several of my books, the lawyer George Thomassy, and Gunther Koch, a sixty-year-old Viennese psychiatrist. Dr. Koch is lecturing Thomassy, a successful trial lawyer, about how to detect jurors who might disadvantage Thomassy's case. The lawyer reacts to being lectured:

Thomassy didn't take this kind of shit from a judge, why the hell
should he take it from this accent.

The word "accent" characterizes not Koch but the speaker Thomassy.
He deprecates Dr. Koch because he doesn't like being lectured. The
trace of prejudice against foreigners is especially meaningful because
Thomassy has tried hard to repress his own immigrant background.

If there is a common error among inexperienced writers, it's that they
say too much, they try to characterize with an excess of detail instead of
trying to find the word or phrase that characterizes best.

The words you select depend on the circumstances under which you
introduce the character. For instance, when we first see a character at any
distance, physical size makes an instant impression. If we are seeing a
character at closer range, we often notice the eyes first. What inexperienced writers often do is give us the color or shape of eyes. That's not as
effective as conveying how the character uses his eyes. If on meeting a
person he averts his eyes, it usually connotes something negative. Good
eye contact is usually perceived as positive. Unrelenting eye contact can
be negative to a shy or withdrawn character:

> I couldn't make eye contact with her. She was looking for invisible
> spots on the wall.

> She said, "I don't love you anymore," but her eyes belied her words.

> She didn't answer me. She just continued to glare as if her eyes
> said it all.

Another error of inexperienced writers—or journalists in a hurry—is to
confine characterization to the obvious physical attributes. For females,
facial features, breasts, hips, buttocks, legs. For males, broad shoulders,
strong arms, chiseled features, and so on. That's top-of-the-head, thought-
less writing. Such clichés are common in speech. We expect better of our
writers.

Instead of clichéd attributes, consider using physical characteristics
that relate to your story. For example, if you are writing a love story between a woman and a man, consider the belief of some psychologists that
a woman's most prominent sexual characteristic is her hair. (If that surprises you, imagine a woman you think attractive as bald. Would she still
be sexually appealing?) The same psychologists hold that the most

important sexual characteristic of a man is his voice (And if that surprises you, think of a man you believe to be attractive and imagine him with a squeaky, high-pitched voice. Would he still be sexually appealing?)

If you want to convey an antisexual attribute to your reader, consider the characteristics of hair and voice in a negative way.

There are at least five different ways to characterize:

1. Through physical attributes.
2. With clothing or the manner of wearing clothing.
3. Through psychological attributes and mannerisms.
4. Through actions.
5. In dialogue.

You'll want to avoid generalizations or similes that have been overused, such as "She shuffled like a bag lady" or "She carried herself like a queen." One of my students described a character this way: "George was a big fellow." That passes on information, but evokes nothing. The student was encouraged to think how he might revise his material to stir a feeling in the reader. This is what he did:

> When George came your way, you thought you were being run
> down by a truck.

We know immediately that George is a big fellow, but more important we feel his size as threatening. The writer has characterized by an action, which is far more effective than characterizing by description.

Characterization should be kept visual whenever possible: **"He walked against an unseen wind"** is visual. Opportunities are available in a character's gait, posture, demeanor, and other physical behavior. For instance, there are a lot of ways that a character can get across a room. Walking is the easy, lazy answer. The writer's aim should be to pick a way that both characterizes and helps the story.

Think of the many ways a character can walk. She can promenade, take a leisurely walk, stroll. She can amble, which means to move easily, to saunter. She can wander aimlessly.

You can pick up the pace, and have a character hasten, scurry, scoot, rush, dash, dart, bolt, spring, run, or race. Each of these words harbors a nuance that can help both to characterize and to convey a visual image.

You can even use a metaphor effectively, as in "She flew to the store to get there before it closed."

A writer who always has his characters "walk" is missing opportunities. Variants on walking should be used with caution, however. Their overuse annoys readers. In considering the possible variations for walking, you have been doing what writers should do every day—reflect on the meanings of individual words.

It is also possible to characterize by going into great detail about how a particular character walks. Witness the following from a John Updike story:

> She didn't look around, not this queen, she just walked straight on slowly, on these long white primadonna legs. She came down a little hard on her heels, as if she didn't walk in bare feet that much, putting down her heels and then letting the weight move along her toes as if she was testing the floor with every step, putting a little deliberate extra action into it.

One author whose work I edited found a way to walk his character straight to bestsellerdom. The story hinged on the relationship of a husband to his wife and his mistress. The novel wasn't working because the husband and wife were characterized successfully, but the mistress seemed to be all sex, a one-note characterization that failed to make her come alive. A triangle doesn't work unless all three participants are characterized fully.

I asked the author to describe how the mistress would walk across the room. He said he saw her walking across the room like a young lion—a male simile that opened up a new way of characterizing the mistress. Male traits were then used to describe her elsewhere in the book. It made her come alive, which in turn made the relationship credible. The book went on to become the number-one bestseller for thirty-seven consecutive weeks.

One can describe a way of moving that gives us a sense of personality:

> Henry moved through the crowd as if he were a basketball player determined to bounce his way to the basket.

The character needn't be in motion. Posture can provide personality:

He had the bearing of a man who had been a soldier a long time ago.

Physical behavior can give the reader a sense of personality: tapping a finger, pointing with eyeglasses, snickering, laughing, clapping hands wildly.

A broad range of psychological attributes is available to the writer. Let's look at one that can create a dramatic effect:

He said nothing.
I demanded an answer and he just stood there.
"Say something," I said.
His silence was like a brick wall between us.
"Come on! Speak!"

That's an example of someone who gets his way by refusing to do something. Psychological attributes can be much more direct:

She bombarded them with questions nonstop as if their answers were irrelevant.

Calvin's glazed expression said, "I'm not paying attention. I'm listening to the music in my head."

She was only nine years old, but she could look directly into your soul as if in a previous life she had been a Grand Inquisitor and your lies were condemning you.

Characterizing through psychological attributes can be rewarding because they often connect to the story:

He dealt with his friends as if they were employees.
He talked and they listened.

If you got in a car with her you'd find that her sentences were at least ten miles long.

At a party he'd come on to a woman—any woman—as if she were the only woman in the room.

Physical and psychological attributes can also be combined for purposes of characterization:

As he moved slowly across the room, age and arthritis made him seem brittle, but when he spoke—anywhere about anything— people stopped to listen as if Moses had come down with new commandments.

If you develop a characteristic that's especially pertinent to your charac- ter, or original, it's a good idea to use it on the character's first ap- pearance, to "set" the character. For instance, if you now know that your character will first be seen walking, then gait is a characteristic that should appear right away. If the character is the kind who always inter- rupts other people in conversation, you might consider introducing that character as he or she interrupts. For instance:

> George and Mary were at the kitchen table, debating how to handle their misbehaving teenager when Alma walked in and said, "I don't know how you people can just sit there talking instead of getting off your butts and giving that child of yours a lesson with the back of your hand."

There are many ways in which characterization can go wrong in the hands of a less experienced writer, but two stand out because they are so common in rejected fiction. There is the protagonist with a weak will, and the villain who is merely badly behaved.

First, consider the "hero" who is not heroic, who lacks drive, a will to attain his objective. Let's face it, readers aren't interested in wimps. They are interested in assertive characters who want something, want it badly, and want it now.

Test yourself. Would you want to spend ten or twelve hours with a wimpish character who is weak and ineffectual? Don't ask the reader to. A wimp in life is a social bore. A wimp in fiction is an obstacle to reader enjoyment.

I have talked to writers whose problems with wimpish characters in their work had a direct link to their own lives. There are children who, damaged by authority, become fighters against authority. There are also people who, damaged by authority in childhood, become relatively pas- sive adults as a means of camouflaging their aggression and anger to save their hearts and lives. Camouflaged anger is useful in stories, but it is the final unleashing of the anger that attracts readers most.

In working with such writers, or with shy writers who produce shy heroes, I have found a way, once they understand the inhospitality of fiction to passivity, to help them get rid of a wimpish protagonist who is de-energizing their fiction. I ask the writer to imagine that he is in his study with the door closed. A person outside wants to come in. The writer orders the intruder to stay out. I ask the writer to imagine a second person outside his door who says to the first, "Get out of my way," then comes into the writer's study without asking. The writer starts to object and this second intruder says, "You shut up and listen for a change!"

That second person is the writer's replacement for the wimp. That's his new protagonist. I urge the writer to listen to the character, rude as he is, and then compose a letter from that new non-wimp character to the writer that is assertive, candid, and at least a touch eccentric.

As to villains, bad behavior on its own is not as effective as mean spiritedness, deriving satisfaction and even pleasure from hurting the hero or preventing him from attaining his goal. (A section on character-izing villains begins on page 68.)

In the course of developing a character, there are some questions I will ask myself. Does he behave differently toward strangers than he does to members of his family? Such a difference is revealing. Would my char-acter behave differently when he met an old friend who is now famous than when he bumped into another friend of the same vintage who is down on his luck and ashamed? I also ask myself if my character ever talks to people in a way they find offensive. Does he realize he is offend-ing them? Does he try to apologize or change? Or doesn't he care? We know that people reveal themselves more when they raise their voices than when they speak normally. If my character had reason to shout, what would we hear? Or if my character is the kind of person who would never shout, what thought is he repressing? It adds to the drama to have contrast between what the character is doing and what he is saying to himself. As you can see, my questions provoke both good and bad characteristics and lead me into the character's relationships and into story scenes.

When I'm planning a character, I also try to listen to his or her dia-logue as if the character were in the room with me. Do they use figures of speech and expressions that characterize strongly? I search for con-scious and unconscious mannerisms of my character. As to a character's clothing, I try to focus on one item that will stand out in the reader's mind, for instance the fact that my character always wears a raincoat even when the sun is shining.

Eventually I have to ask myself about my character's attitude toward himself. If he is sometimes self-deprecating, does he reveal it through some physical tic or in things he says when he first meets people? If he is arrogant, what does he do that will make the reader feel he is arrogant without his saying a word? An arrogant action, I find, works better than arrogant speech.

I have seen talented writers hurt their chances of publication because they persist in writing about "perfectly ordinary people." Of course there have been numerous successful novels in which the main characters were not extraordinary. What the writers mean by "perfectly ordinary people" are characters who are seemingly no different from the run of people we meet who do not seem in any way distinctive.

People who are exactly like other people probably don't exist. But people who seem like most other people litter our lives, and we don't usually seek their company because they are boring. Readers don't read novels in order to experience the boredom they often experience in life. They want to meet interesting people, extraordinary people, preferably people different from anyone they've met before in or out of fiction.

The experienced writer will give us characters—even in common walks of life—who seem extraordinary on first acquaintance. Are there exceptions? Of course.

In my novel *The Resort*, the leading characters are an "ordinary" middle-aged couple, Henry and Margaret Brown, who find themselves in horrific circumstances at the end of chapter one. If Henry and Margaret Brown were truly ordinary, they wouldn't have interested the reader. And so I had Margaret Brown become a physician at a time when few women were in medical school. I also made her outspoken, extraordinarily curious, and smart as hell. And I had Henry, a businessman, spend his off hours in ways few businessmen do.

I made the Browns just different enough to interest the reader, but it was important that they not seem "special." Therefore, when calamity hits the Browns, readers from any walk of life can identify with their plight, which is critical for the story. Stephen King usually has quite ordinary-seeming characters get involved in extraordinary circumstances. In most instances, however, you'll want to make your characters as distinctive as possible rather than "ordinary."

The extraordinary quality of a character should usually be made evident almost immediately after he or she appears in the story, unless the thrust of a story is to have the gradual unveiling of a character's unusual habits or ambition.

Beware of characters who are so extreme as to seem like cartoon characters. Some characters in Charles Dickens's novels seem wildly exaggerated. Such characters are difficult to make credible to readers of mainstream fiction today.

Most authors seek high ground between the character who seems "perfectly ordinary"—and therefore uninteresting—and the wildly exaggerated cartoonlike character. Let's get a fix on the most fertile areas of characterization.

What makes a character extraordinary? Personality? Disposition? Temperament? Individuality? Eccentricity? How much overlap is there?

Let's explore each of those terms in as much depth as we can. My students find that their work in characterization improves markedly after they've considered the full span of meaning of those terms.

First, *personality*. We know that people at a party will cluster around people with personality. Personality refers to the distinctive traits of an individual, a set of behaviors, attitudes, manners, and mannerisms that identify a person. Personality speaks of an individual's makeup, nature, and combined traits, his essence. It means the specialness of a person, which in some may involve likability, power, charm, magnetism, and charisma. The constituent parts of personality are disposition, temperament, individuality, and eccentricity.

I'm not pushing these definitions as definitive. I'm trying to suggest that exploring an important term in depth can produce a stimulating variety of definitions that are valuable tools for thinking about a character.

The *disposition* of a person is her attitude toward the people and places of the world, her customary response, particularly her emotional response. Disposition can involve a person's qualities, outlook, mood, frame of mind, inclination, bent, bias, tendency, and direction, her proclivity, predilection, penchant, and propensity. Today, disposition is sometimes thought of as a predisposition, a mind-set. As you can now see, there are inspiring convolutions of meaning for these words that together define what a writer is trying to achieve in characterization.

Temperament is a person's manner of behaving, thinking, and particularly reacting to people and circumstances, his characteristic way of confronting a new day or a new development. Temperament can also be seen as a person's mettle, spirit, leaning, or inclination. Temperament often connotes a negative tendency toward anger or irritability, though the term "even temperament," of course, means the opposite.

Individuality is the aggregate of qualities that distinguish one individual from others. It connotes that person's distinctiveness, difference, and, most important, her originality and uniqueness. A writer describes a character's singularity with the particulars of concrete detail. These are the characteristics by which an individual is recognized by others. Her differentness is her identity. It can be said that the individuality of a person marks her off, singles her out, sets her apart, and ultimately defines her.

I've left for last a definition that speaks most to the point of giving your characters special and unusual characteristics.

Eccentricity is an offbeat manner of behavior, dress, or speech that is peculiar to a person and greatly dissimilar to the same characteristics of most other people. We think of the eccentric person as odd, a card, perhaps somewhat kinky, a queer fish, a quirky individual different from the other people we know. When we speak of an eccentric person, don't we refer to him or her as a "character"?

The idiosyncrasies of a person are, of course, as seen by others rather than that person, who often believes his or her idiosyncrasies to be "perfectly normal."

Eccentricity is at the heart of strong characterization. The most effective characters have profound roots in human behavior. Their richest feelings may be similar to those held by many others. However, as characters their eccentricities dominate the reader's first vision of them.

If you were to examine the surviving novels of this century, you would find that a majority of the most memorable characters in fiction are to some degree eccentric. Eccentricity has frequently been at the heart of strong characterization for good reason. Ordinariness, as I've said, is what readers have enough of in life.

When a great number of young men take to wearing an earring, that is not eccentricity. When young women iron their hair as many did in the sixties, that is not eccentricity. They are conforming to a widespread group mode.

Eccentric behavior is sometimes said to be nutty behavior, implying strange behavior, which is perfectly suitable for fiction. But "nutty" can also mean crazy, which is not intended here for an important reason. There are two types seldom seen in fiction: people who are psychotic and habitual drunks. Readers find it difficult to identify with their behavior. There are exceptions, of course, as in horror stories. In Alfred Hitchcock's *Psycho,* the leading character is crazy, though we don't know it for certain until quite near the end. Alcoholics sometimes play secondary roles in novels, and there have been several novels featuring alcoholic individuals or couples. But the most memorable alcoholic, who saw a giant rabbit called Harvey, involved a playful use of alcoholism that would probably not be attempted today with the recognition of the severity of the illness.

Dostoevsky's opening of *Notes from Underground* has a character explaining himself. He is so self-contradictory that when I read this opening aloud to students, they invariably laugh:

> I am a sick man. . . . I am a spiteful man. An unattractive man. I think that my liver hurts. But actually, I don't know a damn thing about my illness. I am not even sure what it is that hurts. I am not in treatment and never have been, although I respect both medicine and doctors. Besides, I am superstitious in the extreme; well, at least to the extent of respecting medicine. (I am sufficiently educated not to be superstitious, but I am.) No, sir, I refuse to see a doctor simply out of spite. Now that is something that you probably will fail to understand.

Consider also Captain Ahab in Melville's *Moby Dick*, certainly an eccentric. In Mark Twain's celebrated novels, what captures our attention is not the ordinariness of Tom Sawyer and Huckleberry Finn but their eccentricity. Think of the twentieth-century novels of Hemingway, Faulkner, Graham Greene, Kafka, García Marquez, Fitzgerald, Saul Bellow, Philip Roth, J. D. Salinger. Or the short stories of John Cheever. Their most memorable work springs from eccentric characters.

Think of the most eccentric person you know. What makes him (or her) eccentric? What is the most eccentric thing they have ever done? What might they do that would seem even more eccentric? Then think of your character doing that very thing! Unlikely? Unreasonable? Surprising? All of the above? If such behavior would be out of character for your protagonist, then what variation of it would be in character?

If your character isn't capable of any important eccentricity, you may have picked a character who will not be greatly interesting to readers. People notice the eccentricity of others. They talk about it with their friends. It becomes the subject of gossip and rumination. When people do only what they are expected to do, they don't make us eager to spend a dozen hours in their company.

You may be wondering if I am suggesting too much complexity in characterization. I don't expect you to use it all, but your explorations will stimulate thoughts that add to the potential richness of the characterization. To the extent that the complexity reflects the intricacy of human nature, the characters will come alive to the reader and remain alive in the reader's memory.

One reason characters in transient fiction don't linger in the reader's memory is the shallowness of the characterization. If Ian Fleming's James Bond is remembered, it is as a kind of cartoon character. The reader doesn't concern himself whether James Bond lives or dies except when he is in the middle of reading a James Bond story, and even then he doesn't worry much because the cartoon character has to live another day—for another book!

Sherlock Holmes is a wonderful character. But we don't think about him as we would about a member of our family or a close friend, living or dead. We think of him as a character in a book or film. In the best of mainstream fiction, and in literary fiction, the most complex characters seem to graduate to a permanent place in our memory, as good friends do.

The same is true of villains. Professor Moriarty doesn't occupy our lives except when we are reading about him. But the reader carries the memory of Iago and Lady Macbeth for a lifetime.

Contrast is a useful technique for characterization. It sometimes has the extra virtue of surprise. I recall attending a convention once where I sat in back of a large room. Several rows ahead of me sat a woman dressed in an immaculately tailored gray suit, her hair kempt, her posture markedly straight, and she was picking her nose. What helped characterize her for me was the contrast between her appearance and her nose-picking.

Characterizing through unusual clothing or the manner of wearing clothing is another often neglected possibility. What it requires is to avoid the easy description that first comes to mind. "Jerry always wore his cap backwards" isn't writerly. It can be improved:

> His cap worn backwards was a message to the world: Jerry did things differently.

A layman might say, "Ellen looked terrific in her gown." That's top-of-the-head writing, which can be improved:

> In her gown, Ellen looked like the stamen of a flower made of silk.

The first description doesn't say anything particular about either Ellen or the gown. The second is visual and tells us how Ellen and the gown came across in a way that made them both look good.

One of my students took the easy way out in describing his character Martin. "Martin was an informal dresser who didn't like other men getting all dressed up." I persuaded him to rethink the sentence:

> Martin referred to men who wore shirts and ties all day not as people but as "suits."

An important technique that is used too seldom by novelists is to give a character life by introducing attributes that go against the character's dominant behavior in the scene to come. Early in *The Best Revenge* there is a scene in which the hero, the Broadway producer Ben Riller, whose current play is in severe financial difficulty, goes to see Aldo Manucci, the moneylender Ben's father used to go to many years earlier. In the scene, done from Ben's point of view, Ben is in the position of pleading for money, and Aldo presumably has the power to save him. Therefore, in characterizing Aldo on his first appearance, I gave him a variety of weaknesses:

> At last she wheeled him in, a shrunken human stuffed by a careless taxidermist. He was trying to hold his head up to see me, an eye clouded by cataract. He took an unblinking look, then let a rich smile lift the ends of his mouth as his voice, still bass though tremulous, said, "Ben-neh!" which made my name sound like the word "good" in Italian.

A common fault in fiction is the portrayal of characters as all good or all bad. Therefore, when introducing a character who will be in a position of power in a scene, suggest that character's vulnerability before the character exercises power. Conversely, when introducing a character who will be hurt emotionally or physically in the scene to come, show the character's strength at the outset.

In a short story there is usually time for only one event or episode. A character comes to life, the event takes place, the story's over. There is room for a change of attitude toward something specific. Most often there isn't room in a short story for a character to experience enough to cause a profound change.

In a novel it is common and desirable for the principal character to change by the end of the book. If the protagonist is a risk taker, he may step into adulthood by learning that some kinds of risks are foolhardy. If the protagonist accepts certain conditions as a part of life, he may have learned that some of those conditions can change. And the protagonist who at the start is a pessimist about human nature may discover that a single human being can make a difference for a large number of fellow humans.

These are just a few examples of how a character might change in the course of a novel. The writer has to ask, is the change consistent with the character as portrayed? A change can be surprising, but it should not seem out of sync with what we know about the character.

Somerset Maugham said, "You can never know enough about your characters." When you have trouble improving a particular characterization, you need to know more. The remedy may lie in viewing your character from a different perspective.

Another way is to have your character complain bitterly about something. In life, complaining is more effective when it is done in a normal voice, the words speaking for themselves. However, bitter complaining connotes an emotional overload. At such times, your character is speaking, as it were, from the gut or the heart rather than the head. Listen to the character in that state. It will help you with the part of characterization that is normally hidden from public view.

Imagine your adult character secretly dressed in children's clothes. Why is he doing that? What you want is not your answer, but the character's answer to that question. The child in an adult character may have a poignant memory of a lasting hurt. Or a marvelous secret to reveal.

Yet another way is to visualize your character as suddenly rather old. How would that change her appearance, dress, walk? Is there anything that you can incorporate in your characterization at your character's present age? Some people preserve characteristics of their childhood, others seem prematurely old in some way. So do some characters.

Imagine your character in an armchair talking to you. Ask your character questions that are provocative. Let your character challenge you. Disagree with your character. Let him win the argument.

Unfetter your imagination. Can you see your character flapping arms, trying to fly? Or trying to kiss everyone at a party? Or walking in the snow without shoes? Readers are interested in the out-of-the-ordinary. All these questions involve the character in action, the ideal way to characterize.

Last, imagine your character in the nude. This one almost always works if you portray your character in the nude honestly and in detail. People in the nude become especially vulnerable. This doesn't mean you should necessarily portray your character actually in the nude. Your character may not want to get undressed, or may want to dress quickly to cover up. Or your character can just be thinking in the bath or shower. An author of mine, Edwin Corley, had a remarkable success with a first novel called *Siege*, which started with a scene of a black general in his bathtub. Everything the general did later was more believable because a person seen realistically in the nude is immediately credible.

CHARACTERIZING VILLAINS

Once upon a time, readers tolerated mustache-twirling villains with no countervailing virtues in their makeup. Today's readers can be roughly divided into two groups, those who accept the fantasy villains of childhood, as in the James Bond stories and Arnold Schwarzenegger films, and those who insist on credibility. In life, villains do not uncurl whips and snarl. They seem like normal human beings. But normal humans are not villains. What distinguishes the true villain is not just the degree to which he hides his villainy under an attractive patina to snare his victims, but his contact with evil. There is no social solution to the true villain's villainy, he cannot be reeducated and become a nice guy. His villainy is an ineradicable part of his nature.

In the successful TV series *NYPD Blue*, a senior police official from outside the precinct makes the precinct captain's life miserable at every opportunity. The official is not a nice guy, he is a bad guy. The audience dislikes him more than it dislikes the criminals who are brought in. Every time the official hurts one of the good cops, we wish something bad would happen to him. Then, when the official overreaches and blunders, we are exhilarated. The official has boxed himself into a corner. We like that. Finally, when the official has to choose between defending a civil lawsuit he can't win and resigning from the force, we are joyful. The villain is getting his due.

What the writers have been doing with this character all along, of course, is manipulating our emotions, which is exactly what your role is when you are pitting characters against each other to create a story.

Some suggestions to consider in characterizing an antagonist:

Can he have a physical mannerism that would·be at least slightly disturbing to most people, for instance an involuntary blinking of one eye? Or sniffing? Frequent nose-wrinkling? Earlobe-pulling? Elbow-scratching? It is the repetitive nature of such mannerisms that grates on readers.

How does your antagonist behave toward people he's never met before? Does he effuse charm, is he overly deferential, or is he discourteous, uninterested, openly bored, arrogant? All of these are characteristics that would help form the reader's attitude toward your villain.

Another possibility is to have your antagonist do something frequently that most people do only occasionally. For instance, does he blow his nose every few minutes (though he is not sick), does his forehead sweat a lot though it is not especially hot, does he scratch himself, cough unnecessarily, wink at others as if there were some implied meaning in what they or he were saying?

To weave individual characteristics into a story, as much as possible let them come out during or as part of an action. The object is to avoid holding up the story and to keep the writer's explanations out of it. To see how it's done, let's examine a work-in-progress in which a successful young businessman, driving to work in what becomes a severe rainstorm, passes a hitchhiker, then out of compassion and guilt, turns his car around to pick the man up:

> As the man clambered in I could see he was one of those assless thin fellows who hikes his pants up higher than most men do.
>
> The hitchhiker had his hand stretched out to shake. I was of the belief that hitchhikers, like waiters and mailmen, don't offer their hand, but this man's was stuck out there like an embarrassment, so I held on to the wheel hard with my left hand and put my right hand out to shake the man's rain-wet palm.
>
> I could tell the man's breath was the kind that toothpaste didn't cure.

The hitchhiker introduces himself. Even his name has an evil sound. He is characterized by clothing, sight, smell, and now touch:

> The skin of Uck's hand seemed flaked, reptilian. Even when the man tried to smile, his face didn't cooperate. Like Peter Lorre's, his

lips thinned, but that was all. I thought if this man's mother had
pressed a pillow on his nose and mouth when he was a baby, would
anyone have convicted her?

The protagonist is so repulsed by what he sees, smells, and touches of
the hitchhiker, that his mind jumps to wishing the man dead. That puts
the reader's emotion on the defensive. The reader—whatever his conduct in private life—doesn't believe or wish to believe that he would
hope a man would drop dead just because he was repulsive. "Hey," the
reader thinks, "this guy's human."

That's the key, of course. Uck *is* human. We meet his wife and child.
He can be charming if he wants to. Nevertheless, he is fundamentally
evil in the way he attaches himself to the life of the protagonist and
won't let go. He is not just getting a lift in the rain, he is the leech that
cannot be pulled off the skin. Uck has taken the first step in pushing
himself into the protagonist's life and has begun the process of forcing
the protagonist out of his job and home, a true villain.

You need to ask yourself about your antagonist, Is he curable? Is he
bad but can be straightened out? Bad will work, but evil will provide a
more profound experience for the reader.

We have seen that wimpishness is off-putting in a protagonist. We
have a sense that *will*—desire reinforced by ambition—is what makes
protagonists drive us through their stories. In the example just given, the
protagonist is intensely interested in his work that has brought him a
comfortable life, his wife, his house. The hitchhiker who appears in the
rainstorm is set to take that from him and cannot be bought off by
ransom of any kind. From that clash of these two characters, we get the
kind of conflict that attracts readers.

CHARACTERIZING MINOR PLAYERS

Major characters deserve and get our primary attention. That doesn't
mean we should settle for stereotypes for minor characters. Sometimes
they are given a name, a sex, an age, and no characterization. I've seen
minor characters given too much characterization, fooling the reader into
thinking they had some larger role to play. Sometimes all you want is for
the reader to be able to *see* the minor character. Here's how Nanci Kincaid does it:

You think you never saw white completely until you see Roy's butt.

The most efficient technique for making minor characters come alive is to select one memorable characteristic that singles them out from the rest of humanity. This is particularly true for fleeting characters, those that appear and vanish, not to return. Early in Hemingway's *A Farewell to Arms* the reader comes upon:

> The priest was young and blushed easily.

In just seven words, the priest is visible even before his special uniform is described. Note that blushing is an action that characterizes, important here because the priest, in military service, is about to be picked on by a senior officer.

Irwin Shaw, in a story called "No Jury Would Convict," shows us this:

> The man in the green sweater took off his yellow straw hat and carefully wiped the sweatband with his handkerchief.

Simple enough, but what makes us see that man is not a description of what he is wearing but an action, wiping the sweatband.

When a writer characterizes beautifully, we indulge him. Every page of Dennis McFarland's first novel, *The Music Room*, is a delight because it is so well written. McFarland doesn't pass up any opportunity to characterize. Here's how he deals with the most minor of characters, a hotel desk clerk, seen from the point of view of the protagonist, whose brother has just died:

> . . . the man behind the hotel desk, whom I had never seen before—dark, and sporting the handlebar mustache of a lion tamer in a circus—seemed to know me, and to know my trouble. I watched him cheerfully help a man just ahead of me, then turn decidedly sorrowful as he shifted his gaze in my direction. It was with great sympathy that he handed me the pink slips of paper on which my telephone messages were written, and I couldn't help noticing that the skin on his hand appeared a bit too moist and white, and the several hairs on the back of it were a bit too coarse and black, individual, and rooted, as if magnified.

Characterizing a minor character through the eyes of an important character is a valuable technique. Note how Anne Richardson Roiphe does it in *Up the Sandbox!*:

... the dwarf lady who lives in our building is hurrying across the street, her shopping bag filled, her fat legs bare and her feet encased in their usual heavy orthopedic shoes. Her face is round and her features are broad, distorted by thick glasses. I had never seen a dwarf till we moved to this building. It's been four years now, and each time we pass my skin crawls. Despite all the humane teachings I have of course heard, I still feel not considerate, compassionate or easy in the company of cripples. I hold to the medieval conviction that someone has been criminal, perhaps in bed, or maybe only in imagination, but someone has committed a crime, perhaps the victim herself.

Minor characters can not only help characterize the major players in a story, but can also advance the plot. In the first three pages of *The Best Revenge*, I introduced five characters in addition to the protagonist in order to characterize the protagonist, Ben Riller, and to get the main plot line going: Ben is in trouble.

A theatrical producer, Ben is just entering the reception room of his office. An elderly messenger is at the desk of Ben's assistant, Charlotte. She is trying to signal to him, but Ben's attention is on the waiting actors. Let's see how the messenger is used:

The geriatric who'd been wrangling with Charlotte spots me at last. Some of the best actors in the world are close to eighty. Their age-lined faces exude character. In the movies you can do repeated takes, but in theater the scourges of the body haunt eight performances a week. Old people chip at my heart. I see my father, Louie, in every one of their faces. . . . It aches to turn an old man down. I smile as he approaches me. I think he wants to shake my hand.

What he wants to do, it turns out, is to provide me with personal service of a subpoena.

I try to hand it back to him, but he's out the door with a gait a younger man would envy.

I used the messenger to help fill out the characterization of the protagonist, Ben. Characterizing a minor player gives us a chance to characterize a major player.

In that same paragraph, several other things come across. The reader learns the producer's feelings about the theater, age, the differences for actors in film and on the stage. It also introduces the producer's father,

Louie, a major character. The point to note is that when depicting a minor character, you can seize the opportunity to convey much else. The most important thing in that brief bit with the messenger is that it takes us—through an action—into the heart of the plot: the hero, Ben Riller the successful producer, is in trouble.

The point I want to leave you with is that the permutations of character are endless and the techniques for achieving them are many. When you are engaged in the complex task of characterization, consider the techniques in this chapter the equivalent of calling 911.

I have tried in this chapter to convey a variety of ways to characterize both minor and major characters. I have an additional suggestion. Spend some time reading or rereading two or three of the classics in which characterization is both profound and memorable: the novels of Dostoevsky and Flaubert from other cultures; Shakespeare's great plays, particularly the tragedies; such twentieth-century writers as Joseph Conrad, Graham Greene, Henry James, to pluck a few from among the many. You'll find that one of the characters resonates in your memory or speaks to your view of life more than most. As you are readying yourself for sleep, imagine a scene in which that character and the character you are working on have a conversation about the story of your book. Imagine what one says and how the other answers. In due course, let yourself sleep. You might find that in the first moments of wakefulness the next morning, you'll want to reach for a pad and paper at your bedside to record some thoughts about your character, enriched by his or her conversation with a character you loved.

Ultimately, the job of characterization among the best of writers is governed by that writer's understanding of human nature. In the early twentieth century, a novel called *Pollyanna* by Eleanor Porter put a new word into our language. "Pollyanna" has come to stand for a blindly optimistic person. We speak of an ostrich attitude, putting one's head into the sand, pretending what is out there and real does not exist. A writer cannot be a Pollyanna. He is in the business of writing what other people think but don't say, which leads us to markers, the subject of the next chapter.

5

Markers: The Key to
Swift Characterization

Lionel Trilling, one of the influential critics of the midtwentieth century who was also an infrequent but interesting writer of fiction, declared that fiction at its heart involved the differences between classes. While this observation is invaluable to writers of fiction, it is also a match tossed into flammable material. The fact that acute differences exist between social and cultural classes seems to be acknowledged in most of the world, but in the United States, where democracy is often confounded with egalitarianism, even the idea that social classes exist has long been taboo. It is, however, a writer's specialty to deal with taboos, to speak the unspoken, to reveal, to uncover, to show in the interaction of people the difference between what we profess and how we act. Moreover, because touchy subjects arouse emotion, they are especially useful for the writer who knows that arousing the emotions of his audience is the test of his skill.

When we discuss cultural differences, we are not talking about economic differences or equal opportunity. Cultural differences arise from inherited characteristics, upbringing, and individual temperament. The best literary fiction often confronts these differences. Even transient or popular fiction can benefit from an awareness by the writer of this rich lode.

Wonderful stories can be crafted about people's inherited characteristics, upbringing, and individual temperament. Characters, just like people, can strive to overcome this baggage and training. Some people succeed in doing so, some can't, and the same is true of the characters available to our imaginations.

Many dramatic moments in theater and film come from clashes between characters based on differences in background. How can we overlook the source of audience interest in Shaw's *Pygmalion* or its rendering as a musical in *My Fair Lady*? Put the garish and tacky Eliza Doolittle in touch with Henry Higgins, and you have a clash of social and cultural differences instantly recognized by millions.

These differences are at the heart of what is in my judgment the best play by the best American playwright of the twentieth century, Tennessee Williams's *A Streetcar Named Desire*. The play and film derive their power from the cultural conflict between Blanche DuBois, the fallen "lady," and Stanley Kowalski, the blue-collar brute, who strip each other's pretenses, witnessed by Stella, who married beneath her, and found herself in the world of card-playing, beer-swilling male animals.

Characters of different cultural classes caught in a crucible are, of course, ideal for fiction. The dramatic heat generated by cultural differences, inherited or nurtured, added to the differences of individual temperaments, can help writers create wonderful stories. These differences are a valuable resource for scenes as well as entire plots. It is the underlying basis of conflict in fiction.

Most people, regardless of their background, prefer others whom they think of as "their own kind." Which means that there is a widespread prejudice against "the other kinds." While this prejudice can be controlled and even overcome to some degree in life, a vestige of feeling about "otherness" remains even in most people who deny it. That feeling of "otherness" is useful to the writer in plotting because readers' emotions can be quickly committed when they observe two characters of differing backgrounds in the same story.

It is useful for writers to step onto the thin ice of this subject matter with a clear understanding of terms and meanings.

A *culture* consists of the behavior patterns, beliefs, traditions, institutions, taste, and other characteristics of a community passed from one generation to another. The adjective "cultured" is usually used to connote a superior level of aesthetic and intellectual development that results from education and training.

A *class* is a stratum of society whose members share cultural and social characteristics. "Class" used by itself—as in "she had class"—connotes superior style or quality.

Good writers have come from every imaginable social class, and some stand ready to defend their turf. A writer has to squelch his emotional reactions consciously in order to get enough distance to use them in his work as a writer.

People in civil society usually try to overlook the kind of differences we have been talking about. But they don't succeed. Their attempts to cover up noticed differences sometimes fail, hurting others. In general, cultural differences are noticed by almost everybody. When people learn to set aside cultural differences, we speak of them as "open-minded." Yet "open-minded" people sometimes say inappropriate things to make people of other social classes feel "more at home." This makes the others feel less comfortable, not more comfortable. Therefore, despite noble intentions, social and cultural differences can be a source of high feeling and high drama. As we shall see, for plotting purposes, differences are more important than similarities.

Action movies categorize people into good guys and bad guys. In many of the films that are nominated for Academy Awards, the discernment of differences becomes more subtle. That discernment becomes a necessity in the best literary and mainstream fiction.

The butting together of characters of differing backgrounds can be extreme, as in D. H. Lawrence's *Lady Chatterley's Lover*. It can produce comedy if a good old boy joins the ladies and gentlemen of Virginia on a fox hunt. What we expect of a good old boy is that while he, too, hunts for pleasure, it is in the company of men who hunt in packs, dressed in rough clothes, who would laugh at the gaudy dress of traditional fox hunters. Social and cultural differences strike sparks both for the writer and the reader.

In literary fiction, the clash of differences is often more subtle than in *My Fair Lady* or *A Streetcar Named Desire*. One of my favorite stories, which won a place in *The Best Short Stories of 1991*, was Kate Braverman's "Tall Tales from the Mekong Delta." Let's look at the beginning of that remarkable story and observe the clash of background and values:

> It was in the fifth month of her sobriety. It was after the hospital. It was after her divorce. It was autumn. She had even stopped smoking. She was wearing pink aerobic pants, a pink T-shirt with KAUAI written in lilac across the chest, and tennis shoes. She had just come from the gym. Her black hair was damp. She was wearing a pink sweatband around her forehead. She was walking across a parking lot bordering a city park in West Hollywood. She was carrying cookies for the AA meeting. She was in charge of bringing the food for the meeting. He fell into step with her. He was short, fat, pale. He had bad teeth. His hair was dirty. Later, she would

freeze this frame in her mind and study it. She would say he seemed frightened and defeated and trapped, cagey was the word she used to describe his eyes, how he measured and evaluated something in the air between them. The way he squinted through hazel eyes, it had nothing to do with the sunlight.

"I'm Lenny," he said, extending his hand. "What's your name?"

She told him. She was holding a bag with packages of cookies in it. After the meeting, she had an appointment with her psychiatrist, then a manicure. She kept walking.

"You a teacher? You look like a teacher," he said.

"I'm a writer," she told him. "I teach creative writing."

"You look like a teacher," Lenny said.

"I'm not just a teacher," she told him. She was annoyed.

"Okay. You're a writer. And you're bad. You're one of those bad girls from Beverly Hills. I've had my eye on you," Lenny said.

She didn't say anything. He was wearing blue jeans, a black leather jacket zipped to his throat, a long red wool scarf around his neck, and a Dodgers baseball cap. It was too hot a day for the leather jacket and scarf. She didn't find that detail significant. It caught her attention, she touched it briefly and then let it go. She looked but did not see. They were standing on a curb. The meeting was in a community room across the boulevard. She wasn't afraid yet.

"You do drugs? What do you do? Drink too much?" he asked.

The narrator and Lenny come from different worlds. We find out how different as the story goes on. Lenny is invading her world just as Henry Higgins invaded Eliza's and Blanche DuBois invaded Stanley's—with different intent, of course. The reader senses the difference early from the clothes they are wearing, from the woman's fear and need to be polite, and Lenny's impolite, aggressive questioning and assumptions.

The process of identifying different worlds for the reader can be accomplished quickly through *markers*, easily identified signals that to the majority of readers will reveal a character's cultural and social background. Clothing, as we've seen, is a useful marker. A woman in a tailored suit suggests formality. Would we expect to see that woman walking in the street with a man wearing a totally sleeveless "muscle" shirt or a cap with a slogan on it? The reader assumes they are not together because they have the appurtenances of widely different backgrounds. But if they are walking arm in arm, what is the reader to think or feel?

Today, people of every background seem to wear jeans. But if a man wears designer jeans with a pressed crease do we assume he's just come off his job at a construction site? Suppose the reader sees someone on a construction site who is wearing designer jeans with a pressed crease, what does the reader think? He thinks *phony*. Phoniness can be useful to a writer.

While no marker is an absolute designation of background or class (there are exceptions to almost all of them), the reader will feel a reaction to the markers. For instance, if we are in a courtroom where a young man is being charged with a criminal offense, what do we expect to see? We expect that his lawyer will have made him get dressed up, often with a suit and tie. If in that courtroom that same young man is dressed in his usual cut-off blue jeans, dirty sneakers, and a T-shirt with an obscene slogan, what would we think? That his lawyer had neglected to do his job? What would the judge think? Surely the judge knows that lawyers dress up their clients. Will the judge think that the lawyer or client is showing contempt for the dignity of the court? The reaction to clothing is often a reaction to the surroundings in which the clothing is worn. Keep that in mind when you're describing a character in a specific scene.

When in fiction, theater, and film the writer brings together people of differing social and cultural backgrounds, he needs to step back to watch the inherent drama of differences explode. Differences assume opposition. That's what makes writing dramatic. If dealing with social and cultural differences makes the writer uneasy, that's good. Emotion-inciting material is the most desirable kind. If social and cultural differences between characters excite emotion, the tension of any story will surely increase.

Many aspects of cultural class distinction have been used in fiction. Some characteristics that once denoted upper and lower classes have diffused in time.

In countries with diverse cultures like the United States, regional differences sometimes become more apparent than class distinctions. Generational differences also produce changes. For instance, while a conspicuous tattoo still suggests "lower class" to the reader, and the larger the tattoo the lower the class, in recent years some young people of all classes have had themselves tattooed with small objects such as a heart, a rose, or a butterfly.

Though the characteristics that once connoted "lower class" and "upper class" to readers are no longer absolutes, they still work as markers in which readers find connotations and associations. Those markers continue to be invaluable to the writer.

Let's look at some common markers, some of which have been overused:

Hair worn in curlers under a head scarf in public usually connotes "lower class" to readers.

For a woman, fingernails the size of animal claws and garish nail polish used to make a statement about class. Clawlike fingernails and excessive rouge continue to suggest unsophisticated artifice, which can be useful to a writer. Black under the fingernails of a man dressed up to go out might be a marker of a person who does dirty work with his hands and never quite gets them clean. The writer doesn't have to say what I've just said. All he has to show the reader are the fingernails; they are effective markers.

Public conduct with children is an immediate marker. A woman walking with a "dressed-up" child connotes one thing. A woman screaming at her children in the supermarket suggests another.

What does the incessant chewing of gum suggest about a character? What would an ankle bracelet convey to a reader about a character? What about a man wearing multiple large rings, or a diamond ring?

Mannerisms can be important markers. How does the reader react to a male character who publicly picks his nose, scratches under his arms and in his crotch? Would the reader instantly assume that the character is couth or uncouth?

Even the transportation used by a character can be a marker. If a reader knew nothing about a character except that he owned a pickup truck, a motorcycle, and a souped-up car with oversize tires and a noisy muffler, what would the reader think about that character's background?

Food, drink, and the places they are consumed are markers. If the reader knows a character drinks popular brands of American beer, rye whiskey, and chilled red wine, what does the reader guess about the character's background? If the character drinks Scotch, Perrier, and martinis straight up, does the reader have a different view? Of course. These markers are useful. Fizzy wine or coolers would not be the choice of people with educated palates. Nor would you be likely to find people with educated palates on line in a fast-food take-out joint. Conversely, a construction worker, even if dressed in his Sunday best, is likely to feel mighty uncomfortable in one of Manhattan's posh East Side restaurants, where all the waiters are dressed in black tie and the menu is in French.

If your character brought his mouth down to his food rather than his food up to his mouth, the reader would likely draw an instant assumption about his upbringing. However, some distinctions in eating habits are poor markers because they are too complex to describe succinctly. For instance, the British use a fork in the left hand and a knife in the right. The left hand brings the cut food to the mouth. Americans keep switching hands and bring food to the mouth with the right hand. Distinctions of that sort are not good markers for the writer because they require too much description and readers might still not get the point without the author telling them explicitly. A marker should convey its point instantly.

Perhaps the most frequently used marker is found in the vocabulary and expressions of a character's dialogue. If a character uses words like "ostensibly," "exacerbate," "primordial" correctly, and with ease, what would you, as a reader, think about them? That vocabulary is indicative of someone who is well educated. But it could also reflect a pompous person. One of the most common vocabulary markers is heard on television when a police officer talks about a "perpetrator."

In most of my novels I have at least one character with an accent, a distinguishing marker. In *The Best Revenge* at least three characters have accent markers that differ noticeably from each other. Many politicians speak in incomplete sentences peppered with clichés. Street people use four-letter words and vulgar expressions. All of these markers characterize quickly.

The content of a character's speech can also generate markers. If a character displays knowledge of what went on in previous centuries, is interested in international issues, reads books and appreciates them as physical objects, and votes regularly as a matter of principle, what will the reader think about his or her background? Markers provide the writer with an opportunity to show the character's background instead of telling the reader about it.

Attitudes can also be used as markers:

> Arthur came to New York expecting to be insulted or mugged by every passerby.

An inexperienced attitude toward travel can be an important marker, for instance, a preference for group tours, being intimidated by foreign languages and customs, or buying up mass-produced souvenirs. However, be wary of cliché markers such as an American tourist abroad in search of a restaurant that serves hamburgers.

I have a strong preference for action markers, that is sentences that describe what a character does and at the same time reveal something about the character's upbringing or background:

Every time Zelda ate in a restaurant, she found some reason to send food back to the kitchen.

Louis always played it safe by overtipping the waiter.

As usual, Angelica let her food get cold because she was busy watching everyone else in the restaurant.

We have just seen three quite different instant characterizations in the same location, a restaurant.

I have sometimes found that even accomplished writers neglect to ask themselves some fundamental questions about their important characters that could provide useful markers. For instance, what trait inherited by the protagonist has most influenced his adult life? What custom of the protagonist's family still haunts his life? Which personal habit has he tried to break, unsuccessfully, for years? What family tradition has had the most positive influence on the protagonist? What is the single most important factor in the villain's upbringing that contributed to his reprehensible conduct?

If you are presently writing a novel, have you examined it to see if there are some social or class differences between your two most important characters? How do those differences influence the story? If you have neglected such differences, how might you bolster your story by adding some social and cultural differences that arouse emotion?

And now that you're mastering the creation of characters, it's time to ask, "How do you plot that story?"

6

Thwarting Desire: The Basis of Plotting

We are driven through life by our needs and wants. So must the characters we create be motivated by what they want. The driving force of characters is their desire.

Inexperienced writers, sometimes ill read in the great works of their own and previous times, often try to write novels with a relatively passive protagonist who wants little or has largely given up wanting. I have met more than one writer who says that his character doesn't want anything—he just wants to "live his life." That always brings to mind something Kurt Vonnegut said:

> "When I used to teach creative writing, I would tell the students to make their characters want something right away even if it's only a glass of water. Characters paralyzed by the meaninglessness of modern life still have to drink water from time to time."

The most interesting stories involve characters who want something badly. In Kafka's *The Trial*, Joseph K. wants to know why he is being arrested, why he is being tried, what he is guilty of. In Fitzgerald's *The Great Gatsby*, the central character constructs his life with the sole object of reuniting with Daisy, the woman he loves. In Flaubert's *Madame Bovary*, Emma Bovary, her head full of romantic notions, wants to escape the dreariness of her husband and her life. If your character doesn't want anything badly enough, readers will have a hard time rooting for him to attain his goal, which is what compels readers to continue reading. The more urgent the want, the greater the reader's interest. A far future want does not set the reader's pulse going the way an immediate want does. The want can be negative, wanting something not to happen, as in Frederick Forsyth's *The Day of the Jackal*, in which the reader hopes that de Gaulle will escape the assassin's bullet.

In the chapter on characterization, I suggested that some of the most memorable characters in fiction were eccentric. To carry the point a step further, I suggest relating the character's deepest desire to the character's fundamental difference from other characters, especially the character of the antagonist.

Which brings us to the essence of plotting: putting the protagonist's desire and the antagonist's desire into sharp conflict. If the conflict isn't sharp, the tension will be lax. One way to plan is to think of what would most thwart your protagonist's want, then give the power to thwart that want to the antagonist. And be certain there is a two-way urgency: your protagonist wants a particular, important desire fulfilled as soon as possible, and the antagonist wants to wreck the chance of that happening, also as soon as possible.

Those are the three keys: the want and the opposition to the want need to be important, necessary, and urgent. The result should be the kind of conflict that interests readers.

A word of caution: these plotting guidelines are *basic* and to some degree simplistic. They are intended to provide the writer with the easiest route to publication. The well-read writer will be familiar with complex plots that deviate from the norm. What they do not deviate from is the fierce desire of the protagonist and the conflict engendered by obstacles.

The essence of dramatic conflict lies in the clash of wants. You need to be certain that the conflicting wants are connected significantly and are over something that the reader will view as important. For instance, if the hero wants to preserve his valuable stamp collection and the villain has stolen it and intends to sell the items in it piecemeal to conceal his theft, their wants are clearly on a collision course. However, ask yourself, does the reader care enough about the stamp collection? If the stamp collection belonged to President Franklin Roosevelt, an avid stamp collector, the theft of that collection could have interfered with matters of state until it was resolved. The reader will care about the stamp collection to the degree that he cares about the protagonist and what the protagonist loves. That's one of the reasons why the best plots develop out of character.

It is easier for the reader to identify with a want that is close to universal and not too specialized (a stamp collection is relatively specialized). The wants that interest a majority of readers include gaining or losing a love, achieving a lifetime ambition, seeing that justice is done, saving a life, seeking revenge, and accomplishing a task that at first seemed impossible.

In transient fiction (sometimes called "commercial" or "popular" fiction), the wants are less personal and often more melodramatic. Events happen rather than grow out of character. Though my personal preference is for literary fiction, I have worked with a number of highly successful professional bestselling novelists who didn't seem to care whether their characters were remembered years later. They mastered craft; their storytelling was suspenseful and compelling for large numbers of readers. The wants of their characters tended to be different from those in literary fiction. For them and other writers of popular fiction, the following wants were paramount:

- Defeating the plans of a national enemy.
- Blocking an assassin out to kill an important person.
- Rescuing someone close to the hero.
- Solving an important crime.

The clash between your characters can be based on almost anything as long as it is involved with their desires. The most common causes of a clash are money, love, and power. Power connotes control, usually over other human beings. Therefore, in a community of two people, if one has power, the other doesn't have it. Some of the most interesting plots involve a character who has power in one arena up against a character who has power in another arena, and both characters are caught in the same crucible. (We will deal with the crucible in its own chapter.)

When planning your story, it is important to remember that small clashes result in stories that seem relatively trivial. Larger clashes resonate for the reader. Ask yourself these questions: Does the conflict you are working on lead to profound unhappiness, injury, or death? Or is the conflict over an object that is exceedingly valuable to the main character? Is the conflict over an important life decision—to move far away, to change one's career, to leave for another partner, to follow a hazardous opportunity, to avoid intolerable circumstances?

Ask yourself, will the clash between your protagonist and your antagonist seem inevitable to the reader? Have you avoided coincidence as the cause of their clash? Will the clash take place in a highly visible environment so that the reader will see the action?

If you have some concern about the intensity of your plot, ask yourself, Does the conflict you've invented involve the best possible thing that could happen to your protagonist? Is what happens a surprise to anyone? Can you make it surprising by setting up an action and then showing the opposite of what your reader is likely to expect?

Would the conflict you have described result in a verbal or physical struggle? Would that struggle call for strong scenes in which your characters clash in an exciting way? Remember your book is told in scenes each one of which should produce an excited reaction in the reader.

If any scene seems not yet exciting enough, think of introducing a new character into it, which always generates possibilities for conflict, especially if the new character has something important at stake in what is happening in that scene.

If you get stuck, there's another device some writers use. Think of the worst thing that could possibly happen to you right now. Don't censor. A layman instinctively covers up. A writer disciplines himself to uncover.

Now think of your very best friend. Conjure up a picture of him or her in your mind. Remember the good times with your best friend. What is the worst thing that could happen to him or her at this very moment? It has to be something different from the worst thing you imagined happening to you. It should be linked to your friend's character, ambitions, or desire.

Now imagine the same worst thing happening not to your best friend but to the character in your story. Would that create a suitable obstacle in the plot you are developing?

The protagonist's biggest obstacle is usually the antagonist and what he does. But there can be numerous other obstacles that will thwart the protagonist on the way to achieving his goal, including, perhaps, what you imagined happening to your friend.

There are other techniques to get your plotting motor going. By thinking of certain conventional obstacles, less conventional obstacles will occur to you. For instance, your character needs to get someplace right away. The car breaks down. (In a melodrama, the breakdown may have been precipitated by the villain or an accomplice.) Or the weather changes drastically and impedes progress. If the weather won't do, think of any unexpected, uncontrollable event.

Here are some other stimuli. A deaf person fails to hear something. A blind person fails to see something. A recluse refuses to tell what he has seen. An airplane flight is aborted on takeoff. Water is needed immediately for an urgent purpose; suddenly there is no water in the tap.

There are larger obstacles that can stimulate your plotting: a sudden illness of an important character. Help is unavailable. An accident happens on the highway to someone the reader cares about. Or an accident at home—someone falls in the bathtub or off a ladder. A natural disaster (flood, earthquake, hurricane, forest fire) puts your character at great risk.

It's common to think of the obstacles of all being generated by the villain, but we've seen that acts of nature can also be obstacles. And there are always other people butting in. You can devise an unwanted intervention by someone who wants to help but makes things worse. Or you can have an unwanted intervention by someone unrelated to the villain who wants to block the protagonist for reasons of his own. You can have a previously absent person return who causes problems because she is not up on what has transpired during her absence. The list could go on. But you get the point. You can always check your daily newspaper for obstacles in the lives of people in news stories.

One caution. Some obstacles need to be planted ahead of time so as not to seem arbitrary devices of the author.

Writers who feel the need of discipline in plotting can sometimes benefit by preparing a list of every obstacle they plan to use in their plot. They then can ask themselves, is the first obstacle strong enough to hook the reader? Do the obstacles build? That means as each obstacle is faced and overcome by the protagonist, an even greater obstacle has to present itself.

I know novelists who have very strong first obstacles, but they do not follow up with stronger obstacles, with the consequence that the reader feels the story winding down. As a result, the reader either gives up reading before the end or, even if he's persistent, won't rush to get that author's next book.

Some writers I've worked with find it difficult to develop plots because they're not sure their plot ideas would be of interest to readers. Here are some clues to areas of reader interest:

- Reading about enemies trapped together. In life, one of the most uncomfortable experiences people have is being with someone they don't want to be with. In fiction, when readers observe someone else in that predicament, it engages a strong concealed emotion. The reader wants to know the outcome.

- Experiencing a character's embarrassment involves the reader. Causing a character to be embarrassed will almost always create an interesting plot development.
- Experiencing a character's fear creates enormous tension. It can be fear of mortal danger, of course, but experienced novelists generate fear from small things. Eric Ambler's *The Light of Day* has a scene in which the protagonist is chauffeuring a car with a loose door panel concealing smuggled arms. As the screws rattle, so does the reader, afraid that the car's owner in the backseat will hear the rattling. The scene is full of tension.
- Change in a relationship invites the reader's tense interest in the outcome. In life, people get bored when nothing changes even though changes in life are fraught with peril. If the perils of major change happen within the covers of a book, the reader will be absorbed.
- Readers enjoy being surprised. Nice surprises are one of the pleasures of life. We like to receive surprise presents, good news, the announcement of an unexpected visit by friends we want to see. Bad surprises in life bring hurt, sadness, misfortune. But in books readers thrill to the unexpected. A new obstacle, an unexpected confrontation by an enemy or a sudden twist of circumstance all start adrenaline pumping and pages turning. Novels, stories, plays, and screenplays thrive on bad as well as good surprises.

Surprises are not difficult to create. Look at each important incident in your plot and see what you would normally expect to happen next. Then have the exact opposite happen. At least half the time an idea will suggest itself that will surprise your characters as well as yourself.

You can surprise yourself (and your readers eventually) by picking an unusual locale that you know well enough to depict accurately. Then choose a character you have already created who is most unlikely to show up in that locale. Put that character in that locale. Imagine what happens when the character shows up there, and other characters react.

Finally, I would like to suggest an easy means for getting character-derived plot ideas. Sometimes even experienced writers get stuck. I counsel them to examine the classified personal ads, which frequently have the following characteristics:

- They are written by people who want a relationship so badly that they are willing to advertise for it.

- What they want is a mate, which is a high category of desire and the subject of much fiction.
- The ad writers are doing two things at once: they are trying to describe the kind of person they want to meet; they are describing themselves (sometimes unknowingly).
- The ad writers are frequently fantasizing about their ideal as well as about themselves.
- Readers of the ads usually get a far different impression from the one the advertiser intends.

The personal ads I've seen that are useful appear in *New York* magazine, the *Village Voice, L.A. Reader, L.A. Weekly*, and the *New York Review of Books*. Some are available nationally at better newsstands or by subscription. The *New York Review of Books*, a highbrow biweekly with a large international following, is a fine source because some of its ads are quite imaginative. I quote one of my favorites:

VERY UNUSUAL MAN

I'm looking for a very special woman—probably someone who rarely if ever, answers ads. Very well-educated and extraordinarily bright, funny, beautiful, athletic, sophisticated, outdoor oriented, honest, nurturing, vulnerable, financially secure, very sensual and able to be open and present to other people. Someone who is very successful in her own way, courageous and psychologically grown-up. Probably 35–45, with a great appetite for exploring life with another person. I'm extremely well-educated, post-doctoral in humanities, and work at the top of the business community. Handsome, 6', 180 lbs., athletic, very, very successful financially and professionally. I am a psychologically secure, well-balanced man who is totally natural and curious, sometimes brilliant, intuitive, funny, honest, genuine, direct and very open. I spend two to three months a year off doing interesting things other than work. I am a very complex, very special man with deep values and a good heart. I need to find someone who has gotten to the same place in her life and is headed in the same direction. Note/phone/photo a must.

I've read that ad at a number of writers' conferences. Invariably, the audience keeps laughing throughout. They laugh because of the discrepancy between their image of the advertiser and the person's self-image, ideal stuff for stories. If several writers were to choose the same ad as a source for a character-based plot, I can guarantee that they would come up with entirely different plots. Personal classified ads are a good emergency resource.

In this chapter we have covered the elementary essentials of devising a plot. Now let's take a look at some innovative ways of plotting.

7

The Actors Studio Method
for Developing Drama in Plots

A plot consists of scenes. What follows is an excellent way of creating almost any scene.

In midtwentieth century, the home away from home for most superbly talented American actors was a white wooden church on scruffy West 44th Street in New York City that had become the locus of the Actors Studio. The building contained offices and rehearsal areas, but its core was the auditorium one flight up with its makeshift stage and hard seats. The physical environment didn't matter. All who entered there knew they were in the cathedral of American theater, where the most talented aspirants got a chance to be scourged by Cardinal Lee Strasberg and where celebrated stars honed their work.

In time an associated Directors Group brought some of the best stage and film directors to work in the Actors Studio. Missing were writers, the playwrights who needed to see their work-in-progress being performed by professional actors, guided by experienced directors, all willing to commit long hours of rehearsal and performance without compensation except for the arduous pleasure of work and the spurt of hope that once in a great while a scene coming to life at the Actors Studio might turn into a production and a job.

In 1957, along with Tennessee Williams, William Inge, Molly Kazan, and Robert Anderson, I was one of ten founding members of the Playwrights Group of the Actors Studio in New York. As word of the group got around, it expanded to include talented newcomers like Edward Albee and Lorraine Hansberry, and novelists like Norman Mailer who hoped to write for the theater. Writers could now see their new work performed by superlative actors guided by talented directors. During its earliest years, the weekly meetings of the Playwrights Group included a trial performance of a play or a part of a play before an audience of fellow writers, directors, and actors, who would afterward comment on the work.*

For us writers, a high learning time came from the less formal exercises that did not require weeks of rehearsal by actors. In these exercises, writers were transformed into actors for the benefit of their colleagues. I was one of two writers picked by the director for an early exercise. The other writer was Rona Jaffe, the author of several bestselling novels. The director who worked with us that day was Elia Kazan, director of five Pulitzer Prize-winning plays and winner of two Academy Awards. For the writers in the audience—and for the "victims," Rona Jaffe and me— it was an experience that gave us one of the most valuable techniques a writer can have.

We were to improvise a scene for which there was no script. I was to play the part of the headmaster of the Dalton School, a private establishment in New York for the privileged young. Rona Jaffe was to be the mother of a boy who had been expelled by the headmaster. That's what the audience knew.

Then Kazan took me aside, out of everyone's earshot, and told me that the mother of the expelled boy was coming to my office, undoubtedly to try to get the boy reinstated. This incorrigible boy had disrupted every class he was in, did not respond to the warnings of his teachers, and under no condition was I to take him back.

After this briefing, which took half a minute, I returned to the makeshift stage and Kazan then took Rona Jaffe aside. What do you think he told her?

None of the writers—myself included—knew what Kazan told Rona Jaffe till afterward. He told her that she was the mother of a bright, well-behaved boy, a first-class student, that the headmaster was prejudiced against him, had treated him disgracefully, and that Rona had to insist that the headmaster take the boy back into the school immediately!

Rona Jaffe and I were turned loose on the stage to improvise a scene in front of the audience. Within seconds we were quarreling, our voices raised. We both got red in the face and yelled at each other. The audience loved it. We were battling because each of us had been given a different script!

That's what happens in life. Each of us enters into conversation with another person with a script that is different from the other person's

* I deal with the sexual politics, outrageous experiments, glories, and shenanigans of this interesting group in a work-in-progress entitled *Passing for Normal*. Here I concern myself solely with the technique playwrights learned that can be used to advantage by writers of fiction and film.

script. The frequent result is disagreement and conflict—disagreeable in life and invaluable in writing, for conflict is the ingredient that makes action dramatic. When we get involved with other people, the chances of a clash are present even with people we love because we do not have the same scripts in our heads. And the tension is even greater when we are involved with an antagonist.

You are now armed. The secret of creating conflict in scenes you write is to *give your characters different scripts.*

Over the years, in teaching writers at the University of California and at writers' conferences and workshops, I have stage-managed an exercise involving members of the audience that enables these principles to be remembered. In teaching the Actors Studio method of creating conflict, I ask for one male and one female volunteer. I take the male student around a corner out of earshot and tell him that he is to visit a woman he loves and tell her, **"I got your message."** No matter what she answers, he is to insist he got her message. I then take the female student out of earshot and tell her that a fellow she thinks is obnoxious is coming over. She didn't leave a message for him. She just wants the money.

When both students come on stage in front of the group, the male student arrives at a make-believe door, knocks, is let in, and says, **"I got your message."**

The woman, as instructed, answers, **"What message? Did you bring the money?"** The usual reaction is loud laughter from the audience. Whatever the man and woman then say, the audience enjoys their adversarial dialogue, each relying on a different script.

That's what you do with your characters. Whatever scene they are in, give them different scripts and you'll have conflict in the scene and an entertained reader or audience. This technique works well for scenes in both commercial and literary fiction, with the scripts in literary fiction differing more subtly. This craft technique contains a range of possibility for every kind of writing.

Let's clarify this simple procedure. You are imagining a scene with two characters. Before you write the scene, make a note as to the "script" or tack (keep it simple) of the first character and then of the second character. Make sure the scripts are different and at odds. Only you will be privy to the scripts of both characters. Let them play out the scene in front of you as you write. And if you have a third character in the scene, give that character a script different from the other two.

A "script" in this exercise is not the actual lines of dialogue, only *the intent of the character in that scene.* Think of the character as getting instructions from you, the writer. It is important to keep the instructions brief. In the example devised by Elia Kazan, my script consisted of knowing who I was supposed to be (the headmaster of the Dalton School) and that I had thrown out a badly behaved boy. Rona Jaffe's script was equally simple: the headmaster was in the wrong and she was determined to get her marvelous boy reinstated.

One of the values of using this method is that if Kazan had used two different writers for the exercise and given them the same scripts, the audience would have heard different extemporaneous dialogue and perhaps the scene would have taken a different direction than it did with Rona Jaffe and me. If you gave those scripts to a dozen different writers, you'd get a dozen different stories.

As an exercise, jot down the scripts of each of the characters in a given scene of any novel you may be reading. The writer probably wasn't thinking of the character's positions as scripts. The Actors Studio technique is a shortcut to the intuitive and learned processes that experienced writers use in creating dramatic confrontations in stories and plays.

It's a wonderful technique. Use it well.

8

The Crucible: A Key
to Successful Plotting

In the previous chapter, we were privy to the Actors Studio technique, giving your protagonist and antagonist different scripts and letting them tangle. While two characters can have different scripts throughout a book, the Actors Studio technique is most valuable for planning individual scenes.

For plotting an entire work, I especially like the use of a *crucible*. In ordinary parlance a crucible refers to a vessel in which different ingredients are melded in white hot heat. The word has come to mean a severe test, which leads us to its use in plotting fiction. Author James Frey refers to a crucible as "the container that holds the characters together as things heat up."

Characters caught in a crucible won't declare a truce and quit. They're in it till the end. The key to the crucible is that *the motivation of the characters to continue opposing each other is greater than their motivation to run away*. Or they can't run away because they are in a prison cell, a lifeboat, an army, or a family.

The following examples are drawn from memorable fiction that most writers will have read:

- In Hemingway's *The Old Man and the Sea,* the man and the hooked fish are in a crucible: neither will give up to the other.
- In Flaubert's *Madame Bovary,* Emma Bovary is married to a man she loathes. Divorce, then, was impossible. Her marriage is the crucible.
- In Nabokov's *Lolita,* Humbert is in love with a young woman who is still a child. For most of the book Humbert and Lolita are in a crucible because she has nowhere else to go. When a third character, Quilty, provides an exit for her, the crucible cracks.

A crucible is an environment, emotional or physical, that bonds two people. It can be a scene or a series of scenes, but more often the crucible is an entire book. The crucible is a relationship, often one influenced by locale. Two prisoners in a cell are in a crucible because of where they are, and their confrontations are accelerated by the fact that they are thrust into the cell with different scripts. *The Kiss of the Spider Woman* is an excellent example. In my novel *The Magician,* the crucible is a high school. The villain, Stanley Urek, goes to the school, and so does the protagonist, Ed Japhet. Neither is free to go elsewhere. The crux of the conflict between the two boys derives from Urek's role as leader of a gang that extorts protection money from the other students and Japhet's refusal to pay. Both boys must continue in school and live in the same community. The school, and in a sense the community they live in, is their crucible.

In *The Best Revenge*, Ben and Nick start out as archenemies. Ben is producing a play for Broadway that is in deep financial trouble. Nick is a gangster nouveau, a new-style moneylender whose terms are severe, but Ben has no choice except to borrow from Nick and involve him in the production of the play. They are locked in the crucible of the play Ben is producing and Nick is financing. Ben is forced into a relationship he cannot leave. Nor does Nick want to leave once he gets a taste of the excitement of being involved in theatrical production. Remember that the essence of a crucible is that the characters are drawn more to the crucible than to escaping from it. In the end, the enemies, Ben and Nick, become friends, their lives melded in the crucible.

In his book *How to Write a Damn Good Novel*, James Frey came up with some excellent examples of characters caught in a crucible. I have adapted them and added others for use by my students:

- All the people in a lifeboat are in a crucible.
- Business partners, one a workaholic, the other lazy, are in a crucible.
- A wife and husband, bonded together by marriage, love, and duty, remain in conflict until separated by death or divorce. Their crucible is marriage.
- A father and son in conflict are also bonded by a relationship that even death doesn't end. They can walk away from each other, but neither can get the other out of his memory. Their relationship, for better or worse, is for keeps.

Some situations do not lend themselves to creating a crucible environment in fiction, but you'd be surprised how many do. Test the possibilities. If the locale you have chosen for a particular scene does not add the stress of a crucible, can you change the location of the scene, making it difficult for one of the participants to leave? Or is there anything that you can add to the background of either or both characters that would link them in a crucible and thereby raise the stress of their relationship?

Putting two characters in a crucible is an excellent way to proceed in plotting. Some writers, however, prefer to work with a simpler concept, that of a *closed environment*, the locale where the action takes place. Here are some examples to illustrate the difference:

- An astronaut who gets deathly ill during a space mission is in a closed environment. The location is a crucible, but as yet there is no overwhelming relationship that keeps him there. He is caught in a capsule in outer space.
- Robinson Crusoe and Friday on an island are in a closed environment. While their isolation from the rest of the world is the most important fact of their lives, their relationship gradually dominates the reader's interest.
- In *Moby Dick*, Captain Ahab's ship, the *Pequod*, is a closed environment. The most interesting relationship is that of Ahab and the White Whale. Therefore, it is not the ship that is the crucible, it is the vast ocean that contains both Ahab and the whale.
- In Jean-Paul Sartre's brilliant play *No Exit*, which every writer should read, all four characters are in a closed environment, giving the play its dramatic intensity and its theme: Hell is other people.

When devising a locale for a scene, it always pays to give a few moments thought to the possibility of choosing a closed environment. It will invariably increase the tension of the scene. The ideal time to think of that locale is when you are first imagining your characters. What crucible might they be in? If you can find the right crucible, you will be on the way to a mesmerizing plot.

9

Suspense: Keeping
the Reader Reading

Your predecessor, a storyteller of many centuries ago, recited his stories around a fire. If he failed to arouse his listeners' anticipation and droned on, or if his audience guessed what happened next, they either fell asleep or killed him.

You are lucky! If you fail to arouse your reader's interest, the worst that will happen is that is you won't get published. However, if your goal is publication, whatever the nature of your story please pay close attention to what follows because suspense is the most essential ingredient of plotting.

You can have a remarkable style and intriguing characters, but if your writing doesn't quickly arouse the reader's curiosity about what will happen, the reader will close the covers of your book without reading further. *Suspense is achieved by arousing the reader's curiosity and keeping it aroused as long as possible.*

Readers aren't articulate about what keeps them reading a particular work. Some, impatient to find out what happens to the characters next, will say, "I can't put this book down," which means the reader's curiosity is greater than his need to do almost anything else. Suspense is strong glue between the reader and the writing. I remember my pleasure at getting a letter from Barnaby Conrad, founder of the Santa Barbara Writers Conference and author of many books, including the novel *Matador*. Conrad had just finished reading a novel of mine, which, he said, he had been unable to stop reading except once when he "got up to micturate." The function of suspense is to put the reader in danger of an overfull bladder. Of all the reviews of my novels, the line I remember best was in the *New York Times*: "If you bury yourself in a Sol Stein book while walking, you'll walk into a wall." That's the idea: immerse the reader so deeply in the story that he'll let go of the book only when the real world intrudes.

"Suspense" derives from the Latin word meaning "to hang." Think of yourself as a hangman. You take your reader to the cliff's edge. There you hang your hero by his fingertips. You are not to behave like a compassionate human being. You are not a rescuer. Your job is to avoid rescuing the hero as long as possible. You leave him hanging.

Hanging, of course, is an extreme situation from melodrama. Suspense can take many forms, some of them subtle. Suspense builds when the reader wants something to happen and it isn't happening yet. Or something is happening and the reader wants it to stop, now. And it doesn't.

Suspense needles the reader with a feeling of anxious uncertainty. Here are examples of the kinds of situations that create suspense:

- A prospective danger to a character.
- An actual immediate danger to a character.
- An unwanted confrontation.
- A confrontation wanted by one character and not by the other.
- An old fear about to become a present reality.
- A life crisis that requires an immediate action.

The writer's duty is to set up something that cries for a resolution and then to act irresponsibly, to dance away from the reader's problem, dealing with other things, prolonging and exacerbating the reader's desperate need for resolution.

Therefore:

- Don't eliminate the prospective danger to a character.
- Don't let the character overcome the immediate danger without facing an even greater danger.
- If your character is apprehensive about an unwanted confrontation, make sure you hold off that confrontation as long as possible.
- When an old fear is about to become a present reality, don't relieve the fear. Make the situation worse than the character anticipated.
- If a character's life crisis requires an immediate action, make certain that the action backfires. Prolong the crisis.

The point, of course, is that you don't resolve the suspense you've aroused. Your duty is to be mean. You are giving the reader a thrill he yearns for in books and detests in life. You frustrate the reader's expectations.

Let's look at some examples.

Isak Dinesen, a remarkable short story writer, began *The Sailor-Boy's Tale* with a young sailor observing a bird caught high in the rigging, flapping its wings, turning its head from side to side, trying to get loose. The young sailor thinks, "Through his own experience of life he had come to the conviction that in this world everyone must look after himself, and expect no help from others."

The reader wants the young sailor to climb the rigging to free the bird. That action is delayed by the young sailor's thoughts about the past. The delay causes tension in the reader. In the fourth paragraph, the boy is climbing up. The bird turns out to be a peregrine falcon, which has special meaning for the boy. But just as he frees the bird, the falcon hacks him on the thumb, drawing blood. The reader wanted the bird freed, and look what happened.

The reader has to wonder what will happen now to the sailor boy, to the falcon, to the young sailor's notion that "everyone must look after himself, and expect no help from others." In other words, the reader's curiosity is thoroughly aroused by boy, bird, and theme, all in a few paragraphs of a short story that ends not many pages later. The novelist's job is even harder, for he must arouse the reader's curiosity enough to hold him for hundreds of pages. That means that suspense and tension must be constantly renewed.

In popular or transient fiction the author usually relies much more on plot than character to arouse suspense initially, as Frederick Forsyth does in *The Day of the Jackal.*

Forsyth's ingenuity in creating suspense is worth noting. Based on an outline of the plot alone, more than twenty publishers turned down his first novel, *The Day of the Jackal*, I among them, because the plot was about an assassin out to kill General de Gaulle—who was already dead! However, when Forsyth, unanimously rejected, wrote the actual novel, he skillfully held the reader with powerful negative suspense, the reader hoping that the assassin would be stopped before he could kill de Gaulle. In other words, the reader was forced to suspend disbelief for the sake of the plot. And he was made to do so by the author's technical skill in arousing suspense, not through character as much as through the intended action that the reader wanted desperately to see stopped. *The Day of the Jackal* is worth studying for its use of suspense.

* * *

One of the most common complaints heard from editors is that a novel "sags in the middle." By "sag" they mean the story loses its momentum, suspense flags, the reader no longer has his curiosity aroused about what will happen next.

To prevent this problem from happening in the first place, you must understand the ideal organization of a novel and how each chapter can be made to contribute to the suspense of the whole.

In speaking before writers' conferences, I demonstrate a method for achieving suspense throughout a book by summoning eight or ten volunteers up onstage. I ask each person to think of a location for a scene and to announce it to the audience. The likelihood is that we get a series of wildly unconnected places, the desert near Palm Springs, Chicago, Hong Kong, a cave in Virginia, an island off the west coast of Florida, and so on. The audience laughs, enjoying the wild hopping about in space. We enjoy the surprise of moving around to unexpected places.

I organize where each person stands to get the most interesting mix of locations. Then I ask each person in turn to remind the audience where his or her scene is located. I then point out how suspense will work throughout a book consisting of those eight or ten different scenes.

Let us say that the first scene takes place in the desert near Palm Springs. The scene will end with the hero in serious trouble in the desert. Do we then start the next scene (or chapter) in the desert with the hero? Absolutely not. We leave the reader in suspense and go to the next location, Chicago, where we see a scene with a different character, say the hero's fiancée, getting into trouble. We still want to know the outcome of what happened to the hero in the desert, but our attention is now diverted to the heroine in Chicago. At the end of scene (or chapter) two, we desperately want to know what the heroine in Chicago, who is in serious trouble, will do to extricate herself.

We now have two lines of suspense going: what will happen to the hero in the desert at Palm Springs and, most urgently, what will happen to the heroine in Chicago.

We begin the third scene in either of two places. We can go on to a third location, Hong Kong, and leave the reader in suspense about both the hero and heroine, or we can go back to the desert and continue the story of the hero at Palm Springs, leaving the reader in suspense about the goings on in Chicago. Of course, at the end of scene three, the hero is facing an even greater obstacle than he did at the end of scene one, and the reader is left hanging, and in scene four we go back to the heroine in Chicago, or to a third person in Hong Kong.

The places don't need to be as far apart as Palm Springs and Chicago and Hong Kong. The entire novel can take place in Marshalltown, Iowa, with the first scene ending with a bank being held up, and our hero, the bank manager, being tied up and gagged by the daring robber, and shoved into the vault. The second scene can then be, say, in the bank manager's home, where his wife is preparing dinner and wondering why her husband, always on time, hasn't arrived home yet. The wife, nervous, cuts her hand badly. She tries to stop the bleeding but has difficulty tying a tourniquet with one hand. She runs to a neighbor's house. The neighbor isn't home. She gets in her car, and drives to the next neighbor, who is quite a distance down the road, meanwhile getting blood all over the seat of the car. As she arrives at the second neighbor's yard, she passes out in the car. End of second scene.

The reader is now concerned about the bank manager in the vault and even more about his wife. The third scene starts with a local roofer working on a building across the street from the bank. He's an observant fellow and has noticed people going into the bank, but no one coming out. It's none of his business, but his curiosity gets the better of him. He slings his hammer into the leather carryall around his waist, eases himself down from his perch on the roof, and trots over to the bank. He looks in and immediately realizes what is going on and is ready to back off and call the police when the lookout for the bank robbers spots him, and thinking the hammer at his belt is a gun, fires at the roofer, hitting him and alerting the robbers in the bank.

Whew! The reader is now concerned about three things, the bank manager in the vault, the bleeding wife passed out in a distant neighbor's yard, and the roofer, lying shot in the street. All of these events are in the same town, but by starting each scene in a different location and focusing each on a different character, we now have three lines of suspense going at the same time.

It helps to jot down the location of each of the scenes in your book to see if they can be arranged in an order that will take each scene to a location different from the one at the end of the preceding scene. It isn't necessary to do this with every scene in a book. I find that if you change location or character in a majority of instances, you can also, where appropriate, continue the action of a suspenseful scene in the following chapter. The plan should be followed to achieve the purpose of suspense, not to follow a rigid pattern. Many writers also find this exercise useful in imagining different locations, which always increases reader interest.

Making a simple chart like the one that follows will be of help. On each line, note the location (different from the location of the preceding scene, if possible), the principal character in the scene, and, briefly, the action that takes place there. Be brief. (Keep in mind that if there is no action, you don't really have a scene.)

SCENE OUTLINE: LOCATION, CHARACTER, ACTION

Scene 1 _____

Scene 2 _____

Scene 3 _____

Scene 4 _____

Scene 5 _____

Scene 6 _____

Scene 7 _____

Scene 8 _____

Scene 9 _____

Scene 10 _____

One of the frequent failings of novelists is the inclusion of material between scenes. This usually takes the form of a narrative summary of offstage happenings. By using the simple outline above, the temptation to include material between the scenes may diminish. Remember that a reader's interest is in the scenes, not the interstices between the scenes. When I have a group onstage, each representing a locale where a chapter takes place, I have the writers first hold hands in a circle, then drop their hands to indicate visually that transitions between scenes aren't needed. Those transitions almost always constitute the offstage parts that make a book sag. Today's reader is used to jump-cutting.

The next step requires discipline also. Look at your list of scenes and find the weakest one, where your own interest flags. If you eliminate your weakest scene, you will strengthen your book as a whole. It takes guts, but do it!

If you've eliminated the weakest scene, you now have another scene that is weakest. If you've got the guts of a writer, you may now be able to eliminate the second-weakest scene. It's an ideal way to strengthen a book. Remember, your intent is to build a publishable novel. You are not a scene preserver!

It will help to keep in mind the difference between a scene and a chapter. A *scene* is a unit of writing, usually an integral incident with a beginning and end that in itself is not isolatable as a story. It is visible to the reader or audience as an event that can be witnessed, almost always involving two or more characters, dialogue, and action in a single setting. A *chapter* is a part of a longer work that is set off with a number or a title. A chapter may have several scenes or scenelets. When each chapter of a novel (except the last) ends, the reader's interest should be aroused anew, thrusting him forward in the novel. The key is *not to take the reader where he wants to go.*

To refresh our understanding, let's look at that ideal architecture of a suspenseful novel in terms of chapters.

Chapter 1. The chapter ends with a turn of events that leaves the reader in suspense. The reader wants to stay with the characters and action of that chapter.

Chapter 2. The reader finds himself in another place and/or with a different character. The reader still wants to know what happens in Chapter 1. Chapter 2 ends with a turn of events that leaves the reader in suspense. The reader wants to know how Chapter 2 turns out. *Two lines of suspense are operating.*

In Chapter 3, the reader finds himself in a continuation of the suspenseful events in Chapter 1. He is still in suspense about Chapter 2. By the end of Chapter 3, a new line of suspense has been created. *Two lines of suspense are still operating.*

If you keep doing this with successive chapters, the reader will be kept continuously in suspense and there will be no sag in the middle of the book or anywhere else.

If you think this kind of architecture is crafty, you're right. It is an important part of designing a novel to influence the emotions of the reader. And as we know, the emotions of the reader are affected by suspense more than by any other factor.

If you want to group your scenes into chapters, here are some guidelines:

- Short chapters make a story seem to move faster.
- Normally avoid chapters of fewer than three printed pages. They may not be long enough to engage the reader's emotions.
- Ideally, each chapter might end the way the movies used to end their weekly serials: with the hero or heroine in unresolved trouble. If you're not familiar with those serials, use a soap opera as a guideline, with the end of each episode making you want to see what happens next.

One of the best ways of accustoming yourself to the idea of continuing suspense is to study novels that you have found difficult to put down. Pick up any well-known suspense or thriller writer's work and look at the chapter endings. You'll see how most of the time each chapter ends on a suspenseful note and throws the reader forward into the next chapter. The most experienced suspense writers start the next chapter somewhere else or with other characters.

In literary novels, of course, the suspense is often more subtle. All forms of fiction have one thing in common: the chapter endings arouse the reader's curiosity about what will happen next.

Your chapters are not cemented in place. You can reorganize them in any fashion that accelerates the suspense of the whole. Watch out for time shifts that would disturb the reader. Try to keep moving only forward in time until you've had a good deal of experience.

A word of caution. In reorganizing the chapters in a book it is crucial to avoid disimprovement. Whenever shifting locations, keep a copy of your present architecture, then play with rearranging the chapters in another order. You may find that what you will be putting into new places are parts of chapters or scenes within chapters. That's fine.

If you change the sequence of chapters or scenes, you may also have to do some stitching at the seams. Obviously, this rewriting is much easier if you're in an early draft, and still easier if you're in the planning stage.

I cannot overemphasize the importance of architectural suspense. It has been a major factor in the success of writers I have worked with. Mastering this technique can in itself improve the chances of a book's acceptance for publication.

10

The Adrenaline Pump: Creating Tension

Writers are troublemakers. A psychotherapist tries to relieve stress, strain, and pressure. Writers are not psychotherapists. Their job is to *give* readers stress, strain, and pressure. The fact is that readers who hate those things in life love them in fiction. Until a writer assimilates that fact he will have difficulty in consciously creating sufficient moments in which the reader feels tension.

Tension is the most frequent cause of physiological changes in the reader. The sudden stress causes the adrenal medulla to release a hormone into the bloodstream that stimulates the heart and increases blood pressure, metabolic rate, and blood glucose concentration. The result is an adrenaline high that makes the reader feel excited. That excitement is what the reader lusts for. Like all excitement, it is endurable for brief bursts, which is one of the factors that distinguishes tension from suspense. Suspense can last over a long period, sometimes for an entire book. Tension is felt in seconds or minutes. There are occasions in fiction when it lasts longer and begins to border on the unbearable. The best novels have respites in which the reader is allowed to relax so that the tension can ebb, but not for long.

The word "tension" is derived from the Latin *tendere*, meaning "to stretch." Tension is a stretching out. Think of stretching a rubber band more and more. If you stretch it too far it will break. We experience moments of tension as seeming longer because we want the tension to end. Tension produces instantaneous anxiety, and the reader finds it delicious.

The writer's job is to create tension consciously, and in my lectures I sometimes demonstrate how tension is created. Without warning, I will suddenly adopt a stern expression, point a finger at someone in the first row, and in a commanding voice demand, "You! Get up out of your chair!"

For a moment, the person I've singled out doesn't know what to do. The audience is hushed, watching. I order, "Stand up!" The person—face flushed—wonders why I am ordering him to stand. "Stand up!" I repeat. The tension in the room is great as long as he disobeys. When the person finally stands up, the tension in the audience is broken. I quickly point out that the way to create tension is to cause friction (ordering "Stand up!") and to have the recipient of the order not stand up; the tension will continue only as long as the disobedience.

Several times luck has been with me during this demonstration. I order a writer in the front row to stand up, and he remains frozen in his chair. Again I order him to stand up. By this time the rest of the audience is as tense as he is. I step off the stage and come physically closer to the writer. In the voice of a marine drill instructor, I bellow the order to get up. The writer starts to stand, and before the tension can break I shout, "Lie down on the floor!"

Telling someone to stand is not necessarily unreasonable. Asking someone to lie down on the floor of an auditorium full of people seems unreasonable. That's when the tension in the audience breaks. People laugh. Others titter. Finally, the victim in the front row joins in. He doesn't have to lie down. The tension is over.

Our instinct as human beings is to provide answers, to ease tension. As writers our job is the opposite, to create tension and not dispel it immediately. In examining the manuscripts of hundreds of writers over the years, a common fault I've observed is that the writer creates a pressing problem for a character and then immediately relieves the pressure by resolving it. That's humane but not a writer's function. His mission is to manipulate the emotions of the audience, and when it comes to moments of tension, to stretch them out as long as possible.

A common way to create tension in a novel is to simply note a "fact" that is likely to chill any reader. The following is the opening sentence of a thriller I recommended earlier, *The Day of the Jackal* by Frederick Forsyth:

> It is cold at 6:40 in the morning of a March day in Paris, and seems even colder when a man is about to be executed by firing squad.

Does the precise time convince you of the reality of what's taking place? Do you want to know who is being executed by firing squad? Do you want to know why he's being executed? So did millions of readers.

That one sentence creates tension. I recounted the plot earlier. An assassin has been hired to kill General de Gaulle. The reader doesn't want de Gaulle to be killed. That creates negative suspense (wanting something *not* to happen) that lasts almost to the end of the novel. The tension of that first sentence is momentary. The main line of suspense is book-long.

The most important moment of tension in a novel is its first use, which should be as close to the beginning of the book as possible. It puts the writer in charge of the reader's emotions.

You might well say, "Wait a minute, Stein. Isn't my job in the first few pages to create a living breathing character that will interest the reader?" Yes, of course. The closer writing gets to literature, the more likely it is that what fastens us to the early pages is our interest in a character. And then, as soon as possible, the writer creates some moments of tension for that character. Here, in outline, are the kind of plot situations that provide opportunities to create tension:

Dangerous work is involved: The place is postwar Bosnia. A likable demolitions specialist parks his five-year-old daughter with a neighbor watching from a distance and then, a prayer on his lips, goes about trying to dismantle an unexploded shell. The author describes what the man is doing in minute detail. The reader, aware of the man as a human being, aware also of the five-year-old watching from a distance, feels tension mount with every turn of the screw.

A deadline is nearing: Molly knows that at six o'clock the villain will return. At four o'clock the hero, Frank, has not yet arrived, and Molly, glancing at the time, is tense. So is the reader. At five o'clock Molly is beginning to panic. At two minutes to six, the reader's tension is extreme. At one minute to six, Frank arrives breathless.

An unfortunate meeting occurs: The heroine is in a department store elevator. She presses the button for the sixth floor. The elevator stops on the fifth floor, and the dangerously neurotic man she jilted gets on. The reader becomes instantly tense.

An opponent is trapped in a closed environment: The protagonist, who in his youth hunted vermin on a farm, is now seventy years old. He owns the only rifle in the neighborhood, where the citizens are terrified by the rumor that a diseased mountain lion has come down into the town and chased a woman into the basement of her house. The woman has locked herself in the boiler room, and the mountain lion is roaring outside its closed door. The elderly rifle owner is summoned to kill the lion. A younger man offers to take the rifle and go down the cellar stairs to the trapped lion. The old man gives his rifle to the younger man, but immediately sees that the younger man doesn't handle the firearm in an experienced way. He asks for it back, and enters the house. At the head of the cellar stairs, he hears the lion below, but can't see the animal clearly, except for its eyes. The older man has a flashlight, but how is he to hold the rifle with one hand and the flashlight with the other? As he puts the flashlight down, the crazed lion bounds up the cellar steps.

Well, we'll stop right there. What we've done is add one tense moment to another, piling up the degree of tension toward a climax. The temptation for the inexperienced writer is to have the older man go in and shoot the crazed animal right off. That makes short shrift of the tension. By adding the element of the younger volunteer and the flashlight, we add to the tension, stretching it out.

Tension can be as valuable in literary fiction as in thrillers. The opening story in Ethan Canin's collection of novellas, *The Palace Thief*, is called "The Accountant."

At the very beginning, the accountant-narrator tells the reader that his crime was small. We then hear him tell the circumstances and details of his crime. Far into the story, when we are witnessing the crime, we don't want the accountant—whom we've gotten to like as a human being despite his faults—to wreck his life by going forward with the crime. While he is in the process of committing it, the reader becomes extremely tense. As the accountant takes an object that doesn't belong to him, we want him to put it back. This isn't suspense because he told us at the outset that he committed the crime. But there are moments of high tension, stretched out. The reader keeps hoping that any second the accountant will stop the clock, change his mind, not go through with this stupid, unnecessary, trivial, bizarre crime, and yet he goes ahead with it, wrecking his life. "The Accountant" is a story worth reading for pleasure the first time, and worth studying the second time.

Relocating a sentence to increase tension is a valuable technique. The "she" in the following is a young woman who doesn't yet know that a boy she had made love to is dead. She meets several of his friends. Here's the original:

> "Before I got your message, I thought we were going to meet over at Urek's like usual. He in trouble again?"
>
> A fog of silence descended. Nobody looked at anybody else. Finally, Feeney said, "She doesn't know."

I transposed one sentence and created two new paragraphs. Note the increase in tension, though no words have been changed.

> "Before I got your message, I thought we were going to meet over at Urek's like usual."
> A fog of silence descended. Nobody looked at anybody else.
> "He in trouble again?"
> Finally, Feeney said, "She doesn't know."

One of the easiest ways to create tension is by means of dialogue. The best dialogue sparks with friction, generating tension in the reader as it does in life. In the next chapter, we'll see how that's done.

11

The Secrets of Good Dialogue

Success in writing dialogue is one of the most rewarding aspects of the writer's craft. By the time you finish reading this chapter you should know more about dialogue than ninety percent of published writers. The fact is that the majority of writers write dialogue by instinct with little knowledge of the craft.

I was lucky. Plays consist entirely of dialogue. Before I was a novelist I was a playwright and had a chance to see my plays produced on and off Broadway in New York, at the National Theater in Washington, and in California. For many years I lived in a world in which the currency was dialogue.

In the autumn of 1989, I was invited to give a twelve-week course on "Dialogue for Writers" at the University of California at Irvine. In the class, writers of fiction far outnumbered playwrights and screenwriters. When I returned east at the end of those three months, the *Los Angeles Times* reported that the students, some with many books to their credit but still learning, refused to let the course end. They met weekly, insisting that I come back. I did each winter, and many of those writers are still studying with me, perfecting their dialogue and other aspects of their fiction.

Readers enjoy dialogue in stories and novels. Those same readers would hate reading court transcripts, even of dramatic confrontations. What makes dialogue interesting and so much actual talk boring?

Talk is repetitive, full of rambling, incomplete, or run-on sentences, and usually contains a lot of unnecessary words. Most answers contain echoes of the question. Our speech is full of such echoes. Dialogue, contrary to popular view, is not a recording of actual speech; it is a semblance of speech, an invented language of exchanges that build in tempo or content toward climaxes. Some people mistakenly believe that all a writer has to do is turn on a tape recorder to capture dialogue. What he'd be capturing is the same boring speech patterns the poor court reporter has to record verbatim. Learning the new language of dialogue is as complex as learning any new language. However, there are some shortcuts.

First, let's examine some of the advantages of dialogue. As you know from an earlier chapter, fiction consists of three elements: description, narrative summary, and immediate scene. The twentieth-century reader, influenced by a century of film and a half century of television, is used to seeing what's happening in front of his eyes, not hearing about events after the fact. That's why immediate scenes—onstage, visible to the eye—dominate today's fiction. *Dialogue is always in immediate scene*, which is one reason readers relish it.

When talk is tough, combative, or adversarial it can be as exciting as physical action. Listen to this exchange from an early episode of the television series *NYPD Blue*. The central character is a detective named Kelly. In court he sees the murderer of an eight-year-old boy use legal technicalities to win a plea bargain. Kelly is enraged. The judge warns him, "We govern by law, not by your whim." Not bothering to conceal his contempt, Kelly counters:

> Don't tell me how you govern. I work your streets. I clean up after how you govern. The way you govern stinks.

Confrontational dialogue—whether in Shakespeare, a contemporary novel, or a policeman talking back to a judge in a TV drama—is immediate, creating a visual image of the speakers as it shoots adrenaline into our bloodstream.

As the writer of fiction masters dialogue, he will be able to deal with characterization and plot simultaneously. Let's prove that by taking a hard look at just four lines of dialogue and what we can accomplish with them.

First, some actual overheard conversation:

> SHE: How are you?
> HE: How am I? Oh, I'm fine, how are you?
> SHE: And the family?
> HE: The family is great. Everybody's well.

It doesn't take much of this to bore a reader out of his skull. Let's change those lines somewhat:

SHE: How are you?
HE:　I suppose I'm okay.
SHE: Why, what's the matter.
HE:　I guess you haven't heard.

Those simple changes introduce suspense. The second line, **"I suppose I'm okay,"** doesn't sound like the character really is okay. The fourth line makes the reader want to know what happens next.

Let's try another revision of those four lines:

SHE: How are you?
HE:　Oh, I'm sorry, I didn't see you.
SHE: Is anything wrong?
HE:　No, no, absolutely not. I just didn't see you.

With that exchange, we know something is wrong and that the man is lying. We're beginning to get a sense of character.

In life, speakers answer each other's questions. We compliment a speaker by saying he is direct. Dialogue, to the contrary, is *indirect*. The key word to understanding the nature of dialogue is that the best dialogue is *oblique*. Take another look at those first two lines:

SHE: How are you?
HE:　Oh, I'm sorry, I didn't see you.

He doesn't answer her question! He is not direct. His response is oblique. The writers I've coached who learn how to make their dialogue oblique have all taken a giant step toward improving their work.

Let's try one more revision:

SHE: How are you? I said how are you?
HE:　I heard you the first time.
SHE: I only wanted to know how you were.
HE:　How the hell do you think I am?

Characters don't need to make speeches at each other. From just four lines the reader learns that these two people have probably had a relationship in the past that is not resolved, and at least for one of them the relationship is filled with bitterness.

We're not only characterizing, we're building a story out of just four lines. A reader's emotions can be sparked with few words. That's the power of dialogue.

Tension can now be increased not only by the substance of their relationship but also by incidental matters. For instance:

HE: It's beginning to rain.
SHE: What do you suggest?

The conversation can now go in a number of directions. He can say, **"Why don't we talk some other time."** Or **"Why don't we go in for a cup of coffee."** Or **"Come sit in my car for a few minutes."** Each of these would take the plot in a different direction.

We've come a long way from the original, boring four lines.

If you need proof that dialogue and spoken words are not the same, go to a supermarket. Eavesdrop. Much of what you'll hear in the aisles sounds like idiot talk. People won't buy your novel to hear idiot talk. They get that free from relatives, friends, and at the supermarket.

What is the most frequently used word in real speech? Uh. It's what people say to borrow time to think of what they want to say. "Uh" is totally useless to a writer. Dialogue is a lean language in which every word counts.

Count for what? To characterize, to move the story along, to have an impact on the reader's emotions.

Some writers make the mistake of thinking that dialogue is overheard. Wrong! Dialogue is invented and the writer is the inventor.

Elmore Leonard is considered a superb practitioner of dialogue, but does anyone in life talk the way his characters do? Elmore Leonard's dialogue is invented, it is a semblance of speech that has the effect of actual speech, which is what his readers prize.

If you're relatively new to dialogue, you might try an exercise I've developed that is used by screenwriters as well as novelists. Let's imagine two characters, Joe and Ed. Joe says, **"Ed?"**

What is Joe trying to accomplish by that one word?

There are several possibilities:

- Joe wants to get Ed's attention.
- Joe has heard somebody and wants to know if it is Ed.

Now imagine that Joe adds one word and says, **"Now Ed."** What is Joe's intention?

If there were a comma between "Now" and "Ed," it might mean "The time is now, Ed." But there isn't a comma or pause. There are a couple of possibilities.

- **"Now Ed"** is a reproof.
- It's a warning.

We don't know which unless we know the context in which the two words are spoken. But what is clear is that those two words in context can mean a lot—an admonition or a warning.

Let's try one more. What does Joe mean by repeating Ed's name three times: **"Ed, Ed, Ed"**? If a dozen readers were to pronounce those three recitations of Ed's name, you'd probably get a dozen different intonations but only one meaning: Joe's feeling of disappointment in Ed's conduct, derived from one word repeated three times: **"Ed, Ed, Ed."**

With this exercise we are learning to listen to what words mean. The reader can get all the words he needs from a dictionary. What the reader gets from your fiction is the meaning of words. And most important, the emotion that meaning generates.

We've learned that *what counts is not what is said but the effect of what is meant.* If you keep a journal, that's worth writing down.

When I worked with Elia Kazan on *The Arrangement*, we tested dialogue by reading lines aloud to each other. As I noted earlier, the best way to judge dialogue read aloud is to read it in a monotone without expression. The words have to do the job.

When I examine dialogue in chunks, mine or someone else's, I ask myself the following:

- What is the purpose of this exchange? Does it begin or heighten an existing conflict?
- Does it stimulate the reader's curiosity?
- Does the exchange create tension?
- Does the dialogue build to a climax or a turn of events in the story or a change in relationship of the speakers?

The next step is to check if the lines spoken by each character are consistent with that character's background. Then I remove clichés that are out of character. I remove any echoes that slipped in.

Talk is full of echoes. Echoes don't belong in dialogue. Here's an example of echoing conversation from a cocktail party scene:

SHE: Boy, am I glad to see you.
HE: I'm glad to see you, too.

It fails as dialogue. Here's how it was rewritten:

SHE: Boy, am I glad to see you.
HE: You finally got your contacts in.

Let's imagine a cocktail party at which a man is trying to come on to a woman he has just met. He might say:

"You are the most beautiful woman in the world."

Her instinct is to be polite. She might answer:

"Why, thank you."

That is boring. Nothing is happening. Watch what happens when her response is oblique:

HE: You are the most beautiful woman in the world.
SHE: I'd like you to meet my husband.

Most conversation is square, and therefore turgid. There is no story. In the example of dialogue above, the man makes a verbal pass, and the woman declines it. *Something is happening.*

In creating oblique dialogue, the questioner must provide the respondent with an opportunity to be oblique. Otherwise, it might seem that the respondent didn't hear or didn't understand. Certain forms of question call for a response. For instance:

"Why are you giving me the third degree?"

Since the question is direct, a lack of direct response may be noticed by the reader. We expect questions to be answered. A simple change in the question can open the gate wide for an oblique response:

"What's this third degree?"

It is highly unlikely that you have a group of friends all of whom speak exactly alike. If they were a group of characters in a work of yours, you'd want to differentiate each one's speech. Most writers recognize this, yet the chief fault of many television and film scripts as well as novels is that the dialogue of different characters sounds the same. Even some experienced writers are unfamiliar with the techniques available to them for differentiating characters through their speech.

The richest means of such differentiation are *speech markers*, signals that are quickly identifiable by the reader. Vocabulary is an important marker. Throwaway words and phrases are markers. Tight or loose wording is a marker. Run-on sentences are markers. Sarcasm is a marker. Cynicism is a marker. Poor grammar is a marker. Omitted words are markers. Inappropriate modifiers are markers. Consider all these a mine for the jewels of dialogue.

Vocabulary encompasses different kinds of markers, such as polysyllabic words and professional jargon. Polysyllabic words like *intricate, oxymoron*, and *antediluvian* indicate the speaker is well educated or pretentious, depending on the context. The point is that the character's speech can be differentiated from others' with just a word or two. Be warned. The words have to fit the character you've created. Otherwise, the special vocabulary will jar the reader.

Jargon is a two-edged marker that usually identifies the character's profession and at the same time conveys a negative impression of the speaker. There is a tendency among people within a profession to use or create words whose meanings are clear only to others within their narrow group and obscure to the rest of the world. This tendency in all specializations is a barrier to communication and a support of self-serving secrecy in an "in" group. Writers have an obligation to defend their language against the assaults of jargon.

A simple example most people have been exposed to comes from the fields of psychology and social services, where "interpersonal relationships" is an overblown expression for "relationships," which means the same thing. The field of medicine is notorious for its jargon. This provides an opportunity for writers, particularly of comedy. For instance, a pretentious health worker might say, "This capsule is suitable for oral administration." The patient might reply, "You mean I can swallow it?" Jargon is a marker of stuffiness. One must be careful in its use. A touch is plenty. A surfeit of jargon quickly becomes caricature instead of characterization.

Certain throwaway words and phrases are useful markers. "Actually," "basically," "perhaps," "I dare say," "I don't know what to think," "it occurs to me," "you see," "anyway" are all words that can be cut unless you are choosing to use them as verbal tics of a particular character.

Tight or loose wording functions as a marker. "Beat it. Go home" is obviously tight wording. "I would appreciate your leaving now" is loose wording. They each give different signals to the reader about the character speaking.

Run-on sentences can be useful to characterize a nonstop talker:

> "The minute I was through the doors of that store I was a fish in a barrel of minnows, my eyes bulging out of my head at the fancy vests, scarves, jumpers, prints, knits, it seemed as if everything was on sale except the clerks, and one of them, the way he came up to me and whispered in my ear, maybe he was too."

Also sarcasm:

> "Anybody who can spend money the way you can must be printing it."

Or:

> "You own the whole country or just this store?"

Poor grammar is an easy marker.

> "If you was the last man on earth . . . "

Diction refers to the writer's precise choice of words for their effect. I've pointed out that when a policeman uses the word "perpetrator" it comes across as pretentious. When a teacher of young children uses the word "albeit," that, too, comes across as pretentious. Literary work as distinguished from transient work is marked by a careful choice of words, but when it comes to dialogue all writers must attend to diction. Even the simplest of examples demonstrates how diction can differentiate one character from another. "May I know your name?" comes across as a polite and perhaps excessively formal marker. "You, what's your name?" sounds impolite and aggressive.

Spelling out pronunciations (for instance, "Anyone see my seester?" as an attempt to indicate a Latino accent) is almost always a bad choice. I would also like to caution against a use of dialect in which speech is differentiated from the standard language by odd spellings. Though dialect was used quite extensively in earlier periods, today it is seen as a liability for several reasons. Dialect is annoying to the reader. It takes extra effort to derive the meaning of words on the page; that effort deters full involvement in the experience of a story. For example, Cockney, a dialect of British English, is difficult for many English-speaking people to follow in film and TV, and on the printed page. Dialect is offensive to some readers. Moreover, people do not hear their own dialect or regional mode of speaking; only listeners from other communities hear it. That means you are reducing your potential audience by the employment of dialect. As a substitute for dialect use word order, omitted words, and other markers. James Baldwin made a breakthrough in fiction conveying the speech of blacks by word order and rhythm more than by dialect.

For many kinds of ethnic characters, in addition to word order and rhythm, errors in speech, particularly the omission of words, are useful:

"How you get so big?"

In addition, you can use the wrong verb, leave out the articles "the" and "a," devise incomplete or slightly malformed sentences, use vocabulary oddities, and the occasional foreign word that would be understood in context. Content references can also help; for instance, in *The Best Revenge*, when the ancient Italian Aldo Manucci refers to actresses it is to Gina Lollobrigida and Anna Magnani. Note the construction of his speech:

"You a much big man now," Manucci said. "In papers all time Ben-neh Riller present, Ben-neh Riller announce, Ben-neh Riller big stars, big shows. You bring Gina Lollobrigida here I kiss her hand. I kiss her anything," he laughed. "Magnani, you know Magnani, she more my type."

Manucci's American-born son might say, "You're a big man now." Aldo says *much* big man, using an inappropriate modifier. He pronounces Ben in two syllables, *Ben-neh*:

"Know something, don't give half that much to one party even when I was king around here. Never mind. Nineteen seventy-nine dollar nothing. When you was boy, Ben-neh, five cents buy big ice cream, five dollars get someone off street for good."

Note the details again. "Know something" would not be used by someone schooled in good English, ethnic or otherwise. Aldo leaves out the subject "Do you." He doesn't say "today's dollar," he describes it by the year. Aldo uses the wrong verb and leaves the article out. Not "When you were a boy" but "When you was boy." And so on.

Small changes in speech can make a big difference in characterizing any speaker, but especially ethnic characters.

The addition of a syllable to convey ethnic speech is used effectively by Joe Vitarelli, an actor who has a strong talent for writing fiction. As a mob chieftain in Woody Allen's film *Bullets Over Broadway*, Vitarelli refers to Shakespeare's play as "Ham-a-let" and to a steak as a "sir-a-loin."

Monologue, or direct address to the reader by a character speaking in the first person, uses the same principles as dialogue, though in self-characterization there is a great danger of making a character sound as if he or she were answering a questionnaire instead of talking. Even fine writers like E. L. Doctorow can stumble. The first chapter of *World's Fair*, headed "Rose," the name of the Russian immigrant speaking, starts this way:

I was born on Clinton Street in the Lower East Side. I was the next to youngest of six children, two boys, four girls. The two boys, Harry and Willy, were the oldest. My father was a musician, a violinist. He always made a good living. He and my mother had met in Russia and they married there, and then emigrated. My mother came from a family of musicians as well; that is how, in the course of things, she and my father had met. Some of her cousins were very well known in Russia; one, a cellist, had even played for the Czar. My mother was a very beautiful woman, petite, with long golden hair and the palest blue eyes . . .

Doctorow's monologue sounds as if Rose were answering a questionnaire. It doesn't come to life. Here's how a monologue by a Russian immigrant sounds when it doesn't just rattle off biographical facts but reveals character, and has other features of dialogue:

Of course I'm a wanderer! Moses wandered, Columbus wandered, should I have rotted in the old country? Should I have stayed in my *shtetl*, a subject not only of the Czar but of every Cossack who wanted a Jew to beat? You don't need to be an Einstein to know that nothing plus nothing equals nothing. I got out because in Russia the future is for others. If I'd stayed, would I have met a woman like Zipporah from a big city like Kiev? Would this woman and I have produced an impresario like Ben?

Note that in the above speech by Louie Riller, a character in *The Best Revenge*, the character's ethnic background is evident not from defects in speech but from the content, including the use of one Yiddish word whose meaning is relatively clear even to people who don't know it.

The art of dialogue is a vast subject, itself deserving of a book. Before leaving that complex subject, I want to add a word about dialogue of earlier periods for those writing historical novels or stories.

Historical novels placed in the Middle Ages do not use Beowulf's or Chaucer's English because both would be unintelligible to the contemporary reader. John Fowles, whose novel *The French Lieutenant's Woman* takes place in the nineteenth century, points out that writing dialogue for an earlier era involves invention, not just research and mimicry. Fowles, in commenting on his own work* reinforces the point that dialogue is a *semblance* of speech rather than an attempt to duplicate it:

In the matter of clothes, social manners, historical background, and the rest, writing about 1867 (insofar as it can be heard in books of the time) is far too close to our own to sound convincingly old. It very often fails to agree with our psychological picture of the Victorians—it is not stiff enough, not euphemistic enough, and so on; and here at once I have to start cheating and pick out the more formal and archaic (even for 1867) elements of spoken speech. It is this kind of "cheating," which is intrinsic to the novel, that takes the time.

In my dialogue classes I have often had some fun with my students by redoing well-known speeches of previous centuries in the argot of today. They not only sound absurd, but often the students cannot guess the original, though the content remains the same. I can convey the idea most

* In *Afterwords: Novelists on Their Novels,* edited by Thomas McCormack, New York, 1988, St. Martin's Press.

simply with an example from my baptism with the semblance of historical speech. My play *Napoleon* takes place in France during the early nineteenth century. Its cast includes the important figures of the time, Talleyrand, Metternich, and of course Napoleon and Josephine. In a confrontation between Talleyrand, the aristocrat who survived his kings and adversaries, and the upstart Napoleon, Talleyrand provokes the younger man into a flash of anger. Talleyrand couldn't say "Don't get so hot under the collar" or "Cool it" in the argot of today. He says, "Save your blood the journey to your face, I meant no harm." You won't find anything like that in any of the recorded conversations of the time. It is dialogue invented to suit a period, as John Fowles said, a form of "cheating" in which writers use a newly minted language to simulate an old.

P.S. An often overlooked advantage of dialogue in novels and stories is this simple: it provides white space on the page that makes the reader feel that the story is moving faster because the reader's eyes move quickly down the page.

12

How to Show Instead of Tell

I recall the time Shirl Thomas of the Southern California Chapter of the National Writers Club phoned to say that numerous speakers had advised their members to "show, not tell," but nobody told them *how* to show. Would I address their group on that subject? That's what this chapter is about: how to show.

When we're young, before we can read, we get used to the idea that someone is "telling a story." A child being read to can experience a story, of course, but the child is also aware of the person reading, whose skill as a reader is a factor, who may read too fast or too slowly, who cannot imitate animals as well as the child's imagination can, who is in control, who can stop—unreasonably from the child's perspective—when the child wants to go on. Important also is the fact that the child is hearing what's happening in a book, as it were. If and when the child becomes an avid reader, when he controls the reading unhampered by a senior outsider, he is more likely to experience a story as an adult does. It is an active experience. It is not about something, it is something.

Growing up, the child hears from others about what has happened elsewhere, stories purportedly true, or gossip embellished by imagination. In school, the child is asked to write about what happened elsewhere, during the summer vacation, or at Christmastime. Stories are relayed rather than consumed as experience.

All of these early exposures to offstage happenings contribute to the belief that stories are *told*. They can be a liability to writers later in life because the writer has to change his mind-set from telling what happened somewhere else to creating an experience for the reader by *showing* what happened.

Twentieth-century readers, transformed by film and television, are used to seeing stories. The reading experience for a twentieth-century reader is increasingly visual. The story is happening in front of his eyes. This transformation from stories told to stories seen should not be surprising. Who would deny that sight is our primary sense? We prefer to witness an event to hearing about it afterward secondhand. Which is why I urge writers to "show a story" instead of "tell a story." One of the chief reasons novels are rejected is that the writer, consciously or not, is reporting a story instead of showing it.

The advice "Show, don't tell" existed well before the age of film and television. Henry James gave that counsel.

The late John Gardner, in his excellent book *On Becoming a Novelist*, insisted that the one danger area for "telling" is what a character feels. That may be the most important, but it's not the only hazard.

There are three areas in which the writer is particularly vulnerable to telling rather than showing: when he tells what happened before the story began; when he tells what a character looks like; and when he tells what a character senses, that is, what he sees, hears, smells, touches, and tastes. Those are all places where the author's voice can intrude on the reader's experience.

What happened before the story began, sometimes called "backstory," should be shown rather than told about either in narrative summary or in a flashback. What happens offstage can also be brought onstage and shown. This is a large subject, and is treated separately in the next chapter.

What a character sees, hears, smells, touches, and tastes can be shown through actions rather than described. And feelings, of course, are best shown through actions.

Here's the silliest way that "telling" crops up:

"Henry, your son the doctor is at the door."

One character should never tell another character what the second character already knows—unless it's an accusation. If this kind of telling intrudes, it is really a dodge for the author to convey information, which can be done subtly. For instance:

"Do you think Henry would look more like a doctor if he grew a beard?"

That is sufficient for the reader to learn that Henry is a doctor and sounds like something that one parent might say to another.

The following is a more common way that writers "tell":

> Helen was a wonderful woman, always concerned about her children, Charlie and Ginny.

There is nothing for the reader to see, therefore the reader feels that he is being told about Helen. Here's an example of showing the same thing:

> When Helen drove her kids to school, instead of dropping them off at the curb, she parked her car and, one hand for each of them, accompanied Charlie and Ginny to the door of the school.

We are shown Helen in action without being told that she's a mother who is especially concerned about her children.

The reader wants an experience that's more interesting than his daily life. He enjoys and suffers whatever the characters are living through. If that experience is interrupted in order to convey a character's background, or anything else that the author seems to be supplying, that's telling, not showing, a major fault because it intrudes upon the reader's experience. Put simply, the reader experiences what is happening in front of his eyes. He does not experience what is related to him about offstage events. If his experience is interrupted, he gets antsy. "Telling" starts the reader skipping. Elmore Leonard said he avoids writing the parts that readers skip.

To better understand how to show instead of tell, look at some examples:

> **He was nervous** tells.
> **He tapped his fingers on the tabletop** shows.

Sometimes longer is better for showing:

> I put a yellow pad in front of me on the desk. I placed a pen on the yellow pad. This is ridiculous, I'm not going to write anything, just call.

That's a character about to make an important phone call. The reader isn't told he's nervous. The character is given a nervous action. It's useful to remember that an action can often show how a character feels.

Let's look at the evolution of telling into showing in the following examples:

She boiled water tells.
She put the kettle on the stove begins to show.
She filled the kettle from the faucet and hummed till the kettle's whistle cut her humming short shows.
She boiled water in a lidless pot so she could watch the bubbles perk and dance.

As you can see, we have gone from the general ("She boiled water") to showing a kettle being put on the stove, which conveys visually to the reader that the character is boiling water. In the third example, the addition of detail makes the visual come alive with more action. Finally, a different approach to the subject matter adds characterization and distinction, bringing us a long way from "She boiled water." The key to the improvement is particularity, a subject covered in greater depth in a later chapter.

One of the best examples I know of showing instead of telling is in, of all things, the series of television commercials for Taster's Choice coffee that have become famous for their interest as well as their effectiveness. The commercials consist of extremely short episodes of encounters between two attractive-looking neighbors, a man and a woman about each of whom little if anything is known. The viewer immediately wants them to get together. And the coffee provides the excuse. In one episode, the man shows up at the woman's door. To his dismay, another man opens the woman's door. When we learn the other man is her brother, we experience relief (for him, for ourselves). In a later episode, when the neighbors are cohabiting, the woman's adult son shows up, a surprise. In all of these, the dialogue is minimal and much is left to the reader's imagination. The commercials are lean in the writing and subtle in the acting, in contrast to most commercials in which the writing is excessive, pushy, adjective-laden, and unbelievable in dialogue. If you get the opportunity, tape the Taster's Choice commercials so that you can study them. They constitute a short course in subtle showing, in lively dialogue, and dramatic credibility.

In my novel *The Childkeeper*, some important scenes take place in a room that the children of the family call the Bestiary because it contains several large stuffed animals. In the first of these scenes, I wanted to make it evident that one of the children, sixteen-year-old Jeb, bosses the other kids around. I could have told the reader that by saying he was bossy. That's telling, now showing. Here's how I was able to get the idea across by showing:

> In the Bestiary, Jeb, sixteen-year-old caliph, lay stretched on an upper-level bunk bed, fingers twined on chest.
> "Dorry!" Jeb's command filled the room.

"Caliph," which means the head of a Moslem state, conveys the "boss" idea immediately. "Fingers twined on chest" helps the image. And Jeb's one word of dialogue seals the matter.

If a writer said, "Polly loved to dive in her swimming pool," he'd be telling, not showing. Information is being conveyed to us. We do not see Polly. But the writer I quote below is John Updike, who shows Polly to us in a writerly way:

> With clumsy jubilance, Polly hurtled her body from the rattling board and surfaced grinning through the kelp of her own hair.

The author is showing Polly in her "clumsy jubilance," hurling her body; we hear "the rattling board," and see Polly surfacing, grinning through "the kelp of her own hair," the last a marvelously precise image. Note that Updike didn't say "her hair was like kelp" (a simile), but "the kelp of her own hair" (a metaphor), an excellent example of particularity.

When you stumble upon information in your work that sounds like the author's intervention, try to come up with a simile or a metaphor that shows what you're trying to tell.

Let's look at another evolution from telling to showing:

> **He took a walk** tells.
> **He walked four blocks** begins to show.
> **He walked the four blocks slowly** shows more clearly.
> **He walked the four blocks as if it were the last mile** shows more by giving the reader a sense of the character's feelings, which the previous version did not.
> **He walked as if against an unseen wind, hoping someone would stop him** shows most of all because it gives the reader a sense of what the character desperately wants.

One clue to whether a writer is showing rather than telling is to determine if the passage is visual. In WritePro®, the first of my computer programs for writers, there is a protagonist named Beth Reilly. If a hundred writers characterize Beth Reilly, they'll produce a hundred different characterizations. The best ones, however, nourish our eyes.

One extraordinarily successful nonfiction writer, who tried her hand at developing a story with Beth Reilly, imagined Beth as the daughter of Irish immigrant parents, who at eighteen was crowned queen of the Chicago St. Patrick's Day parade, received a scholarship to a fine college and went on to law school, only to have the ill fortune of being seduced by a married neighbor.

As you can see, that is all information passed on in a nonfiction vein. What the writer needed to do was to transform the information into a visual scene for fiction. Here's the result:

> You should have seen the blush on Beth Reilly's freckled face as the Mayor tried to make the too-small crown stay atop Beth's full head of hair. A reporter from the Chicago Tribune handed up two hairpins to the Mayor to keep Beth's crown in place. It seemed as if everyone at the St. Patrick's Day Parade expelled a breath of relief as good Queen Beth curtsied to the crowd and the crown stayed in place. They applauded as she was handed the certificate that would give her four free years at Boston College as her reward. That day it seemed as if she could want and get anything. What she got was a married man introducing himself by handing her an expensive bottle of wine over a fence and with him, a future she kept secret even from her priest.

That's not perfect yet, but conveying the information with visual detail (the blush on Beth's freckled face, the too-small crown, two hairpins) showed the scene to the reader. No longer is the author telling.

Showing need not be complex. Can you show merely by the use of color? One of the students in my advanced fiction seminar, Linda Kelly Alkana, herself a teacher of writing, started her novel this way:

> Beyond the Arctic Circle, the color of cold is blue. But deep beneath the Arctic water, the color of cold is black.

That's an interesting beginning. We see the water. And the change in color is ominous.

As I've repeated often, what we as readers want from writing is to experience it. Receiving information from the author doesn't give us an experience.

Gloria Steinem quotes an Indian saying, "Tell me, and I'll forget. Show me, and I may not remember. Involve me, and I'll understand." I'd like to amend that. "Tell me, and I'll forget. Show me, and you'll involve me. Involvement is the first step toward understanding."

If you are concerned about whether in any passage or chapter you are telling rather than showing, there are some questions you can ask yourself:

Are you allowing the reader to *see* what's going on?

Is the author talking at any point? Can you silence the author by using an action to help the reader understand what a character feels?

Are you naming emotions instead of conveying them by actions? Is any character telling another what that character already knows?

While showing rather than telling is important throughout a work, it can serve as a miraculous cure for the ailing first pages of a novel or story. Showing means having characters do things that excite our interest, making those pages visual, letting us see what happens firsthand.

I have a small suggestion that carries with it a big reward. In a three-word note to yourself say, SHOW THE STORY. Then hang the note where you will see it whenever you sit down to write. Think of it as an antidote to a lifetime of hearing that a story should be told.

13

Choosing a Point of View

If all but one of the instruments on a surgeon's tray had been sterilized, that exception would be a danger to the patient. It can be said that one slip of point of view by a writer can hurt a story badly, and several slips can be fatal.

The term *point of view* as used by writers is misdefined even in good dictionaries. It means the character *whose eyes are observing what happens*, the perspective from which a scene or story is written.

Without a firm grasp of point of view, no writer of fiction is free to exercise his talent fully. This chapter is designed to help you understand the advantages and disadvantages of each point of view so that you can choose knowledgeably which to use to accomplish what you have in mind.

Each point of view available to the writer influences the emotions of the reader differently. Since affecting the emotions of the reader is the primary job of fiction, deciding on point of view is important.

In general, I advise the less-experienced writer not to mix points of view within the same scene, chapter, or even the same novel. It is unsettling to the reader. If you mix points of view, the author's authority seems to dissolve. The writer seems arbitrary rather than controlled. Sticking to a point of view intensifies the experience of a story. A wavering or uncertain point of view will diminish the experience for the reader.

The experienced writer who has mastered point of view can experiment with tightly controlled yet shifting viewpoints. When I started out I used the most neutral kind of third-person point of view. It was only after my confidence increased that I started using multiple first-person points of view in different parts or chapters, with the point of view established and clearly identified at the outset of each part or chapter.

Writers are often confused about point of view when they are presented with an unnecessarily large number of choices. Let's keep things as simple as possible by examining the three main points of view:

> I saw this, I did that.

No mistaking that one. It's the *first-person* point of view. What about the next example?

> My friends Blair and Cynthia were doomed. I could feel their fervor when I saw them embrace, yet in their eyes there was a wariness, as if each of them knew that their happiness could not last. I must tell you what happened the next day.

That is also first person, a story told from the sole point of view of the narrator. He sees what he believes to be in the eyes of his friends Blair and Cynthia, but it is not *their* view of how they feel, it is *his* view.

The narrator can be merely the observer of a story involving other people. This form of first person was more common in the nineteenth century. Today, a narrator is more often the protagonist or a principal character directly involved in the action. He can even be the villain of the piece.

Can you identify the point of view of the following?

> He saw this, he did that.

Third person is correct. The simplest way of understanding third person is that it is the same as first person except that you have substituted "he" or "she" for "I."

What about the second-person point of view?

> You saw this, you did that.

Forget it. Second person is used so rarely that I suggest just shelving it. I think of it as the crackerbarrel mode, the storyteller seeking to involve the reader in the story as if he were a character. The fact is that the reader is quite prepared to be involved emotionally in the story not as himself but through identification with one or more of the characters.

Now let's look at yet another point of view:

Kevin looked longingly at Mary, hoping she would notice him. She not only noticed him, she wished he would take her in his arms. Mary's mother, watching from the window, thought they were a perfect match.

This writer is all over the lot. One moment he seems to be in Kevin's head, the next moment in Mary's, and a second later in Mary's mother's point of view. What's going on?

In that short paragraph the reader knows what Kevin is thinking, and also what Mary and her mother are thinking. The author feels free to roam anywhere. That point of view is called *omniscient*, which means all-knowing.

Let's recap the three main points of view so that we're absolutely clear about the differences. In first person, the character—frequently the protagonist—tells the story from his or her point of view: **I saw this, I did that.**

The easiest way to think of the third person point of view is to substitute "he" for "I": **He saw this, he did that.**

In the omniscient point of view all characters and locations are fair game.

The usual reaction of beginning novelists is "Why can't I just use omniscient and be done with it? I can go anywhere, do anything—sounds great." Imitating God, by seeing and hearing everyone, is tempting, but maturity usually provides leavening. The Deity can't pay attention to everybody all the time, and neither can the writer. A story about everybody is a story about nobody. Before he'll let himself become involved, the reader wants to know whose story this is. He expects the writer to focus on individuals.

Each point of view has advantages and disadvantages.

The advantage of first-person POV (writers usually refer to point of view as POV, so let's call it that) is that it establishes the greatest immediate intimacy with the reader. It is an eyewitness account, highly subjective, and highly credible. When a character speaks directly to us, it's easier to believe what the character is saying. If you are good at impersonating your characters, you will be comfortable with the first-person POV. Better still, once you know the character, you will become expert in talking with that character's voice.

For each plus there is, alas, a minus. The author of a first-person story must constantly be on guard against telling the reader something that will sound like the author rather than the character. Furthermore, many writers see a severe limitation in that the first-person POV can convey to the reader only what that character sees, hears, smells, touches, tastes, and thinks. You can't have scenes your first-person character isn't a witness to. He doesn't know what's going on beyond his ken, although there are ways of circumventing that liability, which I'll demonstrate in a moment.

Another liability of first person is that it's difficult for a character to describe himself without seeming foolishly egotistical. Hundreds of writers, including me, have used a mirror to get around that. Forget it. A character seeing himself in a mirror is a cliché. However, a first-person character can think about his looks, or changes in his looks. Or another character can say something like:

"Are you dyeing your hair?"

This could lead to an exchange about the character's hair. Or:

"Are you getting taller?"
"I'm just stooping less these days."

Dealing with the "I" character's ego is more difficult. If he sees himself as weak, the reader won't have much interest in him as a protagonist. If he sees himself as strong, the reader will think him a braggart. Therefore, in the first-person POV the author relies on action and the speech of other characters to reveal things—particularly good things—about the "I" character. An unreliable or villainous first-person narrator can lend credibility. A first-person commentary by a not terribly intelligent character can provide an experienced writer with opportunities. In any event, first-person POV can be exceptionally rich.

There's something you'll want to watch out for using the first person. If the character takes the reader into his confidence, the character can't "forget" to provide the reader with an essential secret or other important piece of information. When the reader learns that something was withheld, he will feel cheated. The most dramatic way of handling information that the character is reluctant to convey is for another character to strip the secret from him in heated conversation:

I have been wedded to the truth my entire life. What would I be doing at a young person's bachelor party? I told Jonathan flat out, "I didn't go."

"Bullshit, Maurice, you were there."

"On my conscience, I swear I didn't go."

"You don't have a twin brother, do you?"

I told him I didn't know what he was talking about. Jonathan pursued me across the room.

"Was it your twin brother who came out of the john in his suspenders? Maurice, you left your jacket hanging in the stall you were so drunk. You're lucky somebody didn't rifle your pockets before Adam steered you back in for it."

I was barely able to speak. "You were there?"

Jonathan nodded. "I was there."

A point sometimes overlooked by beginners is that if a story centers on the narrator's ability to survive life-threatening dangers, some suspense will be lost in the first person because the character will have to survive to finish the story!

If you examine an anthology of short stories that have been selected for their excellence, you may be surprised by the number that are written from the first-person point of view. Despite the seeming limitations of a single character's perspective, first person well done is immensely rewarding to both experienced writers and experienced readers. The first-person point of view is valuable, for instance, if you've drawn a character who is highly intelligent or perceptive. His or her complex thoughts can be conveyed much more directly and intimately to the reader.

Another advantage of first person is that it can involve the reader's emotions—even empathy—with a protagonist who does horrible things. The *New York Times Book Review* carried an interesting interview with Scott Smith, a first novelist, that accompanied a review of his novel *A Simple Plan*:

> Scott Smith's protagonist Hank commits bloody acts. The reader would find it hard to empathize with Hank if the story were told in the third person. In fact, Smith's choice of first person was "vital to overcoming the reader's natural distaste for Hank's bloody acts." Said Smith, "I think there's something very seductive about a first-person voice, you sort of fall into it, no matter what horrible things the character does, and I wanted to keep that up until the very end, at which point the reader would have to sort of pull back. But no matter what he did, I was sympathetic to him. What's seductive to the reader is even more so to the writer."

Sometimes using the first-person point of view is a necessity. Jerzy Kosinski's first and best novel, *The Painted Bird*, is a story of tremendous power. I once loaned a copy to a man I'll call Michael, a hugely successful businessman who was expert in classical music, a collector of first-rate art, and an avid reader who "never reads fiction." We were vacationing in adjacent cottages and after he'd read only a few pages, Michael rushed over to ask, "Is this true?" I strung him along with "Do you think it's true?" and he kept coming back after several chapters, asking again, "Is this true?" That book converted Michael to reading fiction from that time on.

The amazing fact about *The Painted Bird* is that its language is full of imaginative images and some of the events depicted are bizarre or aberrant, yet because the use of first person is handled so skillfully the emotional experience for the reader is "This is true."

The Painted Bird begins with a preface in third person of less than two pages that sets the period and the locale. (In general I advise against the use of prefaces in fiction. Some readers skip them, and in doing so, miss essential information. I have found that the essential material of prefaces can almost always be skillfully developed in the story itself.)

Kosinski's novel, unlike the third-person preface, is in the first person. The narrator is presumably a ten-year-old boy:

> I lived in Marta's hut, expecting my parents to come for me any day, any hour. Crying did not help, and Marta paid no attention to my sniveling.
>
> She was old and always bent over, as though she wanted to break herself in half but could not. Her long hair, never combed, had knotted itself into innumerable thick braids impossible to unravel. These she calls elflocks. Evil forces nested in the elflocks, twisting them and slowly inducing senility.
>
> She hobbled around, leaning on a gnarled stick, muttering to herself in a language I could not quite understand. Her small withered face was covered with a net of wrinkles, and her skin was reddish like that of an overbaked apple. Her withered body constantly trembled as though shaken by some inner wind, and the fingers of her bony hands with joints twisted by disease never stopped quivering as her head on its long scraggy neck nodded in every direction.
>
> Her sight was poor. She peered at the light through tiny slits embedded under thick eyebrows. Her lids were like furrows in deeply

plowed soil. Tears were always spilling from the corners of her eyes, coursing down her face in well-worn channels to join glutinous threads hanging from her nose and the bubbly saliva dripping from her lips. She sometimes looked like an old green-gray puff-ball, rotten through and waiting for a last gust of wind to blow out the black dry dust from inside.

At first I was afraid of her and closed my eyes whenever she approached me. . . .

This story is seen through the eyes of the narrator. If it were told in the third person, it wouldn't be credible. The fantastic old lady would have seemed "made up." In my judgment, the author didn't have a choice. First person was inevitable. Kosinski chose it and wrote a novel that is now an established twentieth-century classic.

Third person is the most frequent choice of so-called commercial novelists. A majority of the books on the fiction bestseller list at any given time are likely to be written in the third person. It is a popular form for action/adventure and mainstream stories. There is strong precedent for today's third-person stories. Before stories were written, the man who told stories around a fire undoubtedly spoke of the adventures or experiences of others. When man invents myths, he is using the third person. Third person works best when the story is seen consistently from the point of view of *one character at a time*, though the author is free to report what any of the characters hear, smell, touch, and taste. Bottom-line editors and publishers favor third person. Here's an example:

Peter Carmody opened the door of his home, set down his bulging briefcase, and surveyed his domain. The two children were lying ass-up on the carpet, watching television, and didn't turn to greet him.

Were they ignoring him, or had they simply not heard him come in?

He opened the door again and this time let it slam. Twelve-year-old Margaret whipped over and in a second was on her feet running toward his outstretched arms. Ah, he thought, she hadn't heard me the first time.

Jonathan, a blasé thirteen, turned more slowly so that his eye would not lose sight of the television screen until the very last second. By that time Margaret was swarming all over her father,

taking his hat, holding on to his arm as it were the limb of a backyard tree.

There are many variations within the third-person mode, which is often
confusing to less experienced writers. Third person can be close to first
person, telling only the experiences of a single character as that character would know those experiences, but always referring to him as "he."
As the author takes advantage of the third-person form, he can move into
a scene from which the protagonist is absent, and show that scene from
a different character's POV. But be warned: POV has to be consistent
within a scene, otherwise you'll be crossing the line into the omniscient
point of view, which gives you license to go into any character's head at
will but involves the danger of confusing the reader or losing him along
the way.

Plausibility is a major concern of third person. In the first person, a
character can say, "I ate six bananas" and perhaps we believe him. In the
third person, when a character says "Mary ate six bananas," we are inclined to think, "Oh yeah?" We accept things from a first-person speaker
that we would question in a third-person speaker, who has the same distance from the reader as a stranger does in life. The first-person speaker
becomes an intimate. We are inclined to accept his word.

Once the author establishes the limitation of the third-person point of
view, he must stick to it and the limitation becomes an advantage, a re-
straint, a discipline. If you adopt a loose form of third person in which,
say, each chapter is seen from a different character's POV, be sure to
choose for each scene the character *who is most affected by the events of
that scene.*

Though I have written in third person (*The Magician, Living Room,
The Childkeeper, The Resort*), I love writing in the first person and am
partial to it (*Other People, The Touch of Treason, A Deniable Man, The
Best Revenge*).

In the "know-it-all" omniscient POV, the writer can go anywhere, especially into the heads of more than one character even within a scene.
Hemingway in "The Short Happy Life of Francis Macomber" skillfully
gets into the mind of a wounded lion. Look it up.

The omniscient POV allows the author to speak in his own voice, to
say things that would be inappropriate for any of his characters to say.
The author's voice, however, should have personality, authority, some
wisdom, and ideally a fresh sense of humor. The author, in other words,

needs to be quite a character to manage the omniscient point of view interestingly. One of my most talented students, Anne James Valadez, whose work sparkles with originality, prefers the omniscient point of view; her voice is unusually distinctive and exudes the authority of myth.

The danger of the omniscient POV is that the reader will hear the author talking instead of experiencing the story. The omniscient POV lacks discipline. Because the author can stray into anybody's head, it is hard to maintain credibility and even harder to gain a close emotional rapport with the reader. Total freedom can be as upsetting to the writer as to the reader.

Even authors with several published novels to their credit can make errors in point of view. In a novel called *Talent*, the looseness of an uncontrolled omniscient point of view results in passages like this:

> "Driving up here always makes me feel like Paul Newman at the wheel," joked Allison.
> She and Diana climbed quickly to Mulholland, which twisted for miles along the spine of the ridge like a carelessly abandoned garden hose.

The point of view at that moment is presumably Allison's. From the driver's point of view, would a twisting road ever look "like a carelessly abandoned garden hose"? The image is forced. But more important is the fact that it mixes point of view within the same paragraph. A twisting road might look like a garden hose from a helicopter or a low-flying airplane, but from a car?

Readers don't notice point-of-view errors. They simply sense that the writing is bad.

Clifford Irving handles the omniscient point of view skillfully. His novel *Trial* begins with an objective view:

> In Houston, Texas, in the early winter of 1985, a petty thief named Virgil Freer devised a scheme to bilk the chain of Kmart stores.

Virgil's scheme is outlined, but by the end of the first paragraph he was arrested and in jail. Virgil hires a young criminal defense attorney named Warren Blackburn. We get glimpses of what Virgil is thinking. He says to Blackburn,

"You got to help me."

And immediately we are inside Blackburn's head.

I've met a lot worse than Virgil, Warren decided.

In the first few pages, we've heard the author, and we've been inside the head of Virgil and the lawyer he picks. Clifford Irving is using a *controlled* omniscient point of view—with good results.

Let's take a moment to examine the comparative subjectivity of each point of view. In first person, the POV is entirely subjective. Think of it this way: the character talking to the reader is not only conveying everything the reader gets to know, the character is making a case for himself. It's his view of himself, the others, the world.

In third person, the choice is greater. If the story can be told as if from a single character's POV, the reader will have some sense of subjectivity. The writer can even choose to shift the subjectivity to another character, but has to be careful not to shift about carelessly. Back in 1973, John Godey, a thriller writer, published a book called *The Taking of Pelham One Two Three*, about the hijacking of a New York City subway train. Godey wrote in the third person, shifting from character to character every few pages. Every short section was headed with the name of the person from whose point of view he was writing. The problem was that in the first twenty-eight pages, I counted seven characters into whose point of view the reader was admitted for a short period. It was a dizzying experience.

If you use the third-person point of view, you can be a partisan of all the characters or some. You can be entirely neutral or objective, conveying nothing of the characters' thoughts or aims. Complete objectivity tends to be sterile of emotion, particularly the kind of intimacy that readers enjoy in literary novels, but it is useful in stories that are mainly action. Whatever genre you write in, my recommendation is that you focus on the POV of one character at a time, and sustain it, or you're likely to get into trouble. If you've got to let your readers know what everybody thinks, you'd probably be better off using the omniscient point of view, the loosest of forms. You can more readily let the reader know what each character thinks than you can in the third person, as Norman Mailer did in his first novel, *The Naked and the Dead*. The novel starts with:

Nobody could sleep. When morning came, assault craft would be lowered and a first wave of troops would ride through the surf and charge ashore on the beach at Anopopei. All over the ship, all through the convoy, there was a knowledge that in a few hours some of them were going to be dead.

That is clearly an omniscient point of view. The next long paragraph begins with:

A soldier lies flat on his bunk, closes his eyes, and remains wide-awake. All about him, like the soughing of surf, he hears the murmurs of men dozing fitfully.

The reader experiences everything in that paragraph and the next long paragraph from the point of view of an anonymous soldier. That paragraph ends with the soldier coming back from the latrine:

And as he returns, he is thinking of an early morning in his childhood when he had lain awake because it was to be his birthday and his mother had promised him a party.

The reader might expect to be taken back to the anonymous soldier's childhood party. Instead, the next paragraph introduces us to new characters:

Early that evening Wilson and Gallagher and Staff Sergeant Croft had started a game of seven card stud with a couple of orderlies from headquarters platoon.

Then we get a scene of a card game with Wilson, Gallagher, and Croft. We get inside Wilson's head: **He was feeling very good.** In the next paragraph, we enter Croft's head for a second to find out he is annoyed by the hands he's been getting. Soon Wilson **reflected for a moment, holding an undealt card in his hand.** Then we are told Wilson is dejected. We get into Gallagher's head—his conscience is bothering him, he is thinking of his seven-month-pregnant wife back home. And so it goes. We are told things by the omniscient author, and we go in and out of the minds of the three card players. Young as he was when he wrote *The Naked and the Dead*, Mailer's natural talent overcame his lack of experience. His use of the omniscient point of view seems instinctive, but he made it work well because the reader feels the author is in control. The great danger in using the omniscient point of view is the loss of control that is attributable to the lack of discipline.

While an author can write about characters more sophisticated than himself, it is difficult to fashion a character who is more knowledgeable and intelligent than the author, particularly if the author is going into the character's most profound thoughts. That's why characters like scientists, public figures, and intellectuals in some popular novels come across as stilted or fake. Similarly, if the author is writing about people less intelligent than himself, he must be careful not to put thoughts into a character's head that are beyond that character's capabilities.

The major decision, of course, is which point of view to use. Some of the authors I've worked with have an instinct for one or another point of view based in some measure on their experience as readers. Those who write thrillers usually write in the third person. Those whose reading has been mainly literary are more often tempted by the first person. But that still leaves a large terrain in the middle. Mainstream fiction is written in both first and third person. My advice is to try the form that feels comfortable to you. One advantage of understanding point of view is that if your work isn't satisfying you, you can always put the draft aside and rewrite it from another point of view. If you've used third person, try first. If you've used omniscient, try third or first. Or both. Switching points of view has saved novels that were going nowhere.

Earlier in this chapter I mentioned that there are ways to get around some of the limitations of first-person point of view. The most important, of course, is to get beyond the character's horizon and let the reader experience an event where the first person narrator was not present. In the following example, a character named Florence is speaking:

> "The old bitch threatened to blow the party if I was invited, though the occasion was as much mine as Rose's. Helen told me she put her punch glass down in the first minute because the punch tasted as if it were made with grape juice and gasoline. Debbie, would you believe it, phoned me from her car to say the background music was so loud you couldn't hear what anybody said if you didn't know how to lip read. I could hardly hear her because of the traffic noise. Thank heaven Maryanne came zipping straight over from the party to tell me Sally's husband looked like he wouldn't last an-

other day. And Rose, she said Rose's breath kept everyone standing at least three feet away from her, looking for an excuse to escape. I wasn't invited, but I might as well have been. I probably know more about what happened than anybody."

Note that to help credibility, there is a sense of cattiness and conflict in Florence's attitude toward the people at the party. A simpler but perhaps less credible way would be to give the first-person character a legitimate reason to ask about what is for her an offstage event. Or the first-person character addressing the reader can guess what might be happening at that moment elsewhere. The point to remember is that you have to motivate the reporting of offstage scenes. And whenever possible keep the report visual. We see Helen putting the awful punch down. We hear Debbie with difficulty as well as see her use her car phone. We smell Rose's breath.

Finally, here's a POV checklist to use in examining your own work:

- Is your point of view consistent? If it slips anywhere, correct it. If it isn't working, try another point of view.
- Is your point of view sufficiently subjective to involve the reader's emotions? Have you been too objective?
- Have you avoided telling us how a character feels? Have you relied on actions to help the reader experience emotion?
- If you're using the first person, have you used another character to convey in conversation what your first person character looks like?
- Is the "I" character sufficiently different from you?
- Have you told the reader anything that the "I" character couldn't know or wouldn't say? Is the author's voice showing?
- Is there anything in your material that is not likely to be known to someone with your character's background or intelligence?
- If you're using third person or the omniscient point of view, have you used particularity in describing that person?
- Would it pay to narrow your focus so that the reader can identify more readily with one of the characters?
- Have you established limitations or guidelines for your third-person point of view? Have you then adhered to those limitations?

Subjects taught in colleges and universities are called disciplines. Writing is a discipline. And one of its most disciplined techniques is that of point of view. The choice of point of view is yours, but once you've decided, be sure that you stick to it as if your reader's experience of the story depended on it. Because it does.

14

Flashbacks: How to Bring Background into the Foreground

When he was young, Barnaby Conrad, founder of the Santa Barbara Writers' Conference, worked for Sinclair Lewis. Once he asked the master how best to handle flashbacks. Lewis's reply was succinct. He said, *"Don't."*

It is true that even experienced writers sometimes handle flashbacks awkwardly. It is also true that flashbacks are used too often, and frequently remove the reader from the experience he is having. Nevertheless, you sometimes need to use flashbacks, and therefore you should learn how to employ them properly.

Ideally, *all fiction should seem to be happening now*. That sentence is worth pasting on your makeup or shaving mirror or on your computer where you will see it every day.

We don't read in real time. A writer can brush hours aside by one word: "Later . . ." Some stories seem to read fast, some seem to drag. Proust, in *Remembrance of Things Past*, dwells for dozens of pages on thoughts inspired by a cookie. Zola, in his classic *L'Assommoir*, has a sumptuous meal that, as I recall, lasts for fifty pages. If we don't read in real time, why not go back to some previous matter in a flashback? Why are editors so inhospitable to flashbacks?

The reason flashbacks create a problem for readers is that they break the reading experience. The reader is intent on what happens next. Flashbacks, unless expertly handled, pull the reader out of the story to tell him what happened earlier. If the reader is conscious of moving back in time, especially if what happened in the past is told rather than shown, the engrossed reader is reluctant to be pulled out of his reverie to receive information. If we are enthralled, we don't want to be interrupted. Therefore, the art of writing flashbacks is to avoid interrupting the reader's experience. I'll show you how that's done.

Let's be sure we understand each other. *A flashback is any scene that happened before the present story began.*

Note that I said any *scene*. A true flashback, however short, is a scene, preferably with characters in conflict.

If you find that you absolutely must use a flashback, there are a number of points to engrave on your mind:

- A flashback must illuminate the present story in an important way. Otherwise, why bother? If it doesn't enhance the present story markedly, you may not really need it.
- Whenever possible, the flashback should be an immediate scene rather than an offstage narrative summary. The reader needs to witness the flashback rather than be told about what happened.
- You can go into a flashback directly or segue into it. The object is to make the transition to the flashback as unobtrusive as possible. Slipping into the flashback quickly avoids the risk of the impatient reader skipping pages because he sees the flashback coming before it grips him.
- The first sentence of a flashback needs to be arresting.

A flashback is presumably there because it provides information. To the reader that information should not come across as information about the past; it should be as immediate and gripping as a scene in the present. If you're riding in an elevator, you don't want to see the chains and pulleys of the mechanism. The reader doesn't want to see your chains and pulleys, he just wants the ride. Ask yourself:

If the flashback is necessary, can the reader see the action in it as an immediate scene?

Is the opening of the flashback as interesting or compelling as the beginning of a novel or story?

Does the flashback enhance the reader's experience of the story as a whole?

A good flashback is a scene that is depicted exactly as it would be in the present story except for how it is introduced and how the present story is rejoined.

Certain words should carry warning labels for the writer. "Had" is the number-one villain. It spoils more flashbacks than any other word. Most fiction is written in the straight past tense. When writing flashbacks, as quickly as possible use the same tense you're using for the present scenes. That means in almost all cases the straight past tense, not the variants. Instead of saying, "I had been remembering . . .", say "I remembered . . ."

Here's an example of an author who gets tangled up in "hads" that are totally unnecessary:

> I remember when my boss had called me into his office and had said, "Sit down." He had remained standing. In those days I was like a new army recruit, I had taken everything said to me as an order. I hadn't wanted to sit down with him looming over me.

When that author's editor finished, this is the way the text read:

> I remember the time my boss called me into his office and said, "Sit down." He remained standing. In those days I was like a new army recruit, I took everything as an order, but damn if I wanted to sit with him looming over me.

The first example has five "hads." The second example has none.

Sometimes authors double up on a fault with "had had," or use the contraction for "had," and compound the problem with another word to avoid in flashbacks, "then":

> Ellie had had a mother who wanted a boy and who'd made Ellie wear boys' clothes and cut her hair like a boy for years. Then one day . . .

The author should have written:

> Ellie's mother wanted a boy. She made Ellie wear boys' clothes and cut her hair like a boy's for years. One day . . .

In starting a flashback, your aim is to get into an immediate scene as soon as possible. Since dialogue is always in immediate scene, one way of handling flashbacks is to use dialogue early. What most writers don't realize is that you can use dialogue even if the flashback is short. Here's an example from the second page of *The Resort*. Margaret Brown, a physician, is reminiscing about her education in medical school. Watch how the thought of a certain instructor almost instantly becomes dialogue:

Margaret realized much too soon that the ultimate organ, the brain that harbored the mind, was *terra incognita* for most of her fellow students. Her wisest instructor, Dr. Teal, once asked her if brain surgery attracted her as a specialty.

"No," she said much too quickly.

"May I ask why?"

"I find surgeons boring."

Dr. Teal, a surgeon, blushed. Margaret quickly apologized, explaining she meant those of her fellow students who . . .

Inserting those three lines of dialogue helps the rest of the reminiscence become visible to the reader.

There are two ways of introducing a flashback. First is the direct method. An example I point to often is from Brian Glanville's novel *The Comic*. The protagonist is a comedian who is thought to be crazy. On the sixth page, he tells his therapist:

"I've always told jokes, Doc."

The next paragraph begins a flashback in a direct manner:

Which is true. Go back as far as I can remember, and I'm telling jokes. In fact I think he's right, it was a defense; or it began as a defense. At home, at school. My father, big bastard, keeping that pub in the Mile End road, always handy with his belt.

And so on, into the comic's childhood. Brian Glanville hooks us with an intriguing character. We want to know more about this "mad" comic who is speaking to us over the head of his doctor, as it were. We're glad to have his background brought to us by the flashback.

There are equally simple ways of concluding a flashback.

You can use a line space (four blank lines) to mark the passage of time and restart the present scene after the line space. Or you can begin a new paragraph with "One week later . . ."

Or you can restart the present scene with dialogue: "Last week you didn't talk this way."

You can come out of the flashback by a direct statement. John, in bed with Anna, has been remembering (in a flashback) a scene in the past:

The next day John got out of bed as if he had his whole life to live all over again.

It needn't be that direct:

> Without taking his eyes off Anna's sleeping face, John slipped into his undershorts, buttoned his shirt, put one leg and then the other into his pants, but when he sat on the bed to put on his socks and shoes, Anna opened her eyes.

While flashbacks are to be avoided whenever possible, the flashback thought can be immensely useful in enriching both a character and a scene. In life our thoughts interrupt us all the time. Frequently the thoughts are relevant to where we are, what we're doing, what people are saying to us. Thoughts give texture to life and also to novels.

The first three pages of my novel *Living Room* show the heroine, Shirley Hartman, locking the door of her apartment in a Manhattan high-rise, taking the elevator to the top floor, and climbing the stairs to the roof. Then we get her thoughts, which are interspersed with thoughts of the past. Without those thoughts, of the past as well as the present, the scene would lose impact.

Let's join Shirley Hartman one page into the scene, listen to her thoughts, and then examine them closely to see how the effect is achieved:

> Through gaps in the clouds drifting across the charcoal sky, she made out the moon. As a child, she could always decipher its face; now it seemed to have only a scarred surface, crags and mottled ground where instruments had been implanted, sending messages, even now.
>
> A few rectangles of light in the higher building across the street betrayed their occupants' sleeplessness. Shirley leaned over the waist-high parapet, her feet on tiptoe, and dizzyingly saw in the street below a taxi disgorging its passengers. Suddenly she thought of the unwashed dish with the remains of the cottage cheese and fruit. She should have rinsed it off, stuck it in the dishwasher, left things neat. And the diary she kept in her desk drawer, the leather flaking with age, the broken lock, the coded recordings of long ago, the first time she had taken pleasure with herself, the crazy evening with Harry, she should have dropped it into the incinerator! And Al's one letter, she should have flushed it away. Al, that intolerably independent man who could live without anyone, who she thought loved her but didn't need her, how would he react when he heard, would it surprise him, the stoic who pretended never to be surprised by anything?

Its tires screeching, the taxi accelerated away in the streets below.

In the *Times*, she thought, her obituary would rate a picture. In the *News* it might even make the upfront pages, given her occasional notoriety and the scandalous nature of what she was determined to do.

Her father would think what? He'd say something like, *Death can't teach you anything you can use!* In her mind, she touched fingers to Philip Hartman's eyes, closing them so that he could not see.

Pulling herself up onto the ledge she scratched her right knee. She remembered the midtown traffic accident she had come upon and the badly injured woman lying in the street, her dress up, her pubic hair visible to the gaping onlookers; Shirley was glad she was wearing pantyhose, *as if it mattered*. Why was she still holding her handbag? She dropped it to the roof behind her, heard the glass of her mirror break.

What if her hurtling self hit that pedestrian late-walking his dog, or another one unseen, she was not a murderer, the only crime she wanted to commit was against herself. If there were a crowd below yelling *Jump! Jump! Jump!* would she leap into their midst?

It seemed funny to be afraid to stand up on the ledge. She swung her legs around to let them dangle over the side.

Would her limbs flail?

Might her head turn down as she fell? The thought of it striking the pavement first was terrible.

She stood up on the parapet, swaying slightly.

Al said she looked better naked than she did with clothes on, as if that were the ultimate compliment. Al had nothing to do with her decision. It was her life. She wanted out. Shirley held her breath.

Mingled in Shirley's thoughts are the following flashback thoughts:

1. What she thought about the moon when she was a child.
2. The unwashed dish with the remains of her dinner.
3. The diary she should have burned.
4. Al, who loved her.
5. Her father.
6. A traffic accident with a badly injured woman.
7. Al's comments about how she looked naked.

Why the flashback thoughts? If in the first chapter the reader saw an unknown woman trying to commit suicide, the reader's emotions would not be engaged in any important way. You have to know the people in the car before you see the car crash. Shirley's flashback thoughts, added to her thoughts in the present, are how the reader gets to know Shirley and begins to want her not to jump.

Note that the flashback thoughts are part of a visual scene in the present, a young woman up on a parapet, ready to jump. If the flashback element is to consist of more than quick thoughts in an ongoing scene, the writer must be certain to create a flashback scene that stands on its own to avoid the flashback becoming a narrative of something that happened elsewhere. To move from what is happening in the present to a scene from the past without breaking the reader's experience requires segueing to a scene in the past as inconspicuously as possible.

The term *segue* is derived from music. It means to glide unobtrusively into something new. I prefer the segue into a flashback to the more direct method, moving from the present scene to a scene in the past inconspicuously.

Flashbacks normally decrease suspense, but they can be fashioned to increase suspense. For instance, in *The Best Revenge* there is a single scene that runs for three chapters. It is the fierce facing-off of the protagonist, Ben Riller, and the antagonist, Nick Manucci. To heighten the suspense of that confrontation, I inserted three flashbacks into the scene, remembered by Nick, designed to increase the suspense by postponing the outcome of the confrontation. Each of the flashbacks illuminates the long scene and adds to its meaning. And each is segued into and out of as surreptitiously as possible.

In the course of the same novel one learns a great deal more about the antagonist in flashbacks from his wife's point of view. We find out what kind of lover Nick is, why she married him, and what happened to that marriage. An antagonist, characterized in depth, has come to life as a credible human being, a person who holds the reader's interest, however inhumane his methods. Saul Bellow said that Nick Manucci, the villain, was the best character in the book. I believe Nick's flashbacks and those of his wife contributed to that view.

If the ghost of Sinclair Lewis is within earshot, I say flashbacks done correctly can provide richness and depth to a novel as long as they don't read like flashbacks, if they are active scenes slipped into and out of simply and quickly.

If you have a flashback in your manuscript or are contemplating writing one, ask yourself, does the flashback reinforce the story in an important way? Is it absolutely essential? If it's not, you may not really need it.

Can the reader see what's happening in your flashback? Can you give it the immediacy of a scene that takes place before the eye? If your flashback is not a scene, can you make it into an active scene as if it were in the present?

Take a close look at the opening of your flashback. Is it immediately interesting or compelling?

Is the reader's experience of your story enhanced by the flashback or—however well written—does it still intrude?

Has the flashback helped characterize in depth, has it helped the reader feel what the character feels?

Is there any way of getting background information across *without* resorting to a flashback?

We now come to an ideal solution: moving flashback material into the foreground and eliminating the need for a flashback.

The example I'll use brings forward childhood material since that is the most common occasion for writing a flashback:

> "You were a lousy kid, Tommy, a brat from the word go."
> "Hey, man, if you got punished as often as I got punished—"
> "Your old man was teaching you discipline."
> "By yanking my plate away before I'd had a mouthful?"
> "He got through to you, didn't he?"
> "He starved me. What he got through to me was I was hungry and he wouldn't let me eat. I hated him. I wished he'd die."
> "You got your wish, didn't you?"

In this brief exchange in the present the reader gets the following information:

1. Tommy had a lousy childhood.
2. Whoever is talking to him thinks it was Tommy's fault.
3. Tommy's father withheld food from him as punishment.
4. The repeated punishments drove Tommy to hate his father and wish him dead.
5. The speaker is loading Tommy with guilt.

Note that all five points were conveyed in short order *without a flash-back*. You've just seen how information can be conveyed in present dialogue in such a way that the reader is witnessing a dramatic scene that takes place in the present, thus eliminating the need for a flashback.

The example above is entirely in dialogue. Thoughts can accomplish the same purpose, as in the following example in which only one of the characters is speaking, yet all the points are made:

"What's bothering you?" Al asked. "You're not eating."

Tommy poked his fork at the pork chop. He cut pieces off. He raised one toward his mouth, then suddenly put the fork down and shoved his plate away from him.

"Hey, kid, tell me what's the matter," Al said.

The matter, Tommy thought, was you didn't have my father, I did. You didn't have him yanking the plate away as punishment. You didn't go to bed with pain in your gut.

"Hey," Al said, "is it your old man's death? Is that what's bothering you?"

Tommy has said absolutely nothing. We've been privy to his thoughts. And we've got the background we need right in the foreground.

In conclusion, I don't want to minimize the skill that's needed to make flashbacks as involving for the reader's experience as everything that happens in the present, However, I've never seen essential background material that couldn't be made to work as scenes. And more of that background can become foreground than you may suspect. The time it takes to do it right is an investment in the reader's experience.

15

The Keys to Credibility

Credibility is central to much of what the writer does. He creates a world in which the invented characters must seem as real as the people who surround us in life. What happens to them, however extraordinary—and it should be extraordinary—must be believable. The motivations of the characters should be credible. And that provides the occasion for the writer to meet his biggest enemy, himself.

The writer has a natural tendency to act as we all do in life—that is, we question the motivations of others more often than we do our own. When creating fiction, those characters are our selves and we cover for them. This leads to a variety of problems.

I have watched as a bestselling action novelist once again has a character throwing another character over the railing of a ship. Think a moment, how many people do you know who would be capable of lifting a hundred and fifty pounds or more up from the ground high enough to toss that entire weight over a railing? In action fiction, the willing reader suspends disbelief. If one guy throws another over the railing, the reader goes with it. If a writer's concerned about the quality of his writing and needs to say that "Tiny picked him up bodily and threw him over the railing," he will have planted earlier that Tiny is six foot three and a weightlifter.

In fiction, plays, and film, *planting* means preparing the ground for something that comes later, usually to make the later action credible. Planting is necessary when a later action might seem unconvincing to the reader. Not all actions require planting. For instance, if Todd trips Andrew and Andrew then punches Todd, Todd's action does need planting, Andrew's punch does not.

In fiction that has a higher aim, the credibility of every important action in the story is at risk unless the writer is confident that the motivation or ability of the character makes the action credible.

Some inadequate motivation is easy enough to fix. For instance, if a character suddenly gets up to go shopping for the convenience of the author because something is going to happen in a shopping mall, the events in the mall may not be credible unless the motivation for the character going to the mall is planted ahead of time. The planting can be simple enough through a touch of humor:

"I'm not going to go on a shopping spree ever again. After today."

Or you simply need to get a character out of the house. Instead of an unmotivated walk, he could say:

"These new shoes are not going to get broken in if I sit around the house."

Some actions are so bizarre that it may seem next to impossible to motivate them:

We had been married for three years when, one Sunday, Tom dressed, as usual, in a shirt and tie, slipped into his handsome jacket, put on his best cordovan shoes, and left the house without his pants.

What conclusion can the reader come to, that Tom suddenly went crazy? Or is this going to be a wacky comedy about an eccentric? Could Tom be so concerned abut something else that he forgot to put on his pants?

Readers are seldom interested in truly crazy people. It is hard to be moved by their actions because some seem so unmotivated. It is not credible that someone, otherwise all dressed up, would forget to put on pants before leaving the house. We are left with the possibility that this is going to be a farce in which actions are not required to meet any tests of credibility. If this were a story about an eccentric who behaves unpredictably, Tom's strange conduct would require planting. If Thomas's action is not to seem ludicrous, he would have had to have been characterized as someone who could do something as zany as going out dressed up without his pants. Readers will not readily accept the unlikely. Can this character's action in going out without his pants be made to seem credible? Can Thomas's aberrant act be prepared for so that it will seem credible when it happens?

Think of "planting" as preparing the ground in a garden:

Tom and I had been married for three years when, one Sunday, he dressed, as usual, in a shirt and tie, put on a handsome suit and his best cordovan shoes, but forgot to put on his socks.

I decided not to say anything, but the next Sunday he dressed in the same handsome suit, put on his socks before he put on his cordovan shoes, then tied his tie over his undershirt and left the house before I could catch him.

I said nothing. But the third Sunday, he remembered to put on a shirt before putting on his tie, then put on a handsome jacket, and left the house without his pants. I thought I'd better speak to him.

This revision is funnier, and more credible despite the zaniness of the action. Thomas's forgetfulness was planted.

The worst mistake that a story writer can make is to have unconvincing motivation for actions that are central to the story. A married engineer with a well-paying job notices a momentarily unattended carriage in a supermarket and kidnaps the baby. What is the reader to think?

The reader has to guess. Is the engineer childless and desperate? Does his wife refuse to have a child? Still, kidnapping is a contemptible act for which the punishment is severe. What in the engineer's background would have made it possible for him to pick a stranger's child out of a carriage and take it away? How does the man's wife react when she learns of the kidnapping? When he is apprehended, what excuse does he give? There are too many unanswered questions, which makes the reader feel that this comes across as a "made-up" story that the events described didn't happen. Clearly, the kidnapping of a child is a major action that must seem motivated at the time that it takes place.

Coincidence is enchanting when it happens in life. A friend we haven't seen for years walks out of the same darkened movie house as we do, we go for a coffee together, and have a gabby reunion. If this happened in a story, the skeptical reader would say that the author is responsible for the coincidence and that it isn't believable.

Here is an example of how to diminish the appearance of coincidence:

Problem: Sally and Howie are ex-lovers who have not entirely gotten over each other. The author has arranged for Sally to run into Howie in the shopping mall. The reader smells coincidence.

Solution: The reader learns that Sally has been avoiding a particular store she and Howie used to shop in because she's afraid of meeting Howie there. But Sally wants something that store—and no other store in the neighborhood—carries. Before entering the store's revolving door, Sally peers through the window to make sure Howie isn't in there. She goes in, finds what she wants, and hurries to the revolving door, a smile on her face, only to see Howie in the other compartment of the revolving door on his way in. They both register surprise, then laugh.

A coincidence still? Yes, but the way the author arranged it with detail— the special store, Sally peering in to avoid Howie, the revolving door— all help to make their coincidental meeting a true surprise.

There are many other ways of diminishing coincidence. For instance, a third character can arrange for Sally and Howie to meet "accidentally" at an event staged by the third character.

The most dangerous place for a coincidence to occur is at the climax of a story. The protagonist has his head on the chopping block. Suddenly the *deus ex machina,* the god in the machine, comes down for the rescue. Those devices fool no one. They exist for the author's convenience because he can't figure out a credible way of rescuing the protagonist.

It is so difficult for a writer to gain objectivity about his own work, and in no area more so than in judging coincidental matters. I'd like to offer a peculiar strategy that seems to work. You can sometimes get objectivity artificially by making a new title page and replacing your name as author with the name of an author whose work you admire especially. Then read your manuscript with that author's eyes to see if you can catch any action that is insufficiently motivated or that smacks of coincidence.

If that doesn't work for you, try preparing a new title page and replacing your name with the name of an author whose work you dislike. Go at the manuscript with a vengeance to root out unmotivated acts and coincidence. It's astonishing what a change of perspective will do.

Above all, remember that the main actions of your work are like great flowering plants. Put the seed down well earlier and admire the harvest. Leave coincidence to the hacks and the god in his machine.

16

The Secret Snapshot Technique: Reaching for Hidden Treasure

The secret snapshot technique is designed to help writers whose fiction doesn't touch the emotion of readers, who write from the outside looking in, whose stories are uninteresting to experience because they seem "made up."

The characters and themes that lie hidden within each author are the source of work that strikes readers as original and real. How do we jog the author to write from the inside, in touch with subject matter and feelings that will enable him to brush the reader's emotions?

I've used the secret snapshot method in individual conferences with writers and in seminars. In the latter, the author whose work is being discussed comes up front and sits in the "hot seat." The two of us talk. Everyone else is eavesdropping.

I ask the author to think of a snapshot of something so private he wouldn't carry it in his wallet because if he were in an accident, he wouldn't want a paramedic to find it. The snapshot we're looking for is one the writer wouldn't want his neighbor or closest friend to see. Not even a family member. Especially not a family member.

I call them snapshots because I prefer that the writer start with something visual. Some people jump to the conclusion that a secret snapshot is of something sexual. Wrong. In practice many are not. In one that worked for its author, her snapshot was of a rose in a one-flower vase that was put on her office desk by someone whose identity she never learned. In another, the author's snapshot was of an audience he addressed years ago. The image remained like grit in his memory because all the while he talked his undershorts kept slipping down. Later in this chapter I convey in detail how a writer of detective stories turned her book around successfully by a snapshot of her two-year-old sleeping in his bed.

Some writers squirm through the process, shifting uncomfortably in their seats. That's a good sign.

If your reaction to this exercise is "my secrets are nobody's business," that's understandable. But if you want to write something that will move other people, you have to come to terms with the fact that the writer is by profession a squealer. He learns by starting to squeal on himself.

If you're thinking that you may not have the courage to be a writer, I can tell you that's what most writers think when confronted with this assignment for the first time. Few people have the natural ability to open themselves up to strangers. The writer learns how. One of the ways is to write down what you see in your most secret snapshot. If you're tempted to fudge, don't. If you've decided to give us a made-up snapshot, you'll serve your writing better by changing it to the snapshot you're hiding.

Nobody's going to see it. Not yet. Perhaps not ever. What they will see is the *result* of your finding the right snapshot.

Is your snapshot such that any of your friends or neighbors might have one just like it? If so, change it to one that only you have. Your writing is going to be yours, not writing that could come out of anyone else's closet.

Do you think other people would want to see what's in your snapshot if they heard what's in it? If not, you'd better try another.

Please answer truthfully: would you carry that snapshot in your wallet or purse? If your answer is "yes," perhaps it's not so secret. The snapshots that work best are embarrassing, revelatory, or involve a strong and continuing stimulus to memory.

If you're feeling, "Hey, I didn't bargain for this, all I wanted to do was write stories," I remind you that the best fiction reveals the hidden things *we usually don't talk about.*

The stories and novels that get turned down are full of the things we talk about freely—the snapshots in your photo album that you show to friends, family, and neighbors. Readers don't want to see your photo album. They have their own. They want to see what's in the picture you're reluctant to show.

You say, "Why can't I start with other people's secret snapshots?"

You can. It's a longer route to success, but it gives you a chance to build your courage. A writer needs the courage to say what other people sometimes think but don't say. Or don't allow themselves to think.

If you elect to conjure up someone else's secret snapshot, it has to be one that you wouldn't be allowed to see under any circumstance. Can you describe that snapshot? What interests you in that picture? Would your interest be shared by lots of other people if the person involved were a character in your novel? If not, you'd better change the snapshot. Or improve it.

If you're stuck, try this. Everyone except liars has at least one person he truly dislikes, maybe even hates. What kind of snapshot would he carry that he wouldn't want *you* to see? Don't tell me the first thing that comes to mind. Maybe the second.

Would your enemy pay to keep you from seeing that snapshot? If not, try another that's really private.

How much would you pay to see a snapshot from your actual enemy? Nothing? Not much? Then it's not a good snapshot. If you'd pay to see it, maybe people will pay to buy your book.

Here's a snapshot you probably know. It's your best friend's secret snapshot. He or she may have confided in you about it. Or you may have guessed what it might be from a bit of evidence here and there. Or because of your insight.

While you're collecting other people's snapshots, how about one of someone you knew who is now dead? Does it make you feel safer?

This method may seem a bit offputting or uncomfortable at first, but experienced writers will tell you they love this exercise because they know how rewarding it can be. Probing secrets is a key to writing memorable fiction.

A writer submitted for my consideration the early part of what she hoped would be a thriller about the hazardous work of a policewoman who works as a decoy, pretending to be a hooker in order to trap a killer.

The students in the seminar liked the plot, but the story had not involved them emotionally. The author moved into the hot seat at the head of the table. The others all listened while I asked questions and she talked.

It became evident that the writer had been on a police force but no longer was because of something that had happened in her line of work. Interesting. But not as interesting as her revelation of what she felt was the worst moment of each day. It wasn't her hazardous work. It was when she tiptoed into the bedroom of her sleeping two-year-old son to pat his hair before going off into the night to work. That was her secret snapshot.

Hazardous conditions frighten us all. The possibility of premature death haunts our lives. The thought of not seeing a loved one again causes pain. And what love is as binding to a woman as her child, asleep in his innocence, his mother going off to a night's work from which she might not return?

In that snapshot lay the emotional root of her book. After our session, the writer started her novel with a scene in which the decoy was patting the sleeping head of her child before going off to her hazardous work. As a result, the tone of the book changed from an ordinary though suspenseful story told from the outside, to one readers could feel strongly. From that first scene, the reader wanted to say to the woman, "Watch out! Be careful, come back to your child." With every danger the decoy faced, the reader thought of the sleeping child. The reader, full of emotion now, read the novel not as an interesting plot but as a moving experience.

Soldiers have to be brave. So do policemen, firemen, miners, and construction workers who walk on the skeletons of high-rise buildings. Test pilots have to be especially brave because they are flying equipment that hasn't been flown before. Perhaps the bravest test pilots are the men and women who fly into outer space. They see the earth differently than we do, as if they were people from another planet.

Writers who do good work learn to see things with the innocence of visitors from outer space. Their bravest journeys take place when they fly into inner space, the unexplored recesses in which the secret snapshots of their friends and enemies—and their own—are stored.

To provide your readers with insight, you become an explorer. That's what we've been doing here, exploring territory in your memory that has been—and continues to be—hidden from public view, but that can make your stories sing.

17

How to Use All Six of Your Senses

What a waste! In our daily work and play, our senses of sight, sound, touch, taste, and smell define the world for us. Then, as writers, we let three of our senses atrophy, as if our characters had lost part of their humanity and didn't need to touch, taste, and smell.

Never mind that laymen neglect their senses. We writers have an obligation to use all five senses in our work if we are to enrich the laymen's experience.* And we cannot neglect the sixth that haunts our lives and our literature.

I caution you. Even the sense of sight, the one we use the most in our life and work, needs to be honed beyond the everyday needs of the laymen for whom we write. We need to see more acutely so that we can record what is fresh.

We take our senses for granted. When we let their use atrophy, it often takes conscious effort and exercise to restore our awareness of the ways in which we take in the world around us. If you were to shut your eyes and remove your keys from a pocket or purse this moment, could you describe what a key feels like in a way that would be understood by a person who came from a country in which keys were not used?

What have you observed or felt about your keys? If I handed keys to you, by what signs would you know that they were yours and not someone else's? Not knowing our keys from keys that are similar is symbolic of our neglect of our senses. We deprive ourselves and our readers. Most writers use sight and some conventional sounds, and little else. This

---

* I urge every writer who wants to improve his sense awareness to study Diane Ackerman's extraordinary book *The Natural History of the Senses.*

chapter, then, is a course in enrichment of your sensory awareness, and through that awareness an enrichment of your writing.

Is the sound a cat makes *meow* or *mrkneow*? James Joyce, who had an acute ear, used *mrkneow*. Some people contend that the vocabulary of cats is extensive. There's no point to your using Joyce's sound or the cliché *meow*. Listen to your cat and see if you can't come up with something that your readers will recognize but perhaps will never have seen in print before.

Do we listen closely? Is the sound made by a baseball being hit *thwack* or *crack*? Or some other?

There are clichés for most common sounds. I hope to persuade you to describe sounds not in clichés but as you hear them after careful listening. Some of my students have come up with wonderfully original sounds that enhance their work. A young child at the piano: **bonk, bonk, bonk**. Or **the whump of two automobiles coming together**.

Sound, of course, is not continuous. It is interrupted by pauses, by momentary silences, the absence of sound that makes music possible. Let's look at an extreme instance of the use of sound in Jerzy Kosinski's *The Painted Bird*. In it, you may recall, a ten-year-old boy who is abandoned by his parents in Europe during World War II wanders through a nightmare of savagery and love in which he loses the ability to speak because in speaking he might give himself away. After the war, at the end of the book, a skiing accident lands the protagonist in the hospital, where something wonderful happens to his long silence:

[I] was about to lie down when the phone rang. The nurse had already gone, but the phone rang insistently again and again.

I pulled myself out of bed and walked to the table. I lifted up the receiver and heard a man's voice.

I held the receiver to my ear, listening to his impatient words, somewhere at the other end of the wire there was someone, perhaps a man like myself, who wanted to talk with me. . . . I had an overpowering desire to speak. Blood flooded my brain and my eyeballs swelled for a moment, as though trying to pop out onto the floor.

I opened my mouth and strained. Sounds crawled up my throat. Tense and concentrated I started to arrange them into syllables and words. I distinctly heard them jumping out of me one after another, like peas from a split pod. I put the receiver aside, hardly believing it possible. I began to recite to myself words and sentences, snatches of Mitka's songs. The voice lost in a faraway village church had found me again and filled the whole room. I spoke loudly and incessantly like the peasants and then like the city folk, as fast as I could, enraptured by the sounds that were heavy with meaning, as wet snow is heavy with water, confirming to myself again and again and again that speech was now mine and that it did not intend to escape through the door which opened onto the balcony.

The universe of sound available to the writer extends from a simple **bonk, bonk, bonk** to Kosinski's protagonist rediscovering his ability to speak.

Humans see the world. Other animals smell it. Watch a cat investigating anything new, a surrounding, a possible food. It leads with its nose, just as its larger sisters in the jungle do. Cats and other animals define the world first by smell. In some human cultures, the sense of smell is treated as if were an unwelcome adjunct to the "good" senses, fit only to be deodorized or perfumed.

For the writer, the sense of smell provides opportunity. It is important not only to be aware of and use smells, but to be accurate in rendering them. Rubber bands have a marked odor. An old book smells musty. Unseen wind has a smell. If you don't smell anything, what might you smell? A single flower in an imagined vase on your desk?

> What he first noticed about Detroit and therefore America was the smell.

That's the first sentence of a short story by Charles Baxter called "The Disappeared" from the *Michigan Quarterly Review*.

A writer can use the sense of smell to good effect in many ways, for instance, to help a reader experience a setting:

> I could tell we were coming to the kitchen. The odor of fresh-baked bread drifted into the hallway like an invitation to follow where it led.

Smell can be used to establish a relationship:

> Malcolm came through the back door, the football in the crook of his arm, his sweatshirt emblazoned with a dark butterfly of sweat. He put the football down, and positioned his arms around me. I closed my eyes and could smell the earth of the playing field and what I had come to think of as the aroma of his presence.

Characterization can benefit from the use of smell:

> Sally fluttered in, enveloped in her newest perfume.

This tells us that Sally habitually uses too much perfume. Smell can also be used to establish atmosphere:

> Down and down we went. I stopped counting the stairs. The dank smell told me we were well below ground.

Or this:

> Terry glanced skyward and sampled a lungful of the chilled air. The universe smelled fresh, as if everything could now start over.

The absence of smell is also useful to a writer:

> "They've bred the smell out of roses," Gloria said. "Don Juans are my favorite climbers because their touch is velvet and the rose breeders haven't robbed them of their smell. Yet."

A gifted young woman named Ketti McCormick was briefly a student of mine some time after she had lost her sight. She still continued to see colors, not those in her field of vision but those refractions of colors previously seen that remained inside her head. Her contact with the external world, like that of other blind people, was now mainly through the sense of touch, which most of us neglect. Ketti once had trusted her eyes to keep her out of danger. She had to develop a greater sense of trust in others that they would not leave things in her path that she might trip over. She was angry at males who left the toilet seat up.

A blind person surmises how I might look by feeling my face. Try that some time. Blindfold yourself and have someone brought into the room whom you haven't met before and who wouldn't mind if you found out what they looked like by touching his or her face. You might describe each feature—nose, cheeks, forehead, ears, chin, hair—and have someone write your descriptions down. Then, with the blindfold off, look closely at the person and at your description, and offer an apology for your probable inaccuracy. You are in all likelihood deficient in your use of the sense of touch, as we all are. It would benefit our writing greatly to improve how we see with the ends of our fingers.

There's a way to do it. And you won't need a cooperative new acquaintance, just the blindfold, though it might help to have a friend or family member around to empty the contents of your purse or pocket on a table after you are blindfolded. Feel each object with your fingertips, describing it as best you can as if to someone from another planet who wouldn't know what those strange objects are that you carry everywhere you go. You can't say a credit card feels like plastic. You have to particularize. That exercise alone can work wonders in letting you experience your sense of touch:

> As soon as they came in from the cold, Eric reached into his pocket for a slim metal tube and brought it to his lips. He realized that he hadn't uncapped it even before he heard Sheila laugh. He pulled the cap off the tube, turned its base to bring the waxy plug up higher, and rubbed it first across his top lip, and then his bottom lip.

In the example, the sense of touch fortifies the characterization of Eric as absent-minded, an improvement over the author intruding to tell the reader that.

Does the handshake of an athlete feel the same as the handshake of a wimp? Does the hand of a child feel the same as the hand of a seventy-year-old? Does the surface of every wooden chair feel the same? What does water feel like when it is too hot? What does your favorite cat or dog feel like when you are petting it? Would you dare write a love scene omitting the sense of touch?

Your writing can only gain if you attempt to use the sense of touch at least once in every scene.

That imaginary guest from another planet can also be useful to you in cultivating your ability to describe what you taste. Your guest has never experienced the kind of food you are eating. See if, from memory, you can describe in detail the foods that you tasted in the last meal you ate. Your guest has never heard of bran flakes or strawberries. You'll have to invent similes and metaphors to tell your guest what they taste like. It's not an easy exercise, but it will accelerate your skill as a sensuous writer. You wouldn't feed cardboard meals to guests. Don't feed cardboard meals to your characters. Make your reader's taste buds pop, even if he's from outer space.

* * *

We speak of a "sixth sense" as a sensation we cannot identify with seeing, hearing, touching, smelling, or tasting, but which we know is there. "It" can be anything imagined or real, a person or a higher power. Some people refer to the phenomenon as extrasensory perception, or ESP. A writer can make excellent use of a "sixth sense" in mainline fiction as well as in mystery and suspense fiction. You are alone in the house, and you hear a door close. Is it the wind? But there is no wind inside the house.

An exercise to develop your sixth sense is worth trying. Close your eyes. Imagine who is in the room with you. Turn all the lights on. There's no one here. Good. You can relax. Is your watch ticking louder than usual, or are you imagining it? Why is today different from other days, what is supposed to happen? Why isn't the phone ringing? If it does ring, who will it be? Close your eyes again. Are you sure someone isn't in the room with you? What if you're wrong? What if it's . . . ?

It doesn't take much for you to feed your hungry imagination. Through practice, you can establish a link between your imagination and the so-called sixth sense.

I've left the most important sense, sight, for last because it is the one least neglected by writers. Yet improving your eyesight, sharpening your ability to describe the visual, can be productive.

The first thing you see is usually a cliché. We see the tall man, the attractive woman, the room full of people, the clean-cut lawn. These are the easy images that leap to mind. The writer's job is to look for distinguishing detail, the particularity, in visualizing what his reader is to see: the man whose wavy hair wouldn't stay under his cap; the woman who looked ready to shout at just about anyone, the partygoers jammed together as if they were on a crowded subway train; the virgin lawn that looked as if it had never been walked upon.

Ideally, the writer sees something that everybody will recognize but that no one has seen quite that way before.

A technique used too seldom involves changing the sense:

> Zalatnick led me into the shop not as if I was a fellow looking for
> a job but as if I was a friend of a friend. I was sure the men in the
> shop could smell the difference.

"Smell" isn't meant to be taken literally. Switching the sense from seeing to smelling creates a metaphor that gets the point across to the reader quickly.

Here's how one might use each of the six senses to characterize players in a story:

> Gloria kept wrinkling her nose as if she were trying to sniff the truth of what everyone was saying to her. (smell)
>
> Greg knew that his handshake hurt people. (touch)
>
> On the phone Mary's voice was like music. I couldn't hear the words, but I knew what she meant. (hearing)
>
> Lucille shielded her eyes like a make-believe Indian examining the horizon. (sight)
>
> Barry savored each spoonful of melon as if it were ambrosia he would never be allowed to taste again. (taste)
>
> Garret could swear someone had come in behind him, yet hesitated to turn around for fear he would be right. (sixth sense)

If you look at those examples again, you'll note that each of the characterizations is an action. Somebody is doing something. There's no need to stop a story to characterize or to use the senses.

18

Love Scene

The main concern of this chapter is the most common kind of love scene in literature, between a man and a woman. But there are other kinds of love that provide writers and readers with appealing stories: love between an adult and a child; same-sex love affairs; love between a human and an animal; love between children, and love in odd combinations.

To begin with the last, we already know that a major source for writers of fiction involves bringing together people from different social or ethnic backgrounds who meet and fall in love. D. H. Lawrence's *Lady Chatterley's Lover* and L. P. Hartley's *The Go-Between* are outstanding examples. In theater, the vitality of Tennessee Williams's *A Streetcar Named Desire* is attributable in large measure to the clash of backgrounds. Sometimes the differences are bizarre—for instance the love of a monstrously deformed person for a normal-appearing human (or vice versa). It is useful to study the classics such as *Beauty and the Beast* and *The Hunchback of Notre Dame* with an eye toward understanding how emotions are generated in the reader. The interplay in the audience's emotions may arise from the conflict of repugnance slowly overcome by affection. Young people are much more interested in and accepting of the grotesque in such fantasies. If you enter this difficult but rewarding territory, be mindful that your story to be acceptable must be sufficiently different from the well-known classics.

Love stories of great poignancy can be fashioned out of the love between an adult and a child because once upon a time everyone was a child. A child can be desperate for love. Adults are sometimes too busy with the mechanics of living (job, homemaking, the behavior of other adults) to respond to a child's need. The denial of a child's craving for affection touches many readers. Love between a parent and child, or unrequited love between a parent and a child (in either direction), or the belated recognition of parental love or love of a parent, or a child or parent who rejects affection—all are possibilities. However, any sexual conduct involving a child raises the issue of child molestation, a difficult subject for fiction and one involving psychopathology rather than love.

Affection between people and their pets or other animals is frequently the subject of children's books, and has long been important in such adult books as the Tarzan stories and Jack London's *The Call of the Wild*. It takes skill to make an animal believable as a character, and the best method is to give it a particularity just as you would a human character, a distinctive characteristic and preferably one that relates to the story—for instance a cat that jumps up into the lap of everyone but the person who loves it.

A mistake made easily in stories that involve animals is to neglect particularizing the human character. Also, it is important that the animal have a clear want of its own and not be merely the passive recipient of human wants.

The writer who wants to write about the relationship of a human to an animal has to cross two tripwires. There seems to be a greater limit on imaginative story possibilities than in the relationships between humans. So much has been done with human/animal material that innovation becomes difficult.

Also, the trap of sentimentality is present and ready to snap. It may amuse you to know that George Stevens, a long-time editor of J. B. Lippincott, once a venerable American publishing firm, actually wrote a book that contained the three most common ingredients in the bestsellers of his time. He called his book *Lincoln's Doctor's Dog*.

Same-sex love affairs have been the subject of fiction for a long time, though some books, like Radclyffe Hall's *The Well of Loneliness* were often banned, and E. M. Forster's *Maurice* was not published until after the author died. During recent decades, homosexual love stories and homoerotic fiction have come out of the closet. A special market has developed for these stories, and homosexual attraction has made an occasional appearance in mainstream fiction.

Infantile and child sexuality raises profound discomfort and disbelief in many readers, requiring great skill in the writing. However, a child showing immature affection for another child (sometimes called "puppy love") is widely acceptable. This is not a frequent subject of fiction and is difficult to do well.

Which leads us to the principal topic of this chapter, romantic and sexual love between adults. I have some bad news.

Editors will tell you that love scenes are often among the worst-written scenes not only in rejected work but in published work. Such scenes are often mechanical, overly physiological, hackneyed, or sentimental. However, editors know that trying to discuss the flaws in love scenes with their authors is like walking across a mine field. One never knows when a flaw in the writing of a love scene derives from a buried discomfort in the author's life.

In recent decades we have had both a sexual revolution and a counter-revolution. Along about 1960, a prominent publishing attorney named Harriet Pilpel asked me if I was willing to go to jail for Henry Miller. I was then heading an upscale book club whose judges were interested in distributing a forthcoming Henry Miller title that dealt with sexual matters explicitly, and Ms. Pilpel, well known as a civil libertarian, seemed quite certain there was then a real risk of allegedly criminal conduct in distributing works by Henry Miller that are today found in bookshops throughout the world.

A few years later the floodgates opened not only to books that treated sexual conduct openly and with some degree of seriousness, but also to transient novels that mocked adult lovemaking as much as misnamed "adult" movies did.

Adults are in general knowledgeable about the physical apparatus and actions involved in lovemaking, and concentration on these can quickly become repetitive and boring. Some people, and consequently some writers, have never learned that mechanical description of sexual activity does not usually arouse readers who are no longer adolescents. Moreover, female readers, who account for the purchase of most hardcover fiction, often lose patience with male writers who continue to fabricate love scenes solely from a male point of view. Men who write love scenes as if they are dealing with the mechanical parts of an engine should know that such scenes have zero erotic effect and do not accomplish their primary mission of evoking a loving experience between people.

Readers remain interested in passion, if not in the mechanical details. Moreover, any novel accrues an advantage by including a love story. It is one of the easiest relationships to plot, a fact that is most obvious in the field of musical comedy. A handsome young man appears at one side of the stage. A beautiful young woman appears on the other side. The audience immediately wants them to get together. *It is the author's job to keep them apart as long as possible.*

The gestation of love can be the central dramatic event in the lives of characters. The loss of love is one of the most devastating things that can happen to a human being. Both possibilities can generate enormous emotion in life and, if skillfully handled, in fiction.

The gain of love and the loss of love are powerful combustibles. It is doubly powerful to have both gain and loss of love in the same story. Suspense, tension, and conflict inhere in love stories. An endless cornucopia of relationships is available to the writer.

Of course, disadvantages offset this. The prevalence of love in so much fiction requires the writer to exercise his imagination in order to come up with scenes that will seem fresh. Love stories also carry the danger of sentimentality.

The writer invokes sentimentality when he elicits superficial emotions that are exaggerated, excessive, or affected, obviously designed to elicit the reader's sympathy. Sentimentality in fiction usually comes across as patently insincere, mawkish, or maudlin, and should be avoided. A writer's sensibility should be directed toward evoking a depth of feeling in the reader, not to fabricating superficial excesses of emotion on the page.

The main flaw in most love scenes is similar to that of the main flaws in all other scenes: the reader's emotions have been insufficiently considered by the writer. The primary erogenous zone is in the head, and that's where the reader experiences writing.

The reader wants to identify with a character. Love scenes can be especially effective when the reader is identifying with *both* characters— that is, with the hoped-for success of the relationship—experiencing more than each of the characters individually. This can be accomplished if the writer considers the love scene from the point of view of each of the characters even when writing from the disciplined point of view of one of them. The reader needs to understand the relationship between the lovers better than either of the lovers do.

The two most essential ingredients in love scenes are tension and tenderness. A crisis in the relationship or postponing lovemaking, keeping the lovers apart as long as credibility permits, generates tension. It's a mistake to let the reader know early the likely outcome of the scene.

No love scene should be the repetition of a familiar ritual. To sustain the reader's interest in the outcome, the attraction should seem new even in a longstanding relationship.

Interruptions in a love scene can be useful. Not the grocery boy ringing the doorbell, but the lovers themselves noticing a picture, listening to some special music, talking about memories that arouse—all the while postponing the consummation to increase the tension of the scene.

Literary foreplay does not necessarily involve physical contact. If the possibility of contact is in the air, nuances in actions and dialogue can affect the reader's emotions. A woman brushing her hair can have a powerful aphrodisiac effect. Less produces more in the reader. In the following example a couple stand in front of the door of his house. The reader senses that once inside the house, they are going to make love. The writer's first temptation might be to let them in the house, to get on with it. But delay builds anticipation. It can be accomplished by minutiae:

> I was waiting for him to say something. Instead he reached into his pocket and removed a key ring with three keys on it. Holding the first key, he said, "The garage." Then he held the second key, dangling the others, and said, "The back door."
> He must have seen me smile.
> He took the third key between his thumb and forefinger and said, "The front door." Then he handed the key ring with all three keys to me and said, "Welcome."

Among the many advantages of a love scene is that it provides excellent opportunities for characterizing both partners and for creating sympathy or antipathy toward one of the characters.

Love stories exist about each of the seven ages of man. Three of those ages are most useful to the writer.

The youngest lovers may be inexperienced, tentative, nervous, worried about pregnancy, disease, getting caught. Any or all of these can become a writer's Petri dish for brewing conflict and drama. External obstacles loom in abundance. The young lovers may be separated by distance because of school, work, and family. They may have to overcome class differences, family incompatibilities, peer pressure, or rivalry from another young person, or from an older, more experienced individual. Keep in mind that you don't want to tell the reader what they are feeling, but to evoke feelings in the reader as a result of what the young lovers say to each other and what they do. It helps to make each of them vulnerable in a different way.

With adult lovers in the child-bearing age group, one of the most powerful forces of nature is at work, the drive toward procreation, often unknown to or unacknowledged by lovers. The human race is perpetuated by drives that are endocrinal in origin. Romantic love, as it is experienced by most (but not all) people, is a cultural invention. While these are things that the average reader doesn't want to hear about, it is important that the writer know them.* Love scenes deal with the consequences of these physiological drives and cultural customs. Writers need to be knowledgeable about the nuances of human relationships and the origins of feelings; hence, it helps for writers to know and understand as much as possible about the psychology and physiology underlying love—what the pulls are, whether or not the participants are aware of them.

An obstacle commonly faced by adult lovers is the threat of a competing person and the consequent loss of security in a relationship. An adult wandering from a relationship can get involved with persons of questionable character and can blunder into acts of violence. The consequences of infidelity have inspired hundreds of plots. Some obstacles encountered by adult lovers are internal, such as guilt over conduct disapproved of by the person or by society. Also casting a shadow over both old and new relationships is the fear of passing age boundaries, of getting older.

In plotting a love story, a writer must remind himself that plot grows out of character. What happens in a love scene should come out of the writer's understanding of his characters and their motivation, and the clash between such characteristics or motivation in different characters. Some basic questions to ask yourself about your prospective love story:

Does each of your lovers have one thing that distinguishes his or her physical appearance from that of other people? Is there something distinctive in the way your lovers dress?

Keep in mind that the most boring kind of relationship is one in which there are never any problems. He loved her and she loved him, they never quarreled, is the ultimate turnoff. In devising a love story, search for the root conflicts based on character and upbringing, but also ferret out surface conflict by asking yourself if you have depicted your adult lovers at a moment of crisis. If not, can you add a crisis that will increase the tension of the relationship? Does the woman want something reasonable that is refused by the man, perhaps for reasons that he keeps secret and that arouse her suspicions? Does the man want something that is refused by the woman because she is afraid of the result? Whatever your plan, remember that if there is no friction between the lovers, there is no

* As a guide to the probable sources of romantic love. I have recommended to many writers Helen Fisher's *Anatomy of Love*.

interest on the part of the reader. And if there is massive friction, will the reader be convinced that they are nevertheless in love? If they are not, you don't have a love story.

One exercise writers in my classes have found to be exceptionally beneficial is writing an exchange of ten lines of dialogue, alternating between two lovers. The object is to have the reader experience two things from the ten lines: that the characters are quarreling and that they are lovers (not ex-lovers). You might want to try your hand at the exercise yourself. You may use more than one line for each turn, but keep the exchanges short:

Lovers' Quarrel in Ten Brief Exchanges

He:
She:
He:
She:
He:
She:
He:
She:
He:
She:

The "Lovers' Quarrel" exercise is not easy. Some writers, in their early attempts, find it as difficult as rubbing the belly with one hand while patting the top of the head with the other. But that is precisely the kind of thing a writer must do in the best of scenes, have more than one thing going on at a time. Students have been known to revise and rerevise drafts of this short exercise week after week until they achieve the objective: having the reader feel that the characters are in love *and* are quarreling. Let's look at a bad example:

He: Where are you off to now?
She: None of your business.
He: You step out of this door, we're finished.
She: I'm glad you noticed.
He: Noticed what?
She: That we're finished, stupid.
He: You're not taking my car.
She: It's half mine. Community property. Now get out of my way.

He: I'll report the car stolen.

She: I'm sure the cops will love finding out you reported your car
     stolen by your wife.

What's wrong? We have a quarrel but no indication that, though married,
they are still lovers. Let's look at another example:

He: You touched me.

She: I've got a license to touch.

He: I just got home, hon.

She: I know.

He: Hey, I haven't even had a chance to wash up.

She: I know.

He: I'll fall walking backwards.

She: I know.

He: The couch is in the way. Hey!

She: Gotcha!

It's clear that they're lovers. There is tension in the scene, but they are
not really quarreling. The wife's repetition of "I know" is a nice touch,
and the exchange has a coherence, but it is not a lovers' *quarrel*. The
point of this exercise is to learn how to do two things at the same time.

When students develop their skill, I encourage them to add some narrative to the dialogue and even to increase the number of lines, if
necessary, to complete the scene. The following miniscene is what one
of my male students came up with after some revision:

"I never wanted to see you again."

"Then why did you come back?"

"The roses," he said.

She turned in the archway, gilded by rays, back to him, walled,
protected, and stared into the tangle of exploded flowers. They had
opened and fallen back upon themselves like silent film stars, dried
leaves, brittle branches.

"You came to see a dying garden, Ryan."

"We planted it together."

"I didn't know you were coming."

"Meg, I didn't know you would be here."

She felt his eyes on her back. The Bukhara sucked in his foot-
falls as he crossed the room. He edged beside her.

"It needs water, care . . ."

"Maybe it will rain," she said.

"Can't count on rain. It needs . . . some care."

"You were always too busy," Meg said and turned slowly toward him. "It was beautiful once. Wasn't it?"

"Like a meteor shower," Ryan said. "I'm sorry."

"So am I."

We know they are still lovers. At the outset they are having a strong difference of opinion. The reader can't help feeling some emotion when reading this short scene. I encourage you to try this exercise from time to time as your skill develops. You may find a story or even an entire novel blossoming from it.

Another age group to consider is older lovers, perhaps from the age of fifty to the so-called golden years celebrated in the film *On Golden Pond*. The underlying drive toward procreation is at rest. Companionship increases in importance. Shared experience in the past becomes a vital part of the present. Security, both economic and emotional, becomes more important. And there is the omnipresent fear or acceptance of inevitable death. But one should consider certain liabilities of this fertile ground for the writer.

In Western countries, sadly, there is far less respect for the wisdom that comes with age than in Eastern countries. As a result, among the young there is little interest in the aged. When love relationships among older persons are handled expertly, the results are felt by audiences of all ages, but the marketing of such material is encumbered with difficulty. As the population in developed countries lives longer, however, there may be a shift in interest that will make love stories involving older characters easier to market.

Questions to ask yourself if you are considering a story with older lovers:

In developing your love scene, is there a hovering notion that the lovers do not have all the time in the world?

Have you included the need for companionship, often the most urgent need of older people?

Have you included touching or some other physical relationship that will enhance the poignancy?

The key to writing an effective love scene is to imagine it from the perspective of each of the partners. If the writer is a woman, she should give special thought to the perspective of the man in the scene. If the writer is a man, he should give special thought to the perspective of the woman. Then the scene can be written from the third-person point of view, or from the first-person point of view of either of the characters, but the writer will have imagined the thoughts and feelings of both partners, which should enable the scene to be written as richly as possible.

A scene can also be enriched if either of the participants gains an insight about the other person.

What are some of the things a writer can do to enhance a love scene?

You can place an object in the room that is meaningful to one or both lovers. If possible, plant the object before the love scene. Don't let either of the lovers notice it until an important juncture in that scene, when one of them sees the object, turns off, and the other lover has to rekindle the relationship. This is really a modified version of what happens in most stories, with obstacles in the way of the protagonist getting what he wants.

Another obstacle can be the weather. If the lovers are preparing for an outing in the countryside, a sudden storm will interfere with their plans. They seek refuge in what looks like an unoccupied building. But is it unoccupied? Or will a sudden snowstorm keep illicit lovers housebound in a house to which the spouse of one of them will be returning soon? These suggestions, and those that follow, are not meant to be specific plot points for you to pursue. They are examples of the kinds of obstacle one might use to prolong a love scene that can become a love sequence.

A tack you might consider is to have something unexpected happen that causes a misunderstanding. The more one of the lovers tries to clear up the misunderstanding, the deeper it gets. Make it seem that the impasse is unsurmountable. Then introduce a third character, who can make the impasse worse, or who can provide a way of clearing up the misunderstanding.

Another tack would be to have the third character not know that the two are lovers, and the lovers have a reason for not wanting the third character to find out about their relationship. That involves unrehearsed play-acting by the lovers, ripe for mischief.

Conversely, a couple can pretend they are together, when in fact they are not. Then if a third character were to say or do something that makes it absolutely necessary for both the lovers to continue the pretense, you have an interesting development. The moment the third character leaves is a moment of high tension. Will the couple drop their pretense? Or will the pretense have started something they didn't expect?

The intrusion in a love scene doesn't have to be from a third person related to either or both parties. It doesn't even need to be a person that is intruding. We've just discussed the weather intruding. An earthquake, a firestorm, or any other catastrophe can be a mighty intrusion provided it is handled realistically rather than as melodrama. But note this. Though an action is the ideal interruption, a thought can also interrupt, particularly a significant thought or memory, and it can be a lot more effective than the local volcano blowing its top.

A love scene and a sex scene are not the same. A poignant love scene can be written with the lovers not coming close enough to touch. As an instance, consider the prisoner, unjustly tried and accused, who has to communicate with his beloved on visitors' day through a glass shield, speaking on phones, though they are only inches apart physically.

Conversely, a sex scene need have nothing to do with love, as in a scene of casual sex between strangers, or a rape.

If it is your plan to make your love scene erotic, a few points are worth considering. As I noted earlier, the most important erogenous zone is in the head, which means that if a man's head isn't turned on, he won't be able to function. If a woman's head isn't turned on, her failure to experience may lead to faking.

The "rabbit" approach to sex has little to do with the relations between the sexes that can be experienced by readers. The same is true for mechanical recitations of sexual play without regard to what is happening to the emotions of the people involved.

Many years ago I met Maurice Girodias, the French publisher who became notorious as the publisher of sexually explicit novels in English. Those green-covered paperbacks infiltrated into America in the luggage of tourists long before the liberation of sexuality in literature in the late fifties and early sixties. Quite a few of Girodias's pseudonymous authors later made their reputations under their real names.

Girodias was a master at teaching his authors how to handle erotic material. One Girodias-sponsored title had what I remember as the ultimate seduction scene: it held the reader for about a hundred pages before the relationship was consummated. This is not something to strive to imitate. It demonstrates a principle. The point to grasp is that the mere description of multiple sexual acts does little or nothing for the reader. A single act, kept at bay, warmed to, stretched out, can have a marked erotic effect.

In preparing to write an erotic scene, the writer has to be clear about the relationship between the couple, and has to know what he is trying to accomplish in his story through the sexual intimacy. The most common possibilities include an assignation, colloquially a "quickie." Though it has nothing to do with love, this kind of scene can be erotic. But even a so-called quickie can't be quick on the page and have an effect on the reader. It must move the story forward by having an effect on one or the other character. Even a meaningless assignation has to have a meaning for at least one of the characters or it doesn't belong in the story.

More common in fiction is the one-night stand. A brief, not-to-be-repeated encounter has greater potential for a story than a meaningless copulation, but to have an important effect on the reader it, too, has to convey something about each character. Why is each of the participants doing this, and how does each of them react to the experience while it's happening and afterward?

More interesting is the sexual encounter that is the budding of a love affair. Because it is a beginning, the scene can be full of nuances, problems, thoughts, actions. Think of it as a back-and-forth experience and not a straight line. Each digression—if it doesn't take the reader away from the fundamental goal of the scene—can heighten and extend the experience.

My novel *Other People* contains a number of scenes between George Thomassy, a forty-four-year-old lawyer, and Francine Widmer, a twenty-seven-year-old client who becomes his lover. The scene I will refer to runs about six pages. It's not about continuous lovemaking. Other things happen. The interruptions—planned by the author—stretch the tension between the beginning and its consummation. But the interruptions are all part of the story.

Thomassy and Francine were brought together as a result of Francine being raped. Her father, a corporate lawyer, persuaded Thomassy, a criminal lawyer, to help his daughter, who was seeking to get the rapist put in jail. Francine had not had sex since the rape until the scene I am about to describe. An important choice was to write the scene from the woman's point of view.

The scene starts with a detailed description of a meal that Thomassy is preparing for both himself and Francine in his home. The fact that she is in his house in itself sets the stage for the possibility of an erotic scene. That possibility hangs in the air, as it were, over the scene that follows, when they talk and think about other things. Note that what they talk about is specific, for instance a painting that is prominent on Thomassy's wall. From a few words about the artist, Francine's thoughts wander to the idea that good art lingers into posterity, while the work of most people in the professions is forgotten, except perhaps for the rare work of an innovating genius. Francine is surprised that artists aren't hated more by those whose work is by its nature transient. Thomassy, a successful criminal lawyer, responds:

"I'm a salesman. I sell cases to juries. Or to punk D.A.'s."

When Thomassy puts himself down, he is actually raising himself in the reader's eyes. The reader knows how tough and successful he is as a lawyer. The reader's emotional reaction to Thomassy's self-description is something like, "Hey, Thomassy, don't knock yourself. I've seen what you can do."

This technique of elevating by seeming to do its opposite sets Thomassy up as a potentially interesting lover because he has insight into himself, an that usually means insight into others. In the scene, the conversation momentarily turns back to the dinner they are finishing. As to sex, nothing is happening, except in the reader's head. In fact, by this time the reader is liking them as a couple and wants one of them to make a move. The author is not quite ready to oblige.

Thomassy snaps on the TV set for the ten o'clock news, which tells us the evening is getting late. Francine runs water to do the dishes. Thomassy says he'll do them, and comes up behind her at the sink. The entire scene is from her point of view:

The front of his body was touching the back of mine. I felt his lips on the lobe of my right ear, just for a second.

"It's all right," I said. "A woman doesn't want to be admired just for her mind."

He put his arms around me and took the dish I was rinsing carefully out of my hands and put it aside.

"I'll do those later," he said.

"I should be going soon."

He turned me toward him.

"My hands are wet," I said.

He took my head in both his hands and touched his lips to mine, a skim for a split second.

I kept my wet hands wide apart as he kissed me again, this time mouth to mouth.

I broke away. "My hands are wet," I said, breathless.

"I don't care."

And then I put my wet hands around him as our mouths met. I could feel his body's warmth and my own heart pound. And suddenly he was kissing the side of my neck, then below and behind my ear, I could feel his tongue flicker, and then our mouths were together again until, to breathe, I pulled away, feeling the blood in my face, and I was quickly drying my hands on the dish towel when he pulled me into his arms again and I knew we both knew it was no use fighting it any more and we were holding each other tightly and desperately, and then we were moving each other to the couch, not wanting to let go, but we had to, to open the couch, and then it was kissing again and clothes coming off, his and mine, and we were lying clasped, kissing lips, faces, shoulders, then holding on, sealed against each other, until he raised his head and realized there were tears in my eyes and his bewildered look was begging for an explanation.

I could hear the thud of my heart.

"What's the matter?" he whispered.

I couldn't find my voice.

"Tell me," he said.

It was like the anxiety attacks I would get in the middle of the night when insomnia stole my sleeping hours, a fear that my heart would burst from the thudding.

"It's like driving the first time after an accident," I said.

We lay side by side for a while.

At this point, Francine lies there thinking about an incident in high school. The reader is feeling *Get on with it*. Then:

He got up, naked and unashamed, and went somewhere, returning with two elegant glasses filled halfway with something I didn't recognize.

"Madeira," he said. "Rainwater." He took a sip. "Magic," he said, and handed me my glass. "It's a one-drink drink. Safe."

I looked at the glass skeptically.

"It's okay," he said. "Try it."

I took a sip.

"Lovely," I said, licking it from my lips.

"Don't do that," he said.

"What?" I took another sip. He leaned over and licked my lower lip. No one had ever done that. He slid onto the bed, holding his glass upright as if it were a gyroscope. Then he tipped it slightly and let a few drops splash onto my breast. .

"Don't move," he said, and gave me his glass to hold. There I was, helplessly holding one glass in each hand, unable to move, and he licked the Madeira from each breast and from the valley between.

He borrowed his glass back, tipped it lower down, then handed it back, my handcuff. I looked at the two glasses, at the ceiling, then at the soft hair of his head as he licked the drops of Madeira. . . .

I'll stop the scene a couple of pages before the end because I'm certain that by this time you will see how I've stretched the scene, concerned with the reader's wanting Thomassy and Francine to get together, and knowing that my job was to keep them apart. The scene is a literary form of foreplay.

Note that the scene consists of many short sentences. Then, the paragraph in which they move to the couch is long, almost all of it one extended sentence. The tension of arousal is handled with snippets. The breakthrough is written as breathless continuum.

At that point, the specter of Francine's rape arises. The sex is stalled, but not the scene. Thomassy brings her a special drink, to intoxicate her not with alcohol but with what he precedes to do with the drink. The sex act itself is handled the same way. This is a love story, and their first sexual encounter is related to the things that bring them together. We experience love blooming, not just passing fornication.

Lovemaking between a couple that has made love before can be a more difficult task for the writer. Art imitates life. If the likely outcome is known to the participants, it removes an element of suspense. For the experienced writer it may mean creating a delay, or even an event or action that stops the inevitable. A scene between lovers experienced with each other can be helped by a surprise, the opposite of the expected, or an intrusion.

In writing a particular scene in *The Magician,* my design was to portray the sixteen-year-old villain Urek's vulnerability, to create a touch of sympathy for him, and at the same time to give the reader some clues as to the possible origins of his violent nature. His involvement is with a girl called the Kraut, who has been having sex with Urek's gang, usually serially in full view of the others. This time Urek, in trouble, has come to the Kraut's home by himself. The Kraut is surprised when Urek shows up at her place. Urek has committed a crime that has excited him, but he is not an articulate boy and tries to shrug off her questions. She says, "What are you so worked up about?" and he exclaims, "Jesus, I gotta talk to somebody." She puts him down by saying, "How about your mother." Finally, she agrees to listen to him and locks the door of her room. She sits down at her vanity mirror and starts combing her hair. You may recall that in the chapter on characterization I referred to the supposition of some psychologists that a woman's hair conveys a strong sexual force (most men find it disquieting or repulsive to imagine a woman bald or losing her hair). Recall that after World War II, when the French wanted to dehumanize women who collaborated by having sex with the enemy, they shaved their heads.

Urek wants the Kraut to turn around to face him. She says she can't comb her hair if she turns around. That's when he touches her hair. She is sarcastic. "Well, you're getting real romantic." She doesn't expect romance from him.

The author provides a delaying action. The Kraut asks Urek if he's ever talked to a priest. And Urek rants about why that doesn't work for him in a way that draws a touch of sympathy from her. She says, "Come here."

In that context, those two words start the erotic engine. She, still sitting, puts her hands around Urek's waist, then lays her cheek against him and listens to his heartbeat:

> "Hey, you're alive," she said, letting her hand drop and just brush the front of his pants.
> "Whadya do that for?"
> She laughed.
> "Say," he said, "are you really a nympho? Some of the guys say . . ."
> He thought she was going to make him get out. Instead she said, "Your mother and father, they don't like it when they do it, do they?"
> "I never thought about it."
> "You had to. Everybody does. You think any of the old people like to do it?"
> "How would I know?"
> "You ever watch them?"

"What do you think I am?"

"I do. I got a way. It's what gave me the idea before."

"Before what?"

"Before I ever did anything with anybody."

Urek wants her to stop talking. She goes on talking, but unhooks her bra, and says:

"You never once kissed me."

He says, "You mean on them?"

"On the mouth, stupid."

We learn that Urek has never kissed any girl on the mouth. She teaches him:

His head was in a roar. He could feel the needling in his groin, the signal, but couldn't connect the idea of kissing lips and a feeling half his body away.

"Do it to me," she said.

He looked blank.

"What I'm doing to you."

Their mouths met, and despite the slaver and terrified thoughts in his head, he felt himself stiffening with an urgency, the need to rush.

She slipped off her shoes, unwrapped her skirt, let it drop, and stepped out of it. She took her half-slip off.

"You don't have to take everything off," said Urek.

She took her socks off, and then stepped out of her white panties; the hair where her legs met was dark, not blonde like her long hair.

"Arencha going to turn the light off?" he said.

"She shrugged her shoulders and turned the switch. It merely dimmed the light, one of those three-way bulbs now at its lowest setting. Then, completely naked, she sat down in front of her dressing table again, and again combed her hair. He could have killed her.

"You afraid of catching cold?" she said turning. "Take your clothes off."

He got down to his shorts and socks, then stood adamant.

"Take your socks off."

He took off first one, then the other.

"The rest, too," she said. "Want some help?"

He wasn't going to have any girl undressing him. He let his shorts drop to the floor, the hairiness of his body now wholly exposed to her view.

"Well," she said at his preparedness.

He gestured toward the bed.

"What's your hurry?"

She came closer to him, and he gestured toward the bed again.

Her hands were on him, stroking, and he tried now with force at her shoulders, to push her to the bed, but it was suddenly too late, and like an idiot he stood there, coming in spasms.

The Kraut was frightened at his anger. He didn't say anything. She put her arms around him, it seemed to him tenderly, and sat him down on the edge of the bed. She kissed the side of his neck, then his cheek, and then his closed mouth.

He motioned for her to turn the light completely off, which she did, so that she wouldn't see him, but when he lay down, his face in the pillow, she could hear him smothering the shame of his sobs.

In some ways that scene is akin to the classic scene of a boy being initiated by a prostitute. However, this boy has had sex with this girl before in the company of his cronies. This time a special circumstance has arisen. he has come to her after trying to kill the protagonist. The intent of the scene is to enlarge the characterization of both Urek and the girl by showing his vulnerability as well as his anger. Though the girl disdains him, when he fails she shows compassion.

Note how the action in the scene is delayed time and again. For the reader, this continues the tension.

In writing any sexual episode, you have to guard against fashioning a scene of continuous lovemaking. It needs to be broken up by thoughts, actions, digressions, delays that are pertinent to the story. Toward that end, you may find it useful to make a list of each character's concerns during the scene. To maximize tension, those concerns should be different. Keep the Actors Studio technique in mind by giving each of your characters a different script for their love scene. When you revise, test each part of the scene for what you believe the reader is feeling at that moment.

You need to remind yourself until it becomes second nature that you are playing the emotions of an audience. In writing love scenes, you need to let the reader's imagination do a lot of the work.

I want to conclude with a caution. The violence that accompanies sex in some novels, film, and TV is not only offensive in principle but also counterproductive. Small actions, or a few well-chosen words, can move the reader much more than an act of violence. While you are learning to master love scenes, I urge you to find subtleties that will enable readers to fill the envelope you have created, which is the subject of the next chapter.

19

Creating the Envelope

This chapter is short, which is only appropriate to its point: less is more.

Writing fiction is a delicate balance. On the one hand, so much inexperienced writing suffers from generalities. The writer is urged to be specific, particular, concrete. At the same time, when the inexperienced writer gives the reader detail on character, clothing, settings, and actions, he tends to give us a surfeit, robbing the reader of one of the great pleasures of reading, exercising the imagination. My advice on achieving a balance is to choose the most effective detail and to err on the side of too little rather than too much. For the reader's imagination, less is more.

You can't have come this far without knowing that my most urgent message to writers is that you are providing stimuli for the reader's experience. I remember Shelly Lowenkopf, a remarkable teacher of writers, admonishing the author of what was intended as a love scene that her mention of every article of clothing that was being removed read like a laundry list rather than a scene between two people. A more common error is detailing the clothing worn by a character as if preparing a missing persons bulletin, when one distinguishing item would suffice and allow the reader to imagine the rest.

Examine the following sentence from Nanci Kincaid's novel *Crossing Blood*, a trove of good writing. In this scene, children are playing in the yard:

> Their old grandmother looks out the window all the time, her face pressed against the glass.

Does the author tell us what the grandmother is thinking? Or seeing? Not a bit. The reader, given the context, can imagine whatever he likes that fits the story. The more the reader's imagination can be substituted for detail from the writer, the greater the reader's experience will be. The mistake we make frequently is telling the reader what the old grandmother is seeing. The point is that's where the grandmother is spending her time. At the window. Looking.

You can give the reader's imagination room with a few common words in context:

> Most grandmothers prattled on about their grandchildren, but when Bettina was asked about hers she would pause as if reflecting on each of them in turn and then state for the record, "They are fine."

I have sometimes described the reader's experience to students as an "envelope." It is a mistake to fill the envelope with so much detail that little or nothing is left to the reader's imagination. The writer's job is to fill the envelope with just enough to trigger the reader's imagination. For a nonfiction example, let's look at George Orwell's first paragraph in *The Road to Wigan Pier*:

> The first sound in the mornings was the clumping of the mill-girls' clogs down the cobbled street. Earlier than that, I suppose, there were factory whistles which I was never awake to hear.
> There were generally four of us in the bedroom. . . .

Orwell creates an envelope for an industrial town in two sentences, the sound of clogs on the cobbled street and the factory whistles he didn't hear. The reader's imagination fills in the rest. That taken care of, Orwell immediately takes the reader inside one of the houses.

Let's look at some examples of the use of an envelope in contemporary fiction. First, the beginning of Canadian author Michael Ondaatje's Booker Prize-winning novel, *The English Patient*:

> She stands up in the garden where she has been working and looks into the distance. She has sensed a shift in the weather. There is another gust of wind, a buckle of noise in the air, and the tall cypresses sway. She turns and moves uphill towards the house, climbing over a low wall, feeling the first drops of rain on her bare arms. She crosses the loggia and quickly enters the house.

The woman, nameless, is looking into the distance. The reader, who is not told what she is looking at, has to imagine what she might be seeing.

Her first impression that it might rain comes from a sixth sense, then wind, noise, and, finally, raindrops. The author supplies only a minimum amount of information. Inside, the nameless woman enters a room:

> The man lies on the bed, his body exposed to the breeze, and he turns his head slowly toward her as she enters.

We don't know who the man is, but we find out quickly that he is badly burned. How did he get burned? We learn she has been nursing him for months. Who is she? Ondaatje's writing is full of particularities that the reader can see and at the same time allows ample room for the play of the reader's imagination.

The grand master of giving the reader's imagination room to play is Franz Kafka. Here's how *The Trial* begins:

> Someone must have been telling lies about Joseph K., for without having done anything wrong he was arrested one fine morning. His landlady's cook, who always brought him his breakfast at eight o'clock, failed to appear on this occasion. That had never happened before. K. waited for a little while longer, watching from his pillow the old lady opposite, who seemed to be peering at him with a curiosity unusual even for her, but then, feeling both put out and hungry, he rang the bell. At once there was a knock at the door and a man entered whom he had never seen before in the house.

Even at the beginning of the first paragraph we begin to feel Joseph K's anxiety. As you read *The Trial* there is no letup. The reader's anxiety can verge on terror, not the make-believe kind but a terror that the reader associates with things in his own experience. Kafka, master of the envelope, creates the atmosphere of a nightmare that seems real, in which his character is beset by the impersonal forces of authority, the police, and the bureaucracy that will not tell him what he is guilty of.

Less is more when it comes to stimulating strong emotions in the reader. One of the mistakes made by some of the popular thriller writers is that they describe the terror of characters instead of letting the reader feel the terror as Kafka does.

I have been visited a number of times by Joe Vitarelli, a successful motion picture actor who is writing his first novel. The little I've read of it shows a remarkable talent. Some of the things he learned about writing may have come from instruction he received from his father. When he was young, Vitarelli's father said to him, "Nobody can terrorize you as effectively as you can terrorize yourself."

Vitarelli had a character saying, "You have two choices, I can kill you or something else can happen. Why don't you wait and see." End of chapter. The envelope is made. The reader can terrorize himself by waiting, or he can go on reading.

III

Fiction and Nonfiction

20

Amphetamines for Speeding Up Pace

The success of a book is measured by the satisfaction of readers. The measure of a reading experience is often expressed as "This really moves fast" or "This book is slow going." Each describes the *pace*, or tempo, of a book in which fast is good and slow is bad.

I've heard editors, authors, and readers describe books as "a cannonball" or "a zipper," assuming speed to be a virtue. Yet the best of good books have purposeful slowdowns in pace from time to time because the authors know that readers, like athletes, must catch their breath.

Why then the obsession with pace? Because a laggardly pace is characteristic of a majority of novels that get turned down by publishers, and, alas, of some that find their way into print but not into the hearts and recommendations of readers. Most rejected manuscripts move too slowly, encouraging their readers to put them down.

I was tempted to call this chapter "teaching the unteachable" because of an event that happened many years ago. Five editors from New York publishing houses, myself among them, were on a panel at a meeting of the American Society of Authors and Journalists. Amid the many faces staring up at us were quite a few belonging to professional nonfiction writers who wanted to try their hands at fiction. When one questioned the panel about "pace," my four colleagues suggested in turn that pace was a matter of ear or instinct, and hence unteachable. I answered last and said in as inoffensive a tone as I could muster, "Here's how it's done." There was an immediate rustle of writers reaching into their briefcases for pen and paper.

There are quite a few techniques for stepping up the pace of fiction, ranging from the simple to the quite complex. Most of these techniques are adaptable for nonfiction also.

Journalists know that short sentences step up pace. They also know that frequent paragraphing accelerates the pace. Short sentences *plus* frequent paragraphing step up pace even more.

Those are simple observations that come to fiction writers only belatedly. And when nonfiction writers turn to fiction, they often forget these simple rules.

In fiction, a quick exchange of adversarial dialogue often proves to be an ideal way of picking up pace by the use of short sentences and paragraphing. Here's an example.

Ben Riller, Broadway play producer, has been ducking phone calls from a reporter named Robertson. When Robertson calls again, Riller decides to take the call. Note how the brief exchange starts with a relaxed paragraph and how the pace picks up as the sentences get clipped. Also, note that there are twelve paragraphs in this brief conversation:

> "Hi, Mr. Riller. I've been trying to reach you about a little item we're running in tomorrow's paper about the show. I'd just like to get your comment to the story around town that *The Best Revenge* may never open."
>
> "Mr. Robertson?"
>
> "Yes?"
>
> "If I tell you you're wrong, your story will say 'Producer denies show folding,' right?"
>
> "Unless you'd care to confirm that it is folding or make some other comment."
>
> "I do," I said.
>
> "Slowly, please," he said, "so I can take it down."
>
> "Mr. Robertson," I said, "does your wife have syphilis?"
>
> Robertson's voice shrilled, "What the hell kind of question is that?"
>
> "I'll tell you," I said. "I've got an AP wire service reporter here finishing up an interview and he'd like to run a story saying 'Post reporter denies wife has syphilis.' We'll, has she or hasn't she?"
>
> I could hear Robertson breathing. Then he said, "You win, Mr. Riller," and hung up.

It isn't necessary to use dialogue to pick up the pace; short sentences and frequent paragraphing alone can do the job. Here's a rather extreme example:

> The alley was dark. I could see a rectangle of light at the other end.
>
> I had no choice. Joad was gaining.

The clop-clop of my shoes echoed as I ran. Damn these high heels.
Suddenly a figure filled the rectangle of light up ahead.
Was it Leach?
Or a cop?
I stopped. The silence was awful.
Over my shoulder I saw Joad enter the alley, boxing me in.
There were no doors. I couldn't climb the brick walls.
I dug in my purse for the police whistle.
A deep breath, I told myself.
The whistle was ice cold against my lips. I blew, again and again
till my ears hurt.
Joad's laugh echoed down the alley.
The figure at the other end laughed, too.

Note that in addition to stepping up the pace, the clipped sentences and frequent paragraphing increase the tension.

Skipping steps can also increase the reader's sense of pace. The following example provides information in what might be described as a normal pace:

In the morning he would shower, brush his teeth, shave, dress in a suitable business suit with shirt and tie, get down to the kitchen in time to have his coffee and then rush off to the station, but he'd frequently miss his train anyway.

Here's how my friend and neighbor John Cheever did it in his celebrated story "The Country Husband":

He washed his body, shaved his jaws, drank his coffee, and missed the seven-thirty-one.

Eliminating about two thirds of the words steps up the pace brilliantly. I call this "skipping for effect."

A technique for stepping up pace in fiction that isn't used enough is flipping forward past a scene *that never appears in the book.*

Not too many decades ago, when a door closed on a couple getting into bed, the chapter would end. When the next chapter started, the coupling was long gone. The bedroom scene existed only in the reader's imagination. The effect on the reader was that of the pace quickening. Here's how the same effect can be achieved in today's less prudish environment.

In my novel *The Magician,* there is one scene in which four rough teen-agers meet with an older girl for beer and sex. That chapter ends with the girl saying, "Okay, who's first?" The next chapter goes to a different location with other characters. The scene that the reader anticipates *never happens.* I was not being prudish. I did it to step up the pace. Though the book had several million readers, none ever complained about the missing scene. The point, of course, is that the more that happens in the reader's imagination, the greater his appreciation of your story. This applies to any kind of scene.

There's an extra benefit to picking up pace by skipping a scene. In revising your manuscript, you may find some scene that doesn't work as well as you had hoped. Consider skipping that scene and turning a liability into an asset if removing the scene propels the pace of your story.

In the chapter on suspense, I showed how suspense can be prolonged throughout an entire book by following each cliffhanging chapter ending with a chapter that moves to a different location or has different characters. While that technique of scene-switching is designed primarily to sustain more than one line of suspense throughout, it also has the effect of increasing the pace of a story.

I mentioned earlier a technique widely used in film called "jump-cutting." It works just as well in novels as it does in movies. With this technique, a story moves from one scene to the next without the in-between matter that would be part of getting from one place to the next. In life, you might leave your apartment, go down the stairs and out into the street, get into your car, drive to your destination, and enter a restaurant. Showing all of that in a movie, or including it in fiction, would be a drag and boring.

In jump-cutting, the viewer of a film might see a character close the door of a house and immediately appear in a restaurant, perhaps even at a table in the middle of a meal. Viewers have no trouble with jump-cutting. And it makes the film seem to move fast. In a novel, a character might close a door. This would be followed by a line space. The next scene is in a restaurant.

Jump-cutting is also available to the nonfiction writer. Skipping in-between matter increases the reader's sense of an agreeable pace, and keeps him turning the pages.

There are three more techniques for stepping up pace that are inherent in the process of deleting the flab in a manuscript. That is the subject of the next chapter.

21

Liposuctioning Flab

It was a reviewer for *Publishers Weekly* named Jeffrey Zaleski who first suggested in print that a forthcoming book needed liposuctioning. It's a perfect description of an important part of the editorial process. Flab is not only the enemy of anyone with excessive flesh, it is the enemy of every writer. Superfluous words and phrases soften prose. Fortunately, there is an antidote.

Flab-cutting is one of the best means for improving the pace of both fiction and nonfiction. When eliminated, the loss of fat has the welcome side effect of strengthening the body of remaining text.

Flab, if not removed, can have a deleterious effect on the impatient reader, who will pay less attention to each word and begin to skip. Skimming—trying to pick out the best parts of text while reading—is as unsatisfactory as trying to pick out the seeds of raspberry jam.

The quickest way of increasing the pace of a manuscript and strengthening it at the same time is to remove all adjectives and adverbs and then readmit the necessary few after careful testing. One of the students in my seminar who had an adjective habit found that after eliminating all unnecessary adjectives and adverbs from his book-length manuscript, it was seventy-three pages shorter and considerably stronger!

Mark Twain said, "If you catch an adjective, kill it!" Take his incitement to murder as a measure of his conviction. The depth of his feelings about adjectives is understandable. He was attempting to pierce the resistance of writers. Most writers erect a Great Wall against the process of eliminating all but a minimal number of adjectives and adverbs. I will guide you through the process of examining them knowing that Twain is dragging you by one arm as I am by the other.

Most adjectives and adverbs are dispensable. The easiest ones to dispense with are "very" and "quite." Word processing programs make the process simple. Find and delete all the *very*s and *quite*s that crept into your first draft.

Waste adjectives are entirely unneeded. Here's an example of a waste adjective that needs dumping:

> The conspicuous bulge in his jacket had to be a weapon.

You don't need the word "conspicuous," and the sentence is stronger without it.

Adjective surgery can be painful until you practice it rigorously and examine the results. Let's try some less painful preoperative procedures first.

Go through your text and find any place where you have used two adjectives with a single noun, such as "He was a feisty, combative reporter." Eliminate one of the adjectives, keeping the stronger one. In the example, I'd keep "feisty" since it's more evocative than "combative." Experience proves that when two adjectives are used, eliminating either strengthens the text. The more concrete adjective is the one to keep. Or the one that makes the image more visual.

Let's think together about the following sentence:

> He was a strong, resourceful warrior.

If we delete "resourceful," we have a strong warrior. If we delete "strong," we have a resourceful warrior. Each would give us a different meaning. A strong warrior is commonplace. A resourceful warrior might be a more interesting choice, but the meaning we are striving for would dictate our choice. The point is that the elimination of either adjective would lend strength to the sentence. And in context, the cut would help improve the pace. Quite apart from eliminating one out of six words, the comma goes too, and commas tend to slow the reading process.

Here's another example of the use of two adjectives with a noun:

> He was a very strong, very powerful tennis player.

The first step, of course, is to take out those "very"s. What's left is:

> He was a strong, powerful tennis player.

Still too much. Which adjective do you eliminate to strengthen the text? You have a choice:

He was a strong tennis player.
He was a powerful tennis player.

Each is better than the original. "Powerful" has a special meaning in tennis—someone who hits the ball hard and has a hard serve. A "strong" tennis player would be one who plays well tactically, and delivers excellent strokes. Few players are both. The choice should not be arbitrary.

In addition to eliminating unnecessary words, I am focusing on using words for their precise meaning, which is the mark of a good writer.

Here's a more difficult choice. What would you remove from the following sentence?

As he walked away, he seemed to be rocking, swaying from side to side like Charlie Chaplin.

Your choices are several. You could remove "rocking" or "swaying" or "swaying from side to side." In this case, whether you remove "rocking" or "swaying," it might be advisable to keep "from side to side" because it is visual, even though it is implied by either "rocking" or "swaying." In cutting excess verbiage, keep words that help the reader visualize the precise image you are trying to fashion.

Here's a two-adjective sentence that needs improvement:

What a lovely, colorful garden!

Which of those two adjectives, "lovely" and "colorful," would you eliminate?

You would be better off with the elimination of *either* adjective. However, if you take out "colorful" and keep "lovely," you would not be making the best choice because "lovely" is vague and "colorful" is specific and therefore gives the reader a more concrete image to visualize.

Examining your adjectives provides an opportunity to see if you could possibly invoke the reader's curiosity with an adjective that is better than either one you now have. What adjective could you use instead of both "lovely" and "colorful"?

There are several curiosity-provoking adjectives you might have chosen:

What a curious garden!
What a strange garden!

What an eerie garden!
What a remarkable garden!
What a bizarre garden!

"Lovely" and "colorful" don't draw us in because we expect a garden to be lovely or colorful. If we hear that a garden is curious, strange, eerie, remarkable, or bizarre, we want to know why. An adjective that piques the reader's curiosity helps move a story along.

Of course it needn't be an adjective that provokes the reader's interest. For instance, consider:

She'd never seen a garden quite like this one.

Any word or group of words that makes the reader ask "Why?" or "How?" also serves as an inducement for the reader to go on.

Like any good rule, using one adjective in place of two has exceptions. Sometimes two adjectives or an adverb modifying the adjective are necessary to create a specific image:

Meryl Streep stood the way a heavily pregnant woman will, in two motions, out of the chair and then up.

"Pregnant" alone wouldn't give you the same image.

There are several rules for determining which adjectives to keep:

- An adjective that is a necessity. Example: "His right eye kept blinking." If you didn't keep "right," it might sound as if you were talking about a one-eyed man.
- An adjective that stimulates the reader's curiosity and thereby helps move a story along. Example: "He had a pursued look" wouldn't work without the adjective. Moreover, the adjective raises curiosity about why he had that pursued look.
- An adjective that helps the reader visualize the precise image you want to project. "The spoon left a line of froth on his sad mustache." Without "sad," the line is merely descriptive. With "sad" it characterizes both the person described and, by inference, the speaker.

An adjective, of course, modifies a noun. An adverb modifies a verb. Most adverbs require the same tough surgery as adjectives:

Leona wished he would call soon.

The meaning of "soon" is implied. The adverb is unnecessary. The sentence is stronger without it.

A frequent error is the use of two adverbs. Which of the two adverbs in the following sentence would you eliminate?

She really, truly cared for him.

Would you eliminate "really" or "truly"? You could take out either. "She really cared for him" is okay. "She truly cared for him" is okay too. But best of all is "She cared for him." It is direct, and picks up the pace.

Small as these changes seem, cumulatively they have a powerful effect on prose.

Using more than one adverb is a common fault. Here's an example from a current bestselling author:

John got up quickly and walked restlessly to the window. He turned suddenly, smiling confidently. Then he sat down slowly, heavily.

That makes six adverbs in two sentences! Watch what happens when you eliminate five of them:

John got up and walked to the window. He turned suddenly, smiling. Then he sat down.

The pace is improved not only by eliminating five adverbs, but also by shortening the sentences.

Before you begin eliminating all adverbs by rote, keep in mind that sometimes adverbs can be helpful. There are two adverbs in the following short sentence. Each conveys something different:

He ate heartily, happily.

"Heartily" connotes eating a lot, "happily" connotes taking pleasure. If it is the author's intention to convey both meanings, the adverbs should be retained. "He ate" without either adverb tells us little.

I hurriedly scribbled the number down on the pad.

Why get rid of "hurriedly"? Because scribbling connotes hurry.

If not all adverbs should be cut, what is the purpose of this exercise? It's to get you to pay close attention to whether each word is helping or hurting your intention. Most of the time two adverbs slow down the pace and weaken the sentence they're in. But changes should not be made mechanically.

I have two rules for testing adverbs to see if they are worth keeping:

- Keep an adverb that supplies necessary information. Example: "He tried running faster and fell." If he's already running, you must keep "faster." If you remove the adverb the sentence means that he fell as soon as he started running.
- Keep an adverb that helps the reader visualize the precise image you want to project. Example: "She drove crazily, frightening the oncoming traffic."

Don't let these exceptions make you lose sight of the fact that most adverbs can be eliminated.

Verbs can also get in the way of pace. Here's one example:

He was huffing and puffing as he climbed the steep street.

The one adjective in the sentence, "steep," shouldn't be removed because if the street isn't steep, why the huffing and puffing? It's the "huffing and puffing" that spoils the sentence because that phrase is a cliché, a tired, overused, familiar conjunction of words. It would be perfectly acceptable to say:

He was puffing as he climbed the steep street.

Can you detect the flab in the following sentence? Two of the six words are unnecessary:

This idea is an interesting one.

Do you find the following sentence stronger?

This idea is interesting.

The flab words are "an" and "one."

Removing flab may seem a simple procedure, and in fact it is once a writer gets the habit of looking for the waste words as if he were an editor. Which words would you remove from the following sentence?

> There is nothing I would like better than to meet an interesting person who could become a new friend.

Here's a clue. To quicken the pace, delete ten of the nineteen words. Don't go on until you've found all ten words. Be as tough on yourself in eliminating unnecessary words as you think I might be if I were editing your manuscript. The best writers of the hundreds I've dealt with over the years were also the toughest on themselves. If you don't find all ten dispensable words, try again until you do.

I've bracketed the words that could be deleted:

> [There is nothing] I would like [better than] to meet an interesting [person who could become a] new friend.

More than half the words have been eliminated!

Certain words frequently constitute flab and can be eliminated: "however," "almost," "entire," "successive," "respective," "perhaps," "always," "there is." Each writer can compile a list of his own, words he uses from time to time that contribute nothing but flab to a text. Your own made-to-order list will serve as the best guide.

You've undoubtedly heard it said that the best writers make every word count. Not always. They, like us, sometimes slip up. Here's an example from Pete Dexter's excellent novel *Paris Trout,* which won the 1988 National Book Award for fiction:

> In the moment of illumination, though, he saw him. Buster Devonne was counting his money.

Check those two sentences. Can you detect three bits of flab? Try to find those words before you go on.

Perhaps you found the same words I did. They are in bold face:

> In the moment of illumination, **though**, he saw **him.** Buster Devonne **was** counting his money.

This leaves us with a shorter version that seems stronger than the original:

In the moment of illumination, he saw Buster Devonne counting his money.

Note how much faster that sentence seems to read than the two-sentence version that contained the flab. And that's from a prize-winning book, the author making a slip that you will not make when you've mastered the advice in this chapter.

Let's take a look at some sentences from which we want to eliminate flab. The protagonist in this story is proud of his house, where he has had meetings with important people. He is also a do-it-yourselfer. Here's the first draft of his thoughts as he comes home one day:

> The best scenes of my private and public life have been enacted here. Over the last fifteen years every room has been improved by my labor.

What excess words would you remove? Try to find them before going on.

> The best scenes of my [private and public] life have been enacted here. [Over the last fifteen years] Every room has been improved by my labor.

Note how much the pace increased after the author took out the bracketed words:

> The best scenes of my life have been enacted here. Every room has been improved by my labor.

The word "life" encompasses private and public. "Over the last fifteen years" provided unnecessary information that weakened the sentence.

The next sentences come from the same novel. A successful loan shark is intent on hiring a lawyer named Bert Rivers:

> I went there to kind of smell out what he was like. That was the last time I was in Bert Rivers' office. From then on Bert Rivers came to my office.

What I did in revising was quite simple. I cut the entire middle sentence, which didn't add anything. The deletion strengthened what was left and stepped up the pace:

I went there to kind of smell out what he was like. From then on Bert Rivers came to my office.

At chapter endings, cutting can be especially important. The following is from the point of view of a mother who has learned that her sixteen-year-old son has been killed in a fight. Here's the original:

> I looked up at the ceiling, knowing above the ceiling was the roof, and above the roof was the sky, and somewhere in the sky there was a power who knew your secrets, a power who emptied out the days and gave your kid to the maggots. What does a mother do with her love? It wasn't fair. Why did God do nothing?

In revising, I thought the sentence "What does a mother do with her love?" excessively sentimental. And "Why did God do nothing?" was too abstract to leave the reader with a suitable emotion at the end of the chapter. I cut both sentences. Here's how the chapter now ends:

> I looked up at the ceiling, knowing above the ceiling was the roof, and above the roof was the sky, and somewhere in the sky there was a power who knew your secrets, a power who emptied out the days and gave your kid to the maggots. It wasn't fair.

The author I have spent more time editing than any other is Elia Kazan, winner of two Academy Awards and director of five Pulitzer Prize plays who turned to fiction and became a number-one bestselling novelist. In his autobiography Kazan said, "I was now in a new profession. My publisher Sol Stein was my producer, and my editor Sol Stein was my director. . . . He saw quickly . . . that I delighted in saying the same thing over and over, thereby minimizing its impact ("One plus one equals a half," Sol would say)."

Eliminating the redundance was an important factor in his novel *The Arrangement* remaining number one on the bestseller charts for thirty-seven consecutive weeks.

I've been teaching my strange formula "One plus one equals a half" for a long time. It has been of value even to the most talented and successful of writers. The formula gives beginners insight into one of the factors that hurts chances for publication.

Catching "one-plus-ones" is a function of what is called "line editing." Shouldn't writers rely on editors to catch things like that? The hard fact is that editors do a lot less line editing than they used to. If a novel requires a lot of line editing, it is less likely to be taken on by a publisher, who has to consider the cost of editing. Which is why is it incumbent upon writers to become, in effect, their own editors. This also applies to nonfiction writers and to writers of screenplays and TV dramas.

On television, the program *In the Heat of the Night* had a glaring example of one-plus-one when Virgil Tibbs's wife said to him, "My parents, Mom and Dad . . ."

Who else might her parents be besides "Mom and Dad"? The script writer should have kept one or the other, not both.

Most often the one-plus-one has the repetition put in a slightly different way. Here's an example from an American classic:

> He was dirty. Everything about him was unclean. Even the whites of his eyes were soiled.

What did the author fail to eliminate? Before you go on, why don't you try your hand at being his editor and bracket what you'd leave out.

You could have eliminated either of the first two sentences. My preference would be to eliminate the second sentence because the short first sentence sets up the effective last sentence better:

> He was dirty. Even the whites of his eyes were soiled.

That example of one-plus-one comes from Sherwood Anderson's classic, *Winesburg, Ohio*.

Here's another example:

> It was a dreadful situation, a time of purest humiliation.

Here the choice is clearer. The first clause is general and familiar. "It was a time of purest humiliation" is more specific. All you have to do is delete the words "a dreadful situation" and you have a more specific sentence that doesn't say the same thing twice.

The following is an example of one-plus-one from a recent book by a much admired and successful novelist:

> He had time to think, time to become an old man in aspic, in sculptured soap, quaint and white.

Now let's think about that sentence. There are two images, "an old man in aspic" and an old man "in sculptured soap." What's wrong?

Both images convey the same thing. A person in aspic is immobilized. A person in sculptured soap is immobilized. Two images that convey the same thing make the reader conscious of the images instead of letting the reader experience the effect. And by cutting one of the two, the pace speeds up. If the author chose the second one, the old man "in sculptured soap," he should have eliminated "quaint and white." We usually think of soap as white unless a color is indicated. And "quaint" means "odd in a pleasing way" or "old-fashioned." Neither definition really helps the image in this context. "An old man in sculptured soap" is strong. "An old man in sculptured soap, quaint and white," is weaker. If the author felt he had to elaborate on sculptured soap to make the image work, perhaps he should have chosen "an old man in aspic" instead.

Sometimes a one-plus-one is created by an unnecessary repetition:

> I noticed the finesse with which Mr. Brethson held the creases in
> his trousers as he sat down. I was always fascinated by what people
> did to keep dress-up clothes in shape.

The first-person narrator notices how Brethson holds the creases in his trousers. The narrator's generalization of what he sees is distracting. In the editing, the second sentence should come out.

Earlier in this book I have several times expressed admiration for the work of a new novelist, Nanci Kincaid, whose *Crossing Blood* was published in the autumn of 1992. Her effective characterization, often accomplished in a stroke, deserves high praise. But she's evidently had no training in eliminating one-plus-ones. In fact, here she demonstrates one-plus-one-plus-one equals one third! Let's look at what she does one sentence at a time:

> Sometimes I wished I had run after Daddy, hugged his leg like a
> boa constrictor.

Not bad, though perhaps the image of a boa constrictor is more negative than the author intended, as the context would seem to indicate.

> Sometimes I wished I had run after Daddy, stuck to him like a
> Band-Aid.

A nice image.

Sometimes I wished I had run after Daddy, locked myself around him like a ball on a chain, like I was the law and he was the prisoner.

Fine. The only problem is that Nanci Kincaid used *all three images*, one after the other. The passage from her novel reads:

Sometimes I wished I had run after Daddy, hugged his leg like a boa constrictor, stuck to him like a Band-Aid, locked myself around him like a ball on a chain, like I was the law and he was the prisoner.

Any one of the three images would be stronger than all three strung together. And the pace would, of course, quicken. The images don't reinforce each other. Once again we break our experience to become conscious of words on paper.

It's time for a word of caution. The "one plus one" guideline does not apply to a conscious piling-up of words for effect. Here is an example of a purposeful piling-up first of verbs and then of adjectives, taken from a recent nonfiction book:

Their object is to tear down the individual in the eyes of the court, to deprecate, denounce, defame, condemn, and revile him, and to besmirch whatever reputation he may have had. Their intent is to leave him demoralized, disheartened, discouraged, depressed, and shaken.

Clearly, this intentional piling on of verbs or adjectives is done consciously for effect, unlike the "one-plus-ones" that diminish the effect rather than add to it.

In this chapter, we've learned to look closely at what we write, to test each word and phrase both for accuracy and necessity. We've also learned to eliminate most adjectives and adverbs as unnecessary flab. And we've found out that even successful writers trip up and reduce the effect of their work with unnecessary repetition.

Removing all forms of flab, including one-plus-ones, increases pace, helping a reader to feel that "this book moves fast."

I trust you've enjoyed improving the pace of classics and bestsellers and knowing that you won't be making the same mistakes.

22

Tapping Your Originality

One of the most important things a writer of fiction or nonfiction can do over time is to find his individual voice, style, and view of the world. The author's "voice" is made up of the many factors that distinguish an author from all other authors. Recognizing an individual author's voice is like recognizing a voice on the telephone. Many authors first find their "voice" when they learn to examine each word for its necessity, precision, and clarity, as we are doing here. The originality of some of the writers I have worked with was immediately apparent: James Baldwin and Bertram Wolfe come to mind. Among my recent students, a young man named Steve Talsky began his work this way:

> I am the way, the answer and the light, through me all things are possible.
> He had written this once as a joke on the headboard of his bed.

No one else I know—published or unpublished—could have written that beginning. More recently, when I saw the early pages of a completed novel by Anne James Valadez, my spirits rose in the hope that she could sustain the promise of those early pages, a thoroughly believable scene of two trees who were once lovers and now, rooted in place, can only report what goes on beneath their branches. Despite the rootedness of the trees, the story is anything but static. It is a work of remarkable originality.

An extremely small percentage of writers show signs of an original voice at the outset. It usually develops over time, and has two components, the originality of what is said and the originality of the way it is said.

Over the years, I encountered writers who felt they didn't make their mark because what they wrote was not sufficiently different from what other writers write. I developed a teaching strategy, a way for writers to discover what they alone can do. It is a high-risk, high-gain experiment. Though it can be accomplished in minutes, it takes hard thought and perseverance. If the exercise works for you, it could tap your originality.

I ask you to imagine yourself on a rooftop, the townspeople assembled below. You are allowed to shout down one last sentence. It is the sentence that the world will remember you by forever. If you say it loud enough, everyone in the world will hear you, no matter where they are. Think of shouting the sentence, even if you seldom shout. What one thing are you going to say? If you'd like to try that exercise now, write down the sentence.

Is your sentence one that could have been said by any person you know? If so, revise it until you are convinced no one else could have said that sentence.

When you've reworked your original sentence, consider these additional questions:

Is your sentence outrageous? Could it be? Is your sentence a question? Would it be stronger as a question?

Make whatever changes you like. I have still more questions:

Would the crowd below cheer your sentence? Can you revise it to give them something they'd want to cheer?

As you can see, I am asking question after question to help you strengthen and individualize your sentence. I continue:

Suppose the person you most love in all the world were to strongly disagree with your sentence. Can you answer his or her disagreement in a second sentence? Please add it.

Some writers will try to get out of further work by saying that their loved one would agree with the sentence. People have different scripts. If your sentence is original, the chances of another person—even your closest loved one—agreeing with it without the slightest exception is extremely unlikely.

Has your second sentence weakened your first? It usually does. If so, make it stronger than the first.

When you've done that, you now have the option of choosing one or the other sentence. There may be value in combining and condensing them.

Finished? Now imagine that you look down and see that the crowd below you is gone. You see only one person, your greatest enemy, who says, "I didn't hear you. Would you repeat that?"

It is a fact that given one last sentence, addressing one's enemy can light up the imagination more than an anonymous crowd can. You don't want to give your enemy the last word or let him respond in a way that would demolish what you've said. Can you alter your sentence so that your statement will be enemy-proof?

This, of course, continues the exercise with one of its most difficult phases, creating an original sentence that is strong and to the best of the writer's ability, seemingly incontrovertible.

Suppose you found out that the only way to get your message across would be if you whispered your sentence. How would you revise it so that it would be suitable for whispering?

It isn't always easy to change a shouted sentence to one that can be whispered and heard, but it sometimes produces intriguing results and shows how the intent to whisper can produce words that are stronger than shouted words.

The last thing I'll ask is for you to look at all of the versions of your sentence. Is there a prior version that is actually stronger than the last? Can the virtues of one be embodied in another? And most important, which sentence now strikes you as the most original, the one least likely to have been written by someone else?

The first attempt at this exercise may not produce your ideal original expression. Save your results and try again. But my experience has been that often the first run of this exercise will direct you to a theme or expression of a theme that is uniquely yours. You have begun to tap your originality, to find your voice. In the meantime, you've had another lesson in the value of shunning the sentence that comes first, and honing, changing, polishing the words of a single sentence to test all of its possibilities. That is, after all, the writer's work.

23

The Door to Your Book:
Titles That Attract

One day in 1962 an elderly woman with a marked Greek accent came to see me in my apartment in New York. Elia Kazan's mother arrived holding in her hand an advance copy of her son's first book, *America America*, which I was about to publish. Her voice betraying a slight quiver, she said that when the plays her son directed won Pulitzer Prizes and his direction of films twice won Academy Awards, her friends were not impressed because they, also Greek immigrants, did not go to the movies or see Broadway plays. Now, she said, holding *America America* up triumphantly, at long last she had something that she could show her friends!

The book, which had a modest first printing, was selected by the Reader's Digest Condensed Book Club, reprinted in mass market paperback, translated into many languages, made into a film, and widely reviewed as the best fiction ever on the uniquely American theme of immigration. All of that might not have happened. When the manuscript arrived, Kazan's name for it was *The Anatolian Smile,* which, I thought, closed the door against a wide readership. *The Anatolian Smile* was not a title designed to attract readers, nor did it resonate with the book's grand theme, how a young man, beset by the hardships of the old world, determined to emigrate to America, and stopped at nothing—even murder—to get to the United States.

Given Kazan's considerable reputation as a director and his known ability to say no in a voice designed to quash an opponent, others might have been tempted to go with the original title. Kazan's first book also happened to be the first book that I would be publishing under the Stein and Day imprint; my idealistic determination was to make every book a winner. That title, *The Anatolian Smile,* would not help. I contributed one word twice, the title *America America.*

I have met many talented writers who insulate their books from the public with titles that are not likely to arouse a reader's interest or to promise a rich experience. That stubbornness is persistent. Many years after Kazan's book left my care, he recycled his original title and had another publisher, perhaps less willing to oppose his strong will, issue a novel with the title *The Anatolian*. That was the first time one of his novels missed a run on the bestseller list. The author was the same. The quality of writing was the same. The title, an avoidable mistake, may have turned off the many millions who were part of his longstanding audience. The novel quickly dropped from sight, its door closed.

A book's life depends on reviewers, booksellers, and readers. Picture a reviewer standing before shelves loaded with the many dozens of review copies that arrive from publishers each week. He can review only one. Which does he pull down from the shelf to see if he might be interested in reviewing it? Would he pull down a book called *Argghocker*? And how will people know *Argghocker* is wonderful if it doesn't get reviewed?

Venture into any bookstore and look at the titles of new novels on display. Take note of your reactions to the titles of books by authors you don't know. You'll see how many books *don't* tempt you to pick them up because of their titles, and which titles intrigue you enough to want to take them down off the shelf and read the flaps.

Titles are equally important in nonfiction. While the subject matter of an ordinary nonfiction book is often enough to attract initial interest to it, a lively title will help even a how-to book. As nonfiction ascends in ambition and achievement, the title becomes as influential as for a novel. One of the authors I worked with closely over many years was Bertram D. Wolfe, whose best work became classics. Wolfe wanted to do a biography of Diego Rivera, one of the great twentieth-century painters Wolfe had known well. The hitch was that two decades earlier Wolfe had already written a biography of Diego Rivera that was published by Alfred A. Knopf, one of the finest publishers in America. The book was titled simply *Diego Rivera*. Though published in a beautiful edition, it did not do well. Wolfe put forward that Rivera had lived another eighteen years after the first biography was published, the events of those years unrecorded. Moreover, Wolfe asserted, in the intervening years he had acquired more insight into the artist and his work. And so he embarked on a new biography, which he titled *The Fabulous Life of Diego Rivera*.

Consider this: The author was the same. The subject was the same. But the title had a power and a resonance that the earlier title lacked. The new book was selected by a book club, nominated for a National Book Award, sold well, and became a standard work. I attribute that success in large measure to the excellent title of the second book. *The Fabulous Life of Diego Rivera* promised the reader much more than the earlier title.

How do you go about finding the right title for a book? Let's look at a spectacular example of a bad title and how it was changed. In the early eighties, one of my editors brought in a manuscript by Cecil B. Currey, a graduate of the U.S. Army Command and General Staff College, a professor of military history, and the author of eight previous books. The book described, sometimes in harrowing moment-by-moment detail, the destruction of an American infantry division in World War II. The manuscript, based on previously classified documents and firsthand testimony from both German and American survivors, demonstrated the tragic consequences of inept commanders. Despite the book's importance, I thought the author's straightforward title for it would kill sales. He called it *The Battle of Schmidt.*

First, nobody had heard of a place called Schmidt, much less of a battle fought there. And Americans, including the members of our editorial board, couldn't keep from laughing at the sound of *Schmidt,* not an appropriate response to a serious book. What we needed was an intriguing title with the right resonance.

Many effective titles have come from poems and songs, and I thought of a song that would likely be remembered by a prime audience for the book, the tens of thousands of infantry officers of World War II. In Officers Training School at Fort Benning, Georgia, young men sometimes kept their spirits up during the "eighteen weeks of hell in Georgia" by singing a ditty someone anonymous had composed to the tune of the Cornell University alma mater, "High Above Cayuga's Waters." See if you can pick out the words that became the title of Cecil Currey's book:

High above the Chattahoochee
Near the Upatoy
Stands an old abandoned shithouse
Benning School for Boys.

Onward ever, backward never
Follow me and die
To the port of embarkation
Next of kin goodbye.

As you may have guessed, *The Battle of Schmidt* became *Follow Me and Die,* with the subtitle *The Destruction of an American Division in World War II.* "Follow me" was the motto of the Infantry School, and the cynical use of it in the song had the perfect reverberation for the book, which went on to be selected by the Military Book Club, and had a life in hardcover and later in paperback, none of which would likely have happened with the original title.

Nonfiction titles are usually easier to come by because in the great majority of cases the author can and does fall back on a short description of what the book is about. If Henry Kissinger calls his book *Diplomacy,* that's enough. But *Diplomacy* by an author whose name is not widely known would be what book sales reps call "a tough sell."

What many nonfiction writers neglect is the appeal more imaginative titles hold for readers. Take the simple matter of making a book of shorter pieces of previously published nonfiction. Saul Bellow, whose novel titles are admirable, in 1994 published a collection called *It All Adds Up.* Some of the content is vintage Bellow, but if you're not familiar with Bellow's shorter nonfiction, would you hurry to look inside a book called *It All Adds Up?* (The subtitle is no better: "From the Dim Past to the Uncertain Future.") John Updike published a collection that he called by the blah title *Picked-Up Pieces,* which seems to minimize the content. Long ago I published a collection of such pieces by Lionel Trilling, which he called by the charming title *A Gathering of Fugitives.* There is no reason to give any book a handicap in its title.

Titles by academicians are sometimes intentionally dull in order to sound serious. However, Allan Bloom, a professor at the University of Chicago, presumably knew that a typical academic title might restrict his readership to other academicians. When he wrote a book on "how higher education has failed democracy and impoverished the souls of today's students," Professor Bloom called it *The Closing of the American Mind,* which surely contributed to the book's becoming a bestseller.

Can an imaginative title help a how-to book? Indeed it can. I recall several people resisting the title of Jo Coudert's first book, *Advice from a Failure.* "Who wants to listen to advice from a failure?" is what they said as we deliberated over the title. The author and I stuck with her provocative title. *Advice from a Failure* turned into a long-lasting, popular success.

Even better as a title was one that came with a child-care manuscript from a pediatrician with sound advice and a sense of humor. He called his book *How to Raise Children at Home in Your Spare Time*. It was taken by twenty-eight book clubs, and I'm certain the title helped.

One of the more influential nonfiction editors of our time, Alice Mayhew, has a particular talent for devising resonant titles for major books. Witness *All the President's Men, Den of Thieves,* and *Parting the Waters.*

Good article titles can help catch the attention of the reader browsing through a periodical. An intriguing title is sometimes sufficient to promote an article to the front cover of a magazine. James Thurber called one of his pieces "The Secret Life of James Thurber." Readers are attracted to secrets the way anteaters are attracted to anthills. Edward Hoagland attracted attention to an article by calling it "The Courage of Turtles." Most readers would not think of courage in the context of turtles. The title arouses curiosity. Long ago, William Hazlitt entitled an essay "On the Pleasure of Hating." Hatred as a pleasure? The reader's curiosity piqued, he wants to see what the author has to say.

A title that people respond to can spur completion of the work. For years I'd been writing an autobiography called *Passing for Normal,* which I began working on seriously only after the title became known to my friends and they responded enthusiastically without having read a word.

I recall asking participants in one of my Fiction Weekends for their titles, and at least two of them were so good I hoped their novels-in-progress made it to publication: *Driving in Neutral* and *Scenes from a Life in the Making.*

Good titles are hard to come by, even for some writers of the first rank. Consider a book once called *The Parts Nobody Knows.* Is it a medical text? The talented author retitled the book, *To Love and Write Well,* which sounds amateurish, though the author was by that time world famous. Still struggling to find a title for the book, he tried again, this time calling it *How Different It Was,* which might excite some curiosity about what "it" is, but is a weak title nevertheless. The author, still searching, went from not so good to much worse, coming up with yet another title, *With Due Respect.*

With due respect, that title is simply awful. Then the author made his final decision, and called the book *The Eye and the Ear.* That had to be his final choice because Ernest Hemingway died before the book was published.

His widow, Mary, had a better ear for titles. She took the book's final title from another manuscript. The book was published as *A Moveable Feast.*

Hemingway, one of the great innovators of twentieth-century American fiction, was often inept when it came to titling his work. One novel he at various times called *As Others Are, The World's Room, They Who Get Shot, and The Carnal Education.* Another title for that book was *An Italian Chronicle,* later changed to *The Sentimental Education of Frederick Henry.* By now you may have guessed that the book's final title was *A Farewell to Arms,* a resonant metaphor that lingers in the mind. And there you have the first clue as to what many great novel titles have in common, the use of metaphor.

Another American author, winner of the Nobel Prize, had a novel that for a while he called *Twilight.* Not exactly a grabber that invites you to open to the first page. The author is William Faulkner. Does *Twilight* conjure up the energy of *The Sound and the Fury?*

One way of enticing a reader is to title a novel with the name of the leading character plus an energizing factor. Saul Bellow's *The Adventures of Augie March* promises more than the name Augie March. His *Henderson the Rain King* resonates; the name Henderson would not. D. H. Lawrence discarded an inadequate title, *Tenderness,* before he called the book *Lady Chatterley's Lover.* It's hard to imagine that Scott Fitzgerald used *Hurrah for the Red White and Blue* before he hit on *The Great Gatsby.* What makes that title intriguing is the adjective "Great."

When an author successfully builds a wide audience for his work, the "title" for his next and future books is usually his name. After *The Naked and the Dead,* any book of Norman Mailer's was sold as "Norman Mailer's new book" rather than under its title.

New York magazine once had a competition for its readers to turn good titles into bad titles. Someone suggested downgrading Norman Mailer's *The Naked and the Dead* to *The Nude and the Deceased.* Though the words mean the same, the latter title for the same novel might have quashed the book's chances in the marketplace.

An author presumably controls the title of his book, but he is subject to heavy influence from people on the publisher's staff. They are the money and the power. An author doesn't always get to exercise his prerogative when it comes to titles.

I lost out once. I had a novel I called *A Stopping Place.* The jacket design included a swastika as a prominent feature. The title, in the presence of a swastika, had exactly the kind of low-key resonance I wanted for the book. However, shortly before press time *Publishers Weekly* carried an announcement of a novel by an author in India who called his book *A Stopping Place*. Titles can't be copyrighted (only motion picture titles can be protected by registration). I wanted to go ahead with my title but the publisher was afraid there might be confusion in the marketplace. Reluctantly, and because everyone was in a hurry for a title change, I okayed the publisher's suggestion of *The Resort* as a title, though I never liked it. It had no resonance.

The point to remember is that the primary function of a title is not to provide the locus of a story, but to entice the reader. Would you believe *The Heart Is a Lonely Hunter* was once called *The Mute*? Or that *The Red Badge of Courage* was originally titled *Private Fleming, His Various Battles*? Or that *The Blackboard Jungle* went by the name *To Climb the Wall*?

Is there a factor that above all others contributes to making a title intriguing and memorable? I've studied the titles that have captured the public imagination during my lifetime. Add to *The Heart Is a Lonely Hunter, The Red Badge of Courage*, and *The Blackboard Jungle* the following titles that almost everyone seems to like, and ask yourself what they have in common:

> *Tender Is the Night*
> *A Moveable Feast*
> *The Catcher in the Rye*
> *The Grapes of Wrath*

All seven of those titles are *metaphors*. They put two things together that don't ordinarily go together. They are intriguing, resonant, and provide exercise for the reader's imagination.

A beginning writer might say, "Stein, those are all books by famous writers. What can we do?"

A great deal. A good title, as I've said, can inspire a writer's work. One of the students in my advanced fiction seminar had problems with his work until he came up with an intriguing title, *The Passionate Priest*. He backed it up with an excellent first chapter that fit the title. Then, after our discussion about the metaphoric resonance of so many good titles, he came up with an even better one that drew immediate approval from all of his colleagues: *A Heart Is Full of Empty Rooms*.

Are there questions you might ask yourself about the title of your work? Yes.

Does it sound fresh and new?

Does it, like a metaphor, bring together two things that haven't been together before? If not, is there a way of doing that with a variation of your present title? Can you use the name of the principal character in an interesting context?

The point to remember is that the primary function of a title is not to convey meaning as much as to sound enticing and if possible exude resonance.

Sometimes one is tempted to wax cynical about titles. Raymond Chandler once said, "A good title is the title of a successful book." That is certainly borne out by the book that won the 1993 National Book Award for Poetry. Its title was *Garbage*. Occasionally, a book with an awkward or bad title will somehow make it in the marketplace. Since my aim is to ease the reader's path to publication, I'll fall back on my experience as a publisher: a good title is like coming to a house you've never been in before and having the owner open the door and say "Welcome." A good title can make a tremendous difference in the early acceptance of a book.

IV

Nonfiction

24

Using the Techniques of Fiction
to Enhance Nonfiction

It is immensely valuable for the journalist, biographer, and other writers of nonfiction to examine the techniques that novelists and short story writers use. In editing many articles and hundreds of nonfiction books over the years, I worked on almost every conceivable kind from child care to philosophy, from books that with hindsight probably should not have been published to works that zoomed high up on the bestseller lists or that became standard works. For our purposes here, I will divide all nonfiction into just two categories: practical and literary. There is some overlap, of course, but the basic distinctions are as follows:

Practical nonfiction is designed to communicate information in circumstances where the quality of the writing is not considered as important as the content. Practical nonfiction appears mainly in popular magazines, newspaper Sunday supplements, feature articles, and in self-help and how-to books. The subjects tend to be instruction, guides, tips, collections of facts, "inside" stories about a particular industry or locale or celebrated personalities, so-called inspirational material, popular psychology, medical and other self-help for the layman. The vocabulary of practical nonfiction is usually as simple as is permitted by the subject matter.

Literary nonfiction puts emphasis on the precise and skilled use of words and tone, and the assumption that the reader is as intelligent as the writer. While information is included, insight about that information, presented with some originality, may predominate. Sometimes the subject of literary nonfiction may not at the outset be of great interest to the reader, but the character of the writing may lure the reader into that subject.

Literary nonfiction appears in books, in some general magazines such as the *New Yorker, Harper's,* the *Atlantic, Commentary,* the *New York*

Review of Books, in many so-called little or small-circulation magazines, in a few newspapers regularly and in some other newspapers from time to time, occasionally in a Sunday supplement, and in book review media.

It should be no secret to readers of this book that I favor work in which the writer presents his best not his quickest, and where the language used comes not from the top of the head but from a consideration of precision, clarity, euphony, and alternatives.

Reporting in nonfiction can be accurate, like a photograph taken merely to record. The best of nonfiction, however, often sets what it sees in a framework, what has happened elsewhere or in the past. As the recorded events march before the reader, a scrim lifts to convey other dimensions, sight becomes insight, reporting becomes art.

Like fiction, nonfiction accomplishes its purpose better when it evokes emotion in the reader. We might prefer everyone on earth to be rational, but the fact is that people are moved more by what they feel than by what they understand. Great orators as well as great nonfiction writers have always understood that.

Nonfiction concerns itself with people, places, and ideas. Ideas seem to attract readers when developed through anecdotes involving people. Some nonfiction writers say they are jealous of novelists who create their characters; they are stuck with life, the characters in the news, the people they have to interview. No matter, the techniques for rounding the characters and making them come alive are similar.

When the nonfiction writer reports to the reader about a living person, the writer has two options. He can characterize the person the way a layman would or he can strive to give the person life on the page. In biography, the choice is clear. If the characters do not breathe, the exercise of assembling the facts of their lives may be of use to scholars but not to readers. When it comes to making the people we write about in nonfiction spring to life on the page, the techniques are useful for all nonfiction writers, not just biographers and historians. Too often, though, what we get in newspapers and magazines is the person's name and title and little else, sometimes a photo or drawing. We may know what the person looks like, but we don't yet know the person. Characterization matters. The reader's attention to a story and the pleasure he derives from it is often measured by how alive the participants seem, which stems, of course, from the skill with which they are portrayed.

It doesn't take much to make people come alive on the page. Novelists learn to provide vitality to minor characters in a sentence or two, usually by selecting one characteristic that is unusual. You will recall the beginning of Budd Schulberg's *What Makes Sammy Run?*, in which the sixteen-year-old protagonist is described as "a little ferret of a kid." Our dictionaries are full of animals, fish, birds, and insects that can be used in the characterization of people: the wolf as predator, or someone who wolfs down food; the yearling as innocent; the toucan as beak-nosed; falcons and hawks as high-fliers; the bat whose sonar for staying out of trouble is more effective than the sonar of most politicians. Plants, from the prickly cactus to the abrasive nettle, are also useful to help characterize. Live-forevers, weeds, invasive clover, fast-growing fescue, wildflowers are among the suggestive names of plants that a writer can use for brief and colorful characterizations.

The best way to make a person come alive is by rendering the person's appearance with some specific detail. Here are some examples from articles, news stories, and books. See if you can detect the key words or phrases that characterize the person:

> The garage attendant's hat was parked perilously on an excessive amount of hair.

This characterization has a touch of humor in that the verb "parked" is used for the garage attendant's hat. The visual image is of an ill-fitting cap that might fall off at any moment. It's enough to enliven this passing character.

How do you enliven an accountant?

> His accountant is an owl of a man who keeps one eyelid half shut not because of an affliction but because there is much in this world he is not prepared to see.

Note the key words and phrases. "Owl" characterizes the man physically, the rest of the sentence characterizes him psychologically.

John Updike, who writes much nonfiction in addition to his celebrated novels, can characterize in a sentence:

> His face is so clean and rosy it looks skinned.

A layman might describe a man as being dressed all in black. The image is vague, it gets the fact across, but not the feeling. It could have been written by anybody. Here's what Updike did, again in a nonfiction work:

He sits by the little clubhouse, in a golf cart, wearing black. He is Greek. Where, after all these years in America, does he buy black clothes? His hat is black. His shirt is black. His eyes, though a bit rheumy with age now, are black, as are his shoes and their laces. Small black points exist in his face, like scattered punctuation.

Markers that signal a person's background can be as useful to writers of nonfiction as to novelists, though few think of markers as a matter of course. Writers of articles, features, and books are more likely to use markers than journalists preparing copy on the run. If reporters try to use markers consciously a few times, it can become a rewarding habit.

As an example of the use of markers in nonfiction, I've chosen excerpts from a front-page story about the hapless treasurer of Orange County, California, Robert L. Citron, from the *New York Times* of December 11, 1994:

> He was the type to wear, along with patent leather shoes and belts, red polyester pants and a green blazer at Christmas, pastels at Easter, and orange and black on Halloween.
>
> The license plate on Mr. Citron's car is LOV USC; and, until it broke, the horn was programmed to play the school's fight song.

These markers—there are more—fit the main point of the story, that the Orange County treasurer who managed and lost billions was not a sophisticated Wall Street type, but a homespun local with unsophisticated tastes. The story focuses on the Santa Ana Elks Club, where Citron came for lunch routinely, arriving at ten past noon and leaving at ten minutes before one. Even the dining room of the Elks Club is described with markers:

> The decor is heavy on Formica, Naugahyde and Styrofoam. On the tables, the only centerpieces are Keno coupons and bottles of Heinz Ketchup and McIlhenny's Tabasco sauce.

These markers of Mr. Citron's private time contrast with his role as "a sophisticated, aggressive and daring investor" whose "high returns . . . made him not only a legend in financial circles nationwide but a hero to local politicians desperate to do more with less." Quick bites of television and the usual news stories told of Orange County's financial disaster but did not capture the human drama of the man behind the collapse. The memorable account by reporter David Margolick that I am quoting ends with a comment from a man by the name of Fred Prendergast, "a regular at Mr. Citron's table at the Elks":

> "To go to a man's home Sunday afternoon, intrude in his personal life, and practically force him to resign, is the most cowardly thing a person could do," he said bitterly. "All they had to do was wait for eight o'clock in the morning, or seven in Bob's case, and he'd have been right in his office, where he's supposed to be. They treated him like an animal."

With the aid of markers and particularity, Margolick made Robert L. Citron visible the way photographs of the man do not and gave a news story a human face and the ring of tragedy. The nonfiction writer who becomes aware of the emotions elicited by cultural differences can use this power in representing people by well-chosen class markers.

Often the writer's job is to characterize public figures in depth. I've selected an example from a work of history, a classic that has sold far more copies than many bestsellers.

Most people have at least an idea as to what Lenin, the founder of the Soviet Union, looked like. Paintings, and sculpture, seen in books and on TV, have carried the often romanticized image. Some photographs bring us closer to the truth. But a skilled writer can give us not only exact images but a sense of personality. In the following paragraph, both Lenin and his brother Alexander are characterized:

> Alexander's face was long and brooding; his skin milky white; his hair, thick, turbulent, frizzy, deeply rooted, stood up in all directions from a line far down on his forehead. His eyes, set deep and on a strange angle in a knobby, overhanging brow, seemed to turn their gaze inward. It was the strongly chiseled face of a dreamer, a saint, a devotee, an ascetic. But Vladimir's head was shaped like an egg, and the thin fringe of reddish hair began to recede from the forehead before he was twenty, leaving him bald, like his father, in young manhood. His complexion was a blend of grayishness and full-bloodedness; his eyes tiny, twinkling, Mongoloid. His whole aspect, except in moments of intense thought or anger, was jovial, humorous, mischievous, self-confident, aggressive. Not knowing him, one might have taken him in later years for a hard-working kulak, a rising provincial official, a shrewd businessman. There

227

was nothing in his build or appearance or temperament to suggest
kinship with his brother Alexander.

The excerpt is from Bertram D. Wolfe's *Three Who Made a Revolution*. One of the strengths in the description of Lenin is the evocation
of what he looked like earlier and later. That's a technique all writers can
employ under appropriate circumstances. Note the liberties taken by the
author. Alexander's hair is turbulent. It is also deeply rooted (how could
the author know?), which conveys its permanence as contrasted with
Lenin's baldness. Lenin is compared to three different types: a kulak (a
well-off farmer), a provincial official, a businessman.

Is taking risks, as this author has, irresponsible in nonfiction? The
dean of American literary critics of this century, Edmund Wilson, referred to the book from which this paragraph was taken as the "best
book in its field in any language."

It's worth taking risks. If it doesn't work, it will be apparent when you
revise.

What if the subject of an article or a book is well known to at least part
of your audience, as would be the case with, say, Franklin D. Roosevelt?
What can a nonfiction writer do that is fresh and new in characterization
when dealing with someone whose history has been the object of inten-
sive research by many writers? One interview, with Betsey Whitney, is
the basis for the extraordinary first paragraph of Doris Kearns Goodwin's book, *No Ordinary Time*:

> On nights filled with tension and concern, Franklin Roosevelt per-
> formed a ritual that helped him to fall asleep. He would close his
> eyes and imagine himself at Hyde Park as a boy, standing with his
> sled in the snow atop the steep hill that stretched from the south
> porch of his home to the wooded bluffs of the Hudson River far
> below. As he accelerated down the hill, he maneuvered each famil-
> iar curve with perfect skill until he reached the bottom, whereupon,
> pulling his sled behind him, he started slowly back up until he
> reached the top, where he would once more begin his descent. Again
> and again he replayed this remembered scene in his mind, obliter-
> ating his awareness of the shrunken legs beneath the sheets, undoing
> the knowledge that he would never climb a hill or even walk on
> his own power again. Thus liberating himself from his paralysis

through an act of imaginative will, the president of the United States would fall asleep.

The evening of May 9, 1940, was one of these nights. At 11 p.m., as Roosevelt sat in his comfortable study on the second floor of the White House, the long-apprehended phone call had come . . .

That paragraph, like much of the book, is filled with visual particularity and action. Goodwin's book is worth studying for its technique in using research, all of it documented, not only to characterize historical persons but to provide the reader with a rich experience.

Here is a checklist of questions you can ask yourself when characterizing:

- Would the reader be able to identify the person you're writing about if he was seen in a group of ten people?
- Have you done anything with the person's eyes, the way they are used, to look at a person or to look away?
- Have you given the reader a sense of how that person feels through describing an action rather than by stating the person's feelings?
- Does your person have a habit like tapping a finger, pointing eyeglasses, laughing too loud, waving his hands in a particular way that would make him more visible?
- Is there anything individual about the gait or posture of the person?
- Can you lend resonance to your characterization by invoking other matters in which your person was involved?
- Has your person changed much? In a longer work, can you use that change?

Setting a scene goes hand in hand with characterization. Suppose someone described a scene from history this way:

Mary Stuart came into the great hall, followed by her retinue. She climbed the steps to her chair, faced her audience, and smiled.

The reader gets the information, the facts, but not the essence of the occasion, and it is the essence that conveys truth. There is no reason why nonfiction writers cannot do as well as novelists in conveying a scene.

Witness what historian Garrett Mattingly did in introducing Mary Stuart in *The Armada*:

> She entered through a little door at the side, and before they saw her was already in the great hall, walking towards the dais, six of her own people, two by two, behind her, oblivious of the stir and rustle as her audience craned forward, oblivious, apparently, of the officer on whose sleeve her hand rested, walking as quietly, thought one pious soul, as if she were going to her prayers. Only for a moment, as she mounted the steps and before she sank back into the black-draped chair, did she seem to need the supporting arm, and if her hands trembled before she locked them in her lap, no one saw. Then, as if acknowledging the plaudits of a multitude, though the hall was very still, she turned for the first time to face her audience and, some thought, she smiled.

How much Mattingly gets into part of one paragraph, all of it designed to make a scene *he never saw* real to the reader.

The difference between ordinary nonfiction and extraordinary writing, as in Mattingly, is often in the resonance:

> Against the black velvet of the chair and dais her figure, clad in black velvet, was almost lost. The gray winter daylight dulled the gleam of white hands, the glint of yellow gold in her kerchief and of red gold in the piled masses of auburn hair beneath. But the audience could see clearly enough the delicate frill of white lace at her throat and above it, a white, heart-shaped petal against the blackness, the face with its great dark eyes and tiny, wistful mouth. This was she for whom Rizzio had died, and Darnley, the young fool, and Huntly, and Norfolk, and Babington and a thousand nameless men on the moors and gallows of the north. This was she whose legend had hung over England like a sword ever since she had galloped across its borders with her subjects in pursuit. This was the last captive princess of romance, the dowager queen of France, the exiled queen of Scotland, the heir to the English throne and (there must have been some among the silent witnesses who thought so, at this very moment, if she had rights) England's lawful queen. This was Mary Stuart, Queen of Scots. For a moment she held all their eyes, then she sank back into the darkness of her chair and turned her grave inattention to her judges. She was satisfied that her audience would look at no one else.

Note how Mattingly conveys the strength of her presence in the last lines of that paragraph. He is characterizing a strong queen for whom many had died. Is he making things up? The writing—quite apart from Mattingly's considerable reputation as a historian—convinces us that the author has feasted on every scrap of eyewitness testimony and on paintings to convey that scene.

Lest you conclude that resonance is available only to the writer of history, here is a paragraph from James Baldwin's essay about his father from his first published nonfiction book, *Notes of a Native Son*. Note how the drive to the graveyard blossoms into so much more:

> A few hours after my father's funeral, while he lay in state in the undertaker's chapel, a race riot broke out in Harlem. On the morning of the third of August, we drove my father to the graveyard through a wilderness of smashed plate glass.
>
> The day of my father's funeral had also been my nineteenth birthday. As we drove him to the graveyard, the spoils of injustice, anarchy, discontent, and hatred were all around us. It seemed to me that God himself had devised, to mark my father's end, the most sustained and brutally dissonant of codas. And it seemed to me, too, that the violence which rose all about us as my father left the world had been devised as a corrective for the pride of his eldest son. I had declined to believe in that apocalypse which had been central to my father's vision; very well, life seemed to be saying, here is something that will certainly pass for an apocalypse until the real thing comes along. I had inclined to be contemptuous of my father for the conditions of his life, for the conditions of our lives. When his life had ended I began to wonder about that life and also, in a new way, to be apprehensive about my own.

25

Conflict, Suspense, and Tension in Nonfiction

A re the techniques of plotting any use to the nonfiction writer?

All storytelling from the beginning of recorded time is based on somebody wanting something, facing obstacles, not getting it, trying to get it, trying to overcome obstacles, and finally getting or not getting what he wanted. What has interested listeners, readers, and viewers for centuries is available in the conscious use of desire in nonfiction.

In life we prefer an absence of conflict. In what we read, an absence of conflict means an absence of stimulation. Few things are as boring as listening to uncontested testimony in a courtroom. Few things are as interesting as a courtroom clash. If Marjorie and Richard lived happily ever after, the reader's response is "So what?" In articles, newspaper stories, and books, the reader's interest often flags because the writer did not keep in mind that dramatic conflict has been the basis of stories from the beginning of time.

Conflict does not have to involve violence. Conflict can be low key. It can exist by innuendo. What it takes is a mind-set when examining the cast of a prospective piece, whether it is to be an article or a scene in a book. Are there two people, two parties, two organizations, or two entities of any kind that are in conflict? If the conflict might not be immediately apparent to the reader, can the writer provide some help by bringing the conflicting elements closer to each other and by highlighting the conflict, actual or potential?

Conflict can arise from a thwarted desire, but the desire must be planted. Here's a simple before-and-after example:

Terence McNiece, 14, was arraigned yesterday in Town Court for allegedly stealing a bicycle belonging to a neighbor.

Watch what happens when desire is added:

> According to the testimony of his mother, Terence McNiece wanted
> a bicycle more than anything in the world, but she couldn't afford
> to buy him one. Terence, age 14, was arraigned yesterday in Town
> Court for allegedly stealing a bicycle belonging to a neighbor.

In the first part of the example, the information that a boy has been arrested for stealing a bicycle comes across as dispassionate fact. It's
rather blah. The revised version, in which we learn that the boy wanted
a bicycle more than anything else in the world and that his mother
couldn't afford to buy him one, tugs at the reader's emotions. What has
been activated is the boy's desire for the bike, which is more powerful
than the act of stealing. A news story or a nonfiction piece can move a
reader more if the writer remembers that desire, wanting something important badly, can be a force.

The more important the objective, the bigger the conflict will seem to
the reader if there are obstacles in the way of gratifying the want. The
thing that's wanted may not be possible. Nevertheless, the reader can
have his emotions stimulated by that unrealistic and unattainable want.

When the writer has his material and is ready to begin writing, that's
the time to determine whether any of the people in the story he is about
to write want something badly. Bringing that material up to the beginning could help touch a match to the reader's emotions.

One of the best guides for planning nonfiction is the Actors Studio
method for developing drama in plots that I described in Chapter 7. It involves giving each character in a scene a different tack. That technique
can be adapted to nonfiction. In preparing to write any passage or scene
involving two people, if the writer focuses on their differing intentions
(or "scripts"), he will immediately see the dramatic advantages of posi-
tioning their conflict in many kinds of adversarial situations in which
conflict is inherent in the circumstances.

Doris Kearns Goodwin's remarkable book *No Ordinary Time* focuses
on the home front in World War II and on Franklin and Eleanor Roosevelt.
All couples in a relationship have differing scripts, but the Roosevelts are
a dramatic example of the point. Eleanor was motivated by humanitarian
causes, Franklin by politics. Their intentions clashed frequently, made
more complex by their extramarital friendships. Yet as a public couple,
especially as Franklin became governor and president, they were trapped

in a crucible. (You will recall from Chapter 8 that crucible is an emotional or physical environment that bonds two people and that characters caught in a crucible won't declare a truce. They're in it till the end. Their motivation to continue opposing each other is greater than their motivation to run away.) The story of the Roosevelts, in expert hands, is as moving as the exemplary novels whose characters are trapped in a crucible.

Though the crucible is as applicable to confrontations of people as it is to fictional characters, I have never known a nonfiction writer who employed the idea consciously. Yet it has been used in countless histories and biographies, both of which invite scenes in which two adversaries are locked in a situation that holds them together more than anything that would drive them apart. Nonfiction writing would be more dramatic and tap the reader's emotions more if the crucible were considered more often in the planning stage.

Suspense is a valuable technique for the writer who wants to make his reader keep turning pages. It occurs when the reader expects something to happen and it isn't happening yet because the author is holding off. For instance, if a person has been characterized in an interesting way and the reader learns that the character is in danger, the reader wants to know how the person gets out of danger. If that information is withheld for a while, the reader will be left in suspense. If trouble is in the offing, the reader hopes that the person will find out in time to prevent the bad event from occurring. A variant occurs when the reader wants something to happen to a character and it isn't happening yet.

Nonfiction writers do not think of suspense as a conscious method for enhancing reader interest in their work, though some writers use suspense instinctively. Let's look at a simple example, from a newspaper story, of how suspense can be implanted:

> A bus carrying thirteen passengers to Mount St. Vincent yesterday evening careened off the road into a gully. One of the passengers, Henry Pazitocki, died before the ambulance reached the scene. Six other persons were hospitalized, two critically.

There is no element of suspense in that first paragraph. The story continues:

> Three of the passengers with minor injuries told patrolman George Francese investigating the accident that the driver may have been

drinking. A spokesperson for the Tri-State Bus Company denied those allegations.

Accusation and denial rendered, no suspense. Here's how a writer conscious of the benefit of suspense might have written the same story:

> A bus carrying thirteen passengers to Mount St. Vincent yesterday evening careened off the road into a gully. One of those passengers never made it to Mount St. Vincent.
> A spokesperson for the Tri-State Bus Company said, "The driver is a teetotaler. There is no evidence that he was drinking despite what some of the passengers said. It was an accident."

The first sentence tells what happened to the bus. The second sentence arouses curiosity as to who was the passenger who didn't make it. The purposeful repetition of "Mount St. Vincent" helps set up the suspense. The second paragraph doesn't tell us who the person is. The switch to a different part of the story (the spokesperson for the bus company) heightens the suspense. The reader wants to know more. Another element of suspense is introduced: was the driver drunk or not? The last paragraph of the story reads:

> Patrolman George Francese, investigating the accident, said, "Three other passengers with minor injuries complained that the driver appeared to have been drinking. Rosella Carew, who was sitting just behind Henry Pazitocki, the man who was killed, said, 'I had doubts about getting on the bus when I saw the driver's eyeglasses in his lap and he didn't even seem to know it.'"

This method of handling the story not only provides conflict for reader interest, at the end it lets the reader draw his own conclusion.

The following true story demonstrates how suspense can be built and maintained in nonfiction through a consistent point of view in which the reader learns only what the narrator knows, and learns it when the narrator learns it:

> A friend of ours let us have the use of her condo in Florida during a period of icy weather in the east. It was a cozy place, fully

equipped, with only one problem. The dishwasher disgorged water all over the kitchen floor.

My wife went down to the superintendent's apartment—his name is Roger—and knocked on the door. He didn't answer. This was Friday, could it be his day off?

I met Roger the first day we were there. He helped us with our luggage. I tried to tip him for helping us with the bags, but he waved the bills away. I guessed Roger to be in his late thirties, maybe a couple of years older. Later, from the window I watched him washing the cars of residents, which seemed to give him a lot of pleasure. No car wash in the world could do the job as meticulously as Roger did. I saw him doing small repairs around the place. Whenever I passed him, I stopped to exchange a sentence or two. I think Roger was slightly retarded, a nice man with a personality a lot more pleasant than most of the people around him who had all their marbles.

Come Saturday morning, my wife went down to Roger's apartment again. Still no answer. I thumbed through the Yellow Pages, and after four tries got a plumber who was working on Saturdays and who promised to show up in an hour. He showed up three hours later, did a quick fix on the dishwasher, but cautioned us that a pipe leading to the dishwasher needed replacing and urged us to tell the superintendent.

I didn't see Roger around at all on Saturday.

On Sunday I looked out of our second-story window and saw several policemen clustered around the door of Roger's apartment. I hurried down and was intercepted by a neighbor.

"Roger's dead," he said.

"Where?"

"In his apartment."

All I could think was, "He's so young!" He seemed strong and healthy the way he hoisted our bags.

The policemen weren't saying anything except that the body was still in the apartment and they were waiting for the coroner.

Hours later, from my window I saw the body bag being carried out. By the time I got downstairs, the police were gone.

Two days later I was about to drive out of the underground garage, when I saw Roger and a young girl moving stuff out of his apartment. I thought he was dead! Who was in the body bag?

I stopped the car and got out to tell Roger how glad I was he was alive and to find out what happened. The man had a stammer. I didn't remember Roger stammering.

It turned out that the man was Roger's twin brother, who'd come a distance, and with his daughter's help was piling Roger's belongings onto a pickup truck.

"Not the bed," the brother said, shaking his head.

From him I learned that Roger had suffered a silent heart attack, probably on Thursday night since he didn't respond to my wife's knock Friday morning. Because he must have felt very cold, Roger put one electric blanket under himself and another on top. He burned all day Friday, Saturday, and Sunday.

"The funeral," the twin brother said, "will be closed casket."

If I had started to recount what had happened by saying, "The superintendent of the building I was staying in burned to death last weekend," I would have spoiled the story by telegraphing the outcome. That's what we do in life. Our instinct is to give the conclusion first. As storytellers, we have to hold back by telling the story from a consistent point of view—in this case, mine—and showing what happened as I learned about it. I didn't refer to Roger as "the superintendent." I called him by his name. I said a couple of things to humanize him. I particularized as often as possible. But most important, I stuck to one point of view. I didn't say more than I found out at any time. I conveyed what I learned in the same order that I learned it, thus giving the entire story a consistent point of view.

In considering suspense, you might want to refer to the following checklist:

- Can your first paragraph arouse curiosity by withholding a piece of information till a bit later?
- Does your story set up a question or controversy and not answer or resolve it immediately?
- Are you loading in facts that unnecessarily diminish suspense early?
- Have you described an action that may arouse curiosity but that isn't explained in the same paragraph?
- Can you convert any sentence to a question that will arouse curiosity rather than satisfy it?

In considering the creation of tension in nonfiction, let's keep the difference between tension and suspense in mind. Suspense arouses a feeling of anxious uncertainty in the reader about what might happen, or a hope that something bad won't happen. Tension usually involves the sudden onset of a feeling of stress, strain, or pressure. As I've pointed out earlier, we deplore suspense and tension in life and enjoy them in writing.

Tension can be created by the simple mention of a time or date. **"It was four o'clock in the morning"** creates tension because it's an hour when most people are asleep. Therefore, anything that happens at four in the morning is in itself tension producing or could be. It's the "could be" factor that creates tension in the reader because he expects tension as part of his experience.

Two authors whose books I edited, Gordon Thomas and Max Morgan-Witts, collaborated on a number of nonfiction "disaster" books that were hugely successful. They specialized in moment-by-moment reconstructions of cataclysmic events in such books as *The Day the World Ended, The San Francisco Earthquake, Shipwreck*, and *Voyage of the Damned. Voyage* was the story of the luxury liner *St. Louis,* one of the last ships to leave Nazi Germany before World War II erupted. We know at the outset that the 937 passengers, all Jews fleeing Nazi Germany, are in danger. If Cuba does not let them in, the ship will return its human cargo to the Nazis and many will die. The first chapter is headed **Wednesday, May 3, 1939**. That prewar date in itself is enough to put tension to work. The second chapter is headed **Thursday, May 4, 1939**. The tension increases. Therefore, each time a date appears, the reader's pulse quickens. That's tension at work.

Let's examine how tension can be induced in a simple sequence. Here's the way it was originally written:

> The suspect refused to obey the policeman's order to come out of his automobile.

No tension. Now the same event as edited:

> The policeman ordered the suspect to come out of his automobile. The suspect didn't move.

What creates the tension is separating the two parts of the action. The separation in the example is momentary. The continuation of tension over paragraphs and pages comes from stretching out a tense situation, often a confrontation between persons or groups. Let's look at the cop and the suspect again:

The policeman ordered the suspect to come out of his automobile.
The suspect didn't move.

Bystanders reported that the officer then drew his gun and in a loud voice said, "Get out, now!"

The suspect shook his head and stayed put.

You can see how stretching out a sequence of acts produces tension that the reader finds pleasurable. Short sentences and short paragraphs help increase tension. A common error is the writer's temptation to rush to a conclusion. In life we savor good experiences and long for them to continue. The rush to end a good experience is counterproductive. The writer must discipline himself to hold back.

26

Quoting What They Say

Dialogue is an area in which the interests of fiction writers and nonfiction writers diverge. For the novelist, dialogue provides immediacy to a scene and is a major contributor to the experience of fiction. For the writer of articles and books as well as journalism, dialogue is a danger unless one uses direct quotes that sound real and can be substantiated. Those are two quite different matters.

Recording what people actually say does not read well. It is frequently hesitant, wordy, repetitive, and ultimately boring as court transcripts prove. The nonfiction writer has remedies.

If you quote anyone for more than three sentences, that's a speech. Break it up with something visual. It needn't be elaborate:

> Craig Marshall was the first to speak. "The issues—count on it—are threefold," he said. "In two sections of the village, tap water is the color of, call it mud. Been that way for thirty years and the incumbents have done nothing about it." Marshall coughed against his closed fist.
>
> "Item two," he continued, "is the traffic nightmare from the sports complex. Anybody in this village has a heart attack when the traffic's letting out can count on the ambulance getting to him in two or three hours." He looked pointedly at the mayor. "That's a death sentence for somebody because as far as I can tell the Almighty hasn't given this community an exemption from heart attacks."

The writer has broken up the quote with seemingly inconsequential things like a cough and looking at somebody. The first interruption humanizes the speaker and adds to the reality. The second—a glance at the mayor—invokes a suspicion of conflict by seeming to blame the mayor for the problems the speaker is talking about.

I saw the first draft, in which the speaker had two windy sentences that contributed absolutely nothing of importance and made the speaker sound like Dwight Eisenhower searching for the end of a sentence. The reporter left them out not to protect the reputation of Mr. Marshall but to prevent his copy from being boring. In reporting spoken words, it is not a writer's obligation to reproduce all of the words as long as the speaker's meaning is preserved.

Few people speak in complete and grammatical sentences. Moreover, perfectly formed sentences often come across to the reader as made up. In this instance, the reporter did a good job of catching the flavor of what was said. In quoting, the writer has to beware of cleaning up a speaker's sentences.

In 1975, just thirty days before Jimmy Hoffa, icon of the Teamsters Union, disappeared from the face of the earth, he came to lunch, bringing along, at my suggestion, the man who was ghosting his autobiography. Hoffa's material had been recorded on tape. The material as spoken by Hoffa was fascinating and colorful. That same material, with Hoffa's rough language cleaned up and sentences straightened out, was unreal and boring. The purpose of the meeting was to insist that the writer restore Hoffa's words, including the expletives and grammatical howlers. I wasn't arguing for a verbatim transcript of the tapes but for a *retention of their color,* which I succeeded in getting, and which all writers who deal with the spoken words of others should strive for.

When you're reporting the results of an interview, you will likely end up with with too much quotation. You want to keep those parts that reveal the character of the speaker or that define subject matter. You want to preserve comments that are confrontational, colorful, or especially appropriate, and ditch the rest.

That brings us to the second matter. Never intentionally misquote. And never invent dialogue.

Invented dialogue is usually a highly visible sign of untrustworthy writing. A few writers of nonfiction commit the same errors as some historical novelists. They provide dialogue that would have been impossible for anyone to record. I know of cases in which books were rejected by editors because some piece of attributed dialogue was so apparently contrived that it cast doubt on the reliability of the author for facts that could not easily be confirmed.

Don't tempt rejection by an editor or a lawsuit from a person quoted inaccurately. If you find yourself inventing dialogue, write a play, novel, or movie.

27

Guts: The Decisive Ingredient

$\mathbb{A}$ long time ago I took an oath never to write anything inoffensive.

In working with literally hundreds of authors over a period of many years I concluded that the single characteristic that most makes a difference in the success of an article or nonfiction book is the author's courage in revealing normally unspoken things about himself or his society. It takes guts to be a writer. A writer's job is to tell the truth in an interesting way. The truth is that adultery, theft, hypocrisy, envy, and boredom are all sins practiced everywhere that human nature thrives.

What people who are not writers say to each other in everyday conversation is the speakable. What makes writing at its best interesting is the writer's willingness to broach the unspeakable, to say things that people don't ordinarily say. In fact, the best writers, those whose originality shines, tend to be those who are most outspoken.

Do shy men and women ever become superb writers? Yes, after overcoming their natural reluctance to say the things they think. Fig leaves have no place on either the bodies or the minds of the best writers. I like the way Red Smith put it: "There's nothing to writing. All you do is sit down at a typewriter and open a vein."

On the issue of candor, is there something nonfiction writers can learn from novelists? Yes, there is hardly anything about the secret, sometimes mischievous, cruel, evil, outrageous, defiant, and glorious acts and thoughts of human beings that has not appeared in the novels of the last few decades. And there is little about the private acts of people that has escaped reporting—and not only in the sensational press. The novelist has it easier. He hides a little—just a little—under the presumption that he is making things up. We all know that the most truth-bearing parts of superior fiction aren't "made up." They come from the novelist's obser-

Guts: The Decisive Ingredient

vation and understanding of human nature. The nonfiction writer who dares to dare is more exposed. The assumption of his readers is that he is writing fact. He may have to prove his assertions to an editor, or worse, to a court. He needs the courage of a soldier or firefighter because often the more he reveals that is interesting to his readers, the more exposed he is. Readers are curious about the inmost secrets of others. The subjects of factual writing—if they are not publicity seekers—don't want anything embarrassing on public display. It is no accident that some of the best nonfiction writing of the century has come from writers who are also experienced novelists.

Mary McCarthy, whose novels brought her fame, early on earned a reputation for keen observation and a sharp tongue for her critical writings. George Orwell's nonfiction is far superior to his fiction and exceptionally outspoken. Critics have called him the best nonfiction writer of this century. V. S. Naipaul's nonfiction, once sampled, will lead you quickly to conclude that he has the courage to see and say what, for instance, politicians almost never say. His nonfiction makes waves by being sharply observant and truthful in territory that frightens off lesser writers. Rebecca West, whom *Time* magazine called "indisputably the world's No. 1 woman writer," started out as a novelist and six decades later was still writing fiction. However, her great reputation rests largely on her shrewd, brave, and intelligent factual writing. Most writers know Scott Fitzgerald's *The Great Gatsby* but haven't read his gutsy nonfiction in *The Crack-Up*.

Writers read writers, and if being outspoken is a problem for you, I suggest you immerse yourself in the work of the writers I've mentioned, and also try the work of contemporaries like Gore Vidal and Joan Didion, even if it's just to sample how they deal with candor.

Vidal, who has never wanted for vitriol much less candor, begins one piece about Tennessee Williams by passing the candor chalice to Williams, whom he quotes saying, "I particularly like New York on hot summer nights when all the . . . uh, superfluous people are off the streets." Borrowing the candor of another has been useful to Joan Didion also. I quote from *Goodbye to All That*, a memoir of her pilgrimage to New York when she was twenty-three:

> I remember once, one cold bright December evening in New York, suggesting to a friend who complained of having been around too long that he come with me to a party where there could be, I assured him with the bright resourcefulness of twenty-three,

"new faces." He laughed literally until he choked, and I had to roll down the taxi window and hit him on the back. "New faces," he said finally, "don't tell me about *new faces*." It seemed that the last time he had gone to a party where he had been promised "new faces," there had been fifteen people in the room, and he had already slept with five of the women and owed money to all but two of the men.

Next let's sample someone not as well known. Gayle Pemberton, a black writer with a Ph.D. from Harvard, wrote about the time she was going broke in Los Angeles on a temporary typist's revenue, and signed up to work for a caterer on three successive weekends. What she later wrote about it made the experience worthwhile:

> Our caterer was one of a new breed of gourmet cooks who do all preparation and cooking at the client's home—none of your cold-cut or warming-tray catering. As a result, her clients had a tendency to have loads of money and even more kitchen space.
>
> Usually her staff was not expected to serve the meal, but on this occasion we did. I was directed to wear stockings and black shoes and I was given a blue-patterned apron dress, with frills here and there, to wear. Clearly, my academic lady-banker pumps were out of the question, so I invested in a pair of trendy black sneakers— which cost me five dollars less than what I earned the entire time I worked for the caterer. Buying the sneakers was plainly excessive but I told myself they were a necessary expense. I was not looking forward to wearing the little French serving-girl uniform, though. Everything about it and me were wrong, but I had signed on and it would have been unseemly and downright hostile to jump ship.
>
> One thing I liked about the caterer was her insistence that her crew not be treated as servants—that is, we worked for her and took orders from her, not from the clients, who might find ordering us around an emboldening and socially one-upping experience. She also preferred to use crystal and china she rented, keeping her employees and herself safe from a client's rage in case a family heirloom should get broken. But on this occasion, her client insisted that we use his Baccarat crystal. We were all made particularly nervous by his tone. It was the same tone I heard from a mucky-muck at my studio typing job: cold, arrogant, a matter-of-fact "you are shit" attitude that is well known to nurses and secretaries.

As Pemberton was drying one of the Baccarat glasses, it shattered in her hand, a happy accident in that she used it as the fulcrum of her piece.

Characteristic of another kind of nonfiction gutsiness is that of Seymour Krim, who wanted, as many writers do, to be a major novelist and instead made exemplary nonfiction his calling. "One life was never quite enough for what I had in mind," he says and means it, as he lays his life bare. Listen to the individual sound of his voice:

> You may sometimes think everyone lives in the crotch of the pleasure principle these days except you, but you have company, friend. I live under the same pressures you do. It is still your work or role that finally gives you your definition in our society, and the thousands upon thousands of people who I believe are like me are those who have never found the professional skin to fit the riot in their souls. Many never will. I think what I have to say here will speak for some of their secret life and for that other sad America you don't hear too much about. This isn't presumption so much as a voice of scars and stars talking. I've lived it and will probably go on living it until they take away my hotdog.

The voice picks up speed:

> America was my carnival at an earlier age than most and I wanted to be everything in it that turned me on, like a youth bouncing around crazed on a boardwalk. I mean literally everything. I was as unanchored a kid as you can conceive of, an open fuse-box of blind yearning, and out of what I now assume was unimaginable loneliness and human hunger I greedily tried on the personalities of every type on the national scene as picked up through newspapers, magazines, movies, radio, and just nosing around.

It should be evident by now that forthrightness doesn't involve sensationalism suitable for the exploitation tabloids. What it requires is honesty of a kind that gets self-suppressed by the public. Doctors are part of that public, but not doctors who are good writers. Witness Richard Selzer's chapter, "The Knife," in his book *Mortal Lessons: Notes on the Art of Surgery.* He does what no surgeon has done before, with precision, clarity, grace, imagination, and candor:

> One holds the knife as one holds the bow of a cello or a tulip—by the stem. Not palmed nor gripped nor grasped, but lightly, with the

tips of the fingers. The knife is not for pressing. It is for drawing across the field of skin. Like a slender fish, it waits, at the ready, then, go! It darts, followed by a fine wake of red. The flesh parts, falling away to yellow globules of fat. Even now, after so many times, I still marvel at its power—cold, gleaming, silent. More, I am still struck with a kind of dread that it is I in whose hand the blade travels, that my hand is its vehicle, that yet again this terrible steel-bellied thing and I have conspired for a most unnatural purpose, the laying open of the body of a human being.

Are readers ready for this kind of candor? In 1994 another physician who writes well, Sherwin B. Nuland, published a book called *How We Die*. It was selected by a book club, became a bestseller, and won the National Book Award for nonfiction.

Did I have to search through my library to find the examples of frankness quoted in this chapter? They are all from one section of a single anthology I recommend to you, *The Art of the Personal Essay,* edited by Phillip Lopate. That book starts with the forerunners, Seneca and Plutarch, picks up Montaigne and Samuel Johnson and Hazlitt en route to the Americans of the present century, and that journey reveals an evolution toward the candor with which our writers tell us like it is.

The audience is ready. The question is "Are you?"

V

Literary Values in Fiction and Nonfiction

28

Commercial? Popular? Literary?

The commercial novelist is a storyteller who is most concerned with plot and plot gimmicks, with maintaining a high level of suspense and physical action. The success of commercial novelists is usually derived from tapping an area of adventure, romance, espionage, or whatever may be popular at the time, creating characters with sufficient skill that the reader is willing to suspend disbelief and follow the hero as he triumphs over unambiguous antagonists.

John Grisham's bestseller *The Firm,* for instance, is an adolescent fantasy, the story of a young lawyer straight out of law school who is offered a job with too much pay, an expensive car, a house, and finds himself working—of course—for the Mob, who won't let him quit. The rest is a chase scene. The market for adolescent fantasies is demonstrably huge. And it cares little about the quality of the writing. Mitch is the beleaguered hero of this fantasy:

Mitch almost felt sorry for her, but he kept his eyes on the table.

In a box? What he kept on the table was presumably his gaze.

He stared at Royce McKnight and exposed a mammoth chip on his shoulder.

That's not a log, it's an attitude.

Mitch ripped two ribs apart, slinging sauce into his eyebrows.

Did his wife, Abby, sitting across the table from him in the restaurant, notice? She says:

"We just moved in this morning."

A fact he already knows, so Mitch says:

"I know."

On a business trip, Mitch, happily married to Abby, is the object of seduction by a woman named Julia in words like these:

Julia drooled at him and moved closer.

She rubbed her breasts on his biceps and gave her best seductive smile, only inches away.

When a private school is mentioned, we learn:

Affluent parents signed the waiting list shortly after birth.

Precocious as well as affluent? According to Grisham, the people Mitch meets have interesting though repetitive characteristics:

He frowned sincerely, as if this would be painful.

He was stocky with a slight belly, thick shoulders and chest and a huge, perfectly round head that smiled with great reluctance.

When he talked the water dripped from his nose and interfered with his enunciation.

Tammy arrived from trip three out of breath and with sweat dripping from her nose.

In this kind of commercial writing, lack of precision is not the only carelessness:

Coffee? Yes, he said, black. She disappeared and returned with a cup and saucer.

The coffee itself was presumably forgotten by the author. And so it goes. The public was forgiving. Or, more likely, didn't notice as *The Firm* topped the bestseller lists.

The most distinguishing difference between "commercial" writers like Grisham and literary writers is the attention paid to the individual meanings and resonance of words and the respect shown for the reader's intelligence. In this chapter my concern is with the craft of the writer who aspires to permanence, who has not an occupation but a calling.

Publishing, the work of bringing words to the marketplace, is, alas, sloppy in its attempts to distinguish books of a certain quality from everyday product that is designed to sell. The latter are called "popular" and "commercial," though books of high quality are sometimes popular, and when they endure, prove their commercial viability by continuing to sell long after their commercial contemporaries are out of print. Both kinds of books can entertain and instruct, though they appeal to different audiences.

A prevalent way of describing the difference is calling the successful commercial book "a good read," whereas the other is likely to be referred to as "a good book." The implication is that one confers a transient experience on the reader, whereas the other may be durable, deserving the permanence of a hardcover binding and a place on a bookshelf, to remind one of the experience, or be reread.

I wanted to clarify the distinction for a practical reason. In the end, you write what you read. If you read literary fiction with pleasure, that's what you will attempt to write. If you read thrillers or romances, you will in all likelihood end up writing for the audience of which you are a part. The same is true for nonfiction—not merely the field of interest, but the quality of language and insight you require of your books, read or written.

The literary novelist is concerned primarily with character understood in depth and engaged in activities that are resonant with the ambiguities and stresses of life. The richness of the best literary fiction is derived primarily from the creation of characters who will persist in the reader's mind after the reading experience is over. Those novelists and nonfiction writers who strive to produce durable work share an interest in precision and freshness in the use of words, in insights into human nature and the physical world, and in resonance. These writers usually develop a "voice" or style that is distinctive.

The writer of commercial nonfiction is often an expert craftsman in a hurry to meet a deadline who measures the effort put in against the monetary reward. He is writing not for the ages but to put bread on the table. Perfecting a piece beyond the requirements of the editor to him means more work for the same amount of money, work that could well go into another piece for another publication. Beyond a certain point, quality is not cost-effective for him.

Fiction writers who don't improve their work beyond the requirements of their editors or the public do not have an interest in perfection because they are deaf to the sound of words and have no instinct or training to hunt precise nuances. They are what they read.

I have edited and published both kinds of writers and both kinds of books. I have worked closely with writers of each kind who have made millions from a single work. What I have never witnessed is a writer's work succeeding notably in a field he doesn't habitually read for pleasure.

Diction is a word laymen associate with clear pronunciation. Its other meaning is the one that is important for writers. Diction involves the choice of words for their precise meaning and sound, the arrangement of those words, and their selection for effect. Excellence in diction is the most important characteristic of fine writing.

The precise meaning of words matters, a notion in disuse by the majority of people, including their presumptive leaders. The inattention to diction is pervasive, endemic, and has reached into surprising places.

On the morning that this chapter was written, the *New York Times* published a review of a biography of General H. Norman Schwarzkopf, the leader of Desert Storm. The coauthors were both journalists. The review tells us that the authors, in their introduction, say they "will paint a picture of a man who is 'human, blunt, clear, idealistic and swiftly effective.'"

I was stopped by the first adjective: human. I hadn't thought of the general as vegetable, mineral, or other species of animal. What did these two journalists intend by leading with the word "human"?

We'd have to guess. Surely they didn't confuse it with the word "humane," which means something quite different. Did they mean Schwarzkopf was what in colloquial parlance we call "a regular guy"? And if so, what is meant by "a regular guy"? It's a verbal trunk into which a hundred readers would pile many meanings relating to their own experience.

In the best of newspapers the best of journalists are usually forced to write quickly—"off the top of the head" is the convenient expression—and that's where an imprecise use of "human" comes from: speed and a minimum of thought, for surely both experienced authors of the Schwarzkopf biography know better.

Poetry and fiction share certain characteristics. In fashioning poetry, a common beginner's mistake is to emote instead of to evoke, to convey the writer's emotion rather than to stimulate an emotion from the reader. One way to a reader's emotion is to bring two words together that have not been together before. Therefore precision is achieved in poetry by the creation of a new grouping of words rather than by using each word for its exact meaning. Precision in poetry is abetted by the sound of words, which is why poetry is sometimes so difficult to translate. The work of Dylan Thomas, possibly the best poet in the English language of this century, is full of newness, words juxtaposed for the first time to create a new meaning. In one, "Fern Hill," he speaks of "the lilting house." Lilt means a tune having a pleasant rhythm. A poor poet might have written "happy house," which is direct and obvious. The "lilting house" evokes the happiness. If it's hard to judge out of context, treat yourself to some time with Dylan Thomas's poems.

Poetry usually involves austere compression. The most famous poem of Delmore Schwartz, "In the Naked Bed, in Plato's Cave," mixes ordinary description ("A fleet of trucks strained uphill, grinding") with fresh metaphor ("The street-lamp's vigil"). The street-lamp is given a human characteristic—vigilance—with a single word. In fiction, the group of words that evoke an emotion in the reader can range from a few words, as in poetry, to paragraphs or sections.

In commercial fiction, the sound of words is rarely considered except for the occasional—and inaccurate—"splat" or "rat-a-tat-tat." In literary fiction, the sound of words can contribute to the effect, though that is rarely noticed by readers. Literary fiction thrives on subtlety and particularity.

"Particularity" is a word my students hear often. Once the word from editors was "be concrete." But to be specific is not as precise as to be particular, which is much more advantageous to the creative writer. Particularity deserves its own chapter, which comes next.

29

Particularity

In his book *On Becoming a Novelist*, John Gardner said, "Detail is the lifeblood of fiction." My only quarrel with that statement is that detail is also the lifeblood of nonfiction. And I want to go a step further. It is not just detail that distinguishes good writing, it is *detail that individualizes*. I call it "particularity." Once you're used to spotting it—and spotting its absence—you will have one of the best possible means of improving your writing markedly.

During the decades that I served as an editor and publisher, what drew my attention to a piece of work more than any other factor was the use of apt particularities, the detail that differentiates one person from another, one act from another, one place from any others like it.

Let's look at some examples of particularization in sketching characters, actions, and places. To characterize, particularity is used to show how an individual looks, dresses, or speaks without resort to clichés or generalizations.

Early in *The Touch of Treason*, the lawyer Thomassy is confronted by Roberts, the patrician district attorney. Watch for the words that particularize:

> Thomassy could see Roberts's handshake coming at him all the way down the aisle, above it that freckled face proclaiming I can be friendly to everybody, I was born rich.
> Roberts's smile, Thomassy thought, is an implant.

The cop-out would have been to say that Roberts had a fake smile. That is a tired expression and a generalization that doesn't particularize. The particularization is achieved in two steps. First, his **freckled face proclaiming I can be friendly to everybody, I was born rich.** Then

Thomassy's thought, that the smile is **an implant.** Note the use of metaphor to particularize. It doesn't say Roberts's smile is *like an implant,* Thomassy thinks it *is* an implant. Of course, Thomassy doesn't believe that literally. In just a few sentences, we know that in Thomassy's view, Roberts is a pretentious prig. The particularization, though brief, is enough to convince the reader. That helps set up the adversarial exchange that follows. Let's observe an action that particularizes:

> Thomassy moved his gaze from Roberts's confident eyes to Roberts's blond hair, then Roberts's chin, then Roberts's left ear, then Roberts's right ear. The four points of the cross. It was what made witnesses nervous. They couldn't figure out what you were doing. You weren't doing anything except making them nervous.

The reader quickly understands that Thomassy disconcerts his opponents. Roberts must loathe Thomassy, the arrogant son of an Armenian immigrant. When they encounter each other in the courtroom, the reader is prepared for a battle that is motivated by more than the case.

Now let's examine the use of particularization in describing a place:

> The renting agent said it was their last best chance of finding an apartment in the neighborhood that wasn't as cramped as the place they had now. Elizabeth and Joe hurried up the stone steps to the parlor floor. The agent stepped aside to let them in. Their first impression was a vast emptiness in which the echo of the agent's voice reverberated.
>
> "It's fourteen feet high."
>
> They followed the agent's gaze to the ceiling, with its tiny plaster angels around the perimeter.
>
> Joe said, "There's room for astronauts. How do you change the light bulbs?"
>
> Elizabeth said, "With a ladder, dummy."
>
> The agent, glad to see the wonder on their faces, said, "Wait till you see the bedroom."
>
> "Is it in the same town?" Joe said, squeezing Elizabeth's hand.

A lazy author might have said, "The apartment was bigger than they ever expected." The reader would not have been able to experience the wonder of its size. By stretching out the particulars (the echo of the agent's voice, the height of the ceiling, the carved plaster angels), the reader experiences the place along with the characters. In addition, the dialogue also particularizes one of the characters. Joe, for instance, has a sense of humor.

If an ordinary object is important to a story, particularization will help call attention to it. Let's look at a before-and-after example:

> "You have an envelope?"
> He put one down in front of her.

This exchange is void of particularity. Here's how that transaction was described by John le Carré:

> "You have a suitable envelope? Of course you have."
> Envelopes were in the third drawer of his desk, left side. He selected a yellow one, A4 size, and guided it across the desk, but she let it lie there.

Those particularities, ordinary as they seem, help make what she is going to put into the envelope important. The details do not consist of waste words; they have a purpose in making the transaction credible.

It should be clear by now that particularizing sometimes takes more words than a quick generalization. For several decades there has been pressure in nonfiction to clip language short, to simplify sentences. The movement seems to have started back in 1946 with Rudolf Flesch's book *The Art of Plain Talk*. Simplification is useful and can be a great aid to those business persons and academicians who tend to inflate their sentences with excess verbiage and pompous jargon. However, simplification is not necessarily appropriate if one's aim is to provide an experience for the reader. "The apartment was large" doesn't do it. Nor does putting an envelope in front of somebody. The extra words are not wasted because they make the experience of the action possible and credible.

Excellence in particularity tells the editor that he is in the hands of a writer. I've seen the use of particularity make an article on a mundane subject sing on the page. The nonfiction books I edited that became classics all had the quality of particularity. And for fiction, particularity is not an option because even transient fiction requires some particularity to succeed with readers.

Perhaps my favorite example of particularization is the first sentence of one of Graham Greene's masterpieces, *The Heart of the Matter*. It has three words every writer would do well to remember:

> Wilson sat on the balcony of the Bedord Hotel with his bald pink knees thrust against the ironwork.

The crucial words, of course, are "bald pink knees," a particularization that makes the character and the place instantly visible and in the reader's experience unique. If we were to eliminate the words "bald" and "pink" how diminished that opening sentence would be:

> Wilson sat on the balcony of the Bedford Hotel with his knees thrust against the ironwork.

By removing the two most particular words, the sentence becomes ordinary. Moreover, though the image is still visual, there's nothing especially memorable about it. The balcony and the Bedford Hotel are also particulars, as is the ironwork, but "bald pink knees" is fresh, original, and immediately makes Wilson visible. Those knees against the ironwork make the hotel visible, too. All of that is accomplished in a single sentence.

Particularizing is also useful if you have occasion to repeat something—like a character laughing—and don't want to bore the reader by repeating a phrase like "She laughed" several times within the same few pages:

> She looked like she was enjoying herself mightily.

> If he laughed behind you suddenly in a darkened room, you'd be frightened.

> His face beamed like Santa Claus. His barrel chest moved up and down, but I couldn't hear him laughing.

> She seemed about to giggle like a schoolgirl, but controlled it. She'd been out of school a long time.

> His response was a sound somewhere between a guffaw and a chortle. Later I learned it was a kind of trademark with him. Nobody else in the world laughed like that.

The temptation is always to use either a cliché or a generalization, what I call "top-of-the-head writing." In this chapter we are trying to fashion sentences that are writerly, that particularize in an interesting way. Here's a top-of-the-head description that doesn't tell us much:

> Cecilia wore short skirts.

It doesn't take much to turn that ordinariness into a sentence that characterizes and particularizes:

Cecilia's skirts were three inches shorter than her age allowed.

Here's another ordinary—I'm tempted to say lazy—sentence:

Vernon was a heavy smoker.

And now several ways to convey the same point with particularity:

Vernon coughed from the ground up.

When a waitress heard Vernon's voice she always guided him to the smoking section without asking.

Vernon looked like those fellows that have one rectangular breast where he kept his pack of Marlboros tucked into his shirt.

Here's a sentence that doesn't give the reader anything to see. It's too much of a generalization:

He didn't know what to do with his hands.

If you're going to deal with a character's hands, give them something to do, as this author did:

Every few minutes his right hand checked to see that his reproductive organs were still in place.

A useful technique for particularizing a character in fiction, a person in nonfiction, or a setting in either is seeing the individual or locale first at a distance and then closer. For the reader the experience is similar to seeing a full-length view of a person and then a close-up in which more detail is noted:

Corrigan's bulk filled the doorway.
I said, "Hi," and got up from behind my desk quickly to shake his hand.
I stopped. His right arm was in a sling. He wiggled the fingers at me.

"Break it?" I asked.

His lips, trying to smile, quivered.

"What happened?" I said, motioning him to a chair.

He turned his face toward the window. I saw the freshly stitched cut that ran from his right cheek straight down into the collar of his shirt.

When a person comes into view, the writer's temptation is to describe him all at once. It's more effective to delay part of the description. Start at a distance, then notice more. It enhances the tension. The same technique of particularizing in stages works for places as well as people.

Elmore Leonard, best known for his dialogue, is also a master of particularity:

> Robbie Daniels was also forty-one. He had changed clothes before the police arrived and at six o'clock in the morning wore a lightweight navy blue cashmere sweater over bare skin, the sleeves pushed up to his elbows, colorless cotton trousers that clung to his hips but were not tight around the waist. Standing outside the house talking to the squad-car officer, the wind coming off the ocean out of misty dawn, he would slip a hand beneath the sweater and move it over his skin, idly, remembering, pointing with the other hand toward the swimming pool and patio where there were yellow flowers and tables with yellow umbrellas.

My favorite particularity in the passage we just read is "he would slip a hand beneath the sweater and move it over his skin, idly, remembering, pointing with the other hand toward the swimming pool and patio where there were yellow flowers and tables with yellow umbrellas." I suppose Rudolf Flesch of *The Art of Plain Talk* would have had Elmore Leonard say something like "He scratched his skin under his sweater," but the quality of the writing would have flown with the rest of the words.

In writing, the word "diction" refers to the choice of words, which is the activity of the writer as he is particularizing. The requirement is precision of meaning, *le mot juste,* exactly the right word. Here's an example from a recent newspaper story:

> Pickpockets board trains, wait until the exquisitely perfect last second and then step off. If anybody else does it, he's a cop.

The lazy writer's cliché would have been "Pickpockets wait until the last second." Instead, the journalist avoided the cliché and sharpened the meaning by calling it "the exquisitely perfect last second." His diction has brought a freshness to the piece.

Books of quality that make the nonfiction bestseller list and earn considerable sums for their authors almost always employ as much particularity as possible. They deserve study. An hour spent in the library just looking at opening pages of memorable recent nonfiction can be instructive. Here is the opening of the book that fared better than the other D-Day books commemorating the fiftieth anniversary of that event in 1994, *D-Day June 6, 1944: The Climactic Battle of World War II* by Stephen E. Ambrose:

> At 0016 hours, June 6 1944, the Horsa glider crash-landed alongside the Caen Canal, some fifty meters from the swing bridge crossing the canal. Lt. Den Brotheridge, leading the twenty-eight men of the first platoon, D Company, the Oxfordshire and Buckinghamshire Light Infantry Regiment, British 6th Airborne Division, worked his way out of the glider. He grabbed Sgt. Jack "Bill" Bailey, a section leader, and whispered in his ear, "Get your chaps moving." Bailey set off with his group to pitch grenades into the machine-gun pillbox known to be beside the bridge. Lieutenant Brotheridge gathered the remainder of his platoon, whispered "Come on, lads," and began running for the bridge. The German defenders of the bridge, about fifty strong, were not aware that the long-awaited invasion had just begun.

Note the particularity with which Ambrose engages the reader. Particularity is not only the essence of fine writing, it is sometimes rewarded by the gratitude of reviewers and readers, who can make bestsellers and classics of books whose authors pay attention to detail and the precise meaning of words.

A book can be said to be an accumulation of paragraphs. You work on one paragraph at a time. If you perfect a single paragraph, you have a model for a book. Such is the paragraph I'd like you to look at next. It's not by a famous author, it's by a student of mine, Linda Katmarian, who has yet to publish her first work. Observe how she uses particularity:

Weeds and the low-hanging branches of unpruned trees swooshed and thumped against the car while gravel popped loudly under the car's tires. As the car bumped along, a flock of startled blackbirds exploded out of the brush. For a moment they fluttered and swirled about like pieces of charred paper in the draft of a flame and then they were gone. Elizabeth blinked. The mind could play such tricks.

What's going on here? She's breaking rules. Adjectives and adverbs, which normally should be cut, are all over the place. They are used to wonderful effect because she uses the particular sound of words. The low-hanging branches *swooshed* and *thumped* against the car. Gravel *popped*. Startled blackbirds *exploded* out of the brush. They *fluttered* and *swirled*. We experience the road the car is on because the car *bumped along*. What a wonderful image—the birds fluttered and swirled about *like pieces of charred paper in the draft of a flame*. And it all comes together in the perception of the character: *Elizabeth blinked. The mind could play such tricks.*

Many published writers would like to have written a paragraph that good. That nearly perfect paragraph was achieved with a small amount of editing and revision. The value of writing that paragraph lay, first, in giving her proof that she could do it, and, second, in giving her a benchmark for rethinking and revising the rest of her book.

A good place to practice particularizing is in letters to friends. Once upon a time, letters were an art form. Today, many people write top-of-the-head letters, full of generalizations and clichés. Many of us think of clichés as something we learned all about in school. The fact is that some of the best-educated writers fall back on clichés both in their speech and work much more often than they realize. For a fiction writer, learning to avoid them and finding those that slip in are important steps toward learning one of the most important aspects of original creative work: examining each word for its precise meaning and the likely effect of every group of words on the emotions of the reader.

For a writer, top-of-the-head writing, even letter writing, is dangerous because the habit could carry over into your work. If you work at particularizing in all of your personal correspondence, the recipients will enjoy what you write much more—and you will be practicing what you need to perfect to get your books published and to build an audience for your writings.

* * *

You'll remember my saying that commercial fiction, too, can benefit from particularity. If you'd like to have some fun putting your knowledge of particularity to the test, you'll need pen and paper or have your word processor turned on. Here are the first two paragraphs of a novel I will ask you to improve:

> At half-past six on a Friday evening in January, Lincoln International Airport, Illinois, was functioning, though with difficulty.
>
> The airport was reeling—as was the entire midwestern United States—from the meanest, roughest winter storm in half a dozen years. The storm had lasted three days. Now, like pustules on a battered, weakened body, trouble spots were erupting steadily.

That opening lacks particularity. "Meanest, roughest," and "trouble spots" are generalizations. The simile "like pustules on a battered, weakened body" is an inaccurate analogy, and is off-putting in the opening paragraphs of a book. Given the generality of a long-lasting snowstorm and your likely experience of airports, how would you revise those two paragraphs to give the opening of the novel particularity? Feel free to change or discard as much as you like. Your revision can be shorter or longer. Remember what John Gardner said: "Detail is the lifeblood of fiction." Use actions if possible. If people are in your opening, have them talk or think in particulars. Make locale, objects, and people distinctive and visible. Use other senses if appropriate. And make it ominous if you can. Stop when you're pretty sure you've improved the opening.

If you like your version better than the author's original, I have a surprise for you. You have just revised the opening of one of the biggest bestsellers of our time, *Airport* by Arthur Hailey.

I tried my hand at a more particularized version of Arthur Hailey's opening based on the author's own facts, scattered in the first three pages of the book. Note how particularizing and introducing a character help increase the tension of that opening paragraph:

> Runway three zero at Lincoln International was out of service, blocked by an Aereo-Mexican 707, its wheels mired in waterlogged ground near the runway's edge. Incoming traffic from Minneapolis, Cleveland, Kansas City, Indianapolis, and Denver

was stacked up overhead, some low on gas. On the ground, the wings of forty planes chafing to take off were icing up.

At the Snow Control Desk high in the glass-walled control tower, Mel Bakersfield, the airport's general manager, drummed his fingers on the glass and peered into the darkness, as if he could will United's Flight 111 from Los Angeles to appear. The plane was due at half-past four. It was now half-past six.

30

Similes and Metaphors

Similes and metaphors are the wonders of writing, and like all wonderful things carry a price. If figures of speech are overdone, they backfire. For instance, here's Martin Cruz Smith in his bestseller *Polar Star* straining to get a metaphor and a simile into two successive sentences:

> In the glare of the lamp, Volovoi's crew cut was a crown of radiant spikes. Of course, Karp, who was doing all the heavy labor, perspired like Vulcan at the forge.

What we see is not Volovoi's crew cut or Karp's perspiration but the author laboring to provide comparisons unsuccessfully. At one point, he stages a fight, and hero Arkady gets shoved into a bookcase, which inspires this simile:

> Paperbacks fluttered out like birds.

I'll bet. The simile is imprecise. Smith can't restrain himself. Here he goes again:

> Her black eyes balanced anxiously on enormous cheekbones.

When read aloud, the vision of black eyes balancing on cheekbones always draws a laugh. That's not a simile or metaphor, just plain overwriting. Which leads me to the principal advice I have for writers striving for color. Try, fly, experiment, but if it shows strain, if it isn't accurate, cut it.

Inaccurate similes and metaphors have the effect of deflecting the reader's attention from the story to the words on the page. Yet when carried off, especially when a simile is original and a metaphor sings, there is no greater glory in the practice of words.

In school we learned that a simile is a comparison of two unlike things, usually joined by the words "like" or "as." Perhaps the "unlike" throws off writers. What is meant is that the writer shows by simile the similarity of two things that were previously not connected:

> *Simile:* She sprang up like a jack-in-the-box when the doorbell rang.

We identify a jack-in-the-box popping up with suddenness, but if it said "She sprang up suddenly," we'd lose the savor of the comparison.

In a metaphor, a word or phrase is applied to something that is figuratively rather than literally similar. This figure of speech results when words or phrases are brought together that do not ordinarily belong together, yet by their proximity convey a fresh meaning:

> *Metaphor:* His bicycle had wings.

The bicycle was going so fast it seemed like a bird in flight or it was pedaled with élan as if it were airborne.

As we've seen earlier, some of the best novel titles are metaphors. *The Heart Is a Lonely Hunter.* We easily recognize the truth of such analogies.

In commercial fiction, the author often uses top-of-the-head similes and metaphors:

> *Simile:* He felt like a million dollars.

> *Metaphor:* It was food for thought.

Those examples are clichés, tired from overuse. Most good writing is characterized by a careful use of precise and sometimes original similes and metaphors:

> *Simile:* He felt as if he were a teenager for whom illness and death were abstractions.

Metaphor: The thought hovered over him, waiting for his permission to descend.

One of the hazards is, of course, the mixed metaphor, in which two or more unrelated metaphors are unsuccessfully combined:

He was dog tired but still feeling his oats.

Nanci Kincaid knows how to pick the right metaphor for her barefoot youngsters:

"Melvina's wild boys were all just barefoot as the day is long. Not wearing shirts, most of them. Just raggedy shorts and *bulletproof* feet . . ."

"Bulletproof feet" is a striking metaphor, the boys walking around in bare feet as if nothing on the ground could harm them.

My students know that I am fond of quoting similes and metaphors from one of John Cheever's best stories, "The Country Husband." The first is an extravagant simile:

The living room was spacious and divided like Gaul into three parts.

The next simile is both accurate and original:

Francis limited herself to two week-night parties, putting a flexible interpretation on Friday, and rode through the weekend like a dory in a gale.

Cheever uses metaphor to set a mood:

The sky was overcast, and poured down onto the dirt crossroads a very discouraging light.

Metaphors can enhance nonfiction also. Witness:

In some cases, generally around public buildings like the White House and State Department, the protective cordon was Saran-Wrap tight.

One of my favorite metaphors was spoken by Clive James in his television series *Fame*.

Hirohito was a 15 watt bulb.

That metaphor is worth examining. It's a long stretch from the Emperor of Japan to a light bulb, but it sure makes its point instantly.

I've suggested that you check your manuscript for similes and metaphors that strain too much. I'll add to that. In examining your work, can you find spots of "bare bones" writing that could be improved by a simile or metaphor that you hadn't thought of when you were getting your early draft onto paper?

31

Increasing the Effect on the Reader Through Resonance

R*esonance* is a term borrowed from the world of music, where it means a prolonged response attributable to vibration. In writing it has come to mean an aura of significance beyond the components of a story. Resonance can come from biblical associations. "Call me Ishmael" instantly reverberates at the opening of *Moby Dick*. In this chapter I show the many ways in which resonance can be produced—by names, by reference to religious sources, by invoking life and death, by a bold conclusion, by hyperbole, by naming the parts of a book, by the use of aphorisms and epigraphs, and ideally from the writing itself, by the writer's skillful use of similes and metaphors. Examples are drawn from important twentieth-century writers of both nonfiction and fiction.

Writers who recognize resonance when they encounter it sometimes still have difficulty in providing reverberations in their own work. Help is on the way. Let's examine the ways of producing resonance through their sources.

We have seen how the opening words of *Moby Dick,* "Call me Ishmael," have instant resonance because of the biblical associations of Ishmael. The same would be true of other memorable names from the Bible, whether used for characters or in appropriate phrases.

Some commercial fiction has derived resonance from the use of public or historical characters. Put an Eisenhower or a Kennedy into a story, and it resonates, especially if he appears fleetingly. I say "fleetingly" because most writers who try to reproduce historical characters at length, including their dialogue, usually fail. It's an area where a near miss is like taking just one misstep off a cliff's edge. Jack Higgins's career zoomed when he began using historical characters briefly in his thrillers.

By Referring to other religious sources. Evan Hunter, who writes also under the name of Ed McBain, is a superb craftsman. His novel *Vespers* draws some resonance from its title, but I would urge you to read at least the first four and a half pages of that book to see how liturgy lends stunning resonance to a scene that involves a killing.

By Invoking death. In T. Correghessan Boyle's 1987 novel *World's End* the author lends importance to a day by the use of a metaphor drawing on the possibility of the death of the earth:

> The day was typical of April in the vale of the Hudson—raw and drizzling, the earth exhaling vapor as if it were breathing its last.

In the last of his Rabbit Angstrom books, *Rabbit at Rest,* John Updike invokes his protagonist's death at the outset:

> Standing amid the tan, excited post-Christmas crowd at the Southwest Florida Regional Airport, Rabbit Angstrom has a funny sudden feeling that what he has come to meet, what's floating in unseen about to land, is not his son Nelson and daughter-in-law Pru and their two children but something more ominous and intimately his: his own death, shaped vaguely like an airplane.

By a bold conclusion. To see how V. S. Naipaul, one of the outstanding writers in the English language in our time, uses a bold philosophical statement to lend resonance to the opening of his novel *A Bend in the River*, let us look at the second sentence first:

> Nazruddin, who had sold me the shop cheap, didn't think I would have it easy when I took over.

No resonance. But that sentence is preceded by this one:

> The world is what it is; men who are nothing, who allow themselves to become nothing, have no place in it.

That first sentence lends resonance to the sentence and paragraphs that follow, perhaps to the book as a whole.

By Invoking a setting that has greatly influenced the life of a person. Some writers of biography will describe the subject's birthplace in detail, but miss an opportunity for resonance. Bertram Wolfe begins his biography *The Fabulous Life of Diego Rivera* with a setting that goes a long way toward explaining a source of Rivera's work:

> Guanajuato is flooded with light. The sun beats down with brilliant intensity upon its flat-roofed houses, fills with purple darkness their windows and doorways, gives bulk to solid forms, draws clean the line that separates surrounding hills from light-drenched sky. The valley in which the city dozes is seven thousand feet above the sea. Narrow cobblestone streets circle through the old center, then begin to climb into the hills. At the outskirts trees become discouraged; ridges rise bare and brown into a sky deep, remote, free from haze, standing out sharp against the light-filled emptiness of space.
>
> He whose eyes have been nourished on these clear forms, solid volumes, and light-filled space will never be altogether at home in the pale yellow sunlight and soft outlines of Paris treetops and towers, where the light is diffused by haze that forever hints of rain. A boy born here may get lost for a while in the Paris fashions of his day and experiment inadequately with fugitive flecks of light and blurring washes of haze in which outlines waver, planes merge, and objects lose their volume; but he can never really find himself as a painter until he has rediscovered the strongly defined forms, pure colors, clear atmosphere, and omnipresent flood of light that gives solidity to all the objects it illumines without seeming itself to appear upon the scene at all.

You can imagine how I felt editing line by line a writer who used resonance to give the reader pleasure and instruction simultaneously the way Wolfe does.

By Hyperbole. A hyperbole is, of course, an exaggeration that is not meant to be taken literally. For the novelist, it presents an opportunity to lend resonance to what might otherwise seem ordinary. Here is Rebecca West's opening of *The Fountain Overflows*:

> There was such a long pause that I wondered whether my Mamma and my Papa were ever going to speak to each other again.

By the end of the first paragraph, Papa is apologizing to Mamma, but the perception by the child narrator of a pause that seems terminal has magnified the importance of the moment of silence. For children, a pin drop of tension between parents can resonate like a thunderstorm.

By Naming the parts of a book. Omens are important in seeding suspense. The prolific British novelist Francis King lists five parts for his novel *Act of Darkness.* The first is titled simply "Omens." It lends a touch of resonance even before the reader encounters the first sentence.

A greater value can be derived from naming chapters in nonfiction. Orville Schell's 1994 book on China, *Mandate of Heaven,* has some chapter titles that invoke resonance twice, in the table of contents, and at the heads of chapters:

"A Hundred Flowers Fade" evokes its familiar opposite, A Hundred Flowers Bloom.

"The Graying of Chinese Culture" derives its effect through a metaphor that resonates.

"Shanghai on Commercial Fire" also uses metaphor to resonate.

By the thoughts and speech of a character. In *The Blue Afternoon,* a remarkable and highly praised novel by William Boyd, an early section is narrated by a character named Kay Fischer, an architect. She speaks in the first person. At one point, she says:

In architecture, as in art, the more you reduce, the more exacting your standards must be. The more you strip down and eliminate, the greater the pressure, the import, on what remains. If a room is only to have one door and one window, then those two openings must conform *exactly* to the volume of space contained between the four walls, the floor and the ceiling.

My aesthetic mentor, my inspiration, in all this was the German architect Oscar Kranewitter (1891–1929). He was a friend of Gropius and like him was heavily influenced by the austere ideologies of Johannes Itten.

The reader absolutely believes that this narrator, Kay Fischer, is an architect. She is, of course, an invention of the author. Her thoughts about architecture provide the resonance that confirms her reality.

Many years ago I invented a character called Dr. Gunther Koch, a foreign-born psychiatrist. In *The Magician* I had him assert his theory of the three categories of people, those who set their own goals, those who are followers content to obey instructions, and those who burn with frustration because they refuse to follow, can't lead, and don't know what they want. When the book first appeared, I heard from psychiatrists who asked to be referred to the professional literature in which I had found that theory. I hadn't found it. I invented Dr. Koch's theory as resonance to authenticate Dr. Koch and his profession. In commercial fiction today, technobabble is used in a similar way. One of my students, a noted inventor, confirms that what writers do in these instances is the same as what inventors do, though the writer's inventions only need to seem to work.

By the use of Aphorisms. I can't recommend aphorisms as a technique for everyone, though my penchant for their creation has given me much pleasure. I use aphorisms in my characters' dialogue. Here are a few examples from *The Best Revenge* as spoken by Louie, a character who is dead when the book begins, which hasn't stopped him from rendering advice:

> "Of course the Bible was written by sinners. How else would they know?"

> "Experience is what enables you to have a guilty conscience when you do something you know is wrong because you've done it before."

> "If you think something is a coincidence you don't know how God works. Pay attention, He doesn't have time to give you private lessons."

> "The best way to move is like a duck, calm on the surface, paddling like hell underneath."

> "Save your breath. It's the Devil who negotiates. God never made a deal with nobody."

There are two points to remember about the use of aphorisms: If they are in the author's voice, the point of view has to be either the third-person or the omniscient author's point of view, not the first-person point of view of a character. If they are in a character's dialogue, as in the case of Louie, you had better be sure the character you've created is the kind who could and would spout aphorisms on occasion.

By the use of Epigraphs. While aphorisms are your own, epigraphs can be other people's aphorisms and thoughts that lend a touch of resonance to your work. An appropriate epigraph can convey the larger import of a novel, without the novel itself becoming didactic. For instance, in *The Magician* I used two epigraphs, one short, one long, both about the true subject matter of the novelist, human nature, and designed to lend resonance to the story even before it begins.

The sources for epigraphs are many. There are quite a few collections of quotations on the market, with *Familiar Quotations* by John Bartlett, now updated by Justin Kaplan, the best known. There are also quotation collections available in software. If you haven't used the collections in book form previously, I would suggest a trip to your local library. Browse through Bartlett and any others they might have on hand. If you take to the experience, you might invest in buying a book of quotations. I've found that browsing for possible epigraphs can sometimes provide additional reward in the paths it opens in a work-in-progress.

Occasionally a book will seem to be buying resonance insurance. William Styron, an admirable novelist, prefaces *The Confessions of Nat Turner* with:

1. An "Author's Note" in which Styron briefly relates the historical background for his novel.

2. A three-page preface to a public document, a pamphlet published in Richmond in 1832, with the same title as Styron's novel.

3. A part title, "Judgment Day."

4. A five-line epigraph.

An excess of preliminaries might be interpreted as defensive. Don't overdo it.

The ideal resonance comes from the writing itself. Brooklyn-born Bertram D. Wolfe, whose biography of Diego Rivera was quoted from earlier, was a master of language who never wrote a word of fiction, but I have on occasion shown exemplary passages of his work to novelists for their instructive value. Here is how Wolfe began his masterpiece, *Three Who Made a Revolution*:

> The great Eurasian Plain opposes few obstacles to frost and wind and drought, to migrant hordes and marching armies. In earlier centuries the plain was dominated by vast Asiatic empires, Iranian, Turkish, Mongolian. As the last of these melted away, Moscovy expanded to take their place, expanded steadily through several centuries until it became the largest continuous land empire in the world. Like the tide over limitless flats, it spread with elemental force over an endless stretch of forest and steppe, sparsely settled

by backward and nomadic peoples. Wherever it met resistance, it would pause as the tide does to gather head, then resume its inexorable advance. Only at the distant margins does the plateau end in great mountain barriers: the snowy summits of the Caucasus; the Pamirs, roof of the world—where two of our three protagonists have peaks named in their honor, thrusting up over four miles each into the sky; the Altai, Sayan and Stanovoi mountains forming China's natural wall. How could a people not be great and not aspire to greatness, whose horizon was an unlimited as this Eurasian Plain?

The visual sweep introduces a work of history with resonance that stems from the skill of the writing. Perhaps that is too much for a beginner to hope for, though I have read the work of relative beginners whose work already embodies the magic of resonance.

VI

Revision

32

Triage: A Better Way of Revising Fiction

The biggest difference between a writer and a would-be writer is their attitude toward rewriting. The writer, professional or not, looks forward to the *opportunity* of excising words, sentences, paragraphs, chapters that do not work and to improving those that do. Many a would-be writer thinks whatever he puts down on paper is by that act somehow indelible.

Hemingway said it succinctly: "First drafts are shit." Judith Applebaum quotes Hemingway as saying to an interviewer, "I rewrote the ending of *A Farewell to Arms* thirty-nine times before I was satisfied." Asked what stumped him, Hemingway said, "Getting the words right."

Of the most successful authors I have worked with, I can think of only one who fiercely resisted revising—for the first thirty minutes of each day that we worked together. Unwillingness to revise usually signals an amateur.

A. B. Guthrie, Jr., tells the story of a beginner at writing who asked him to criticize his manuscript. The work showed so much promise, was so close to being publishable, that Guthrie prepared a long list of suggested improvements. Three months later, he happened to meet the writer and asked how the manuscript was coming. "Oh that," the man said. "I haven't had time for it. I'm almost finished with a new novel." Guthrie reported that none of the man's work has ever seen print.

It is natural to resist rewriting. Every writer wants to be done with it, to cry, "Finished!" If you set a limit on how much rewriting you will do, you are merely devising an artificial barrier between your work and success. I have never encountered a writer who achieved a fully perfected manuscript in a first draft. In fact, the majority of published writers I have known write first drafts that are riddled with craft errors and embarrassingly bad writing compared to the version that finally sees print. They know that writing is truly rewriting.

Even some of the most experienced authors are not aware of a better way of revising than repeatedly starting at page one and going through to the end. That front-to-back process means the writer is rereading his book as he looks for places in need of revision, a word or two here, a paragraph there, a section that needs relocation, an unmotivated action, dialogue that isn't quite in character, a section that sags. After this process, the writer, having gone through his entire book, is likely to grow "cold" on his manuscript, particularly if he soon has to read it all again. He will have disabled himself from viewing the manuscript again objectively.

I call my method of revision "triage" after the system for treating battlefield casualties to provide maximum benefit with limited facilities. Doctors and nurses sort incoming casualties quickly to give priority to those whose lives can be saved by prompt medical treatment as against those who are likely to die in any case and those who will get better even if not treated. In the conventional method of revision, going from first page to last, the writer is dealing with trivial corrections one moment, the next moment coming up against a major problem, then more small matters, in a random process. The problem with that kind of tunnel revision is that the fixing of important problems may necessitate changes earlier in the manuscript, which requires clumsy backtracking; if new material is written, it will be in first draft and have to be looked at again, which means revising the rewriting on yet another front-to-back go-through. That procedure is like treating casualties on a first-come, first-served basis without regard to priorities.

What follows is a guide to the triage method of revision, which gives priority to those matters that are the principal causes of rejection by editors.

The steps I am about to propose are not written in stone. Their order can be changed, as long as the principle is maintained: major matters are attended to first.

Even if you use a computer, I recommend that you have a hard copy of your manuscript to consult for the simple reason that seeing what you wrote on paper will give you a fresh impression of your work. If you follow the steps I am about to suggest, reprint the appropriate section after making any major changes so that you are working with clean copy when you finally go through the manuscript from beginning to end. It is easy to be distracted by your own editorial changes.

* * *

The first step is to make a judgment about your main characters. Do you find yourself thinking about them in situations that are not in your book? If so, good! That means your characters are alive in your mind and should come alive in the minds of your audience. If you can't think of an important character in situations away from the story, that character may need more work. Character problems should be dealt with before beginning a general revision. I am about to ask you some questions about your protagonist that will help you decide whether or not that character needs work.

- What is it about your character that you like especially? Does that happen to be also a trait of yours? If it is, that may be a symptom of the autobiography trap, creating a character that is too like yourself, which hurts the distance that every author needs from his creations. One way to ameliorate the problem is to give the character a distinctive trait—positive or negative—that you are absolutely sure you don't have.
- If you were about to take your only vacation of the year, how would you feel if your character were going along? You would probably be seeing your character at mealtime and in between, day in and day out for a week or two. Honestly now, would you look forward to that? You are asking your reader to spend a good number of hours with that character. You may need to add some sparkle to your character, some interesting eccentricity, perhaps a personality characteristic that will make his company more enjoyable.
- How well do you understand your character? One way to find out is to imagine that you have just won a lottery jackpot of two million dollars. Your character doesn't know you've been playing Lotto, but he is likely to hear about it on the news. People have mixed feelings about the sudden success of friends. Would it be better for you to tell your character the news yourself? How is your character likely to take the news about your new wealth? Would any of his reactions be useful in making him more interesting?

This method of revision makes certain that you have humanized your characters by giving them the kind of thoughts—not always "nice" thoughts—that people have in life. The danger is portraying a person that nobody wants to spend time with.

I have a confession to make. When I finished the first draft of *The Magician*, a highly regarded editor I showed it to said the sixteen-year-old protagonist was such a nice, dull, uninteresting kid that he almost didn't exist.

After all that work? My confidence shattered like a broken teacup. However, I pulled myself together and went back to work. I ended up giving Ed Japhet a more rounded personality at the outset by his denying his father a chance to see him perform at the high school dance. The reader's sympathies are with the father. He wants to see his son perform. The son denies that to him. Not nice, but it helped to make the son credible. Later in the book, Ed refuses to cooperate with the district attorney when Ed's assailant is being prosecuted; he doesn't want to have anything to do with the justice system. He had views, convictions, and was no longer a dull sixteen-year-old. I owe the long-lasting success of *The Magician* in many languages to the revision of its central character. Do take a look at yours.

Does your main character change in the course of your novel? In the climactic scene of *The Magician*, Ed gives evidence of a change in himself, a change so shocking that one editor, reading the manuscript for the first time, actually screamed, causing others to rush to her office thinking there had been an accident. In a story the length of a novel, it is essential that the protagonist undergo change. If yours at present does not, it isn't too late.

The next step in revision is to take a hard look at your villain or antagonist. Note that I use the singular—"villain" or "antagonist." If you have more than one, you may be diffusing the impact of the character's villainy by spreading it. Is your antagonist morally bad, not just badly behaved? Does your antagonist enjoy doing wrong to people? Is your character not just mischievous but malicious? What I'm getting at is the degree of villainy. Is your character just badly behaved or a truly evil person? The choice, of course, is yours. But readers find morally villainous characters more interesting.

Now let's swing the other way. Does your villain have something that charms or entices people? The mustachioed antagonists of yesteryear only provoke laughs today. If the villain isn't intriguing, interesting, lifelike, and believable, he may not be a worthy villain. No villain can attract victims unless he has charm, charisma, position, or wealth.

When I really like a villain of mine, I find that critics and readers like him, too. I liked one of my villains so much, he overshadowed the protagonist, and I spent a long time rewriting the hero to bring him up to the stature of the villain!

If you're having difficulty making your villain charming or interesting, try seeing him through the eyes of someone who loves him. Or at least cares a lot about him. The villain will be a more effective adversary if he has been humanized.

The trap I spoke of earlier applies to villains, too. It is an easy temptation for the writer, consciously or not, to use an enemy as a model for a villain in a story. The writer may lack sufficient distance from the character to write a villain who is both truly bad and at the same time interesting and perhaps even charismatic and charming. Novels are not a place to get even. Think of yourself as in the business of creating characters who are more interesting than the nasties you know in person.

The next step is to give some thought to your minor characters, who are often not minor if the credibility of a scene depends on believing their verisimilitude (lifelikeness). Just one special characteristic can make a difference. An easy way to help characterize minor players is to use one of the senses you may have neglected.

The next step is to be sure you have a credible conflict between your protagonist and the antagonist. Stories from time immemorial have consisted of people overcoming obstacles against high odds and strong adversaries. If you've followed a different course, your plot may not be strong enough to sustain the reader's interest. If your plot needs strengthening at any point, the guidance in Chapters 6, 7, and 8 will help.

The next step is to evaluate the scenes. What is the most memorable scene in your book? Don't go to your manuscript for clues. If you can't remember the scene, it isn't memorable! Then ask yourself what is the least memorable scene? You may have to browse through your manuscript until you find it. That's okay, just don't start reading word for word. That's what makes you grow cold on your book.

What in the scene you selected as most memorable made it work so well? What does that suggest about the least memorable scene? This comparison in itself may spark an idea for revision. Don't be disappointed if you can't think of a radical revision of your least memorable scene. The usual remedy is to cut it! If cutting it removes some piece of information the reader needs, find some other way of conveying that information in an existing scene.

Once you've revised or done away with your least memorable scene, you now have a *new* least memorable scene! You need to subject it to the same tough scrutiny. Would the book be stronger without it?

In dealing with many authors over the years, I found it desirable to set a standard. If any scene falls below that standard, out it goes. The process stops when the remaining scenes all seem to contribute strongly to the work as a whole.

Is it painful to cut a whole scene? Yes indeed. Why, then, should you do it? Because like a surgeon you are interested in preserving the body of the work by cutting out a part that's not working properly or that's causing harm to the body as a whole. What if you are blind to its faults and can't find a weak scene? Put the manuscript aside for a week, a month, or longer (the longer the better), then look again. The weakest scene will jump out at you, staring you straight in the eye until you decide whether to let it live or die.

Once you've dealt with scenes that weaken your manuscript, the next step is to test motivation. First, from memory, jot down what you believe to be the three most important actions in your novel. Is each action motivated in a way that you would accept if this story were told by somebody else? The credibility of your work depends on the three main actions being motivated to your satisfaction. If you find it difficult and need help, remember that motivation has to be either provoked by circumstance or planted ahead of time. Motivation can usually be established by planting it ahead of the scene in which the action takes place.

Chekhov said that if someone has a gun in the first act, the audience knows that the gun must go off in the third act. Among playwrights that's known as the obligatory scene. If a gun is seen in the hands of someone who is not known to carry a gun and then almost immediately fired, it will seem as if the author's heavy hand is at work. If the gun is planted much earlier, the use of it becomes almost inevitable. In fact much suspense can be derived from its *not* being used when the audience thinks it will be.

The news too often brings us cases of serial or mass killings that seem to have no reason behind them. Then follow-up stories deal with the investigation of the backgrounds of killer and killed because *we want reasons for actions*, not just to prosecute the killer but to understand human behavior, especially when it is not like ours.

The motivation of important deeds is not an option but a necessity. Writers of so-called commercial fiction often rely on coincidence. They assume their readers suspend disbelief more readily than the readers of literary fiction. Motivating actions takes work, and using coincidence is much easier. But coincidence is the mark of transient works, and I have met few novelists who are satisfied to think of their work as merely temporary entertainment.

After you've dealt with the three main actions of the book, the next step is to review any other significant actions, ferreting out poor motivation and anything that might seem to happen just because the author wants it to. Is there any action in your manuscript that is not in keeping with the character? Is there any action that under examination sounds far-fetched? It might be fixed by planting a motive in a prior scene. Do this before undertaking a general revision so that you can judge the success of your revision as you read through from beginning to end.

Until testing motivation comes easily, I suggest rereading Chapter 15. That will help anchor in your mind the means of establishing credibility. The examples in that chapter will help remind you that motivation can often be derived from something simple.

You are almost ready to undertake a general revision of the entire manuscript. Take the first page and put the rest aside out of sight. Next do something else. Anything else. Take a walk. Take a drive. Play tennis or golf. Visit a neighbor. Make a cup of coffee. Whatever you do, try not to think about your manuscript. Then come back and make a new title page that looks like this:

Your Present Title

by
[Insert the Name of a Contemporary Author You Admire]

Now read the first page as if it were the other author's manuscript. After reading the first page, would you go on to the next page?

If there isn't a compelling reason to go to page two, it usually means that you haven't sparked the reader's curiosity. If that's the case, you need to go back to Chapter 2 of this book and see if you can use its guidelines to improve your opening.

Of course, if your first page as presently written compels you to read on, congratulations! You are ready to begin the general revision of your manuscript that I've kept you from by suggesting all of these other steps first.

* * *

Embarking on a general revision calls for starting on page one and working through the manuscript to the end, reading as a reader and an editor, not as a writer. If you're not used to the process, and if the fun we had with the title page didn't give you enough distance, try to think of the manuscript this way: It was recommended to you by a friend, but you doubt the friend's judgment. He or she has previously recommended books you found wanting. Maybe this manuscript will turn out to be the same. You are going to read it critically, like a tough editor.

Before you begin, I want to caution you not to disimprove what is there. *If in doubt about a change, don't make the change.* Instead, make a note to yourself for later consideration. I find that when I look at such notes days or weeks later, many of those questionable ideas for revision get discarded.

Your first objective in a general revision is to tighten the manuscript. I know of only one novelist who writes tight first drafts that need expanding in revision. The others need cutting, lots of it. It is perfectly normal to overwrite in first drafts. The test of a writer's skill is in recognizing on later reading what can be eliminated, and then having the guts to do the cutting.

One of the students in my advanced fiction seminar had a manuscript acceptable to his agent but not to him. He knew it was too long. He took advantage of his computer. Every time he came to a paragraph he wasn't sure contributed to the book, he marked it and with a block move transferred it to the end, after the last page. When he finished he found that he had transferred dozens of paragraphs and that only one or two, in modified form, deserved a place in the text. It's a useful strategy. I've tried it and it works.

Your second objective is to watch out for the between-the-scenes material, especially the offstage recounting of actions not seen. Try to eliminate as many of these as you can, or make them active and interesting in themselves. If this needs clarification, reread Chapter 3.

If you're not used to extensive revision, you may feel as if you're trying to do too many things at once. I want to assure you that over time you will be able to do it. In the meantime, do as many as you can and then go back over the manuscript for the others. Remember, I am trying to keep you from growing "cold" by keeping down the number of your reviews of your work.

In your general revision, cut words, phrases, sentences, or paragraphs, pages, or whole scenes that seem not absolutely necessary. Watch for places where your own attention flags. That's usually a sign that something needs to be revised or cut.

If your sentences are all approximately the same length, the effect will be monotonous. Vary the length of sentences. Ideally, follow an especially long sentence with a short, even abrupt sentence. Don't do this all the time. A pattern of short-long-short-long can get almost as monotonous as all long or all short sentences. One of my students writes naturally in a mellifluous cadence. It's her greatest fault. An unbroken mellifluous cadence, lovely for a few sentences, if kept up will put a reader to sleep.

Unless you are consciously trying to slow things down between fast-moving scenes, be relentless in moving the story forward. If you find it bogging down at any point, it could be for many reasons: perhaps too slow a pace, not enough happening. If you don't see an immediate fix, mark the place in the margin and write down what you think might be wrong. Come back to those places later.

If you catch the author talking at any point, or a mix of points of view, mark the section so that you can return to Chapter 13 for guidance.

Are your characters under stress from time to time? Does the stress increase? Keep reminding yourself that fiction deals with the most stressful moments of the characters' lives.

As you go through, cut every unessential adjective and adverb. Cut "very." Cut "poor" for everything but poverty. Make every word count.

If you've said the same thing twice in different words, pick the better one and cut the other. If you find yourself using the same uncommon word twice within a few pages, use your thesaurus to pick a synonym. And in your read-through, mark every cliché for excision.

One of the most common improvements I find in line-editing a writer's manuscript is changing the order of words, phrases, or independent clauses in a sentence. The simplest instance is where you put the identification of who is speaking. Do you write,

George said, "They treating you okay?"

Or:

"They treating you okay?" George said.

If there is any chance that the reader won't know who is speaking at that point, the "George said" should come first. If it is clear who is speaking, "George said" can follow what he says or be omitted.

In my own work, I make transpositions hundreds of times in a book-length manuscript. Sometimes it is to let the emphasis of a sentence fall in a different place. Here's an unedited sentence:

> Josephine Japhet of course knew why her son was a reader in a universe of listeners to rock music.

That puts the emphasis on rock music. I transposed the phrase "her son was a reader" to the end of the sentence, since that was where I wanted the emphasis to fall:

> Josephine Japhet of course knew why, in a universe of listeners to rock music, her son was a reader.

In another scene, Ed Japhet is in school, outside the room where his father has just finished teaching and is trying to get away from a student pestering him with questions after class. Ed shows his impatience this way:

> Your old man teaching in your school was bad enough. Depending on him for a ride home was the pits. *Come on, Dad, move it.*

The thought was improved by transposing the last of the three sentences to the beginning of the paragraph, so that it read:

> *Come on, Dad, move it.* Your old man teaching in your school was bad enough. Depending on him for a ride home was the pits.

After a fight, a boy is lying in the snow, badly hurt. See if you can spot the glitch in this sentence:

> The other cop slid out of the car, knelt beside Urek, fingers feeling for a pulse in the neck.

Because readers will undoubtedly have had experience with a pulse being taken at the wrist, they may suppose that immediately on reading the word "pulse." Immediately, they read "in the neck" and have to change their first view. That kind of glitch can momentarily disturb the reading experience. To avoid it, I simply transposed a few words:

The other cop slid out of the car, knelt beside Urek, fingers feeling the neck for a pulse.

It pays to transpose sentences for clarity. In the following example, a woman who is not always articulate, on the phone to a lawyer expresses her concern about what will happen to her if her husband is convicted:

"If Paul goes to jail, I won't have anywhere. I can't pay the mortgage on my own. He listens to you. Please come over."

In my opinion, the phrase "I won't have anywhere" is not immediately comprehensible in its present location. Transposed, it works well:

"If Paul goes to jail, I can't pay the mortgage on my own. I won't have anywhere. He listens to you. Please come over."

"Purple prose" means writing that is overblown. It turns off editors and readers almost immediately. Here are some dreadful examples of purple prose:

The cry of a soul in torment, swept by a tide of anger and outrage.

Terror plucked at her taut nerves.

Jagged laughter tore at her throat.

Ghastly red spatterings, viscous red-streaked gobbets of his brains.

Fierce rending triumph.

Enough? Nobody writes that way? These are all from the bestseller *Scarlett*, Alexandra Ripley's sequel to *Gone With the Wind*.

A phrase need not be "purple" or "flowery" to be conspicuous, by which I mean that every time you pass it, it jumps off the page and pleases you. When you "love" certain images or sentences, they are frequently so conspicuous as to interfere with the story. If they are, save them in a special box that you'll look into five years from now, and thank me for having asked you to remove them from your manuscript, though it may have hurt at the time.

Root out sentimentality, which is an excess of response to a stimulus. It makes writing "flowery." Your job is to stimulate emotions in the reader. An excessive response turns off the reader, just as it does people in life:

"Why Fred, I am so excited to see you I just can't bear it."

That kind of gushing is just as incredible in fiction as it is in life. *Underplay* to evoke emotion in the reader:

I looked at her eyes. They were dry.

Given the right context, that would evoke more emotion than something overblown like "She was ready to cry her heart out."

As you read through, look for imprecision, when the word you used is not exactly the word you needed. Consult a dictionary. Consult a thesaurus.

Until you are in the habit of making sure that there is something visual on every page, while reviewing the draft put a small V in the lower right corner of every page that has something visual on it. This provides a discipline as you develop the experience of reading with an editor's eye. If a page has nothing visual, mark NV and return to it later to introduce a visual element. If you have two or more consecutive pages with nothing visual, you may have a larger problem that needs remedying, perhaps too much narrative summary where an immediate scene is needed.

In dialogue sequences, if your characters usually speak in complete sentences, fix it so they don't. Have you used enough dialogue? Remember that one of the virtues of dialogue is that it makes scenes visible. If your dialogue sufficiently confrontational? If any dialogue runs longer than three sentences, break it up with an interjection from another character or a thought or action. Check to see that responses in dialogue are oblique, at least from time to time. If any exchange of dialogue seems weak or wrong in comparison to other dialogue exchanges, mark it for later improvement or excision.

In your general revision, catch the places where a character "muttered," "screamed," and the like instead of "said." Substitute "he said" and "she said" for language that tells the reader how the lines are spoken. That's the dialogue's job.

Can you now see why I suggested you perform triage on major matters before your general read-through? If you are new to the process, you'll want to make a checklist of all the things I've suggested catching during general revision. If you find that you just can't do everything in one pass, save some things for a second pass later on. In time, if you do a good job of triage, you'll be able to handle most remaining matters in one reading.

Does that mean you're finished? You are never finished rewriting until you receive galley proofs. You will still make essential revisions, but professionals try to do all the revising they can *before* the book is set in type (the cost of "author's alterations" beyond a minimum is borne by the author). When you've completed triage and then a general revision, you still have work to do. You may want to ask yourself, if you were to bring a strong scene forward, would that provoke the reader's curiosity more than the scene that presently starts the book? Having revised the manuscript, all of it will be fresh in your mind, which will make it easier to identify a strong, curiosity-arousing scene that might be brought forward.

You might consider at this stage whether the ending of your book is a high point of satisfaction for the reader. If not, is there another scene or circumstance that might make a better ending?

After finishing your revision, let the manuscript lie fallow for several days or longer. Don't rush to show it to a friend or family member. Let it cool down. Go on with other work, then come back to the manuscript and read it with your changes. As you become more expert at revision, you will be a better judge of your work than laymen who love you and don't know anything about craft.

For your next read-through, work with a clean manuscript in which the changes you've made are not visible as changes. (One of the great advantages of working on a computer!) This time, as you read, watch for anything that momentarily makes you see words on the page and takes you out of experiencing the story. You are aiming for the reader's *total immersion.* You should be able to spot these flaws after you have made the kind of changes I've suggested.

If all this checking seems excessive, ask yourself would you fly in a plane in which the experienced pilot felt so cocksure that he didn't actually perform the checklist that makes flying safer for all of us?

If you're of a mind to ask, "Stein, do you do all this revision yourself?" I'll report that *The Best Revenge*, a novel of mine I've quoted many times in this book, was turned in to my publisher in its eleventh draft. It was accepted without a single change. Then, on my own recognizance, I did two more drafts.

33

Reprieve: Revising Nonfiction

How many times in the course of a lifetime do we wish we could relive some conversation or event, do it differently? Revision provides that opportunity. First drafts of nonfiction can be flawed in organization, quality control, interest, and language. Lucky for us writers, this is the one place in life where we get a reprieve.

Perhaps if we did get a second chance in life, we'd blunder right back in and muck things up again. That's what can happen in revision unless we have a plan of action. I will attempt to provide a plan here.

Attitude is important. If you review what you've written and exclaim, "Oh my God, this is awful!" you'll only dispirit yourself. The experienced writer knows his first draft will be flawed, that he will get a chance to employ his editorial skills in fixing it. During my decades of editing, I met only one professional writer who believed that his first drafts were graced with perfection. And who is to argue with a man's religion, as long as he takes his manuscript somewhere else?

Just as in revising fiction, the nonfiction writer is in danger of growing cold on his manuscript quickly if he starts revising at the top of page one and goes through paragraph by paragraph to the end. To avoid growing cold, I advocate fixing major things before starting on a page-by-page, front-to-back revision. This will confer two advantages. If you fix the larger problems first, you will in all likelihood make some first-draft infelicities in the new material that you will then catch on your subsequent page-by-page revision. In addition, by working on specific problems, you will not have grown cold on the manuscript when you tackle the read-through.

A good way to begin is to personify your subject matter in an incident involving an individual. Sometimes the germ of such an anecdote is buried elsewhere in the draft. If so, examine it to see if it has the potential of being made stronger than your present opening.

Also ask yourself if your opening is sufficiently visual to be seen by the reader. You may recall that in Chapter 3, "Welcome to the Twentieth Century," I explained the differences among the three main components of fiction—description, narrative summary, and immediate scene—and pointed out that understanding the differences could be of immediate help to a nonfiction writer also. Most important, the nonfiction writer who learns to use immediate scenes wherever he can will also find a dramatic improvement in the readability of his work. The ideal place for your first immediate scene is on page one.

Before you settle on a beginning, ask yourself if it provokes sufficient curiosity in the reader. How soon after your beginning will the reader comes upon the "engine" of your article or book, the place at which the reader decides not to stop reading?

If you are writing an article, does it make one point after another on a plateau, or does it build toward a climax? If it is a book, does the end of most chapters point toward the next?

Have you summarized material that would make interesting visual passages if you converted the summaries to events the reader could see? If there are summaries you cannot or don't want to convert to scenes, can you shorten them in order to avoid losing the reader's attention? If you want to "jump-cut," the reader will go along with you.

Have you created occasional suspenseful interest by raising a question and withholding the answer for a while? Can you recall any place where this might be done now?

Does your work have reverberations of other times or places, of important events or influential people? The most mundane subjects can be given a lift by the use of resonance. There are a number of reference books that go through history, period by period or year by year, giving you the highlights of the time, its influential people, and significant political and cultural events. Browsing through one of these books can sometimes provide you with a few relevant facts that will lend resonance to your work. You can refresh your recollection of other sources of resonance in Chapter 31.

Have you consciously tried to create stress for the reader, some delicious tension? Would it help to look at Chapter 10, on tension for fiction writers, to see if it sparks any ideas for tension in your work? Some of the suggestions can be adapted for nonfiction quite easily.

If you were the editor of your manuscript and it was written by someone else, what would you choose as the weakest part? Look at that section now and see if you can eliminate it. If you can't cut it entirely, can you condense it? Is there anything you can add to the beginning of that section that would arouse the reader's curiosity? Consider your most memorable passage. What makes it so good? Does that provide a clue as to what you might do with your weakest part?

Surprise: If you've cut or changed the weakest part, you have a new weakest part. In retrospect, do you know why it is weak? Can you improve it? Can you cut it and stitch together what comes immediately before and immediately after?

When you've considered those questions and fixed whatever needed fixing, it may be time for a focused reading, by which I mean a reading of your manuscript in which you read not as a reader but as a hunter for specific errors and omissions as if on assignment to do so. If you wrote the manuscript on computer, I suggest working with a clean hard copy of your manuscript. It will seem fresher to you, and faults you may not have noticed before will be suddenly apparent.

Is there something visible on every page? If you are reviewing what you wrote in hard copy, pencil a V in a lower corner of every page that has something visual, and on pages without a V, see if you can create something visual, even if it is a leaf falling from a tree.

Have you eliminated most adjectives and adverbs, and the unnecessary words we call flab? Go after them as an editor, not as the writer.

Cut every cliché you come across. Say it new or say it straight.

Can you spot any similes or metaphors that show signs of strain and should now be cut?

If you've never done this before, you may find it difficult to look for all these things at the same time. If so, you may need to check the following list every once in a while until you are used to the process:

- Add something visible.
- Cut most adjectives and adverbs.
- Cut clichés.
- Replace or cut similes and metaphors that don't work.

As you work along as an editor, do you see any places where the author might have padded the manuscript with unnecessary digressions, overly extensive patches of description, or anything else that strikes you as filler? You always strengthen text when you remove the padding.

As to the last, an anecdote. At a New York party long ago, a nonfiction writer whom I knew by reputation but had not met came up to me, well into his cups, and asked could he come see me with a manuscript he had kept secret from everyone. One hears things like that at parties. They seldom mature into appointments. This writer phoned for an appointment and showed up with a large scrapbook under his arm. What was the "secret" manuscript with which he had intrigued me?

The writer published regularly in a magazine that paid him a generous monthly advance against his articles. The advance, much like an account at a company store, was paid down at so much per published word. The scrapbook contained his articles in the magazine. In each he had bracketed in color the many sections of padding that he had added in order to produce more published words and thereby to decrease his indebtedness. He was now interested in publishing a book of his pieces minus the padding. For reasons lost to time, I no longer remember why this project did not proceed, but its lesson about padding remained in my mind, as I hope it now will in yours.

Now that you've fixed the larger problems and hunted and killed the smaller ones, take some time away from the manuscript and then read it as a reader, not an editor. But keep an editorial pencil handy, just in case.

VII

Where to Get Help

34

Where to Get Help

(British readers please see page 302)

BOOK DOCTORS

Some decades back if your work was talented and thought to be eventually publishable, your book could be bought and an editor assigned to work with you on any necessary revision. As bottom-line management took over most publishing houses, detailed and especially prolonged editing was viewed as not cost-effective, and agents were expected to submit manuscripts that were as final as possible. That change occasioned the development of a new profession, book doctors, mainly individuals who are experienced editors or writers or both who evaluate and work on manuscripts and bring the authors up to speed That help does not come cheap, but the hourly rates are a lot lower than, say, lawyers charge. Many book doctors charge by the assignment, whether it's an evaluation, a long memo of recommendations, or actual line-editing of an entire manuscript. Some book doctors advertise in *Writer's Digest*, some do not advertise anywhere. I can only refer writers to the small number of book doctors whose work I know. Readers of this book can obtain a list of them, with addresses and phone numbers, from the Internet by going to htp://www.writepro.com, then on the menu click on "Book Doctors."

DICTIONARIES

If you've come this far, you know that the quality of a written work is in large measure dependent on the precision with which words are used. The more words I learn, the more I use a dictionary. Over the years I have become increasingly impatient with writers for whom the approximate word will do. The serious writer is addicted to the precise meaning of words in his own work and admires *le mot juste* in the work of others. For him, the approximate word is never satisfactory, and he delights in the tools that enable him to be as precise as possible.

I suggest keeping at least two dictionaries handy while you work, a desk dictionary for convenience, and a larger dictionary on a stand or on top of a chest-high bookcase for easy turning of the pages. Page-turning ease is not a light matter. Many writers will use any excuse not to lift a heavy tome and riffle through its pages. (I refuse to use the two-volume Oxford unabridged dictionary I own because of the inconvenience of tracking its minuscule type with a magnifying glass.) I no longer need to resort to my Webster Unabridged because of the excellence of *The American Heritage Dictionary of the English Language*, which I now use more often than any other, not only for my writing but also to look up all the medical jargon physicians use to communicate with each other in reports that their victims are not supposed to see.

LITERARY AGENTS

An extensive listing of agents can be found in the *Literary Market Place*, the huge annual directory better known as the *LMP*, published by R.R. Bowker. *The Writer's Handbook*, edited by Sylvia K. Burack and published by The Writer, Inc., has a smaller listing. Several other paperback books on the market contain evaluative material on a number of literary agents, but some of the important agencies decline to be listed. A free copy of the brochure "How to Get a Literary Agent to Represent Your Work" by Sol Stein is available by sending a business-size (#10) stamped and self-addressed envelope to FREE AGENT BOOK-LET, The WritePro Corporation, 43 South Highland Avenue, Ossining, NY 10562.

SOFTWARE

While I have taught writers at universities on the coasts and in the Middle West of the United States, the advent of the computer and its almost universal use by writers have enabled me to clone myself in several computer programs. As a result, writers in thirty-eight countries are now able to plug me into an ear, as it were, while they write and revise their work. In these quasi-interactive programs, I function not only as teacher but also as editor, guiding the user step by step. Those programs, thanks to supportive reviews in over a hundred newspapers and magazines and to distribution by the Book-of-the-Month Club and the Literary Guild, have reached a great many writers I have not had the opportunity of meeting in person.

All the programs have a two-minute, automatic installation process, come with their own built-in word processor, and save everything you write automatically, so that you can concentrate on your writing and not on computing.

The first, an award-winning program called WritePro®, is a tutorial program to which I direct beginners, though it has been used success-fully by experienced and published writers, The author of some nineteen novels said in a review that he used the program to remind himself of all the things he didn't know he'd forgotten. I want to call your special attention to two things. You cannot get writer's block while using WritePro, a great help to beginners. Steve Bass, who is president of the Pasadena, California, IBM Users Group as well as a journalist who reviews software, wrote that his "absolute favorite" function was the Flab Editor™, a copyrighted computer software invention that enables the user to strengthen his writing by highlighting individual unnecessary words on a page under guidance, and with a keystroke make them dis-appear so the writer can see how much stronger the text is without them. The words can be brought back at will or deleted with a keystroke. The Flab Editor ™ is in WritePro's Lesson 5, but the technology is usable in all WritePro lessons.

You can obtain a free WritePro lesson by phoning 00 1-914-762-1255 9-4 eastern time weekdays, or by writing to the WritePro Corporation, 43 South Highland Avenue, Ossining NY 10562. They charge only the nominal shipping and handling cost. The lesson on disk, with the man-ual, is free if you tell them you own *Solutions for Writers*. Be sure to specify whether you want the DOS, Windows, or the Macintosh version. The people at the same number and address can also provide you with further information about the lessons. If you wish to purchase the lessons, tell the order taker you own this book and you will receive the highest available discount.

FictionMaster™, also selected by the Book-of-the-Month Club, enables writers to improve their characters, plot, and dialogue by trans-ferring chapters from their manuscripts to the program and editing them under my instruction. FictionMaster can also be used as an interactive tutorial on most of the subjects in this book; you master a technique by using it in your own work. Though FictionMaster is the most advanced program of its kind available anywhere and is used by published writers, it is designed so that a smart beginner can use it also. Phone 00 1-914-762-1255 or e-mail http://www.writeprony@aol.com and ask to receive all of the FictionMaster menus, which will give you a clear idea of the areas covered. They are free. Be sure to include a postal address.

FirstAid for Writers® also enables the user to transfer his own writing into the program, fix anything in need of fixing with my advice, and transfer it back out to his word processor. In addition to its four modules for fiction, FirstAid for Writers contains a complete module for nonfiction that is used by journalists and nonfiction book and article writers. You can obtain a free schematic map of the more than sixty subjects included in this program from the WritePro office.

AUDIOTAPES

An audiotape that writers find useful is "Dialogue for Writers." It contains the essence of the twelve-week course on dialogue that I gave at the University of California at Irvine.

Another audiotape, "What Every Author Should Know About Publishing", is based on my one-day crash course on "Publishing for Authors" given at the University of California.

If you identify yourself as a reader of this book, you can receive a free copy of either tape with the purchase of any WritePro computer program.

THESAURUS

Most writers use computers now. A day doesn't go by in which I fail to use two different on-line thesauruses, marvels of convenience and speed. A thesaurus does not provide as many words with precisely the same meaning as it does words with *similar* meanings. The thesaurus that came with my most frequently used word processor is racy and inexact, producing distant cousins of the word I'm looking up. Which is good. That on-line thesaurus often surprises me with a word that I would not have thought of on my own and that gets me thinking in a different direction. I also keep memory-resident The American Heritage Thesaurus, which is scholarly and prissy. Checking the two thesauruses against each other is fun and a stimulant to the imagination.

For example, a student of mine had a story in which the word "harlot" was overused. My prissy thesaurus came up with the synonym "prostitute" and that's all. My other on-line thesaurus came up with no fewer than twenty-one "synonyms"—some near misses and some pretty far off—that enabled me to add color as well as diversity to her text: seductress, temptress, coquette, flirt, nymphomaniac, siren, tart, tease, vamp, wanton woman, prostitute, whore, call girl, hooker, hussy, slut, streetwalker, tart, tramp, trollop, wench.

The book I favour for synonyms is a paperback called *Roget's Super Thesaurus* by Marc McCutcheon, published by Writer's Digest Books, which also contains antonyms in some cases. I also like *The Synonym Finder* by J. I. Rodale, published in paperback by Warner Books. Both books are organized alphabetically. You don't have to look a word up in the back to find out what section up front you might find its relatives in.

WRITERS' CONFERENCES

My students consistently tell me that they find writers' conferences beneficial for learning, networking and meeting other writers. The fact that writers keep coming back to the same conferences year after year attests to that. Writers enjoy the camaraderie of other writers as much as they do the instruction they receive in workshops. If you are relatively inexperienced in the commercial side of writing, writers' conferences are also a good place to hear agents and editors talk, and to meet them. Lists of writers' conferences are available in the *Literary Market Place*, published by R.R. Bowker, and *The Writer's Handbook*, edited by Sylvia K. Burack and published by The Writer, Inc., and in some issues of writers' magazines. A few of the conferences ask to see several pages of your work ahead of time. It's a good idea to talk to another writer who's been to that conference before applying. The conference administration might supply you with the name of someone living in your area who has attended the conference previously. You might want to get your name on the mailing list of conferences that interest you, since the most popular conferences fill up within a few weeks of sending out their annual announcements.

For British Readers

FREE-LANCE EDITORS

In Britain writers do not usually use the term "Book Doctor", but there are many free-lance editors who perform the same function, reading typescripts and reporting back to the authors with helpful advice regarding possible improvements. An on-going relationship can develop with author and editor working together on the book over a period of time.

Free-lance editors advertise regularly in magazines such as *Writers News*, *Writer's Forum*, *Writer's Monthly*, etc., and the advertisements usually give some indication of the individual's background and expertise. Fees are charged either according to the length of the work or on an hourly rate.

A number of the Regional Arts Boards run a criticism service, allowing writers to get a professional assessment of their work, usually including much constructive advice. Contact the Regional Arts Board for your area for further information.

DICTIONARIES

As far as *The Oxford English Dictionary* is concerned, most writers will find *The Shorter Oxford English Dictionary* entirely adequate for their needs, and if they require more abstruse information can consult the complete work in the local Public Library. For a desk dictionary, *Chambers* (used by many crossword compilers, and particularly useful for dialect words) or the *Collins English Dictionary* or the *Oxford Concise* will fill the bill.

LITERARY AGENTS

Nearly all British literary agents are listed in both *Writers' and Artists' Yearbook* (published by A. & C. Black) and *The Writer's Handbook* (published by Macmillan). Both these reference books give brief details of the agents' requirements, and their date of founding (which can sometimes be a helpful indication of the firm's standing), and indicate by an asterisk membership of the Association of Authors' Agents. Both also list a number of U.S. literary agents, and *Writers' and Artists' Yearbook* includes in addition some firms in a number of other countries.

SOFTWARE AND AUDIOTAPES

Readers of this book outside North America can obtain the free material offered in this chapter by sending their requests by e-mail to http://www.writeprony@aol.com, by fax to the USA at 00 1 914 762 5871 or by airmail to The WritePro Corporation, 43 S. Highland Avenue, Ossining, NY 10562, USA. Be sure to include your postal address as well as an e-mail address if you have one. The free WritePro lesson can be downloaded from the WritePro web site at http://www.writepro.com. If you require a disk and the brief printed manual, please enclose $13.50 for airmail shipping and handling in U.S. Funds or charge it to a U.S. credit card.

There is a section on the WritePro web site called "Tips for British Writers". If you have access to the Internet, you can find it on http://www.writepro.com.

THESAURUS

Both *Roget's Thesaurus* (now published by Penguin Books), which is arranged by subject, and *Collins Concise Thesaurus*, arranged alphabetically, like a dictionary, pass the "harlot" test, and *Roget* does so brilliantly. J.I. Rodale's *The Synonym Finder* (published by Warner Books), recommended earlier in this chapter, is available in Britain. Various thesauri, including *Roget*, can be found on the Internet, and the *Collins* is available, together with their dictionary, on CD-ROM.

WRITERS' CONFERENCES

Many annual conferences for writers take place in Britain. The best known and longest established is the Writers' Summer School, which has been in existence for over fifty years, and is held at Swanwick, Derbyshire, in mid-August. Others of note include the Scottish Association of Writers' Weekend Conference at Crieff in April, South East Writers Association Weekend at Leigh-on-Sea also in April, Southern Writers' Conference at Chichester in mid-June, Annual Writers' Conference at Winchester in late June, Writer's Holiday at Caerleon in late July, and Scarborough Writers' Weekend at Scarborough in October or November. Details of all such conferences are to be found in the various magazines for writers. Although the large number of conferences now available means that it is not so difficult to be sure of booking a place as it was some years ago when only one or two a year were held, early application is still advisable.

Writers' Circles exist all over Britain, and many writers find them stimulating, not only because those who attend the meetings (usually fortnightly) share the same interests, but because helpful advice can often come from fellow members. Your local Public Library will be able to tell you of the Writers' Circles in your district.

Virtually all Local Authorities include Creative Writing among the courses run under their Adult Education programmes. Their tutors are usually authors with a body of published work. Similarly, non-residential courses in Creative Writing are available at a number of universities.

The Arvon Foundation offers people over sixteen a chance to work with well-known authors in an informal way during a weekend. The courses take place at the Arvon centres in Yorkshire, Devon and the North West Highlands. Grants towards the fees can sometimes be obtained from the Regional Arts Board for your area.

35

A Final Word

Whatever the effect this book might have on your writing, I trust that it will have made you into a more perceptive reader for the rest of your days.

I hope you will have occasion to benefit from the techniques that I've been passing on to writers for nearly four decades. In time, some of these techniques will improve your chances of successful publication, or if you're already publishing, will enhance your work. Hemingway said, "We are all apprentices in a craft where no one ever becomes a master." We know that's not literally true. Many of Hemingway's stories and some of his novels are masterly. He meant we can always learn more. You can return to this book like an old friend for guidance and support whenever you feel the need.

In the course of reading this book, you may have come to the correct conclusion that a writer is a manipulator for whom the end justifies the means, a teller of white lies, a deceiver, all to a good end. He is also a shaper of the destinies of the characters he brings to life, a creator of golden idols he hopes some readers will worship. Hence the form of the following advice.

TEN COMMANDMENTS FOR WRITERS

1. Thou shalt not sprinkle characters into a preconceived plot lest thou produce hackwork. In the beginning was the character, then the word, and from the character's words is brought forth action.
2. Thou shalt imbue thy heroes with faults and thy villains with charm, for it is the faults of the hero that bring forth his life, just as the charm of the villain is the honey with which he lures the innocent.

3. Thy characters shall steal, kill, dishonor their parents, bear false witness, and covet their neighbor's house, wife, manservant, maidservant, ox, and ass, for reader's crave such actions and yawn when thy characters are meek, innocent, forgiving, and peaceable.

4. Thou shalt not saw the air with abstractions, for readers, like lovers, are attracted by particularity.

5. Thou shalt not mutter, whisper, blurt, bellow, or scream, for it is the words and not the characterization of the words that must carry their own decibels.

6. Thou shalt infect thy reader with anxiety, stress, and tension, for those conditions that he deplores in life he relishes in fiction.

7. Thy language shall be precise, clear, and bear the wings of angels, for anything less is the province of businessmen and academics and not of writers.

8. Thou shalt have no rest on the sabbath, for thy characters shall live in thy mind and memory now and forever.

9. Thou shalt not forget that dialogue is as a foreign tongue, a semblance of speech and not a record of it, a language in which directness diminishes and obliqueness sings.

10. Above all, thou shalt not vent thy emotions onto the reader, for thy duty is to evoke the reader's emotions, and in that most of all lies the art of the writer.

When you get the good news of a book contract, let me know and share the pleasure.

SOL STEIN

Glossary of Terms Used by Writers and Editors

Action: In fiction, action connotes something happening that is not necessarily physical movement. Adversarial dialogue is action.

Architecture: In the design of a larger work such as a novel, the purposeful order of scenes.

Aria: In any creative form, a longer speech designed to evoke an increasing emotional effect on the reader or viewer. See **speechifying.**

Backstory: The characters' lives before the story, novel, or film began.

Book doctor: A person who provides a free-lance editorial service to writers for a fee. Book doctors critique book manuscripts and shorter material; some do detailed suggestions and line-editing of complete manuscripts, services previously supplied by publishers. They charge by the hour or by the nature of the assignment.

Cliché: A hackneyed expression, tired from overuse.

Coincidence: In fiction, something that happens by chance and is insufficiently motivated.

Crucible: In fiction, a situation or locale that holds characters together as their conflict heats up. Their motivation to continue opposing each other is greater than their motivation or ability to escape.

Diction: Choice of words, probably the best identifier of quality in writing.

Eccentricity: An offbeat manner of behavior, dress, or speech peculiar to a person and dissimilar to the same characteristics of most other people.

Echo: In dialogue, an answer that repeats the question.

Engine, Starting of: The moment when the reader's curiosity is so aroused that he will not put the book down or turn to something else. It usually carries an intimation of conflict, a character threatened or wanting something badly that he can't have.

Episodic fiction: A story told in parts in which one event happens after another without seeming to be integrated into the whole.

Flab: Extraneous words, phrases, and sometimes lengthier matter the elimination of which strengthens prose.

Flab Editor™: A copyrighted computer software function enabling the user to highlight individual words and hide them or bring them back at will to see the difference their excision makes in the strength of text. See the Software section of Chapter 34.

Flashback: A scene that precedes the time of the present story.

Handle: A short description of the book designed to evoke interest in it.

Immediate scene: A scene that is visible, as if being filmed.

Jargon: Words or expressions developed for use within a group that bar outsiders from readily understanding what is being said. The purpose of language is to communicate or evoke; jargon obfuscates or hides.

Line space: Four blank lines in a double-spaced manuscript, used within chapters to indicate a break, usually of time, or a shift to a different location.

LMP: The initials of the *Literary Market Place*, the directory of the American book publishing industry, listing book publishers, editorial services, agents, associations, events, and industry yellow pages. This huge, expensive directory can be consulted in many public libraries. It is invaluable for the writer whose work is ready for the market.

Marker: An easily identified signal that reveals a character's social or cultural class, heredity, or upbringing.

Metaphor: A figure of speech that results when words or phrases are brought together that do not ordinarily belong together, yet by their proximity convey a fresh meaning. One thing is spoken of as if it were another. Some of the best novel titles are metaphors (e.g., *The Heart Is a Lonely Hunter*).

Motivation: The source that impels an action, the reason that something is done.

Narrative summary: Offstage action usually conveyed in general terms.

Oblique dialogue: An indirect reply not in line with the preceding speech, not directly responsive.

Omniscient: Describes the point of view in which the author roams everywhere, including the minds of all the characters.

One plus one equals one half: A formula designed to remind writers that conveying the same matter more than once in different words diminishes the effect of what is said. A corollary of this equation is that if the same matter is said in two different ways, either alone has a stronger effect.

Particularity: A precisely observed detail rather than a generality.

Point of view: The perspective from which a scene is written, which character's eyes and mind are witnessing the events.

SAE: Seldom spelled out, it is an abbreviation for "stamped, addressed envelope." To receive whatever is being offered, you are required to enclose such an envelope with your request or the item or information will not be furnished.

Scene: An integral incident with a beginning and end that in itself is not isolatable as a story. It is visible to the reader or audience as an on-stage event, almost always involving dialogue and other action.

Segue: Derived from music, it means to glide as unobtrusively as possible into something new.

Showing: Making fiction visible to the reader as if it were happening before his eyes, moment by moment.

Simile: A figure of speech in which two unlike things are compared, linked by "as" or "like" (e.g., "He's fit as a fiddle").

Speech signature: Within dialogue, a tag that is characteristic of the speaker, such as Jay Gatsby's "old sport."

Speechifying: Monologue of one person that runs too long.

Static: Describes a scene lacking visible action or dialogue that moves the story forward.

Suspense: The arousal and sustaining of curiosity as long as possible. Involves anticipation and sometimes anxiety about what is going to happen.

Tags: The means by which a speaker is identified, most commonly "he said" or "she said."

Telling: Relating what is happening offstage, or during an earlier time.

Tension: Delicious moments of anxious uncertainty. Derived from the Latin *tendere*, meaning "to stretch."

Vanity press: A firm that advertises to writers, offering to publish their books for a fee. Usually the service is that of manufacturing a small edition and providing scant notice to the public that the book is available. A few of America's most prestigious publishers have kept a well-guarded secret: they also publish books under "vanity press" conditions. Consider it a last resort for a book a writer must see in print whatever the cost.

Voice: The author's "voice" is an amalgam of the many factors that distinguish a writer from all other writers. Many authors first find their voice when they have learned to examine each word for its necessity, precision, and clarity, and have become expert in eliminating the extraneous and imprecise from their work. Recognizing an individual author's voice is much like recognizing a person's voice on the telephone.

AI SHAW

DELTA FORCE VAMPIRE: INSURGENCY

ALEX SHAW

Published in the USA with consent from Hetman Publishing

Date of first UK publication November 2012

Copyright © Alexander William Shaw 2012

First published in the United Kingdom by Hetman Publishing
www.hetmanpublishing.com
Date of first US publication November 2012
ISBN-13 978-0-9561592-6-7
ISBN-10 0-9561592-6-5

II

This book is dedicated to my wife Galia,
my sons Alexander & Jonathan
and my family in England and Ukraine.

ALEX SHAW was head of Drama at Pechersk School International, Kyiv, Ukraine, in the late 1990's before leaving to start his own Kyiv based 'consultancy' dealing specifically with the markets of the former USSR. He was subsequently head hunted for a division of Siemens where he was tasked with business development in the former USSR, the Middle East and Africa. Hetman was Alex's first novel and took twelve years to complete. Published in 2009 it gained critical acclaim in the 2010 Amazon Breakthrough Novel Award (ABNA) and later became a #1 UK Kindle bestseller. Cold Black was published a year later. It followed the success of Hetman, gaining critical acclaim in ABNA 2011 and rose to #6 in the Kindle UK bestseller list. Both books have also now become top 10 Kindle Bestsellers in the USA. In July 2012 Cold Black became a #1 German Kindle bestseller; Hetman reached #4 in April. The third Aidan Snow thriller will be released in November 2012.

When not writing Alex works as a freelance consultant (clients include the UN), dividing his time between his two homes in Kyiv, Ukraine and West Sussex, England. He is married to his beautiful wife Galia and has two fantastic sons, Alexander and Jonathan.

Alex welcomes feedback and comments from readers and can be contacted via his website www.alexwshaw.com you can also follow Alex on twitter: @alexshawhetman

Praise for Alex Shaw

'He won't be stopped now. The book will become popular among Kyiv's expats; some of them will even recognize themselves.' **Kyiv Post on 'Hetman'**

'A strong aspect of **HETMAN** is Shaw's knowledge of Ukraine & Special Forces operations. The character of Bull felt real on the page, you don't get better than that.'
2010 Amazon Breakthrough Novel Award Review

'Thrillers really aren't my cup of tea…but I loved this!!!'
2011 Amazon Breakthrough Novel Award Review

'Something has clicked with audiences as Shaw's books frequently hit #1 on International Kindle charts.'
What's On Kyiv

DELTA FORCE VAMPIRE: INSURGENCY

ONE: Deh Rawod District, Uruzgan Province, Afghanistan

As the blood slipped down his throat Krasnov felt a fire ignite within. The weakness left him to be replaced with a strength that no mortal could match. He was ready to fight. The blistering Afghan sun had been replaced by a hunter's moon and tonight Krasnov would start his hunt again. The Americans under the banner of 'ISAF' were going to assault the cave complex; it would be their missiles that would enable him to complete his own mission. A quarter of a century had passed since he had been face to face with his enemy. Becoming a vampire had taught Krasnov patience but it had also taught him how to kill. It was not that he hadn't killed men before, but that had been different. Those kills had been sanctioned by his country, by his government, by the mighty Soviet Union's war machine. Now he killed so that he may feed. Now the killing was for personal need. But tonight's kills would fulfil a different type of need, vengeance. Krasnov had not asked to become a vampire; to be 'made monster' by the cold Russian who used men like him to destroy. Krasnov had made it his mission to eradicate those who had created him and murdered innocent Afghans all those years before. Their demise would be salvation for Krasnov's crimes. He moved nearer to the opening of the tunnel and felt the presence of an all but silent American UAV in the sky above. Within minutes a Hellfire missile would slam into the Taliban base below. The Americans were about to start their attack and would either discover or destroy the facility. Krasnov collected his Kalashnikov and moved deeper into the mountain.

Brad Black call-sign 'Peter Pan' focussed down the sight of his Barrett M82A1. A Taliban fighter holding an RPG against his shoulder, stood squarely in the Delta operative's crosshairs. A thin smile spread across Black's lips as he imagined the imperceptible whine above of the first Hellfire missile. Launched by an almost silent RQ-170 Sentinel, the USAF's latest model of 'stealth' unmanned drone, the impact would be sudden and shocking. There was a squelch in his ear piece, the ready signal. Operating far closer to the target than any 'green' army unit, the Delta team were risking being caught in a 'blue on blue'. Black collected his Barrett and slithered backwards down the wadi, a mere eighty meters away from the Taliban base. The camp itself was not the target, it was the suspected cave network beneath and what it may contain. It was a hard and deeply buried target or an HDBT in Pentagon talk.

Black imagined the missiles hurtling towards the camp, ever narrowing the distance between target and destruction. And then the impact came…even though he was wearing a helmet and had his palms pressed over his ears, the noise was deafening. One explosion; a moment later a second and then a third. Black scrambled back up the bank of the wadi and re-took his eyeball on the camp. He scanned the smouldering site for targets. A figured staggered out of a cave entrance. He was on fire. Black took him out in an instant, the single shot from his

Barrett all but vaporising the Talib's head. Black then acquired a group of fighters moving towards the entrance of another cave, now visible after the airstrike. He managed to get two before they disappeared inside. There were shouts as armed fighters raced out of the only building to remain intact, firing wildly into the milky dawn light which was now streaked with flames. Black's Barrett barked again and almost immediately the nearest fighter vanished, hurled backwards as a huge hole ripped through his torso. Black acquired his next target and sent another .50 cal round into the tall Afghan. Black estimated ten men in total now scurrying around the camp like ants, badly trained and poorly equipped. He picked off two more who were attempting to set up a Russian PKM. Disbelief raced through Black's head, if this was the best that the Taliban could manage how did they still exist?

There was a hiss in his ear. "Time to kick some Tali-but?" Gonzalez, the team leader, call-sign 'Giant', gave the action command for the rest of his assault team to move in.

More high velocity rounds from 'Minute Man', the second Delta sniper now joined the grunts of HKs. Through the dust and dark smoke there were more figures still moving, moaning, and screaming. The remaining Taliban were dispatched in a sickening hail of lead. All visible targets had been eliminated. Black felt no remorse for the dead men in front of him. Their al-Qaeda allies had chosen to attack the US and the Taliban had chosen to enslave the people of their own country.
"Minute Man to Peter Pan. Time to join the party." Another hiss in his earpiece informed him.
"Peter Pan, Minute Man, confirmed over." Black slung the Barrett 'light fifty' across his back and picked up his own secondary weapon, an HK-416. Moving tactically into the camp, he was on alert for any possible IEDs or remaining Taliban.

Minute Man, real name Marvin Styles strode towards Black with his HK in its ready position. "You missed a couple of 'runners'."

The rivalry between the two Delta snipers was friendly, if intense. "I got mine."

"Yours, huh? Don't go collecting any ears."

The two operatives purposefully moved towards the nearest cave. Gonzalez, Eaton and Flagon had taken the second cave at the far end of the camp. The last member of their six man team, Miller, threw a pair of flashbangs into the cave entrance. They took cover as two explosions erupted from inside.

"On me." Lowering his NVGs Miller advanced inside.

Black pulled down his own Night Vision Goggles and cursed. They were dead. Moving into the inky darkness of the cave, Black started to get a strange feeling. The comms network crackled as Miller attempted to contact Gonzalez. There was a sudden, piercing, whining, noise in his ear piece. Wincing he pulled it out. Night suddenly turned to day as an explosion tore through the tunnel. Both Styles and Miller were briefly illuminated before the shockwave threw them to the ground. Black's head hit a rock and stars erupted before his eyes.

He'd been out for what felt like hours but was in fact only seconds. The Delta sniper rolled onto his front. His back was in agony from landing on his rifle and his neck felt numb. Moving forward in the darkness, he tried to reach out for the others. He found a body and pulling himself to the head, whispered in the ear. "Marvin, that you?"

"Shit man, can't see nothing." Styles groaned. The explosion had been blinding in the NVGs.

"You hurt?"

Styles sat up, blinking. "No. You?"

Black lied. "No." He grunted as he got to his feet. "Stay here."

"What option do I have?"

Miller, a few feet ahead, was crouching behind a large boulder his NVGs raised. "Peter Pan, ready?"

Black followed Miller, ever aware that death was only a second away from a grenade, a round from an AK or a blade thrust towards him in the darkness. They followed the rock face until it suddenly fell away. Miller held up his fist, his arm at a right angle. 'Stop'. This was it; this was the moment of maximum exposure. Miller pulled down his NVGs, retrieved a new flashbang from his webbing and threw it into the darkness ahead. Both Deltas again screwed their eyes shut and put their hands on their helmets and pushed tight against their ears, but the explosion felt all the more deafening in the confined space. Millisecond's after the flash the Americans darted into the abyss, weapons up ready. Their HK's took different arcs, scanning for any sign of movement. Black removed a pair of snap sticks from his webbing twisted them and threw them. An eerie green glow illuminated the space ahead. The chamber was a storage room for Taliban equipment and Intel suggested the regional commanders assault plans. But at the far end there was another opening caused by a rock fall. Both Deltas moved forward to inspect the find.

Miller raised his goggles. "What the hell have we got here?"

They were standing at the entrance of a high ceilinged room, man-made, excavated with heavy machinery. A dim green glow came from the walls casting enough light for them to see. To the left, several Taliban fighters lay, still smouldering, sprawled against fallen rocks like bundles of rags. Another was still alive and crawling towards them, his shattered legs leaving a trail of blood which glowed in the unnatural light. There were strike marks on the rock floor. The men had set off an IED.

Miller whispered into his throat mike. "Target X secure." He then kicked the Taliban fighter hard, rolling him over onto his back. Miller held his HK-416 against the fighter's head and spoke in Pashtun. "What is this place?"

The fighter groaned. Miller pushed harder. "Answer my question, or you'll join your friends, and where you're going they won't be any virgins!"

The fighter turned his head and spat. He spoke in accented English, British, Midlands. Black tried not to laugh, the guy sounded like Ozzy Osbourne.

"You feenk I'm afraid to die, you fooking American? I'll be a martyr…"

"Enough." Miller pressed the muzzle harder into the Brit's head. "You either tell me what I want to know or I'm throwing you to the pigs."

The fighter's face contorted with rage. "You have rules. I have rights I do; I'm a prisoner of war…"

"Pick him up."

Black pulled the fighter to his feet. Miller hit the fighter in the jaw with the stock of his HK. The Brit went limp. Miller secured the man's hands with plasticuffs, and grinning said to Black. "Winning hearts and minds."

"What the…" Styles drew level with them, goggles off blinking taking in the man-made expanse in front of him.

"Nice of you to join us. Here, take this and stay with." Miller pushed the prisoner towards Styles. Together they put him in the recovery position on the floor. With mock concern Miller added. "We can't let him choke, he has rights."

Black moved to the other side of the cave. He could now see several more corpses but these were not Taliban. He prodded the nearest with his desert boot. "This one's been beheaded," he took another step, "so has this one."

"Mercs?" Miller drew nearer and looked at the body.

The corpses were uniformed and Black noticed a Red Star. "Russians?"

"Almost." Miller got on his haunches. "Yah ah, these guys' been dead for a long, long time. We're looking at the Soviet Union's best. But there's no decay, it's almost like they've been mummified. I saw a documentary about it once; it's all about the gasses in the soil."

Black shrugged. "Weird shit, c'mon time to take pictures for the Pentagon."

Miller retrieved a digital camera, put it on video setting and started to record. Standard ISAF intelligence gathering missions were recorded by miniature helmet mounted cameras but this time they had been give specific instructions not to wear any. They were to secure the target and then start 'rolling'. Miller moved away, towards the back of the cave, making sure that he captured some close ups of the bodies and the assorted equipment which now in the light from the camera he could see scattered amongst them.

Styles heard a feint groan and spun, weapon raised. There was a sudden movement, something sprang at him. Instinctively his finger applied pressure to his HK and rounds flew at the advancing shape. At point blank range the rounds tore into the dark figure, causing it to convulse in mid-air and land heavily in a heap on the floor. "Peter Pan, to your six!"

Black turned as Styles' HK spat again. A shadowy shape hit Black's shoulder causing him to fall. The attacker got on top of him. Black grabbed his assailant's arms and rolled over. The eyes of the man were blood red. The attacker bared his teeth like an animal and pushed down, his mouth snapping. Black was paralyzed; something was stopping his arms from working, he tried to shout but no sound came. The attacker clamped his hands on Black's head, forcing his skull into the ground. Black's vision blurred, he started to grey-out. Then the pressure stopped as the attacker was ripped away. Black tried to move but before he could a pair of razor sharp teeth pierced his neck and his world disappeared into darkness.

Fire Base Python, Pasaband District, Ghowr Province, Afghanistan

The mood at the de-brief was sombre. Delta had one man MIA presumed KIA, his body had not been recovered, and a second was in a critical condition. Gonzalez hurled the nearest chair in disgust.

"Control yourself Sargent." Colonel Matthers, the SF liaison officer stood in the entrance of the briefing room. He had flown in from Camp Bastion for the de-brief. "The loss of your man is regrettable but our objective was achieved."

Gonzalez glared at the Brit, righted the chair and sat heavily. "Fuck your objective."

Matthers, showed no emotion but the US officer accompanying him bristled. "The War on terror is our objective, soldier."

"Sir." Gonzalez stared at Major Rockbridge. The man was an ass-kisser.

Matthers addressed the four remaining members of the Delta team. "The data you have provided us with has confirmed our belief that this was a staging base for foreign fighters, the British prisoner is proof of that. We have also gained valuable intelligence regarding the Taliban's use of tunnel networks. Both of these pieces of information have seriously diminished their ability to operate in the area."

Rockbridge cut in. "We hit them hard. Well done boys."

There were no cheers or back slapping. The Deltas were not happy. Gonzalez broke the uneasy silence. "Before he passed out, Minute Man said something about his attacker. I want to see the film. I want to see what attacked him and Peter Pan."

Rockbridge's eyes flashed and he glanced at Matthers who tried to placate the team leader. "Sargent Gonzalez. The film has now been sent off to the Pentagon."

Gonzalez shook his head something was not right. "The Pentagon? So you are telling me that we carried out a classified mission but haven't got a security clearance high enough to see our own footage?"

"Correct."

"This is Bullshit." Eaton added.

"Eaton!" Rockbridge pointed a finger.

"You point that at me again and I'll snap it off." Eaton growled. There was no love lost between Delta and their 'appointed in country' CO.

"Gentlemen please." Matthers held up his hands. "I give you my word that we will recover Black's body."

Rockbridge, face now a beetroot red glared at Eaton who grunted but said nothing more.

Matthers continued. "Now I can't offer any of you a beer but I suggest that you get some serious down time before your next operation. Gentlemen."

Matthers left the pre-fabricated hut, Rockbridge followed and pointed again at Eaton.

"This is Bullshit." Eaton stated again as the door closed behind the officers.

Gonzalez stood. "You don't think I know? But you heard him."

Miller shook his head. "We messed up. I should have been faster. I just couldn't stop it in time."

"It?" Gonzalez said.

"Them, the Talibs." Miller corrected himself.

"And since when does the US of A's Delta Boys take orders from a friggin Brit?" It was a constant complaint from Eaton.

"Hey, we come under JSOC but we're here as ISAF remember that." Gonzalez said flatly as Eaton shook his head.

Flagon saw movement outside. "Here comes the Doc."

A medic entered, he had a strange expression on his face. "Styles is awake."

"Say again?" Gonzalez wanted to be sure.

"I said Sargent, that your man is awake. It's a miracle but he is sitting up and asking for food."

"Let me guess, steak well done?"

The Delta team shared a smile. Styles was a ravenous carnivore whose idea of a gourmet meal was an 'all you can eat buffet' at a steakhouse.

"No. He's asking for it 'blue'."

"That doesn't sound like him."

Miller nudged Eaton "Blue means bloody."

"Thanks. We didn't have fancy words on the ranch."

Gonzalez moved towards the door. "C'mon, let's go beg steal or borrow him his steak."

"From friggin where?" Eaton threw his hands up.

Unknown location, Afghanistan

"Drink."

Black felt a warm liquid touch his lips. Moments later his body felt as though it was burning. His eyes snapped open. Disorientated Black looked around as he started to focus. A bearded figure was crouching in front of him.

"You will have many questions but I am afraid that my answers will not please you."

Black found his voice. "Who are you?"

"Sergey Krasnov."

"A Russian?"

"Ukrainian actually, but that is not important."

As Black's eyes cleared he realised that he was in a sparsely furnished room. It was dark and there were heavy shutters at the window. "Where am I?"

"The name will mean nothing to you, it is just a village."

Black tried to sit up but discovered that he was chained to the bed. "What are you, a mercenary?"

"A Red Army deserter, actually. I have lived here for twenty five years."

Black looked into the face of the man, he seemed no more than thirty. "So you take me captive then what, ransom me off to the Talibs?"

Krasnov shook his head. "I tied you down for safety reasons, your safety and mine."

"Unchain me."

"Of course." Krasnov produced a key and undid a padlock at the foot of the bed. As the chains loosened Black sprung to his feet, his own speed surprising him. He took a step towards the Ukrainian. His captor stood up slowly.

"Again. Who are you and why am I here?" Black scanned the room for a weapon.

"You were attacked, I rescued you."

Images flashed in Black's mind from the cave, a man with red eyes snapping at him with open jaws and then darkness. "From whom?"

Krasnov's eyes bore into him. "A dead man."

Black noticed a Makarov pistol on the crude wooden chair in the corner. He lunged for it.

Krasnov made no attempt to stop him. "That is my Spetsnaz issue side arm. It is over thirty years old, but like me has been very well preserved."

Black held the Soviet pistol in a two handed grip and aimed it at the head of the Ukrainian. "Which way is it to the nearest ISAF base?"

"South, two days walk."

"You don't have a car?"

Krasnov lied. "The Taliban took it when you Americans scared them away."

"I'm going to need all the water you have."

"No you will not."

"I don't want to shoot you, but I said I need water."

Krasnov shrugged. "If you insist upon it there is a well outside."

"Now I'm going to leave."

11

Black moved towards the door and pushed it open, instantly feeling the warmth of the sun on his face. He stepped outside and saw the well. As the rays of the sun touched his neck he felt his throat constrict and then his whole body start to shake. Black fell to his knees and put his hands in front of his face, his fingers were starting to smoke - the skin bubbling. The Ukrainian grabbed his shoulders and dragged him back into the shadow of the hut. Krasnov slammed the door and then pulled the American into a sitting position against the wall. He handed Black a glass bottle. "Drink."

Hyperventilating, Black looked down and saw that the content of the bottle was blood red. He put it to his lips and then knew that it was indeed blood. He tried to remove it but something inside stopped him. He hungrily drained every drop. Again his body shook but this time a wave of cold surged through him followed by a sheet of fire. "You've poisoned me?" Black stood then lunged at Krasnov.

The Spetsnaz commando stepped sideways and using a Sambo move hurled Black against the far wall. "Yes."

Baring his teeth, something inside told Black to attack again. "I'm going to kill you."

Black leapt and collided with Krasnov. The pair seemed to tussle in the air for a second before landing in a heap. Black now saw that the other man's eyes were blood red and that he had fangs. Black hit him with force in the neck and rolled away. Krasnov got to his haunches, rubbed his neck and stared. Black scrabbled for the Makarov still lying in the doorway and pulled the trigger. The roar was ear-splitting in the small room. The round travelled across the space in a millisecond and hit Krasnov in the chest. The Ukrainian grunted and stumbled backwards. Black fired twice more in quick succession, a double tap to the head. Krasnov fell and lay still.

"Shit." Black wiped his brow and tried to steady his ragged breathing. The man had given him no choice. He prodded the

Ukrainian with his boot although he already knew the man was dead. The Delta operative backed away shaking his head; whatever weird gig Krasnov had been part of was nothing more do to with him. He looked around the small room, his eyes seemed to be more adjusted to the gloom now and he started to search for anything that may be of use. He found a map on the table and was surprised to see that Firebase Python was clearly marked, circled in red ink. The map also showed the location of the target Taliban camp and caves. There were notes in Cyrillic at the bottom and a diagram. As he strained his eyes to make out the markings, the letters seemed to make sense and he was able to read them. Black turned the map to orientate him-self and then smiled as he realised that he knew where he was. Looking around once more, Black saw nothing else of importance or anything intelligence worthy. As he left the hut the Afghan sun still burned but he no longer felt the heat. Map and pistol in hand, Black took a deep breath and started to walk he had a long way to go.

Firebase Python, Pasaband District, Ghowr Province, Afghanistan

"How ya feeling soldier?" Gonzalez asked as he and the rest of the team looked down at Styles.

"Like I've been eaten, chewed up and spat out." Styles held his hand against the bandage on his neck; he could feel the vein below throb.

"You got a nicked artery, the Doc said you lost a lot of blood and were lucky you didn't bleed out."

"What time is it?"

"Half three, but it's gloomy as hell in here so you wouldn't know." Gonzalez moved to the widow and pulled the heavy curtain. Rays of bright sunlight streaked across the room falling on the foot of Styles' cot. Unseen by all an imperceptible smoke started to rise.

"Don't! Don't open them. The Doc says that my eyes need to adjust."

"Sure do look red." Eaton peered down at his buddy, who's head started to slump. "Whoa. You ok Marv?" Eaton moved his hand to place it on Styles' shoulder, but before he could do so Styles' left had shot across his body and grabbed his wrist. "Whoa, take it easy!" Styles looked up, for a millisecond his pupils were crimson before he blinked and they returned to their normal blue. Eaton unlaced Styles' fingers from his wrist; they had left a red mark. "If you wanted to hold hands you should have joined the SEALs."

"Performing seals, maybe." Flagon chuckled.

"Yeah, yeah, make fun of the invalid!" Styles rubbed his eyes.

Gonzalez became serious. "Do you remember what happened?"

"Didn't you see the film?"

Gonzalez shook his head. "Taken and sent to the Pentagon."

"Oh." Styles screwed his eyes up. "Something jumped on me, must have been a runner from the camp we missed. How many were there Ghost?"

"I couldn't tell, they kept moving. Sorry. I messed up." Miller was despondent.

"Hey we all missed him. The bastard was like an animal, clawing at me and then," Styles touched his neck, "he bit me!"

"Love bite?" Flagon asked.

"He must have mistaken you for a SEAL." Eaton added.

"There was no one else in the cave, no one else alive that is." Styles paused as if realizing that the team was one short. "Where's Peter Pan?"

There was a moment's silence, Gonzalez spoke first. "Brad didn't make it."

"What?" Styles sat up.

Miller nodded gravely. "There was a secondary explosion that brought down part of the roof. I saw him get buried. Nothing I could do. You were lucky I got you out. It missed us by inches."

"But I can feel him…" Styles' voice trailed off.

Gonzalez looked at his team. "We're going to go back there and find him. I'm not going to leave a man in the field."

Styles swung his legs out of the bed and stood. For a moment he swayed unsteadily before regaining his balance. "Did any of you bring me a steak?"

***

It was night. There was a firm knock at the door. Rockbridge looked up not expecting anyone, annoyed at being disturbed and weary from a long day. "What?"

"May I come in?" The man with black hair asked in accented English.

"And you are?"

"Vladimir Dratshev, GRU."

"Russian military intelligence?"

"Yes."

Rockbridge stood. "Please come in."

The Russian entered. "Thank you. From your expression I sense that you were not expecting me?"

Rockbridge noted the man's rank insignia. "No General. But that is nothing new; my small team here is ignored by ISAF. We just do the dirty jobs and are not important enough to know what else is going on. But it is always a pleasure to meet our international colleagues." Rockbridge extended his hand, Dratshev shook. The grip was firm but the Russian's hand cold.

"I am afraid that the reason for my intrusion is a serious matter."

"Oh? Please take a seat, General." Rockbridge nodded at a small fridge in the corner of what was laughingly referred to as his office. "Can I get you a drink, a coke perhaps?"

"No, thank you."

"So what is so serious that warrants a visit from a General of the GRU?"

"War crimes."

"What?" Rockbridge was puzzled and somewhat concerned. "Please explain."

"Of course. A team of your 'operatives' recently discovered a cave within a Taliban camp."

Rockbridge felt the hair on the back of his neck stand up, the mission was classified no one outside of his chain of command should have known of its existence. "I'm sorry General; I really can't discuss any operational details with you, without express permission from the Pentagon."

"Here." Dratshev handed Rockbridge an envelope. "I think you will find this is in order."

Rockbridge opened it and read the letter inside. "Ok. It seems that they want me to offer you 'every assistance'." He placed the envelope on his desk, placated but slightly annoyed. He looked at his guest, he'd let him ask the questions but he was dammed if he was going to offer up anything extra.

"In the cave network your men entered, a man-made chamber was discovered. Is this the case?"

"Yes."

"Can you describe what was found therein?"

"Bodies."

"Were the bodies dressed in Soviet uniforms?"

"Yes."

"How many?"

"From memory, six."

"Could you tell what the cause of death was?"

"I'm not a homicide detective General." The Russian remained silent, gaze fixed on Rockbridge waiting for him to answer the question. "Two had been decapitated."

Dratshev nodded. "That is as I feared."

"General I will offer you all the assistance I can, but can you please tell me what this is all about?"

"During the Soviet operation in Afghanistan..."

Rockbridge cut him off. "Occupation."

Dratshev shrugged. "Let us not get bogged down by semantics. During the Soviet, occupation, there were reports of local people being abducted and tortured by Red Army soldiers. Now you in the West may have thought of us as 'red devils' who ate the children of our enemy but we were soldiers like you, just doing our jobs. The fact of the matter however was more serious than that. When the Soviet Union ceased to 'exist' classified documents came to light and certain officials started to cover their backs. I became aware of an unsanctioned covert operation that had been conducted here in Afghanistan. In short it was a biological weapons' testing program, small enough to not be picked up on the radar and hidden by the chaos of war. The man-made cave you found, I believe, is the site of this and the men you found are the Spetsnaz operatives who ran it."

Rockbridge whistled. "What type of biological weapon?"

Dratshev nodded. "As we are being open I can be candid with you. It was an airborne weapon, based on a genetically engineered strain of the Ebola virus. Highly contagious."

Mouth dry, Rockbridge stood and opened the fridge to get a coke. He drank before speaking. "How many more of these dirty little secrets are going to suddenly appear, General?"

"Your guess is as good as mine Major. This is the only such facility I am aware of in Afghanistan. I understand that a video recording was made of the cave's interior?"

"A video was taken, the Pentagon has it. I saw it briefly."

"Is there be anything else on there that you can remember which may be of importance?"

The American finished his can. "Not apart from the headless corpses. What happened there?"

"I do not know for sure. We believe that the cave was attacked by the Mujahedeen, and they beheaded the men you found before triggering an IED which sealed the facility."

"General, four of my men entered that cave. One is in a coma. Could any of them be infected?"

"Yes. The salient reason I am here is to screen your men and offer treatment if needed."

Rockbridge felt the blood drain from his face. "General, my men have not been in isolation since the operation ended. They have been in contact with countless numbers of personnel. If they are infected we will have an epidemic on our hands."

"Please calm yourself Major. This strain of the virus is extremely fast acting, if they were infected you would have seen signs by now. In fact my screening is probably not needed but I want to be completely certain that if any residue of the weapon remained it was not taken out of the cave by your men."

"So what do you need?"

"I need blood samples from each man who entered the cave."

"Done."

"I will also need to go to the cave and asses it. I believe it is in only the neighbouring province? "

"Yes." Rockbridge frowned. How did the man from the GRU know so much? "But you have to navigate 'bandit country' to get there."

The Russian smiled. "They shall have to navigate me."

"So when do you want to test my men?"

"Immediately."

***

Firebase Python was the newest such facility in Afghanistan. It was nothing more than a large area of land containing prefab buildings and tents that had been ringed by a high fortified mud wall. The wall on the outside looked like a medieval fortress but on the inside it had large concrete drums placed against it resembling sea defences. Here however it was the tide of insurgency that was being held back.

Gonzalez looked up at the stars that seemed to shine much brighter than back home. He shook his head. Afghanistan was one of the most ruggedly beautiful places on earth yet for more than thirty years it had been torn apart by war. The Afghans had fought the Russians, the Afghans had fought the Afghans and now the Afghans fought the Afghans who fought the International community. All because of religion, a religion that he did not understand. Gonzalez was a catholic like most Hispanics and wore a crucifix but more out of respect for his mother than for Mary, the Holy mother. Would Afghanistan ever change? He doubted it. The locals would find someone else to fight when the Taliban had finally been vanquished. It was a pity, a real pity. Miller, who was crazy on astrology, joined his team leader. They stood for a moment in silence, contemplating the universe.

"You two wanna hold hands?" Eaton approached with Styles and Flagon.

Gonzalez shook his head. "We should call you Brokeback."

"Just as long as you call me." Eaton mocked.

"Let's eat." Styles was starving.

"The Doc said don't push it." Flagon advised Styles, who to his frustration had been ordered not to leave his bed until he had been given the OK.

To the untrained the inside of Firebase Python resembled a construction site. They left the prefab box that served as the medical centre and headed for the open air canteen. It was here that the Americans and the Afghan National Army chowed down at the start and end of each day. There were food drops from Camp Leatherneck, which usually included some favourite dishes from back home, if they were lucky and if not just more packets of meals ready to eat, MREs for short. The

Delta boys always sat to one side. Styles seemed to have made a full recovery but none the less Gonzalez managed to get him special treatment and a 'blue' steak had been acquired 'no questions asked'. Only Gonzalez knew where it had come from and he wasn't telling anyone about the helo pilot who had owed him a favour. Distinguished by their longer than regulation hair, stubble and relaxed manner, the Delta boys preferred to keep themselves to themselves and a safe distance from the occasional passing journalists. At the moment this consisted of a BBC film crew fronted by a blonde documentary film maker by the name of Paige Turner. Eaton had nicknamed her 'head turner' for reasons that were obvious to all. To one side of the canteen a few members of the Afghan National Army, who now more than ever were integrating with the ISAF forces, were taking part in an arm wrestling contest. This included a huge local who was unbeatable. Rumour had it that 'Hakim', as he was simply known, had been an enforcer for an Opium producer before joining up. Prior to that as a teenager he had battled the Soviets. Whether it was a hatred for the Taliban or a love of his country the Deltas did not know, but built like a pro-wrestler, the man demanded respect and instilled fear amongst the other Afghans. A US green army Lt was currently trying to best him as both Americans and Afghan's looked on. The result was not in doubt; Uncle Sam's finest would lose. The question was how quickly. Hakim smiled, to show a mouth of blackened teeth and effortlessly guided the American's hand to the table top.

"I've heard he took on a Soviet patrol when he was twelve." Miller stated matter of fact.

"What did he do kiss 'em into surrender?" Eaton grinned.

"Halitosis Hakim" Flagon chuckled.

"Hey, back off." Gonzalez warned. "Anyone who managed to survive for forty plus years in this warzone gets my vote."

Styles finished his steak, a small trickle of blood escaped from between his lips. He felt revived. "I could take him."

Eaton nudged Styles in the ribs. "I think his kissing days are behind him, Marv."

"You want to kiss his behind?" Flagon feigned incomprehension.

Gonzalez almost choked on his coke as he supressed a laugh. "Hey pack it in."

"No. I'll beat him." Styles stood and before the rest could stop him, strode across the canteen and swopped seats with the defeated Lieutenant.

Hakim stared at the smaller American. "You want challenge Hakim? You think you beat me?"

"I know I can beat you."

Hakim looked into the American's eyes and his smiled vanished. He felt unnerved; he recognised something that he had not seen since his was in his teens. He felt a chill. The American clamped his hand. Hakim blinked and then the contest started. The onlookers gathered and saw what they had expected. Hakim's hand pushed Styles' sideways and towards the table. Styles remained impassive as Hakim started to shake with exertion as the momentum slowed and then stopped. Hakim pushed harder and nothing happened. The crowd grew as more diners realised that an upset may be on the cards. Styles made eye contact with Hakim, a red glow appearing in his eyes as he slammed the Afghan's paw into the table. Hakim let out a yell and tried to pull his hand away. Styles let go on the second attempt.

With his left hand Hakim drew a knife from the cargo pocket of his fatigues and lunged at Styles. The blade entered Styles' shirt on the right side of his chest. Hakim tried to draw it back for a second strike but as he did so Gonzalez was at the table grabbing the Afghan's arm and twisting it to send the large local crashing to the floor. Immediately two Afghan's sat on their colleague, trying to restrain him. Hakim started to shout furiously in his local dialect. A pair of Afghan National Army officers arrived and hauled Hakim away who was still screaming uncontrollably. The crowd started to disperse and got back to the important task of eating. Styles stood and removed the knife from his chest. He wobbled and Gonzalez caught him and the knife.

"Get me a medic!" Gonzalez yelled.

Styles pushed his team leader away. "I'm OK."

Gonzalez looked at the blooded knife in disbelief; at least three inches had penetrated Styles' flesh. "No, we gotta get you to the Doc."

Styles turned away from the crowd so only Gonzalez could see his face, he lifted his shirt. "See, it's nothing."

Gonzalez shook his head "What the…" The wound was no more than a scratch.

***

Black had no idea of how far he had travelled but he had a raging thirst. He had tried to quench it by swallowing the water taken from the crazy Ukrainian's well, but the taste had been repulsive. He had retched as the tepid liquid hit his throat. That was, he could not think properly, perhaps eight or twelve hours earlier? As he continued to navigate the narrow paths over the mountainous terrain, the searing heat of the Afghan afternoon had changed to the chill of evening. Then the bitter night had come and from somewhere inside he had found more strength in the cold, star filled night. He had walked on past dawn and now the sun at its apex threatened to chargrill him once more. His body screamed at him to stop, to take cover to, lie down on the valley floor that he had finally reached but his mind drove him on. It reasoned that every step took him nearer to the firebase, nearer salvation. On the barren plane he could see for miles all the way to the distant mountains. He did not look back, did not turn around. He kept his head down with his collar up in an attempt to shield the sun until he heard an engine. He held his hand above his eyes and squinted. On the horizon at the end of the valley a dust cloud was getting bigger, a vehicle was approaching. Black took cover. This time both mind and body were in agreement and he threw himself flat against the searing dirt. Attempting to make himself as flat as possible and banking on his digital camo fatigues for concealment, he watched as the vehicle continued to close. It was a white Toyota pick-up with what looked like a .50 cal mounted on the flatbed. One figure in a black turban shared the space with the gun. Black cursed. With two in the cab that made it three against one if things went noisy.

The Toyota neared, coming to within twenty feet of him. He was still unsighted by the enemy when he suddenly lost control of his body. A primal urge surged from his stomach to his throat manifesting itself as 'thirst'. Black sprang to his feet and timing his attack to the millisecond ran at the Toyota as it passed. He leapt up at the flatbed and collided with the turbaned fighter. Black's momentum carried both he and the fighter over the opposite side of the truck and barrelling into the dirt. Black's prey had broken his neck on impact with the desert floor and was like a rag doll under him. Realising what he was doing but not knowing why or how to stop, Black sank his teeth into the sand encrusted neck of the Taliban fighter. He bit down and then felt the blood seep into his mouth as he sucked at the artery. His eyes rolled and his vision reddened. At that moment in time the heat, the exhaustion and the danger vanished. He could hear no sound, could feel no heat from the sun and most importantly did not register the first round from an AK47 tearing into him.

Black was aware of the Toyota carrying on for a few feet before it skidded to a halt. He stood and turned. Two men with Kalashnikovs ran at him. Firing on the move, they peppered the dirt around him. A second, third and then a fourth round hit

Black causing him to convulse but he did not fall. Teeth bared, he sprinted directly at them. As the men closed Black fell as more rounds entered his flesh. For a moment his vision blurred, the beating of his heart was loud in his head then he rolled over and sprung to his feet as the first man came within striking distance. Black landed a fist on the man's bearded chin which caused the fighter's head to snap back. As the insurgent fell, Black grabbed his Kalashnikov and cut down the last remaining man at point blank range. Black steadied his breathing as he went to each man in turn and double tapped their skulls to make sure they were dead. He collected their weapons and climbed into the cab of the Toyota. There he saw several bottled of water. He grabbed one and poured the contents into his mouth. Almost immediately he retched as the water mixed with the blood of his first kill, projected out of his mouth as a crimson cloud. Black poured the rest of the water over his head and hands, washing away some of the blood and sand. It was then that he adjusted the rear-view mirror and saw that his eyes were red and his canine teeth were protruding from his mouth. As he stared in disbelief, images of the thing that had attacked him in the cave flashed before him. He shook his head and slapped his face. Heat exhaustion did strange things to people including causing hallucinations, he told himself. He screwed his eyes shut and then as he opened them saw that both eyes and teeth had returned to normal. He put the Toyota into drive and headed for Firebase Python.

TWO: Fire Base Python, Pasaband District, Ghowr Province, Afghanistan

Gonzalez glared at the Russian whose requests he had been ordered to follow. Rockbridge had told him a sanitized version of the truth, that he and his team may have been exposed to a biological agent. After Gonzalez had pushed, Rockbridge had admitted that it may be Ebola.

"General."

"Good evening Sargent. This will not take long. All I require is a sample of blood. Once I have that Vaha will analyse it and we shall know within minutes if you are or are not infected."

Gonzalez looked at the dark haired soldier who accompanied Dratshev. "Vaha? Strange type of name."

"It is Chechen." Vaha stated and turned away.

"If I could have your arm?" Dratshev held out his hand.

"So are you a scientist or something?" Gonzalez rolled up his sleeve and thrust his arm out.

"Something." Dratshev looked at the veins pulsating. He plunged a needle into the American's arm and drew a sample of blood. "Next."

Gonzalez moved away holding a piece of cotton wool to his forearm as Miller entered the room and prepared to have his blood taken.

Rockbridge appeared in the doorway. "Did it hurt that much Gonzalez?"

"Funny." Gonzalez started to walk away then changed his mind. "The Russian is going to the cave. I am formally requesting permission to accompany him in order to retrieve Black's body, sir."

"No."

Gonzalez felt his face flush with resentment. "Maybe it wasn't a lesson they taught you at West Point sir, but you never leave a man behind."

Rockbridge let his lips curl in amusement. "If your screening is clear, you will accompany General Dratshev, but because I do not trust him. If you happen to retrieve Black's body then so be it. Do you understand, Sargent?"

Gonzalez nodded, satisfied. "Yes Sir."

As planned Styles was the last Delta operative to be tested. Dratshev nodded at Vaha, who immediately shut the door.

***

It had been more than twenty five years since Hakim had sensed their presence, their smell, their cold touch. He had grown older and had assigned their abilities to advanced Soviet training programs, to drugs and technology. He had convinced himself to forget but knew deep inside that it had all been a lie. A quarter of a century ago he had witnessed Hadama attacks and had fought back. He self-consciously touched the scars on his chest caused by the flames he had used against them. At that time he had cared little for his own safety, thought little of his own mortality and had acted. It was revenge for the loss of his family, the loss of his world. He had been the one to lead the raid against the cave; he had been the one who swore that the Soviet soldiers had been buried alive in a burning tomb. But like his memories they were not dead, merely buried. Hakim stared out of the bared window in what at Firebase Python was loosely referred to as 'the stockade'. The Delta operative was one of them. It was proof that they still existed. In the past the other ANA members had humoured him when he had told them his story. Some of them too had heard rumours about the invincible Soviets, stories thrown around camp fires but unlike him they were from different provinces only he had seen them and knew that there was indeed no smoke without fire. Hakim touched his chest again. No one would believe him, no one would help him. He had to escape and he had to stop them.

Usually by now he'd be safely tucked up in his cot but Rockbridge's day had been long and was not over yet. He was scanning the most recent Intel intercept when he sensed movement outside and looked up from his desk. Dratshev stood in the doorway.

"Major, I have finished screening your operatives."

"And?"

The Russian shook his head. "I am afraid that one has been infected. The rest are in the clear."

"Styles?" Rockbridge already knew the answer.

"Correct."

"So what can be done?"

"I have some drugs which may slow the onset of the virus but if he is to stand any chance he must be transferred into my custody and taken to our tropical disease clinic. They have the project's research notes and have been working on a strategy."

"You know that I cannot authorise that. Styles is a serving member of the United States Army, he must be treated in a US facility. Your centre must transfer their research to us."

"My government would never allow that, it would be tantamount to confirming that the project took place, against the Biological Weapons Convention. Leaks happen Major; you and I are both old enough to have experienced this. Your man's only hope is to be taken with me to Moscow."

Rockbridge ran his hand through his bristly grey hair. "Let me talk to someone. These drugs you have with you, they will slow the virus?"

"Yes. If I administer them now we may be able to delay the progress of the virus for a day or so. He must however be immediately placed under quarantine conditions."

"Hell General. Look around, this is a firebase not Camp Leatherneck. We don't have anywhere to put him."

"Use the stockade."

Miller and Eaton carried a sedated Styles on a stretcher to the stockade. Both had been ordered by Rockbridge to wear masks. Captain Osman, the CO of the ANA had Hakim in handcuffs and was leading him away. They crossed on the threshold. Hakim's eyes went wide at the sight of Styles and he shouted at Osman in Pashtun. Osman shouted back and pushed him away. Styles started to groan; Miller and Eaton hurriedly took him inside and placed the stretcher on the bunk. In a well drilled movement both operatives removed the poles and let the material act as a sheet. Eaton leant over Styles and looked at his face. The eyes were still closed, the sedatives working. Miller tapped Eaton's shoulder, signalling that they should both leave. Outside Eaton lifted his mask. "Did you get what he said?"

Both operatives knew some Pashtun but Miller's was better. "I heard what he said but I didn't understand it. He said 'that man is Hadama…Hadama."

"What's that, the Pashtun for 'queer'?" Eaton grinned, his teeth reflecting the moonlight.

"As I said I don't know. The guy's crazy, probably smokes too much of Afghanistan's finest."

Dave Raymond sat in a corner of the tent on his cot and looked at 'the rushes', the unedited tape he had used that day. It had been a routine patrol with the 2nd Battalion, 5th Infantry of the US Army's 25th Infantry Division (Light) who were normally based in Schofield Barracks in Hawaii. Raymond had asked where their 'shirts' were but the Yanks hadn't seemed to get his humour. The patrol had entered the compound of a local Afghan leader who had been very vocal in decrying the Taliban and Al-Qaeda. The elder had gone on to state how safe he felt now with the new base in his backyard. He nevertheless however still employed AK wielding bodyguards. At first the locals found it insulting and then rather amusing to be interviewed by a woman, and Paige Turner was a rather gorgeous one. At five ten with natural blonde hair and a figure that even baggy combats struggled to hide she should have been a model, in the chauvinistic minds of most men she met, but was an award winning journalist turned documentary film maker. She had learnt Pashtun and taken up the plight of Afghanistan's forgotten victims, the women who under the Taliban had been treated worse than dogs. She was asleep on the next cot. She was gorgeous but she snored. Raymond smiled, even Venus must have had her faults, probably farted like a trooper. He raised his eyes from the camera's viewfinder and looked at her bum; the green fatigues cupped her buttocks as though made to measure. He let his gaze linger for too long. He wanted to sleep with her but the problem was that both she and his wife wouldn't allow it. He smiled to himself, maybe he should ask them? He shook his head, it was late and he was fantasying again. Back to business. The documentary they were making was part of a series on the people of Afghanistan and how they had been affected and continued to be affected by the 'insurgency'. In Raymond's opinion 'the Stan' had been done to death, the locals had seen so many film crews that now most of them were eligible for their 'Equity cards'. But, and it was a nice butt, Paige didn't think so and as such the BBC had commissioned the documentary. Raymond came to the end of the day's tape and then started to watch the fight at the canteen that had erupted after the arm wrestling. On film the American sat, looked like he was going to get beaten and then all but broke the Afghan's arm. This satisfied Raymond, Hakim needed to be taken down a peg or two especially after he had made a lurid comment about Paige. Hakim had then stabbed at the American with his knife before being hauled away, but then something didn't make sense. Raymond rewound and slowed the tape. He saw Hakim reach for his knife and thrust it deep into the chest of the American; it hadn't been a glancing blow as he had thought. He watched the American stand shakily and then pull the blade out of his chest. Raymond paused the tape and wished he had his full editing suite with him to enlarge and enhance the frame, he hadn't been as near as he had wished and the canteen lighting had not been the best. But then he also wished that they were more than a two man crew, however with the advances in digital technology he and Paige were all that was needed and the BBC had wanted the footage to have a 'rougher edge'. Raymond leaned nearer the screen and squinted. He was sure that the blade had been driven at least several inches into the soldier's chest, yet the man was able to pull it out as if it had been a comb in his pocket. Raymond started the tape again and saw the second American, the team leader, steady the first and then as if nothing had happened saw the first straighten up. "What the hell have we here?"

There was movement from his neighbour's cot. "I give up! You've been tutting and humpfing for the last ten minutes. I was asleep!"

"I know, you were snoring."

"I do not snore."

"How would you know if you were asleep?"

"Anyway, I'm awake now. What is it?" Turner sat up.

"I was looking at the footage we took of the stabbing."

"Dave you know we can't use that, we can't show the faces or any details about the Special Forces operatives."

"That's why I was having a look before I delete it."

"So?"

"So?" Raymond paused; he always found it hard to concentrate around her. Especially when she was on a bed and looking into his eyes.

"What did you see?"

"Oh…Look at this." Raymond rewound the tape; Turner sat on his cot and leant against him. "There, see?"

"Hakim tried to stab the Delta boy but missed."

"He didn't miss."

"What?"

"Look again." Raymond slowed the footage and paused on the relevant frames. "The blade did go in but the bloke didn't feel it."

"That's not possible."

"Well it happened and he took it out."

Turner leaned forward, her blouse opening slightly. "But the suction from penetrating the chest cavity would have been huge. He pulled it out like…" Her voice trailed off as she made no attempt to stifle a yawn.

"Pity we can't use it eh? Or even talk about it."

"So what, was he wearing some new type of ultra-thin Kevlar or stab vest?"

"No."

"Well whatever 'X File' you've found can wait until the morning." Turner looked at her wristwatch. "It's late. Let's go to bed."

"Paige please, I'm not that kind of boy."

"Yes you are, but I'm not that sort of girl. Now let's go to bed, you in your bed and me in mine."

"Fine, but one request."

"What?" Turner sat back on her own cot.

"Please try not to snore."

Turner picked up her boot and threw it at him. "I do not snore!" Raymond rubbed his arm and feigned injury. He was about to speak when he heard the unmistakable sound of a helo engine start and then the thud…thud…thud of rotor blades. "At this hour?"

"Must be an 'immediate'?"

"Come on." He slipped on his UK Gear PT-03 desert trainers, grabbed the camera and left the tent. Turner hobbled after him pulling on her Timberlands and was just in time to see Rockbridge leave his quarters and head for the Delta tent. "Film it."

"I am, but you know we shouldn't."

"It could be something big."

"They've already found bin-Laden you know."

"Well then maybe they've found Lord Lucan or Jimmy Hoffa. Now let's get nearer."

Staying in the shadows the pair skirted the edge of the camp. As they did so a second helo started up and three Delta operatives ran from their tent towards it at the far end of the firebase. Rockbridge appeared again.

Turner put her hand on Raymond's back. "Stay here, I'll go and 'chat' him up."

"Tart." Replied Raymond as he remained hidden.

Rockbridge watched the Delta team leave and sipped from a water bottle. He hated being woken up, always had done and always would. Dratshev had left the base without warning and without clearance in the helo he had arrived in. Rockbridge had stuck to his word and had wasted no time in ordering Delta to follow, but Gonzalez had been annoyed at having to stay back and oversee Styles. Hearing footfall, Rockbridge turned. He rolled his eyes but then quickly smiled professionally. "And what can I do for you Ms Turner, a cup of coco perhaps?"

"Good Evening Major. What's up?"

Rockbridge liked her bluntness. "We have just received some flash Intel, a possible sighting of an al-Qaeda player."

Turner nodded accepting the lie. "Who?"

"You know I can't tell you that."

"Where?"

"I can't tell you that either." He changed the subject. "I hear you are returning to Camp Bastion tomorrow?"

"That's right; I'm doing one last day patrol with Lieutenant Mullins and then jumping on a helo. But I could stay if something interesting were to pop up."

"If anything 'pops up' I'll be sure to let you know. Good night Ms Turner."

"Goodnight." Turner watched him walk to his prefab quarters. He was hiding something but... but nothing. She was tired, dead on her feet. She wearily trudged back to her cot. Raymond arrived moments later and plonked the camera down on his bed.

"Don't even think of looking at that now." Turner warned him. "Just let me sleep."

Raymond smiled. "Fine, just don't snore."

"We are being followed, Comrade General." Vaha tapped the radar screen.

"It is to be expected. Just keep us at an even pace. There are still three hours of darkness and we shall be in the cave in forty minutes. We have nothing to hide."

Vaha had known better than to question Dratshev earlier, but now as they finally neared their target he could no longer hold back his curiosity. "These men in the cave, they are the originals?"

"They are 'The Vampires', Vaha. The most deadly fighting force this world has ever experienced."

There was a silence as Vaha absorbed this information. Dratshev could hear the Chechen's mind working. "I have commanded some of these men for centuries. Now Vaha, you are to join them."

"I am honoured, Comrade General."

"As well you should be." They continued on in silence. Dratshev thought back on the battles he and his men had fought, some of which had been recorded in the great books of history. Many had died to be replaced over the years with the most promising fighting men, those he had turned 'vampire'. Vaha was one such sire. Battle hardened against the Islamic militants in Chechnya, where Dratshev had relocated his research after the cave had fallen. Vaha would now swell his ranks. Dratshev still however needed others.

"We are here." Vaha announced.

"Do not circle but descend immediately."

"But Comrade General, we must recon the landing strip for the enemy."

"There is no need, I have made arrangements."

With the lightest of touches, a testament to Vaha's ability as a pilot, the Black Hawk landed and Dratshev stepped out purposefully into the night carrying a matte black case. Vaha followed several steps behind, Kalashnikov raised. A full moon illuminated what remained of the Taliban camp. Dratshev saw the outline of the first cave entrance and entered. As he and Vaha strode deeper into the cave the light of the moon faded and their eyes adjusted. Better than any pair of NVGs, both immortals could see as though it were day. They reached the rock fall. Dratshev placed his case on the ground and pushed against a huge bolder. Vaha joined him and it gave slightly. They pushed again, their combined strength that of many mortal men. With a thunderous cacophony the rock slide gave way revealing a gap and the facility beyond. Now hands on the other side pulled and within moments there was enough of a gap for Dratshev to step into the chamber. Four Soviet Red Army soldiers stood in a line to greet him.

Dratshev saluted. "Vampires, welcome to the 21st century!" As they saluted he looked at each in turn, Petro, Kirill, Oleg and Victor. "Your imprisonment is over, now we shall take our revenge." Vaha handed Dratshev the case. He opened it. "But first you must feed!"

The Vampires stepped forwards, took bags of blood from the case and piercing them with sharp teeth fed hungrily, their eyes becoming crimson.

"You left us to rot." Kirill was the oldest of Dratshev's men and had centuries before lost all human emotion, existing now to merely fight and feed.

"I had no choice. The Mujahedeen brought down half of the mountain on both entrances. I could not gain entry until now with the aid of the American missiles."

Kirill continued to drink. The Vampires had suffered a starvation induced coma. Unable to feed they had agonisingly slipped into darkness. It was only the faintest scent of the Taliban blood which had caused them to stir, as microscopic airborne particles entered the chamber. Dratshev understood the anger. Lesser men may have fed from one and other until only one remained alive.

"Who is this?" Kirill asked; his mouth bloody.

"This is our newest brother, Vaha."

"A Chechen?" Oleg questioned.

"I was forced to take our research to Chechnya when we were attacked."

"The Chechens are fierce fighters." Victor's eyes locked on to Vaha's. Vaha nodded and retreated to the outside where he would await the arrival of the Americans.

"How long have we been in this tomb?" Oleg now asked.

"Twenty five years and the world has changed. The Soviet Union is no more; the West's enemy is now Islamic terrorists. Empires rise and fall yet we still live." Dratshev saw the bodies of their dead brothers, respectfully covered and to one side. "They too were great warriors".

"They were young and made mistakes." Kirill's stated in an even voice.

"Which one of you sired the American?"

"I did. I was not strong enough to prevent his comrade from halting my feed." Victor replied.

Dratshev nodded slowly. In their weakened state, after having not fed for many years it would have been almost impossible to overcome several armed and highly trained Special Forces soldiers. "No matter, it has worked in our favour. I have placed him in a strategic position at the Americans base. Where is the second American?"

Petro now spoke for the first time, his voice deep and monotone. "I was too slow, he was taken by Krasnov."

Dratshev's face contorted with rage. "That traitor lives?" Petro nodded. Dratshev shook and bared his teeth, in a swift movement he crossed the cave and knelt beside the two corpses. Just before his escape Dratshev had seen Krasnov execute both men with an Afghan Pulwar sword. Then the main entrance and smaller escape tunnel had been blocked as the Mujahedeen had fired RPGs and hurled grenades into the cave. Dratshev had barely escaped the flames and Krasnov had fallen behind him. Dratshev had believed that Krasnov had been crushed and then incinerated. He placed his hand on the chest of each fallen man in turn. The bodies were years' cold yet preserved due to the idiosyncrasies of the mineral rich environment. They had been young, turned during the hell of Stalingrad but had shown much promise. "We shall find Krasnov and we shall kill him and the American he has sired."

36

Steve Flagon call-sign 'Road Runner' was the first to arrive at the cave entrance, followed by Miller and Eaton. Road Runner saw movement and dropped to one knee. "Identify yourself."
"Vaha Grigoryevich, GRU."
"OK, very slowly now edge forward and show yourself."
Vaha stepped further into the moonlight. "Now please follow me, we have found your man. He is alive."
Behind the glass of his NV goggles Flagon blinked. "Alive?"
"Yes but we must hurry, we need to evacuate as the roof is unstable." Vaha turned and took point, leading the Delta operatives towards the facility. They edged into the darkness, NVGs turning the midnight of the tunnel an iridescent green.
"Stop." Miller, who had now taken point, held up a clenched fist as they spotted the opening to the inner cave. Something was wrong. "Where are the rocks? When we left here the entrance was blocked with a rock fall, it just missed me."
"It was like this when we arrived. Now please let us enter in order to help your man."

Miller lowered his fist and the three operatives followed Vaha into the man-made chamber. They saw Dratshev, back towards them leaning over a body. Miller moved forwards. Suddenly there was a rushing which seemed to be at once all around him. A dark figure picked him up and flung him against the wall. Miller hit hard, the air was knocked from his lungs and slid to the floor. Eaton swung his HK-416 in an arc and in the eerie green light fired at another figure. The target twisted and fell. Flagon too managed to fire a few rounds before he was violently pushed to the floor. Sharp teeth snapped at him and cut into his neck like razors. Before he had the chance to move, the chance to defend, his jugular vein was pierced and his life greedily drained. As Eaton tried to retreat two dark shapes blocked his path. Their eyes glowed brightly and if he had not been wearing NVGs he would have seen that they were blood red. He fired directly at them; they twitched as rounds penetrated their flesh but did not fall. The HK stopped, magazine empty. The two vampires then came at him with fists like claws; their blows fractured bones and sent him to the ground. A second later Eaton's neck too had been pierced. Miller lay on his stomach, dazed. His HK had been knocked from his grip. He got to his haunches and frantically reached for his secondary weapon but as he drew it a thunderous impact from behind sent him face first into the dirt. He tried to turn, to pick himself up but was lifted him like a rag doll. Dazed but not out of the fight he threw his head back and felt his helmet collide with flesh, he imagined rather than heard the cartilage in the nose explode. The hands momentarily loosened their grip enough for him to throw his attacker over his shoulder and onto the floor.

"Stop." Dratshev commanded.

Miller turned, pulled his Glock back by its lanyard and quickly fired a double tap at the Russian's head. Like a blur Dratshev stepped aside and the rounds hit the rock-face before ricocheting off at acute angles. Miller fired again but this time Dratshev lunged forward and grabbed both the American's wrist and elbow joint. In one sharp move he broke Miller's arm. The Glock fell to the ground and Miller dropped to his knees holding his arm. It was folded the wrong way. As a shot of cold surged through his body Miller saw the horror around him. Eaton and Flagon were dead; both had the jaws of Soviet Red Army soldiers clamped to their necks. Apart from the sound of blood being swallowed the cave was disconcertingly silent. Through a wave of pain Miller tried to understand what was happening but all he could think about was his favourite film as a kid 'The Lost Boys'.

"You have displayed impressive survival skills. Because of this I am now going to give you a choice. Would you like to live forever or die?"

Miller grabbed his forearm with his left hand and attempted to yank it back into place. The pain was like no other he had ever experienced. As the edges of his vision greyed out he said the first words that came into his head. "Bite me!"

Dratshev watched the Delta operative collapse into unconsciousness.

Black shielded his eyes and looked up. Overhead a Chinook on its way from Firebase Python passed by, its rotors spinning like the wings of a giant dragon fly. The base was now in sight. Black slowed the Toyota to a halt and stepped out. He knew that continuing on in the vehicle would increase the risk of at any moment being mistaken for a Talib. It had taken almost two days but he had made it back to Firebase Python. He sensed rather than knew when the watchtower first saw him. Black removed his webbing, and raised his arms aloft. He waited motionless for a minute or so before cautiously walking forwards.

Gonzalez stepped out of the stockade, swigged his coke and looked at the heavens. The mid-morning sky was once again an unnaturally beautiful shade of blue.

"How is Styles?" Rockbridge asked with actual concern for a change.

Gonzalez shrugged. "Still asleep but sweating some, sir. Doc thinks he has a fever."

"As I thought the Pentagon says it's a no go on transferring him to Moscow."

"So the politicians are gonna let one of my boys die?"

"Perhaps, but they want to send a team to check exactly what he has. They do not believe that it is Ebola, in fact they don't believe the Russian."

"They said that to you?"

"No Gonzalez, that's a little above my pay-grade. I'm just filling in the blanks. Fact is Styles stays here until the medical team arrives."

"Friggin great."

"No, fucking awful."

Gonzalez turned to look at Rockbridge, surprised by his turn of voice.

"I have opinions too soldier; just don't care to air them."

"Maybe you're not such a ..."

"Dickwad?" Rockbridge knew what some of the Delta boys had said about him. "Look I'm sorry we can't do anything more for Styles, but if your men can't get to Black's body today I'll formally request that JSOC give the go ahead for a dozer or something, whatever it is they need to excavate the site."

Gonzalez looked skywards again. One moment they had been a successfully mopping up the Talibs and the next one of his boys was crushed to death, buried in a collapsed cave. He crumpled his can and hurled it across the compound. "Shit man, what a way to go."

"You know you've got to pick that up?"

Gonzalez gave Rockbridge one of his stares but before he could say anything there was a shout from the watchtower on the perimeter wall. "Major, sir you've got to see this!"

Rockbridge and Gonzalez climbed the steps that had been made in the wall. "What is it soldier?"

The US infantryman pointed. "I see it sir, but I don't believe it. Over there." He handed his binos to the CO of the firebase.

"Is that one of ours?"

"I think so sir. I think it's one of your Deltas sir."

"Give me those, sir." Black took the glasses from Rockbridge. "Peter Pan? It's Friggin Peter Pan!"

"Black?"

"Yes. That's Black all right." Gonzalez focussed the lens. In the distance a figure was swaying as it walked towards them through the bleak desert, a desert which stretched for miles in every direction. "How the hell did he get here?"

Rockbridge shook his head. "I don't know and I don't care. But he made it and that's all that counts."

Within a minute Gonzalez was on a jeep racing to intercept Black who was still some two hundred meters away. He pulled up abruptly, causing a cloud of dust to lift.

"About time, Sarge." Black said weakly before collapsing.

THREE: Pasaband District, Ghowr Province, Afghanistan

"Tell me who it was that betrayed me?"

Sitting crossed legged, Ghulam Ali, the Afghan warlord regarded Dratshev with narrow eyes. He exhaled a puff of smoke from his traditional pipe and waited as it rose slowly to the ceiling of the hut. "It was a long time ago; my memory is not what it once was."

Dratshev dropped a bundle of US dollars at the Afghan's feet. "Who betrayed me?"

"I remember now. It was Krasnov. He gave away your location to my enemy, the enforcer - Hakim who in turn attacked you."

The Russian held grudges. Hakim too would pay with his life for the years of research lost, but he would suffer much pain first. "Where is Hakim?"

"I forget."

Dratshev threw him another bundle of notes. "Where is he?"

"He has joined the glorious Afghan National Army. I believe he is at the new base, not far from here." There was a silence as Ghulam Ali chomped on his pipe. "I have given you information about the ISAF forces, I have told you about the discovery of the cave. I have kept my side of our agreement Dratshev, now it is your turn."

"I will see to it immediately. Bring me a Shahid." Dratshev used the Arabic word for martyr.

"What? You expect me to bring one of my men to be experimented upon? I have a better idea." The Afghan held up his hand and a younger man moved from the side of the room and crouched by his leader's shoulder. Ghulam Ali whispered in the boy's ear. The fighter left the hut and returned pushing a man who had his arms bound behind his back. "This traitor is a spy for the Americans. You may experiment upon him."

"Very well." Dratshev stood and removed a cigar shaped container from his coat pocket. This he opened to display a miniature automatic syringe-gun. "I need his neck."

The captive seemed confused to hear Dratshev speak his tongue. Ghulam Ali nodded and the traitor was pushed towards Dratshev. Ghulam Ali continued to smoke his pipe, but now his eyes were wider with interest. The 'spy' was just under six feet tall, his face was full of fear as he looked up at the taller Russian. In one swift movement that the assembled audience all but missed, Dratshev plunged the needle into the Afghan's neck and depressed it one click. A metered amount of a vampire blood based serum shot directly into the jugular vein. The Afghan's eyes rolled back, his eyelids snapped shut then opened to reveal red pupils. Dratshev pushed the man away.

Ghulam Ali stood. "That is it?"

"That is it."

The Afghan regarded his captive who was now breathing heavily and rolling his head. "How do I know it has worked?"

"Shoot him in the head."

"What? You want me to kill him?

"No. I want you to shoot him in the head."

"Crazy Russian." The warlord bent down and picked up his AK47. He pointed the rifle at the cowering man. Paralyzed by fear and two days of beatings, the captive made no attempt to move merely turned his head and hunched his shoulders. Ghulam Ali depressed the trigger, the sound deafening in the mud hut as a single round hit the man in the chest. The impact sent him stumbling back against the wall, blood seeped from the entry wound but he did not fall.

"I said in the head."

Ghulam Ali's nostrils flared, no one gave him orders. He depressed the trigger again and a round hit the spy in the middle of the temple. The top of the head all but disintegrated. The corpse left a blood trail on the wall as it slid to the floor. Dratshev stood emotionless as every other eye in the room stared at the dead traitor. Suddenly its feet twitched, then the body moved and the man started to sit up. Ghulam Ali's mouth fell open as he saw his vampire's head slowly rise. He watched as the gaping hole started to close. Within a minute the wound had started to rebuild itself. The man stood and touched his head in disbelief.

"That was a 7.62 round at close range; if it had been further away the injury and recovery time would have been less."

Suddenly the spy moved his arms and easily broke the bonds holding them. He swung at the nearest fighter, sending him crashing to the floor, he reached for the man's weapon but Ghulam Ali fired. The vampire stumbled but remained standing, a broad smile parting his face and he started to raise his newly acquired AK47. Ghulam Ali switched his own rifle to fully automatic and unloaded the clip into the vampire who jerked as the rounds hit him and he fell. "You have now given me an immortal prisoner!"

"What were you going to do with him?" Asked Dratshev.

44

Ghulam Ali replied as once again the spy started to twitch. "Put him to the sword as a traitor to the Afghan people."

"Then do so."

The Afghan warlord collected his Pulwar from the corner of the room and held it above the vampire. As the vampire started to rise Ghulam Ali swung the sword severing the head. The body went limp. "This is against Allah and all that we Muslims hold holy!" The Afghan's face softened. "You are truly the devil, my Russian friend. This transformation, is it permanent?"

"Until the head is severed."

Ghulam Ali took a step forward and glared intently at Dratshev. "A quarter of a century ago I was twenty five and you were fifty, now I am fifty but you have not aged."

"I have been fifty for a very long time."

A thin smile creased the Afghan's face. "You truly are a Red-Devil and now you will give me an army of my own devils to crush the infidels!" He punched the air with his sword. "Allah Akbar!"

Every other Afghan in the room chanted as one. "Allah Akbar…Allah Akbar…Allah Akbar…Allah Akbar…Allah Akbar…Allah Akbar…Allah Akbar…Allah Akbar!"

Firebase Python, Pasaband District, Ghowr Province, Afghanistan

Rockbridge wearing a surgical mask looked down at Black. Rockbridge was angry. The Russian could have screened Black, but he had left. Vaha had returned without Dratshev stating that the General had the necessary medicine and screening kit with him and would return with the Delta team. A helo had been sent to retrieve the team, it was overdue.

Rockbridge addressed Black. "This is beyond classified soldier. The chamber you found was built by the Soviets to illegally test biological weapons. One of these utilised the Ebola virus. The Doc's sent your blood off to Leatherneck to be checked by the medical centre there. Until we get your results back you have to be isolated, quarantined. We can't risk moving you."

"Ebola, as in African disease? So I'm going to die?"

"If you have been infected then that is a possibility."

"Thanks for sugar coating it, sir."

"Look Black, I've been informed that the chance of infection is minimal. Styles was the only other member to test positive."

"Styles made it out?"

"He's quarantined in the stockade."

There was a silence as both men considered the situation. The preventative medication administered to Styles by Dratshev seemed to be holding off any noticeable symptoms, but Rockbridge had to get the Russian back and fast. Meanwhile Black wasn't sure what to think. Would being infected explain his strange, almost out of body experiences at Krasnov's hut and with the Talibs in the desert?

Rockbridge broke the silence. "Tell me more about your 'Russian'."

Black was drowsy and couldn't summon the energy to tell his CO that Krasnov was actually Ukrainian. Every word seemed to be an effort and his vision was blurred. "He claimed he was a Red Army deserter who stayed behind."

"Since the 80's?" Rockbridge thought aloud.

"He said that he rescued me from the Taliban in the cave."

"Was he going to hand you over to the Taliban for a reward?"

"I don't think so...I have no idea why he took me." Black screwed his eyes up and tried to sit.

"Black, stay on your back – that's an order."

"Sir..." The sound of a helo arriving cut him off. Its engine note was strained.

Coming in faster than usual the helo kicked up a huge dust cloud as it landed. The rotors continued to spin as Rockbridge saw Miller, followed by Flagon and Eaton leap out and run towards their basha, head's down covering their faces. Through the swirling dust cloud, that seemed to block out the last rays of the late afternoon sun, Dratshev appeared. In double time he headed for Rockbridge who noticed the Russian's face seemed reddened, almost sunburnt.

Dratshev stepped into the safety of the medical centre. "Major."

"General." As Rockbridge spoke the Russian's face seemed to become less ruddy. "We have one more man for you to test. Our missing Delta operative has returned."

A narrow smile appeared on Dratshev's face. "That is excellent news, Major. How did he get here?"

"He walked."

Dratshev could not hide his surprise. Perhaps the soldier had not been sired? But it made no difference; the man would be taken care of. All of the ISAF personnel would be taken care of. "Let us not waste any more precious time."

Gonzalez stood as Flagon entered the tent. "You took your sweet time…" The words fell from his mouth as a tranquiliser dart hit him in the neck. Gonzalez's knees buckled and he was unconscious before he hit the floor. Without a word Petro, dressed in Eaton's fatigues grabbed Gonzalez and hauled him onto his shoulder in a fireman's carry. He exited the tent and hurried towards the helo. Oleg, wearing Flagon's uniform, followed at his side with an HK up and ready.

Rockbridge gestured towards Black's bed. "That's our last guy. Now please hurry."

Dratshev opened his greatcoat and pulled out a syringe. "I will need to take some blood."

"This is General Dratshev from the GRU. He's going to test you for Ebola." Rockbridge informed Black.

"Hold still. This will not hurt." Dratshev reached for Black's arm. Black raised his head and looked into the eyes of the

Russian. Dratshev paused and confusion briefly crossed his pallid face. "You walked back from the cave, through the mountains and the desert?"

Black felt the needle enter. "It was a like Switzerland, but without the grass."

Dratshev smiled thinly. There was something here that he did not understand. "You travelled at night?"

"Night and day…" Black could suddenly feel himself getting drowsy.

In the stockade Styles opened his eyes and called out. The sentry on duty moved nearer, and bent over the cot, his face partly obscured by a white surgical mask. Before the soldier could speak Styles sprang up and sank his fangs into the exposed neck. His victim convulsed, arms flailing, hands grabbing at the Delta operative's head trying to pull him off but to no avail. The soldier became limp as his life drained away. Styles wiped his lips and left the stockade. Dratshev's commands had been clear: disable the communication equipment and then make for the helo. Moving faster than even he imagined he could, Styles sprinted across the firebase and entered the communication's shack. Another pre-fabricated building but this one linked to the world via satellite. As the door swung open two operators looked up, their faces registering surprised more than shock. This changed however when they saw the grenade that Styles rolled into the room before calmly closing the door on them. As Styles moved away there was an explosion and the communications desk and operators were no more. Dratshev's operation had now gone noisy.

Rockbridge instinctively ducked as he heard the explosion. "What the hell was that?"

"A grenade." In a fluid motion Dratshev plunged a needle into Rockbridge's neck. The tranquiliser hit immediately and the CO of firebase Python hit the floor. Vaha appeared. Dratshev pointed at Rockbridge. "Take him to the helo."

"Da, Comrade General." Vaha saluted and with ease lifted Rockbridge into his arms and left the building.

Dratshev looked at Black. After taking a sample of blood he had quickly shot him with tranquiliser. Dratshev shook his head dismissively, the man had not been sired he was mortal and as such was of no value to him. Dratshev had what he had come for, he had his men and he had two HVH's – high value hostages. Now the Taliban could have the firebase and his test would be complete.

Private 1st Class James Anders yawned. He'd been looking at the same piece of terrain for what felt like days but in actual fact had been only four hours. This second tour of 'Asscrackistan' had put him over the edge. Their first tour had been spent operating out of a larger base which had a proper canteen with hot food, showers, laundry and even free internet access at the Morale, Welfare & Recreation Office. At firebase Python, although they got real food more often than many other firebases MREs actually did replace most meals when the helos had more important things to do than ferry in food for the troops. They were not as bad off as some bases where the men lived without coms and even without cold showers, but he had now had enough. Enough of the sand, the dirt and the constant threat of losing parts of himself to an IED. He's seen it happen, out on a patrol right in front of him. A friend shredded, scraped up and put in a bag and all the while jubilant chatter over the airwaves from the Talibs. He thought of Marcy, his girl back home and how every time they had a mail drop he braced himself for a 'Dear John' letter, but she stayed true to him, or at least her letters did. No she was 'his love' and he would marry her, once the tour was over. The question was would she accept life as an army bride or force him to quit and take a job with her father's firm? Selling insurance was not his idea of excitement but then neither was sitting and staring at the desert for hours on end. He'd enlisted to make a difference, to take democracy and the rule of law to those who sought to terrorise the innocent and pervert religion. Yet he felt that he'd done nothing to aid this cause. Endless patrols and smiles directed at sullen locals, who would as soon stab him in the back, had left a bitter taste in his mouth. COIN was the official term for what his unit was doing here, 'counterinsurgency warfare' showing the Afghans that ISAF cared, that the international community cared about them, their mud huts and their goats. They were here to help these people, to rid them of the Taliban and their friends in low places, al-Qaeda. Anders shook his head. This wasn't a war; it wasn't even a fight as these cowards left their bombs and ran, hiding behind women and children. They took pot shots at the ISAF soldiers but would only engage if cornered. The people who did any good, to see any real action were the flyers and of course the 'Delta Boys'. Even now they had a helo – 'rotors hot', ready for some 'Black Op' or other. Anders read a lot, now more than ever since he got his kindle and his books of choice were action and adventure, Alex Berenson, Vince Flynn, Jack Silkstone and Stephen Leather - anything where the Islamic fundamentalists got the wrong end of a 9mm round. He wished the reality of his life was more like the fiction. He wished he was about to head off in a helo…

"Two o'clock, movement behind that second compound. Yeah, looks like a bunch of Talib trucks." Private Errol Jinks excitedly held the NV enabled binos tight to his eyes. In the distance one of the innumerable peaks of an Afghan mountain contrasted against the desolate desert and scrublands that surrounded the firebase. Several Afghan compounds with their ten foot high mud and straw walls, hugged what green zone there was next to an all but dry irrigation channel. Barren and sparsely populated the province had been a haven for insurgents, the firebase taking incoming mortars and RPGs in the first few weeks of its existence, but after a couple of drone lead ops had seen the death of nine Taliban fighters and the capture of three more, the local Taliban had taken the wise decision to just 'watch' and leave the base alone.

Anders looked through his own binos and in the uncanny green NV world counted a convoy of twelve wagons with what he took to be PKMs mounted on the back. "What the hell are they up to? They know they'll never get within range."

"Crazy bastards, looks like they…." The explosion made Jinks drop his binos. "What the?"

Anders spun round and saw the comms trailer ablaze. "Shit…"

The explosion made Hakim's eyes snap open. He tried to get up but then remembered his shackles. Chained to the blast-wall just outside the main ANA tent, Hakim slowly pushed himself back and up until he was standing. Captain Osman, emerged from his own tent rubbing his eyes as the unmistakable sound of gunfire rang out, barks from Kalashnikov's followed by the heavy boom of .50 cal rounds from the watchtowers.

"Untie me, Osman!"

Osman blinked and reached for his belt, doing it up as he continued to pull his pants up over his stomach. "You are a prisoner. You shall stay there until we transport you back to Kabul."

ANA soldiers now poured out of their tent in various stages of undress, some wearing dirty white vests others in uniform shirts but all to a man clutching their shiny new M4's funded by the international community.

Osman shouted at his second in command. "Yusuf, go to the command centre, see what is happening. Men take defensive positions on the wall!"

"Untie me you fool! I am the most experienced man you have!"

"Hakim you are a goat. Now keep your mouth closed or I shall have it gagged!"

Dratshev tapped Vaha on the shoulder. "Go." The Chechen nodded and the Black Hawk lifted away from the firebase. Dratshev looked at the men in the chopper, two originals and two new 'recruits'. The Americans would add new blood, new skills to the Brigada and would aid him in his quest. They would now take the hostages and give them to Ghulam Ali who would do whatever he wished with them to further his own cause.

The warning shots had gone unheeded; in fact the Talibs had returned fire. Jinks sighted the cross hairs on the lead Taliban pick-up and yelled. "Hammer time."

A stream of lead, highlighted by evenly spaced tracer rounds tore towards the Toyota Hi-Lux. The front of the vehicle was ripped to pieces as the grill disintegrated. The fuel tank then went up in a fireball. Two flaming fighters staggered out of the cab and another two fell from the back. Jink's eyes widened as he saw the fighters continue towards them on foot, AKs raised. He depressed the trigger and sent more .50 cal rounds into the insurgents. They went down hard, all but disintegrating under the heavy rounds. He then saw more vehicles emerging from the green gloom. As he swung his binos left and right, trying to make sense of what was happening Lieutenant Mullins joined them.

"A grenade has taken out the comms shack; we don't know where it came from. We are being attacked on two fronts; I need you to keep the Talibs at bay until we can somehow get hold of air support."

"Must be the friggin ANA." Jinks growled; he'd never trusted the native army.

"Just keep the Talibs away." Mullins took the steps down and made for the next watch tower. En route he saw Captain Osman and pulled him to one side, ignoring the fact that the Afghan out ranked him. "The comms are down. Are all your men accounted for?"

"Yes and as you see they are fighting!" Osman waved his arms expressively at the top of the blast walls. Mullins nodded and was about to speak when a round ripped his skull in two. Osman froze; the American's blood sprayed his face. And then he too was hit. A round tore into his back. His legs buckled. Osman fell to his knees over the American's corpse, he felt himself sway sideways and raised his arms to stop himself from falling but his arms would not respond, his arms would not move. His head lolled and he fell into the dirt, his brain blearily registering the impact before darkness enveloped him.

Hakim pulled at his chains as he saw Taliban fighters on the wall above Osman. They dropped into the firebase apparently immune to the impact of the fall and hurriedly searched for targets. Hakim heaved at his shackles but they would not budge. He let his head loll to one side and feigned death as two Taliban fighters came his way, one peeled off and into Osman's tent. The other leaned over Hakim and prodded. Now was the time, a split-second to act. Hakim quickly raised his arms, wrapping the chain around the insurgent's neck and pulled as hard as he could. This move should have at the very least rendered its victim unconscious but the Taliban dropped his AK and wildly grabbed at the chain affixed to his neck. He straightened up and tried to move away, the chain tightened but he pulled again and a link snapped. Both men fell forward and hit the dirt. Hakim landed half on top of the Taliban still holding the chain to his throat. The fighter bucked. Hakim was thrown sideways, his right arm reached the Taliban's AK. He grabbed the pistol grip and pulled the trigger. On full-automatic a cluster of rounds exploded from the barrel and created a large hole in the fighter. Hakim got to his feet, and then saw the fighter move and his eyes open. At that instant Hakim knew that he had been right, he knew what he was facing and he knew what he had to do. He placed the Kalashnikov's barrel against the Taliban's neck and emptied the magazine. The rounds obliterated the neck, severing the head. Hakim had killed his first vampire for a quarter of a century.

"They've breached the perimeter!" Anders yelled as he saw movement along the blast walls. The next tower to them went silent.

Jinks continued to pick off targets with his heavy calibre rounds, but then he noticed something impossible. Some of the targets were getting up and continuing forward. He was hitting the trucks but the occupants seemed to be immune. He drilled more rounds into three Talibs, advancing in a tight group in what should have been tactical suicide. All three fell. One immediately stood up and continued on. And then the Taliban were within AK range. Uncontrolled rounds wildly spun in the night air, without tracer they were invisible to the naked eye. Then grenades started to fly. Anders and Jinks ducked as a metallic object arced towards their position. It exploded in the air behind them. Jinks raised his head, Anders did not. Jinks shook his comrade in arms. "Anders…Anders!"

"W…what?" Anders seemed concussed. "I…I'm fine." He smiled weakly and then his mouth fell open with shock as a round from an AK tore away Jinks' face. Anders scrabbled for the .50 cal when suddenly he was lifted and thrown from his firing position. He landed heavily outside the blast walls. He tried to move but couldn't and then he was held aloft as a Talib with red eyes attacked his neck like a rabid dog. As Anders' world dimmed the last thing he heard was a Black Hawk powering away from the base.

In the darkness far away Black heard what sounded like thunder, as colours started to swim in front of his eyes he realised that it was gunfire. Then another sound attacked his ears, screams. His eyes snapped opened he saw the two camp medics at the windows, using their rifles. He swung his legs from the bed and stood.

"Give me your side arm!" Black yelled at the nearest. Without complaint the pistol was tossed towards him.

Black left the medical shack. Something was very wrong. Uniformed bodies littered the ground. He could see Taliban fighters engaged in hand to hand combat with the firebase's troop. But something was wrong. The Talibs were winning. A turbaned figure saw Black and headed straight towards him. Almost in slow motion, the Afghan loosely aimed his AK and started to spray on full automatic. Black retreated into the doorway as rounds impacted all around him. He paused counted to three and as the insurgent's mag emptied he sprang back out from cover, pistol in a two handed grip and double tapped the Talib. Two holes appeared in the fighter's chest and he stumbled. Black fired again and this time sent a further two rounds into the man's forehead. The fighter dropped. Black advanced and grabbed the Afghan's AK. It had two magazines taped together for quick reloading. Black pulled out the mag, spun it around and drove it back in. A hand grabbed his ankle and almost pulled him to the ground. Amazed, Black sent two more rounds, 7.62mm this time into the Talibs face turning it into a red mess. Black looked for his next target. He shot a second Talib in the back of the head causing him to fall from the roof of the nearest pre-fab. He advanced into the open, a foolhardy but necessary move. His base was under attack and he was not going to let it fall. In the open now he saw the true picture of the attack. The comms shack and several others were billowing smoke, each of the guard-towers were manned but the 0.50 cals' had been made to point inwards and were picking off ISAF targets. Men fell and were instantly set upon by Taliban fighters who clawed at them like wild animals. To his left at the far end of the firebase a group of ANA soldiers had manned a Gimpy and were attempting to make a last stand, to the right he saw three American soldiers retreating tactically backwards in formation firing controlled bursts. Everyone else was dead. The base was lost. Black never thought he would die like this, cut down in his own base but he took a perverse pleasure in the fact that he would be going down fighting. He chose the nearest gun emplacement and charged towards it. Heavy rounds zipped over his head and then he was hit in the chest by something with the force of a sledgehammer. Black was lifted from his feet and slammed to the floor. He lay motionless for several seconds as he realised that he'd been by a 0.50 cal. That was it he was going to die. He moved his hands to feel the wound then looked at his fingers, dripping in his own blood. A white hot rage took over him, it masked the pain. He had no idea how he could, but he knew he could stand again. Pushing himself up Black ignored the fire in his chest and charged at the tower. He reached the rough-hewn steps and without pause took them two at a time. At the top he emptied his mag into the nearest Talib fighter and then threw himself at the second who was manning the .50 cal. The gunner fell sideways and Black pushed his thumbs deep into the man's eye sockets. The Afghan screamed, arms flailing and then became still. Black pushed the corpse sideways and grabbed the heavy machine-gun. Lining up a target he fired. The heavy round tore the head from the shoulders of its target. "Scratch on more Talib!" Black muttered to himself before lining up the next insurgent. It was a target rich environment, but he knew his time was limited. Within seconds twenty fighters, some armed others not were heading his way. Black continued to fire, he felled the first two yet those behind stepped over the fallen and continued to come. Then a trail of smoke raced towards him. An RPG…Black threw himself sideways as the grenade impacted a meter from his position. The explosion was deafening, the shockwave contained within the wall horrific. Black couldn't move and his hearing had gone. Then he felt vibrations, heavy thuds of boots. His entire body leaden he managed to sit as the face of an Afghan appeared above the steps, eyes wild, mouth open to show bloody teeth. Instinctively Black bared his own teeth and for a moment there was stillness then his hearing returned and so did his strength. He grabbed the fighter by the neck and hauled him up. With a power he had not known he possessed, he squeezed the man's neck until he felt the cartilage buckle. Pulling the Afghan nearer he sank his teeth into the exposed neck and felt blood pour into his mouth. His victim thrashed wildly before becoming limp. This act had taken no more than five seconds yet it was enough for two more Talibs to appear at the top of the steps, both now leapt at him.

Hakim raised his head from behind a sandbag, the firing had slowed and the remaining Taliban had moved away from his position. On either side of him dead ANA soldiers lay, they were the brave ones who had chosen to fight or the lucky ones whose lives had been extinguished by a bullet and not the jaws of a Hadama. He was one of only two left. The other ANA soldier to survive was Yusuf. "Now do you believe my camp fire stories?"

Yusuf nodded. He had seen the Hadama for himself. "We must tell Kabul, we must alert the rest of the army!"

"How?" Hakim glanced at the young officer. "We have no communication equipment and if we move they shall slaughter us. What we must do is to stay low and prey to Allah, peace be upon him, that these affronts to Him leave us. It is three hours to daylight then we shall be safe."

"OK." Yusuf nodded his assent to the older and far more experienced soldier. "But what drew them away?"

Hakim said humourlessly. "Perhaps they have found some more American beef to feed upon?"

Black ducked the blade that swung violently at his neck and at the same time stepped into his attacker. Black grabbed the wrist with his right hand and with his left hand he used an open palm strike to the elbow to shatter the joint. The Talib screamed and before he could react further Black grabbed the knife and slit the man's throat. As the Talib fell to the ground the second Talib dived for his comrade's neck, not in an attempt to save him but to feed from him. The steps were now blocked but it would be only a matter of seconds before more Talibs swarmed his way. Like lemmings headed towards the edge of a cliff they would not be deterred. He moved towards the .50 cal and saw that it was now no more than a heap of twisted metal, fused together by the heat of the RPG round. He stood up straight and willed a round to enter his flesh but the base was now in an unnerving silence. To his right he saw movement, two figures crouching behind a hastily arranged pile of sandbags and to his left he saw a solitary US soldier with his standard issue M4 carbine. Black slapped his cheeks and snapped himself out of his immobility. He was now more determined than ever. The American would survive, and so would he. Black dropped to his haunches and then springing forward like a sprinter, launched himself off of the wall and towards the compound floor ten feet below. He landed with a thud but somehow managed to keep moving, keep running. Behind him the Talibs were taken by surprise and momentarily did not follow. Black kept his head down and like a linebacker barrelled two Talibs out of the way who were making for the American. He could now see the eyes of his countryman, wide with fear as he neared him. The American raised his rifle and fired, the round just missing Black's left ear, a second round swiftly followed. A Talib appeared between them. The American had missed and now he was out of ammo. He swung the rifle wildly as the Talib grabbed his arms, and then Black was on him. The Talib was forced into the dirt, Black reached down grabbed the head twisted it and tore it away from the body. Arterial spray bathed his face.

"Y…your SIX!" The American yelled.

Black spun as an AK round hit him in the left shoulder. The full focus of the remaining Talibs was now on them. Black swore. They couldn't win, they wouldn't live. Another round hit him and he staggered. The American next to him fell, screaming, dying. A third round caused Black to drop to his knees. This wasn't how he was going to die; again he stood without knowing how and stared directly at an ugly, red-eyed knife wielding Talib no more than a meter away. The Talib bared his teeth then suddenly jerked left as a round entered the side of his skull. Controlled bursts from an AK felled three more Talibs in quick succession. Black picked up the knife and attacked a further fighter. Around him the Talibs scattered as more and more of them were taken out by AK rounds. As they retreated Black looked up and saw the Ukrainian, Krasnov standing on the blast wall with an AK 47.

"Come with me and you will live!" Krasnov bellowed.

Then Black saw it, another RPG aimed his way. His periphery vision became blurred, he moved quickly as the grenade spun towards him. Black looked down from the blast-wall, the grenade landed where his feet had been a moment before. He had no idea how he managed to mount the wall.

"Follow me!" Krasnov yelled as he stood next to a Toyota pick-up on the ground outside the base.

Black jumped down, rolling as he landed. "How?"

"Just get in; we need to escape the sun!"

Krasnov pulled away, tyres throwing loose stones and dirt into the air. High above there was a whining noise and milliseconds later a Hellfire missile exploded on the other side of the base. The unblinking eye of ISAF had for once blinked.

FOUR: Camp Bastion, Helmand Province, Afghanistan

On the other end of the secure line the two star US General gave his acceptance. "Declare a Critical Mission Status. You have my permission to send in a team. Immediately."

"Thank you General." As the SF liaison officer Matthers was glad the overall boss of ISAF operations in Afghanistan was on the same page as him. He ended the call. The firebase had as far as they could ascertain been overrun by insurgents. All contact with Rockbridge and his men had been lost. A drone had confirmed that Taliban fighters were indeed inside the base. The deployment of a Hellfire missile outside the front gates had done very little it seemed to make the unwelcomed guests leave. Matthers made another call to the QRF team; he would brief them in ten. In fifteen they would be airborne. First he had a few questions to ask the last person to see Rockbridge before the camp went dark, his fellow Brit Paige Turner.

As Turner crossed the base from the journos' 'holding area' she felt a sense of urgency that she had not experienced before. She couldn't put her finger on it but something was happening. She had told Raymond to take his camera and go mobile on the pretence of getting some candid footage that they could cut into. In reality he was attempting to find out what was going on. She had missed the biggest story of her life the last time she had been in 'the Stan'. She had been re-called to London by the BBC on the pretence of assisting with the build-up for the Royal Wedding only days before the capture of bin-Laden. She had gotten too close; someone had 'pulled strings' and had her shipped home. She'd be buggered if she was going to miss another story. She arrived at Matthers' office, a plywood affair topped with sandbags and partly hidden by a blast-wall. Even though she found him extremely dishy to look at, she disliked the man. Perhaps it was his hair that was too well groomed for a frontline command position? He reminded her of an old 'Just For Men' advert. She knocked and entered without awaiting a response.

"You wanted to see me Colonel?"

"Thank you Ms Turner."

"What can I do for you?" This time she noted that he looked unusually stern.

"Please sit." She did so and he stared at a legal pad on his desk. "I'm not going to beat around the bush or try to hide this. We simply do not have the time to waste. We have reason to believe that Firebase Python has been overrun by the Taliban."

Her jaw dropped, she felt it.

He continued. "As of 19:25 we lost contact with the base. We have been unable to raise Major Rockbridge or anyone else."

"But I was just there…"

"That is why I called you in here, Ms Turner. The helo you left on with your cameraman and a handful of other personnel was the last to leave the base. You left at, what was it, 18:00?"

"18:19." She had a photographic memory; it served her well in the supermarket and during arguments. "The pilot made a remark that we'd get to see the sunset if we were lucky on our way here." Suddenly she tried to hold back the tears. Did this mean that the men she had filmed, got to know and shared a joke with were now dead?

Matthers noticed she was shaken but ignored it. "Well just after sunset was when we lost all contact. Ms Turner, what I need from you is to tell me if there was anything you noticed when you left the base, anything strange or unusual at all?"

She reached into her pocket for a tissue and touched the corners of her eyes. "Nothing during the day but there was an unexpected helo departure the night before; I mean the same day – early hours of the morning. About two-ish."

"I was unaware of that."

"It was carrying a Russian from the GRU."

"Your sources are obviously much better than mine. What Russian?"

"That's all I could find out. The Russian got in to a helo and left. A few minutes later a Delta team followed him."

Matthers folded his arms and sat back in his chair. He knew of no JSOC mission or why Russia, a non-member of ISAF would be involved in ISAF operations. "What the bloody hell is going on?"

Turner was surprised by his admission and the tone of it. "You don't know?"

"No I do not. So apart from the 'phantom mission' was there anything else that struck you as strange?"

Turner told Matthers about the fight between Hakim and a Delta who had been in the medical centre a matter of hours before. Matthers jotted down a few notes before dismissing her and running to his briefing.

The enormity of what had just happened momentarily muted Black. As the Toyota continued to bounce away from the firebase, passing the wrecked Talib trucks and then the empty compounds, his brain tried to process what he had seen and what he had done. They skirted the desert plain and took a narrow road into the mountains. He finally looked at Krasnov and only then realised that the Ukrainian had been navigating in the complete darkness without the aid of either headlights or NVGs. Black managed to speak. "I shot you dead."

"You did shoot me, but I have been dead since 1988." Krasnov replied.

"I don't understand. Who are you?

"You should ask me what I am. I am a vampire, as are you."

"What?" Black asked the Ukrainian as he manoeuvred the Toyota in-between two giant boulders.

"We are mythical beings, blood sucking creatures of the night. But you are different, you are Ra-Hodok, you can walk in sunlight."

As if on cue Black felt dizzy, his head fell back against the headrest.

"You need to feed. If you do not feed you shall fall into a coma. Here, take it." Krasnov handed him a flask.

Black shakily accepted it. "Blood? Human blood?"

"Drink it, you know that you must."

In the gloom, Black looked at the flask and for a moment hesitated but as he did so his vision blurred at the edges. Krasnov abruptly stopped the truck and grabbed the American's wrists, pushing the flask to his lips. Black's eyes rolled back in his head as the heavy red liquid cascaded down his throat. His eyes then snapped open and his vision cleared. Black locked eyes with Krasnov, both men's eyes momentarily flashed red.

"You know that I am speaking the truth even though your rational mind does not want to believe it. You can feel it in your heart and in the blood that flows through it."

"I'm meant to believe this? That Vampires are real? Come on, they don't exist, they are made up to sell movies and books."

The Ukrainian shrugged. "Where did these writers get their ideas from? From folk lore, myths and legends which in turn originated from encounters with vampires, from fact. I exist, you exist, we as vampires exist. Those things you fought at the base what were they, figments of your imagination?"

Something inside Black told him that as crazy as it seemed, this was the truth. He had been trying to deny it but no longer could. He had drunk the blood of two Talibs, had survived rounds entering his body and now after this new blood he felt unbeatable. Black shook his head, not sure what to feel, or who or what he had now become. "Shit."

"As you Americans say, 'shit happens'." Krasnov put the Toyota back into gear and they continued up the path. "When we met I told you my name, what is yours?"

"Black, Brad Black."

"And your call-sign?"

"Peter Pan."

Krasnov grunted. "Very appropriate; the boy who never grows old."

Black frowned. "The Russians from the cave, are they vampires?"

"They are 'The Vampires', they are what remains of a Soviet Special Operations unit."

"Spetsnaz?"

"Correct. Our commanding officer was a General Vladimir Dratshev."

"Ours? You were one of them?"

"I was their newest recruit; Dratshev turned me only months before we were deployed."

"Are you seriously telling me that the Soviet Union deployed a Special Ops team of vampires to Afghanistan?"

"Yes."

Black tried not to laugh. "The Soviet Union was using vampires to carry out their dirty work?"

"No. The Vampires were using the Soviet Union. As a war zone Afghanistan was the perfect place for Dratshev to continue with his research. No one misses young men in a war, both sides simply presume that the other has either killed or captured them. We had an unlimited supply of subjects to experiment upon and learn from."

"Dratshev is a scientist?"

Krasnov grunted. "He is many things."

"What was he researching, a cure?"

"No not a cure for vampirism, he did not want to give up his immortality. What he wanted was a cure for the other curse. Dratshev came to the conclusion that all humans carry the vampire gene; it is waiting dormant until it is activated. Dratshev wanted to control it so that the subject would retain the human tolerance for sunlight. Simply put he wanted to find a cure for sunlight."

"But he succeeded; you said I was a Ra-Hodok?"

"The Ra-Hodoks, the 'Sun-Walkers', really are the stuff of legend, or are meant to be, but you are one. And it was not Dratshev but I who made you vampire."

"Why?"

"To prevent you from being crushed to death in the cave and to prevent you from becoming lunch."

A sudden anger tore through Black, the realisation of a life lost. "You bit me, so what am I now a member of the walking dead?"

"Is that how you feel, dead?"

"No. I feel alive." In fact Black felt more alive than ever, he felt exhilarated. A thought struck him. "When I first stepped out of your hut I burnt."

"That is because your first blood had not started to take effect on your system. When you left me, for dead after you shot me, I had no reason to believe that you would make it. I had no reason to believe that you were Ra-Hodok. Somehow your vampire gene has mutated to enable you to withstand sunlight like any mortal man."

"So what are the rules, how can we die? I shot you, I saw you die, the bullets entered you."

"We cannot be killed by normal bullets but silver ones slow us down."

Black frowned. "How?"

"We are allergic to silver; to us it is highly toxic. When a standard bullet rips into us, our bodies immediately start to repair the damage. The silver in a silver bullet prevents our system from starting this repair process. Fill a vampire with enough silver and he will die from wounds sustained, like any other victim of a gunshot wound. I was using silver rounds at the base; that is how I prevented the Taliban from tearing you to pieces."

"So we aren't immortal?"

"We are until we are killed." Krasnov laughed without humour.

"By silver?"

"By silver, a wooden stake through the heart, decapitation or fire. In addition to this I can be killed by sunlight. There is much truth in Hollywood movies."

"What about lack of blood?"

"That cannot kill you; merely put you into a coma."

"So how often must I drink blood?"

"That depends upon how active you are and how much your body needs to repair itself. I feed once every twenty-four hours but you may need to every twelve or more frequently if you have sustained injury or are in a very cold environment. You will soon feel if you need to feed and you will know when to stop."

Black tried to think clearly. "Can I eat normal food?"

"Yes, but you must still drink blood. Human blood is the only blood that will sustain you long term but in an emergency any will do to slow the onset of a coma. To become strong and remain at your strongest you must feed upon human blood."

"So if I drink blood I will never age and never die?"

"Yes, just like Peter Pan." Krasnov almost smiled.

Again Black tried to understand what the Ukrainian had explained, it was the stuff of dreams, a thing of fiction yet it was real. He was immortal. His mind continued to whir as Krasnov led them higher into the mountains. An icy chill blew in through the open windows. Black realised that he was not cold, his skin registered the temperature yet he did not flinch from it nor did his skin form goose bumps. "I'm sorry I shot you."

"You had good reason. Do not worry I will not hold it against you."

Black fell silent, again not knowing what to think. The wind whistled around the pick-up as they continued to climb. "How old are you?"

"In human years I am fifty five, but I stopped aging when I was turned vampire at the age of thirty."

"And Dratshev, how old is he?"

"I do not know for certain but he may well be one of the oldest men on earth."

"One of the oldest? How many vampires are there creeping around?"

"I have no idea; I personally have not met any more since I was left here."

Black felt his head beginning to spin. "Why are you here? Why stay in Afghanistan?"

"There was nothing for me at home in Mother Russia. I am an orphan; I have no family which is why Dratshev chose me. I stayed here because I wanted to repay my debt to this country, but I knew that one day someone would find my group and that when happened, Dratshev would appear to re-activate them. I would then be able to destroy them all."

"But they are your team, your unit?"

"They were never really my team, I was the new boy. I was never trusted, I did not agree with the tests being carried out on innocent locals. This gave Dratshev reason enough to want to have me killed. I hated what I had become but I was the only one to feel this way. I managed to pass on our location to some of the local fighters - Mujahedeen, my enemy. My enemy's enemy became my friend. There was a huge fighter, a giant of a man yet no more than a teenager. He had survived an attack by The Vampires that took away his family. Of course he wanted me dead, but realised that siding with me was the only way to stop Dratshev. We worked together and he attacked the cave from the outside whilst I attacked from within. I took the heads of two of The Vampires before I was stopped. The Mujahedeen managed to seal the entrance, but Dratshev got away via an escape tunnel. I followed him, but he managed to lose me. So that is why you found me waiting in a hut, waiting for the cave to be found and opened."

"The others have been what, hibernating?"

"Like Russian Bears in winter. The facility was designed by Dratshev to be impenetrable but this also made it a perfect tomb. Once it was sealed it became air tight, no living thing was able to survive in there. For The Vampires the lack of blood would have caused the survivors to fall into comas, comas which lasted until you Americans arrived."

"I still don't get why you want to stop them?"

"When a man is turned vampire, he generally takes on the blood lust of his sire. He may behave like him and adopt the same moral code. He loses himself. I am fortunate not to have gained the blood lust of Dratshev. You are not a murderer neither am I. These men are not like me, not like you. They are predatory animals; they have not survived for all these years by being polite and respecting others. They are cold blooded killers, they kill for the blood they crave but they also kill for sport. I have been with them when they have herded men like cattle into a pen and then taken their time to toy with them, tearing off a limb here, a head there. I have no qualms about killing every single one of them. This was not your fight but I am afraid that Dratshev will now be after you. You are the creature he has been trying for so long to create and he will stop at nothing until he has you chained to an operating table."

Black shivered, not from the cold. His mind still tried to tell him this was all nonsense, the nonsense of a lunatic, but from somewhere inside a voice told him to listen. A voice told him that this was the truth, that he was a vampire. It was time to embrace the new. "So what do we do now?"

"We are going to sleep, it will be light soon."

"In a cave?"

Krasnov laughed again, this time with humour. "We may be vampires but we are not savages. There is another hut that I use, it contains supplies and ammunition."

"And then what?"

Krasnov looked Black in the eye. "We find Dratshev and we kill him."

***

The gunfire had stopped as had the sound of men dying. The sound of trucks leaving had given way to an unnerving silence over Firebase Python. Hakim lay motionless under a pile of sandbags, his vision limited to an inch of star speckled sky. He did not know if anyone else had survived the Hadama attack. The sun would be his saviour, once its rays started to heat the earth around him he would move and he would escape. He felt like a coward but it had been the only way to survive, after Yusuf had been hit he played dead burying himself amongst the sandbags. As a teenager he had tried to fight back, had been made to watch as his parents were slaughtered before he had been flung off the side of a cliff. Only Allah himself knew how he had survived, but survive he had and vowed revenge. He had recognised some of the men who had attacked; they were part of the clan headed up by Ghulam Ali. The man whom in his twenties, had sided with the Russians against his own people rather than act as a warrior and drive them out of his lands. Once Hakim and Ghulam Ali had been friends, Hakim had seen him as an older brother a role model...his heart started to beat faster as he saw the sky lighten. He had long given up on his revenge but as he lay protected by sandbags his mind filled again with murderous thoughts. And then the sun seemed to explode into his vision. Hakim threw up his arms and rolled out into the open, he grabbed his AK and warily got to his feet. The vista that greeted him was chilling. The ground was littered with corpses, the buildings that still stood were splattered with blood and strike marks. Then he saw movement. A Taliban, a Hadama, he didn't know what to call it, had spotted him. The Hadama ran out of the darkness of the medical shack. Hakim slowly raised his AK. One step, two steps, three steps four...then the Hadama faltered and slowed. It looked at its hand, smoke started to pour from it, and then flames leapt from the exposed flesh. The Hadama fell to its knees as more flames engulfed its body. A smile crossed Hakim's bearded face. He walked past the burning abomination and saw another Hadama, still in the shade feeding at the neck of an American soldier. Hakim switched the selector on his AK to single shot, aimed and fired a round into the Hadama's head. The Hadama toppled away from its prey and into the sunlight, head hitting dirt and then sunlight hitting head. Immediately the Hadama started to scream as flames engulfed its face. Hakim pumped two more rounds into the vampire and carried on walking. Now he started to hear screams from all directions. He stood in the middle of the base as figures on fire, Hadamas scurried into cover, attempting in vain to beat the curse. He knew that the rounds in his AK could not kill them but it would slow them and prevent any from escaping the sun. As the sun engulfed the entire base it replaced the shadow of night with the fiery death of dawn.

Dratshev watched the monitor linked remotely to the video camera. It was one of three cameras he had positioned strategically to record the attack, the aftermath and collect data. Dratshev had devised the assault plan with Ghulam Ali. The one hundred Taliban vampires to attack the base had been split into three assault groups. One that would lead a frontal assault and two that would attempt to flank the base. It was a very basic military tactic and not one that he would have chosen if he were commanding mortal men, as the casualty rate would be high. He had personal experience of such having witnessed it first with the Romans and then much later with Napoleon. But these were not mortal men, they were vampires and as far as Ghulam Ali was concerned they were unbeatable. However each group had been given a different infusion of vampire blood. One was the control group who had received normal vampire blood, the second and third received different combinations engineered with the aim of producing a vampire immune to sunlight. After the firebase had been taken a percentage of the men had been ordered to return to their own camp whilst an equal number of each group were to stay to maintain control of the Americans base. It was not a perfect test but the biggest yet that Dratshev had been able to mastermind. Roughly thirty vampires were still in the base as the sun came up, they had been told that a real Hamada is immune to sunlight, that the only vampires to burn in daylight were those of fiction. Now with the sun washing the firebase Dratshev watched intently to see which group lasted the longest. He noted, as expected that the control group, whom he had wear black waistcoats immediately immolated themselves by standing in the sun. Their deaths were quick but excruciating as they burst into flames. The second group wore green field jackets, as favoured by the late Lion Sheik Osama. Those that were outside too perished but at a much slower rate, a couple even managed to take cover and may have survived in the shadows but to Dratshev this was of no impart. The remaining group wore the traditional black Taliban turban without either jacket or waistcoat. This was the group that he believed would outlast the rest. He had not taken any pleasure in seeing both the American and ANA soldiers cut down to be fed upon, they were merely lab-rats. He had not expected to see anyone escape, yet he did see one Delta climb over the wall. How the man had done this he did not know but the man had shown highly developed combat skills and deadly speed. As he continued to watch he saw something else that did not make any sense, another figure with a Kalashnikov.

Hakim stood his ground. A couple of Hadamas had run at him, vaporising before they had taken two steps but now one was approaching him that seemed to be immune to sunlight. Hakim felt his pulse start to rise but not with fear. He placed his Kalashnikov on the ground then stood erect and retrieved his knife, he would take this one out like a man; he would prove again that he could beat them. The Hadama came within striking distance; teeth bared its left fist swinging up at his face – a giant haymaker from a drunken fighter. Hakim sidestepped and thrust his knife into the Hadamas neck. The Hadama swung both arms violently; Hakim lost his grip on the knife and was knocked heavily from his feet. He was winded. The Hadama now standing over him tugged the blade free of its neck and leered at him, it raised the knife…Hakim booted the Hadama in the side of the knee causing it to lose its balance and then sprang up on his haunches. Moving swiftly for a man of six foot five he launched himself at the Hadama in turn knocking it to the floor. He grabbed his knife and thrust it down to stab as a flame suddenly exploded from the Hadama's right eye. Hakim rolled clear, up and back to his feet. A flame now shot from the left eye. The Hadama furiously rubbed at its eyes, its feet beating a death tattoo on the ground and then its entire body caught alight. Hakim stepped away and looked around. With the exception of the flames licking a dozen or so bodies he was the only living thing left in the base. Overhead he now heard the rotors of a helo and as he looked up he saw a Black Hawk approach. Hakim became prostrate and thanked Allah for his deliverance.

The dust-cloud kicked up by the Black Hawk made Hakim cover his eyes, as he did so two ropes dropped out of the helo swiftly followed by figures in digital camo fatigues. Immediately on hitting the ground they fanned out, HKs up and ready.

Hakim held his arms aloft and exhausted his knowledge of English. "Afghan National Army...no shoot... Afghan National Army...no shoot... Afghan National Army...no shoot..."

"On the floor!" The command came in Pashtun. "Hands behind your head."

Hakim lay on his stomach as the Americans advanced. He was roughly flexi-cuffed before being searched. One Delta member stood watch over him as the rest searched what remained of the base. Looking visibly shocked the team leader pulled Hakim to his feet. He stared at the Afghan with incomprehension. "What the hell happened?"

Hakim answered with one word. "Hadama."

Unknown Location, Afghanistan

Rockbridge expected to squint as he opened his eyes but found the outside world just as black. He opened and closed his eyes to try to make things clearer but he still saw nothing. In the complete darkness he heard breathing and craned his neck. Yes there was someone else with him. Gingerly he tried to move and found that his hands had been tied behind his back and that his feet were also bound. He twisted his legs slightly and heard a faint tap as the heel of his boot hit something solid. He moved his ankle again, again it connected. A thought then struck him. He had no idea where he was or who was holding him. He could not risk speaking. He would use Morse. He started to tap his heel: . _ _ .... _ _ _ .. ... _ .... ._ _ 'W H O I S T H A T'

There was a moment of silence then a name came back also in Morse: 'G I A N T . W H O Y O U ?'

Rockbridge tapped out his name.

"I am glad that both of you have remembered your training, my Morse is a little rusty which is why I have decided to use my voice."

"Dratshev what in hell's name is going on? Where am I?"

The Russian looked at the two hostages, the darkness to him nothing more than twilight. "You are now the esteemed guests of Ghulam Ali. If you do not make a fuss or attempt to escape, you will be traded back to the ISAF forces unharmed."

"Shed a little light on this for me. Why did you snatch us Dratshev?" Gonzalez's sarcasm cut across the cave.

"We had an agreement, which I had to honour."

"Honour?" Rockbridge's voice was laced with anger. "You disgrace your uniform and then speak of honour!"

"Yes Major, honour. Ghulam Ali upheld his side of our agreement. Now gentlemen I suggest that you both cooperate with your Afghan hosts, you are after all the only two survivors from your base."

"What!" Gonzalez tried to stand.

"Oh, that it correct you were not aware. Firebase Python has been over-run and destroyed by Taliban fighters."

"Impossible, my men and the ANA are more than a match for anything that the Talibs can throw at us." Rockbridge bristled and waited for the Russian to reply but there was silence. He then felt rather than saw Dratshev leave as a slight gust of air moved across his face. Even though they were now apparently alone, neither Rockbridge nor Gonzalez spoke. Sensory deprivation was an effective form of torture, in the pitch black they had no way of knowing if they were truly alone. Another gust of air and then a fist connected with Rockbridge's jaw, he sprawled sideways and fell onto Gonzalez. A pair of hands then lifted him clean off the ground and threw him. Rockbridge did not know when he would hit or if he had been thrown into a void. Before he had time to brace his right shoulder landed first causing him to gasp as his collar bone fractured.

"Major!" Gonzalez broke his silence then wished he hadn't as a heavy boot made contact with the side of his head. Pin-pricks of light erupted in front of his eyes.

"What will you do with them?" Dratshev asked his host.

"Whatever I want." Ghulam Ali eyes glazed, exhaled a cloud of smoke. "What would you do?"

"Eat them."

The Afghan almost dropped his pipe before he pointed his finger at the vampire. "You joke. Come on Russian, tell me your ideas, what would the GRU do with such men?"

"Bleed them slowly for intelligence and then when they could tell us no more we would either trade them or forget them."

"That is as I thought. I have a man, he has many metal tools that once were used to replace horseshoes and now are utilised to open mouths. They will talk."

Dratshev nodded but did not agree. An American lead Hostage Rescue Team would be on its way. It would be implausible for Ghulam Ali or any of his men to survive. It may prove amusing to stay and watch the battle but he had had enough of Afghanistan. He did however have another idea. "You should make a film, setting out your demands."

"Like the Lion Sheik himself?"

"That would draw attention to you as a great man. How many men have ever captured the Commanding Officer of an American base? None."

"You are correct and remember I also have the leader of a Delta Force unit."

"I am certain that both Mullah Mohammed Omar and Ayman al-Zawahiri would be extremely pleased with what you have achieved." Dratshev could see the glint in the Afghan's eye, the idea that he had planted. Humans were so easy to manipulate that he had almost lost all interest in doing so.

"Let us not waste any more time, my friend. I have a film to make." The Afghan stood and handed his pipe to an underling.

***

The hut was part of a deserted compound located in a small valley all but hidden by surrounding mountains. It had been used by a hill farmer who years before had disappeared at the hands of the Russians. The land that he had tried to cultivate had reverted to the wild and successive harsh winters and dry summers had caused what little soil there had once been to erode away giving the surface the appearance of a weathered skull. Now that the sun was high, Black climbed to the nearest summit. He squinted and could just make out smoke on the horizon from the Firebase. Krasnov was asleep in what looked like a black body-bag, behind a locked door, in a purpose built room within the hut. He had not survived in Afghanistan for so long without taking precautions and before going to sleep had shown Black his weapons and ordnance cache. Krasnov had taken standard 7.62 ammo and then added silver jackets. He had also fabricated grenades and claymores filled with silver ball bearings. All were deadly to humans but more importantly would have the same effect on a vampire. As Black sat on the exposed rock and looked into the distance he felt a cool breeze on his face and then his chest. It was only then that he noticed the true state of his uniform. He removed his jacket and counted the bullet holes from AK rounds and a much larger hole from the .50 cal. How the hell could his body have survived, it was beyond belief but now belief he had. Numerous rips in his fatigues were witness to the effects of shrapnel yet his body displayed not a single mark. A thought struck him. He lifted his vest, which too resembled Swiss cheese, and searched for the scar he had gotten as a boy when he fell through a plate glass window. He snorted as he remembered how his mother had become apoplectic, yelling at his father who she blamed for his accident. Black ran his hand over his stomach as he relived the moment and then dared a look. There was no scar. A mark that had been part of him since childhood had been wiped away. His eyes became moist as he remembered again his parents and his sister. Had becoming a vampire caused him to lose the only people he had ever loved? Had they too been wiped away? Black had no idea. It was then that he decided that whatever happened he would fight for them, but first he would fight for his country.

Rockbridge and Gonzalez were grabbed, hauled to their feet and hustled out of the darkness of the cave into the cool night air. Instantly lights dazzled them. As his eyes started to adjust Gonzalez could see that the light came from three pairs of headlights. A makeshift set had been created with a camera on a tripod, facing four chairs positioned in front of the sheer rock-face. To his shock he saw that two seats were already taken by Styles and Miller. Gonzalez could remember Miller returning to the base but after that it all went fuzzy. As they were pushed towards the seats Miller tried to stand and was pistol-whipped by a Talib for his trouble. Without a word from any of their captors, Rockbridge and Gonzalez were made to sit. Rockbridge sat teeth clenched attempting to hide the pain that his shattered shoulder was causing him. Two Talibs, their faces covered by Shemags stood behind cradling AKs. Their leader appeared and addressed the Americans in Pashtun. A much younger Talib, whose beard reminded Gonzalez of pubes, translated.

"He says that Ghulam Ali is a name you and all of the ISAF forces will learn to respect and fear!"

"If you let us go now I can promise that you will be treated fairly by the Government of your country."

Ghulam Ali's eyebrows raised as the translator relayed Rockbridge's reply. The warlord then laughed so hard that his belly shook. After he had regained his composure he replied again via his translator. "You are a famous American comedian, but you shall soon stop joking. Now you shall each read a statement to the camera and then we shall see what your own government says."

Another Talib stepped forward carrying several sheets of paper. He tried to hand one to Styles who snatched the paper, quickly scrunched it into a ball and rammed it into his mouth. Without hesitation Ghulam Ali drew a Makarov pistol from his waistband and shot Styles in the left knee. Styles screamed.

The translator again made the Afghan leader's words clear. "The next refusal gets one in the head. What is it, can you not read? Are you that backward?"

The video camera was now switched on. Apart from Styles' moans the group was silent. Each American was handed their own piece of paper. Rockbridge studied his, the hand was spidery but the English correct. He looked up to meet the eyes of his captor. Rockbridge was under no illusion that the man was capable of murder but would he really risk the loss of such an HVH as himself or one of the Deltas?

Miller must have been thinking the same as without warning he stood. "I ain't reading this. Screw you."

The round hit Miller in the forehead, propelling him backwards. Gonzalez snarled and Rockbridge closed his eyes and said a silent prayer. Two Talibs dragged Miller's body away, his head leaving a bloody trail.

"Read." Ghulam Ali said in thickly accented English as pointed his Soviet sidearm at Rockbridge.

Rockbridge looked at the note again and cleared his throat.

***

In the darkness Dratshev thought about his next move. The serum codenamed 'Chornyi Svet' (black light) had shown promise, at least one subject had displayed signs of photoresistance. The serum was derived from the blood of the elder of a small clan of Ingush in the North Caucasus region of Chechnya. Local legend had put the man's age at well over one hundred and twenty. There were many more legends in other former Soviet territories. This had lead Dratshev to tie longevity with the missing 'daylight' gene, namely the human body's ability to repair dead cells. Following this lead he had undertaken some research in Abkhazia where there had been reports since the nineteenth century of many men living well past a hundred. Some noticeable examples such as Tlabganu Ketsba had claimed to be one hundred and forty. Western science dismissed these claims as lies or mere Soviet propaganda but as with stories of vampires, Dratshev knew there was some truth. He had pursued this link over a century before but without the advancements of modern science had been unable to establish a strong enough tie. In 2008 the war involving Abkhazia, South Ossetia, Georgia and Russia had given him another 'in' but when peace had been established less than a month later Dratshev had been forced yet again to pull out and much of his new research had been destroyed by an errant Georgian artillery shell. Although he was by far one of the most powerful men on earth he was not a god and could not operate with complete impunity. He had managed to keep his existence and the existence of vampires clandestine, although he felt an unseen net slowly closing in. Involving the Afghan had been a risky strategy but he had needed the data and the chance to test the properties of his serum against American soldiers had been too exquisite to pass up. The Americans were coming and would attempt to free the hostages, he'd be a fool not to believe this yet he could not bring himself to leave. He had given the Chornyi Svet serum to the returning fighters and would now see how it would react when mixed with the existing serums within their bodies. Would a double dose of Chornyi Svet prolong the vampire's ability to resist sunlight? His hypothesis was that it would, but if these test subjects managed to defeat the Americans he would take care of them himself leaving no trace, no evidence of the existence of vampires.

Camp Bastion, Helmand Province, Afghanistan

Turner sat in the large open air food hall of camp Bastion and pushed a fry around her plate. At other tables ISAF soldiers of many nationalities happily munched away but she was not hungry.

"If you aren't going to have that then I will."

"Doesn't it affect you anymore?"

"What?" Raymond crammed a fry into his mouth.

"That all those men we lived with and joked with could now be dead."

Raymond shrugged and dipped another chip, as he liked to call them into a dollop of ketchup. "They were, are soldiers. They knew what they were getting into."

"Wanker."

Raymond spluttered. "Yes, but what has that got to do with anything?"

"Don't you care at all?"

"Grow up Paige."

"What!" Now it was her turn to become defensive.

"Of course I bloody care, but what can I do? I was one remember, I used to be a squaddie. I thought I was going to die in Iraq but I had to focus, had to cut away when my mates got mashed up by IEDs. That's what I'm doing now. Paige, keep the tears for the soddin camera, get your BAFTA or whatever it is you want. But for your own sanity just switch off when the camera does. You want to cry? Do so on your own. Me? I'll cry when I get home with a bottle of single malt."

She folded her arms and for a while did not speak as he continued to eat from her plate. "Maybe I'm not like you. I can't just stop thinking about something because I choose to."

"You are a woman." He saw her nostrils flare and held up his hand to stop her from exploding. "What I mean is that as a woman you are more sensitive than I am, you care more."

She took a deep breath, placated. "What do you care about?"

"You. I care about you Paige."

"And I thought you just wanted to screw me?"

Raymond reddened. "I don't know how to answer that."

"Honestly."

"I don't just want to screw you."

"Thanks."

Raymond pointed. "Look."

Turner followed Raymond's finger to the CNN News team who suddenly seemed very excited. The reporter, Greg Salmon was getting ready to do a piece to camera.

"Now what do you think they know that we don't?"

"Looks like something we should know." Turner stood and walked towards their table. "Greg, what gives?"

"What no internet connection Paige? The Taliban has released a hostage video; they've got the CO of Firebase Python and three other Americans." Salmon could see how shocked she was. "Didn't you just get back from there?"

Turner nodded then returned to her seat. She was in shock, actually in shock. Her fears were now confirmed. "The Taliban have Rockbridge."

"Shit...if they've got him it means they've got the base and if that's the case then..."

"Everyone's dead." She felt her whole body start to shake; she didn't want to lose it not here in front of her colleagues and the ISAF soldiers. "Take me to our room."

Raymond nodded and for once did not even think of making any innuendo.

Matthers hung up phone and then hung his head. Why him, why his command? A media coup for the Taliban; the impossible possible. But the Taliban had made a mistake, one that even the most unsophisticated insurgent would have avoided at all cost. The hostage video had been uploaded directly via an Iridium satellite phone and as such the NSA's Echelon monitoring program had 'pinged' it. JSOC had already tasked several drones to overfly the surrounding area and the feed from the US satellites going back twelve hours was being studied. He had no doubt that the hostages would be found it was just a matter of if they would be alive. The demands on the video, even if realistic would not be met as the US 'did not negotiate with terrorists'. As it happened the demands were anything but realistic. The leader of the Taliban group called for the immediate departure of all ISAF forces from Afghanistan, the immediate release of all prisoners held at Guantanamo Bay and the immediate recognition of the Taliban as the true government of Afghanistan by the United Nations. And the time scale for all of this? Immediately, by midnight Kabul time. The hostage takers were nothing if not ambitious but it wasn't their demands that had caught the attention of the world but the fact that they had executed a Delta operative. In the good old days news could have been suppressed but now it was impossible, take down one website and another would instantly pop up to replace it. Matthers stood and paced. It did not make sense. Why get such HVHs and then give away your position? It was almost as if they wanted to be found, as if they wanted a fight. He shook his head; did the Taliban actually believe that they could spring a trap? That they could out-fox the resources of ISAF with a few men wearing dresses armed with AKs? What was the plan, try to take down a helo or perhaps kill the hostages and blame ISAF? He had no idea but he also had no time. He checked his watch; a Delta team would be going in within the hour. They had already been given valuable 'HUMINT' by the only survivor of the attack, an ANA soldier who claimed to know exactly who was responsible and where they were based. This was being crosschecked against the satellite and drone feed. Feed…food; that always helped. He left his office.

***

No sooner had the sun set than Krasnov appeared and readied their arsenal. Now they had taken the Toyota and were en route to attack the Taliban base. It was another cave system known to Krasnov; he had used it before, when he had been an ally against the West. If Dratshev was still in Afghanistan Krasnov had bet that he would be with his pet Taliban warlord, Ghulam Ali.

Carefully strapped to the back of the Toyota their bespoke ordnance could have passed for 'bling' on an MTV rap video. This included two modified RPGs with silver filled and coated shells, a box of silver fragmentation grenades, a Russian Dragunov sniper rifle and an AK47 each with 1000 silver jacketed rounds.

"I've had a long time to prepare for this war; I do not intend to lose." Krasnov stated dryly as they pulled away. "They will expect to be attacked with conventional weapons so we shall have the advantage until they realise that we are outnumbered."

"How many men does this warlord have?"

"Around his base perhaps two hundred, that he can call upon to take arms against ISAF? That could be thousands, remember you Americans are not at all popular here."

"You know this man how?"

"He was in league with Dratshev during the occupation; that is how he survived and gained his power."

"And now he has a vampire army?" Black looked down at the brown robes, the Shalwar kameez that Krasnov had given him to disguise his appearance and smirked. "I've never dressed as a woman before."

Krasnov shook his head. "Is that the American sense of humour? Beware of these 'women' we shall be attacking. They are fanatical fighters and now believe that they cannot be beaten."

"No one is invincible."

"Very true; and not many are immortal but they are and as such are highly dangerous. If you are having second thoughts you need not come. I must go as I have vowed to stop Dratshev. It is my duty."

"And it's my duty to avenge all those Americans they slaughtered like animals."

"That is as I thought. Very well we shall both have our revenge. Remember this, Dratshev is mine."

"O.K." But Black had not agreed. If the Russian came within striking distance then Black would take him out. "How much further is it?"

Krasnov shrugged. "In miles I do not know, but it is perhaps another four hours if Ghulam Ali has not blocked the road or the ISAF forces do not intercept us."

In Black's internal battle to accept himself as a vampire he had forgotten all about IASF's eyes and ears in the sky. They had already sent one Hellfire missile into the Python, they must have been watching. "What if ISAF get there first?"

"Then our task is easier."

"But if they send in troops?"

"Then we shall truly see what they are made of. What did John Wayne say, their 'true grit'."

Black shrugged, his dad used to watch John Wayne films. He preferred Jason Bourne.

From his ledge near the very top of the peak, Ghulam Ali looked down at the valley below. His compound, his home was clearly visible by the light of the full moon. His choice to kowtow to the ISAF forces had been a deliberate one. As a tribal leader he'd had nothing to fear from the ISAF forces but as a Taliban commander they would have eliminated him. He had played the long game of pretending to accept the Americans into his home, of abiding by their 'rule of law' and of giving them just enough information on insurgent activity that they believed him to be on their side. Ghulam Ali had been convincing. He had learnt this skill when the Soviets had first invaded and given an ultimatum to all Mujahedeen to accept the new Afghan government they had installed or find themselves on the receiving end of a red army bayonet. Tribal groups were torn apart as some chose to collaborate whilst others vowed to fight for the removal of 'the Russians'. Ghulam Ali chose to bow to the mighty Soviet Union and it was then that he met Dratshev and was given yet another choice, assist or die. Again he collaborated and was well rewarded. When the Soviets finally left his country he had gained enough status and power that he feared no retaliatory attack by any other Mujahedeen faction and then the Taliban had arrived and another deal had been struck and an allegiance formed. Ghulam Ali viewed himself as a master at hiding his true allegiance, but when ISAF had found Dratshev's cave he decided he no longer cared for the charade. An old agreement had come into force, he

ALEX SHAW

would alert Dratshev. Contacting the Russian had been easy and the reward far exceeded all his expectations. Now he had real power, now he would show the West that Afghanistan was not theirs to control, Allah was his true master. As he basked in the prospect of his future glory he saw a distinctive dark shape in the night sky, an American helicopter. It came in fast, low but almost soundlessly and then seemed to hover just off of the ground, disgorging soldiers into his compound. His anger exploded, consuming his entire being. How dare the infidels, desecrate his house! The last foreigner to see inside his home had been that English woman reporter who was nothing more than a travelling prostitute. He had felt unclean for days after her visit but knew that not to agree to a meeting would have been tantamount to turning his back on IASF. Now however this was different, these men were attacking his house and as such the house of Islam. They would pay heavily for this insult. As he watched he saw one explosion and then another. The flames seemed to be magnified tenfold in the night sky. The IEDs planted around his compound for protection had worked. His anger turned to glee. The Americans were predictable and had thought that brute force alone would prevail.

Silently Dratshev appeared. "I hear the American's have arrived."

"Yes my Russian friend, as you said they would."

Dratshev knew it will not be long until their 'eyes in the skies' found the caves. He had no doubt that their progress had been watched with digital pupils. ISAF, in particularly the Americans relied too heavily upon such trickery. Machines were not men, men died, men made mistakes but machines too failed and they failed to interpret. The machines would lead the Americans to them but would also lead them to their death. Their machines had no answer to his Vampires; some of the Afghan's men too would die from lucky rounds severing necks or perhaps being vaporised by ordnance. And then the American soldiers would arrive, mortals against immortals. It would be a charnel house.

Dratshev looked at the self-important tribal elder. "You will stay here?"

"Of course, my place…is with my men. We shall now make another film, shoot another hostage, perhaps a real one? Show the American's that they have made a mistake by not negotiating."

"I understand." Dratshev had learnt that the Afghan had sent his family to stay with cousins over the border in Pakistan, a safe haven at least from sanctioned ISAF attacks. He had thought the man himself may leave but now saw that Ghulam Ali believed he was unbeatable.

"You have been a man of your word, a true 'comrade'." The Afghan placed his large hand on Dratshev's shoulder.

The Russian vampire nodded but inside he felt nothing. The Afghan was a research tool and nothing more.

Hakim had wanted to enter the compound but the Americans had refused, they were the experts at detecting and dismantling IEDs. Back at Firebase Python Hakim had attempted to tell the Americans of the Hadamas but they had not understood or perhaps not wanted to. They had then checked the bodies of the fallen and the charred remains of the Hadamas but had not believed what they had seen. The Americans had however taken photographs and videos. Hakim had given up with any explanation, if the Americans were going to attack those responsible, then that was all he wanted. He knew the exact location of the caves used by Ghulam Ali; they were the same caves that both men had played in as boys. Now he hoped that their childhood playground would become a tomb for his old friend. The Americans readied to detonate another IED. They were well aware that they were being watched and were acting as a decoy for the assault from the HRT which was about to take place.

"I see the explosion, that's our signal." The pilot dipped the collective and the UH-60M Black Hawk highly modified for Special Forces operations plunged towards the unforgiving rock-face. Ropes dropped and immediately the HRT fast-roped onto the rear of the target. Fanning out they looked for targets as the helo rapidly retreated into the darkness. Motionless they waited and listened. The distant show had taken the attention of the Taliban, covering the Delta teams approach to target. A pair of Talibs appeared on the ridge in front of them; casually smoking their backs were squarely to the Deltas as they stared out over the valley. Another flash engulfed the distant compound and the Talibs were cut down by well-placed silenced rounds. Ibanescu, the team leader call-sign 'Gypsy' then double tapped the skull of each x-ray. The team advanced towards the cave entrance. Hastily acquired surveillance shots had shown them that this was the only entrance. The satellites were wrong. Ibanescu flipped his NV goggles down over his eyes he spoke quietly into his comms mike. "On me."

"How did you know?" Black asked Krasnov as Ghulam Ali's head centred in the Dragunov's telescopic site.
"This place is where 'The Vampires' rid Ghulam Ali of those who would not accept his rule. Some they drained of blood instantly and others they let live whilst they were experimented upon. A lucky few were thrown over the cliffs untouched."
"You were part of this?" Black felt like putting a bullet in Krasnov.
"I was the one who threw them over the cliff, some survived. It was all I could do."
Black focussed again on the Afghan warlord. It was still alien to him to be able see at night without an NV scope. He also had not used a Dragunov before, his .50 cal was a different beast being heavier and packing a larger round, but one thing they both shared was a semi-automatic function. "How does the silver alter the trajectory of the rounds?"

"They are heavier due to the extra jacket and they are of limited use over any real distance."

"Are saying that your silver rounds don't work?"

"Niet. What I am saying is that they may not fly straight. After the silver is cast it shrinks as it cools, it deforms and pits. This poses a problem for accuracy. These rounds are best used at shorter distances on semi-automatic."

Black grunted; it was still better than nothing. He needed to site the rifle with the heavier round but without the chance would just have to aim high and hope for the best. "If I had my Barrett I could take him now."

"If I had breasts I'd be called Olga."

It was the first time he had heard the Ukrainian joke and signalled the last of the pre-mission nerves. As he and Krasnov scanned the cave entrance and surrounding area they counted two vehicles concealed under camouflage netting and grasses on the access road and four sentries. Krasnov's estimate at the size of the opposition made Black worry. If Ghulam Ali had a couple of hundred men where were they? Were they concealed within the cave network, if so that would make the complex potentially larger than even Tora Bora. "So why didn't Dratshev base his research here?" Black asked.

"The cave system was too large not remote enough, he did not want somewhere that the locals knew the layout of better than us. So Dratshev made a cave within a cave. I know what you are thinking, and you are correct there could be several hundred men within that mountain."

"Great."

"The sooner we move the sooner we can start to count them."

"OK, let's do it."

"Davai…Davai…" 'Go…Go…' Krasnov answered in Russian.

Black was about to stand but saw a movement in the distance. He looked again through the Dragunov's scope and spied figures dressed in US fatigues. "Wait one."

"What can you see?" Krasnov hovered on his haunches.

"Looks like an SF team, could be Delta or ST6."

"So ISAF has chosen to attack?"

"Not enough men for an attack, looks more like an HRT."

"Or perhaps a Kill/Capture? We cannot get there before the Americans so we must wait for them to draw the Taliban's fire." Black continued to watch the team move. "Hell no, I'm not going to let any more Americans get taken out."

"What do you suggest?"

"We join them." Without waiting for Krasnov's approval Black stood, slung the Dragunov on his back and picked up a short stock AK47. "On me."

"As you wish." Krasnov grabbed his own AK, slipped an RPG precariously onto his back with an improvised strap and followed Black.

Their vantage point was less than a half a mile away from the cave entrance and only accessible on foot. Krasnov's Toyota was hidden, ironically, behind the rusted and burnt out shell of a Soviet T-72 battle tank on the side of the approach road. They had left some ordnance stashed in the back, taking only extra ammo for their Kalashnikovs and several silver frag grenades each. They tactically approached the target, first climbing down from their peak and then ascending the next. Black felt his thighs burn but Krasnov seemed immune as he moved with the agility of a mountain goat, ignoring the sheer drop on either side. Black raised his hand in a fist and crouched. Immediately Krasnov dropped. A Talib appeared with his AK slung over his shoulder. The man looked around before lifting up his long shirt and urinating. If he had been turned vampire the shadows would offer no concealment for Black or Krasnov. Before Black could react, Krasnov stood and casually walked towards the man as he adjusted his robes. Shocked the Talib tried to reach for his gun as Krasnov thrust his knife into the Talibs throat. The Afghan grabbed his neck and stumbled as blood poured from the large gash. Before he could make a sound Krasnov pushed him over the side of the mountain. If he was mortal he would die and if not he would have a long walk. They paused now and listened before moving on. As they crested a rise the cave entrance came into view as did the Special Forces team. The Americans moved as shadows towards the two Afghans who stood sentry. Soundless muzzle flashes were the only indication at this range that rounds had been fired as the sentries crumpled. The team pushed forwards and into the cave minus two who took the place of the guards. A minute later Black raised his arms above his head as he reached the flat plateau signalling the entrance to the cave complex. Silenced rounds hurtled towards them. Krasnov hit the dirt, flattening himself whilst Black ducked behind a boulder. Barely audible above the sound of the Afghan night feet crunched towards them. Black lay on his stomach; he could smell the rifle now and knew he had a millisecond to react before the shooter decided what to do. As fast as he could he rolled and kicked out with his legs, sweeping the American off of his feet. Black sprung up and grabbed the American's throat with his right hand and his HK with his left.

"I'm Delta, call-sign Peter Pan." Black said as the other soldier struggled but could not move. Black repeated the words again as a rifle but crashed into his shoulder knocking him sideways but not loosening his grip. "I'm…DELTA!" Black hissed.

"Identify yourself!" The order was spoken into his ear as the muzzle of an HK burnt his temple.

"Call-sign Peter Pan." Black let go and was then pushed facedown whilst his wrists were flexi-cuffed.

"You shittin me right?" Gloved hands pulled him into a sitting position.

Black looked at the two Americans, faces hidden by NVGs and nomex hoods. "I escaped the attack on Python, I'm Peter Pan, Brad Black!"

"Black, I know who you are. Nomad, untie Peter Pan."

"DJ, that you?"

Frankie Bones, call-sign DJ nodded. "Affirmative, now what the crap are you doing here?"

Black rubbed his shoulder. "Vengeance."

Dale Hicks, call-sign Nomad tapped Black's shoulder. "Just a kiss."

"I'm fine." Black shrugged him off and stood.

"Was he with you?" DJ pointed to Krasnov who lay face down with several bullet holes in his robes.

"Yes."

"Shit." DJ shook his head.

"Do not worry." Krasnov slowly started to rise until he was standing. "They are better shots than I had expected."

"What the? Never mind. Black, I don't know what you are playing at but you need to stay here. My team's been sent to rescue Rockbridge and the others."

"What?"

"The hostages, dumbass. Now sit tight."

"You don't know what you are up against."

"I think we have a fair idea…" A burst of AK fire rang out. Krasnov turned, saw the two Talib sentries on their feet only meters away and returned fire. The silver rounds from his AK sent them to oblivion.

Black thought fast. "The Talibs are wearing a new type of Russian vest that normal rounds don't penetrate. Look we need in on this."

"OK." DJ pressed his comms switch. "DJ to Gypsy, over."

There was a single squelch of static as a reply.

"Have two to send in, repeat two to send in. Peter Pan and a friendly. Confirm you understand."

Another hiss of static.

"OK, go."

Dratshev remained still whilst Ghulam Ali flinched at the sound of the gunfire below. The real assault had started. The Afghan warlord ordered the hostages to be moved and swiftly scuttled along the escape tunnel towards the trucks. He burst into the night air as the shockwave from a large explosion forced the air out of the cave. Ghulam Ali was thrown against the side of his own pick-up, his temple hit metal and his world became a cold black. Dratshev remained above on the ledge, motionless and listened, his hearing sharpened by centuries of development. The American helo that had delivered the HRT had retreated a safe distance and was waiting, 'rotors warm'. He withdrew into the cave and headed towards the sound of gunfire, lifting his greatcoat he retrieved his Spetsnaz issue Bizon-2, its sixty four round magazine making it a perfect CQB weapon. As he moved deeper into the cave his eyes instantly adjusted to the lack of ambient light, complete blackness became twilight. He heard the groans of the American hostages as they were kicked, shoved and moved, he did not follow rather continued to head for the fire-fight.

Black and Krasnov moved swiftly into the chamber, the fear of darkness and of death did not enter their thoughts. The distinctive barking of AKs in the distance let them know that the Delta team had been compromised. Now that the element of surprise had been lost, the hostages would only be alive if their jailors wished them to be so. The chamber started to dip before it rose and then widened. Cordite fumes scratched at Black's throat as they neared the fire-fight and then they saw the Delta team. The Americans were pinned behind a rock-fall whilst rounds rained down at them from a fortified barricade made up of even larger boulders. Two Talibs were on the ground in between the opposing positions and trying to get at the Americans. Each time either would move another round would floor them again. Meanwhile the other Talibs were firing on full automatic; rounds flew in all directions ricocheting from floor, walls and ceiling.

"Identify yourself!" The command was yelled at Black and Krasnov by the Delta operative acting as 'tail-end Charlie'.

"Peter Pan." Black shouted as they both dropped to their haunches, palms exposed. "Plus one."

"Come." The American beckoned the pair nearer and then pushed them towards the team leader.

"Gypsy!" Black shouted once within yelling distance. He was relieved that he knew the man in charge.

"Can you explain why it's like we're shooting friggin 'bb' guns?" The Delta team leader watched two more rounds hit a Talib who staggered before getting up once more.

"They've got some sort of new vest." Even Black knew it was unbelievable.

"Bullshit."

"Where's your family originally from Gypsy?"

"What? Romania." Ibanescu replied not understanding why Black has asked.

"Which is most famous for?"

Ibanescu turned his head to look hard at Black. "Strigoi – vampires? More bullshit."

"Headshots slow them down, sever the neck and you will stop them."

"Who are you?" Ibanescu pointed a nomex gloved finger at Krasnov.

"Spetsnaz."

Under covering AK fire a Talib jumped over the barricade and ran at them. Krasnov popped up and delivered a three round burst into the Talib who was floored instantly. The Taliban fire intensified and like WW1 trench warfare a group of Taliban fighters charged over the top at the Delta team. Black unclipped a grenade waited for two seconds and then hurled it. It exploded as soon as it landed shredding three of the advancing vampires.

An explosion greeted Dratshev as he reached the first kill zone. Ahead the cave opened up into a larger chamber that had been barricaded by the Taliban to form a bottle neck with two fields of fire. Anyone entering the kill zone would have no chance of survival. The fortification would defeat most conventional weapons. The cave system itself could only be defeated by a thermobaric bomb or a GBU-28, tunnel buster. These however would never be used when American lives were at risk. Dratshev looked on as a solitary grenade gently whistled over the top of the barricade. It hit the rock-face to one side exploded, harmlessly he thought but then something unexpected happened. The nearest group of Talibs started to scream and then one fell sideways. Dratshev moved nearer and came to an abrupt halt. He could see shards of silver that had left one Taliban vampire dead and two more bleeding uncontrollably. As he tried to reason what had happened another grenade dropped. Dratshev ran, using every last bit of his supernatural speed. The shockwave caught the soles of his boots and nothing else. He chanced a look back and saw more dead. This had to be the work of Krasnov! No one else would know about the vampiric intolerance to silver. Dratshev walked away, he no longer had any desire to stay and fight. He would find Krasnov and face him on his own terms.

Stunned Ibanescu told his men to hold their fire as Krasnov and Black went to work. Krasnov nodded at Black and then fired a three round burst, Black leapfrogged the Ukrainian's position and got to the Taliban barricade. He pressed himself against the rock immediately next to a firing position. When the echo of Krasnov's rounds died a Talib stood up to take a shot. The barrel of Black's AK at point blank range sent a silver jacketed 7.62mm round into the vampire's temple. Black vaulted over the barricade and searched for targets. He sprayed a further two vamps who dropped before firing another round. He felt a hot stab of pain in his left leg and fell to one knee. Two more rounds hit him in the back sending him sprawling. A controlled burst of AK rounds just missed Black as Krasnov sought out the attacker. The last remaining vampire crumpled and fell.

"Are you OK?" Krasnov extended his hand.

Black grabbed it and pulled himself up. He tasted blood in his mouth and felt hot daggers of pain ripping at his chest and thigh. "Getting used to being invincible."

Ibanescu joined them. "Which way now?"

Krasnov sniffed the air, Black frowned. "Some senses develop further over time. The Vampires are near. Follow me".

They edged further into the cave complex, a line of the elite lead by an immortal Ukrainian. It was eerily quiet until they came to what Black could only describe as a crossroads, two chambers met with tunnels leading in opposite directions. Krasnov froze then quickly took several steps backwards as he heard the sound of feet slapping the rock floor. A group of 'Talib-vamps' ran past. "That is another exit route."

"The recon imagery only showed one entrance and exit." Ibanescu peered along the tunnel.

Krasnov grunted. "Your satellites are wrong."

"So where are the hostages?"

"Gone."

"How do you know?"

"There scent is no longer here."

"Shit." Ibanescu signalled over two team members and sent them along the corridor.

Black turned to Krasnov. "And Dratshev?"

Krasnov shook his head then put out his arm to block Black's path as he sniffed the air. "Wait, there is another scent."

"What?"

"Non-vampire, human."

"The Afghan boss-man?"

"It is not Ghulam Ali, I would recognise his scent. There are several scents." Krasnov moved again and Black followed. "This way."

The Deltas split into two groups, one headed to secure the exit and contact ISAF whilst the second followed Krasnov's lead. The chamber became wetter and lead Krasnov's group down until they crossed an underground spring. It was then that they heard the moans. Krasnov waded through and ducked under a curtain of low stalactites. Seeing the Afghan prisoners he had no choice but to feed. In a frenzy he bit the neck of the nearest and drank as much blood as he could before Black appeared behind him. They made eye contact before Black turned away repulsed and Krasnov wiped his mouth. The remaining two prisoners stared back at them, blind in the pitch black.

"What the hell?" In the green world of his NVGs Ibanescu saw the two prisoners in chains and the bodies of four others.

Krasnov addressed Ibanescu. "This is where Ghulam Ali keeps those who have offended him, rapists, thieves and adulterers."

"Sadistic shits."

"Your men could take days to survey this cave system and still not find all the Taliban. There are numerous places for an ambush I suggest that we get out and re-group."

"Again, how do you know the hostages are not here?"

Krasnov shrugged. "Would you keep a valuable asset here?"

"Guess not."

After freeing the prisoners the group retraced their steps. The slightest lightening of the gloom signalled that they were approaching the exit and the moonlight. Ibanescu managed to get a signal on the comms net. "ISAF has a drone following the hostages. We are being ordered RTB; that includes you two. Helo ETA in three."

"OK."

Ibanescu exited the cave.

Krasnov looked at Black. "We have two hours till dawn. I could reach the truck but not much further."

Black starred at the Ukrainian. "You killed that prisoner in cold blood. You ate him like a rabid dog."

"No. I fed from him like a vampire. This is the reality of who we are."

Black felt a hard rage tear through him but knew it was the truth. "What now?"

"I cannot travel with you. I shall stay here until nightfall. I have an idea where the hostages are being taken."

"Where?"

"Ghulam Ali has another compound to the East. He is a creature of habit and if I am correct I shall meet you there. Now go and say that you lost me in the darkness."

Black looked at the Ukrainian as he walked back into the mountain.

FIVE: Unknown location, Afghanistan

As the sedative that Dratshev had shot them with started to wear off, Rockbridge became aware of the coughing of a diesel engine. Opening his eyes he realised that he was on the floor of a truck, hog-tied. He had a metallic coppery taste in his mouth and felt nauseous. His vision blurred as the truck bumped over a boulder and his head banged against the floor. He screwed his eyes up absorbing the pain which now came from both his shoulder and temple. Opening his eyes as the wave of pain lessened he saw Gonzalez. "How you feeling?"

"Like a fifty cent ho, used and dirty." The sergeant replied.

"How long have we been out?"

"No friggin idea." Gonzalez pushed himself up into a sitting position against the side of the truck

"The Taliban insurgents can't move us without ISAF knowing." Rockbridge looked around. "That's why we're in an empty truck; if ISAF take it out the Taliban just lose a driver."

Gonzalez rolled his eyes. "That's a reassuring thought Major."

"So where is Styles?"

"Maybe he didn't make it? Maybe the HRT boys got him back – take your pick. Whatever we've got to focus on staying alive long enough to either escape or get rescued."

"My escape and evasion skills are a bit rusty, Gonzalez."

"Then we gotta hope that our boys come and get us."

The truck slowed and there were shouts. The canvas back was abruptly opened and several Talibs jumped up, grabbed the two Americans and manhandled them out. It was still night but the sky had become streaked with the dark blue of pre-dawn light. Gonzalez kept his head down, submissive but scanning his surroundings with alert eyes. They were in a compound containing three single story buildings ringed by mud walls which he estimated to be twelve foot high. A second truck was parked just ahead of theirs. Taliban fighters, their faces covered in dark Shemags dropped out of the tailgate and hurriedly moved towards the smallest of the three buildings. Gonzalez and Rockbridge were forcefully pushed towards the second building and thrown through open doors. Rockbridge twisted in vain but again landed on his shoulder. The crunch was noticeable and the pain severe. He blacked out.

Camp Bastion, Helmand Province, Afghanistan

Matthers continued to watch the feed from the drone. Two trucks had moved slowly in the Afghan night away from the mountains and into the plains beyond. They had been sitting ducks for a Hellfire missile but one or both of them contained the hostages. Now they sat still in a compound which Intel had confirmed also belonged to the family of Ghulam Ali. The images from the drone showed two men being led into one of the buildings. He could not make out which of the three remaining Americans the two men were but he could confirm that they were indeed the missing ISAF men. A plan was already being drawn up, the decoy Black Hawk and the second carrying the HRT had been sent to the nearest ISAF forward operating base to refuel and await further orders. What had gone wrong, Matthers wondered? The HUMINT from the Afghan soldier 'Hakim' had been correct, the hostages had been in the cave complex but the Taliban had been expecting the Hostage Rescue Team. He still found it unfathomable, how had a group of Taliban destroyed a fire-base and taken such High Value Hostages? He didn't have any answers and the reports from both Delta teams made no sense. His spirits however were slightly cheered to learn that there was now a second survivor of the attack on the base, and more importantly he was an American. Matthers would de-brief the survivor in full on his arrival at Camp Leatherneck after the Op. Matthers screwed his eyes up and shook his head in an attempt to ward off his weariness. The BBC film maker, Turner had been sniffing around again, he'd have sent her back to London but he had needed something to look at. He smirked, that was not officer behaviour. He really shouldn't have given her any favours but he had and once then Op was over she would be demanding her interview, her scoop her exclusive or whatever it was these reporters called it. Bugger. He needed a real drink. He sipped his tea, it tasted of dishwater.

"I still don't get it Black, why the hell did that crazy Soviet stay all this time in Asscrackistan?"
In the relative safety of the SF modified UH-60M Helo, Black shrugged. "Maybe he had nothing to go home for."
Ibanescu nodded. "I hear that one. What am I going to do when the Unit finishes with me, ride a friggin desk?"

ALEX SHAW

"Join the Circus, what other option is there for a bearded lady?" Hicks slapped his team leader on the back.

"Yeah, you could follow me as a clown."

The mood on the helo was tense and the banter did nothing to lessen this. The mission had been a failure; the hostages had not been recused, but they had not taken a single casualty, which given the ability of the opposition was remarkable. Black sat in the half-darkness trying to think what to say at his inevitable de-brief. It would have to be the truth, but a sanitised version without any mention of vampires. He felt his head fall forward and fatigue spread throughout his body. His eyes were beginning to close.

Ibanescu shook him awake. "Hey Peter Pan, you ok? You're not looking so good."

Black nodded. "Fine."

Ibanescu touched his headphones as the Black Hawk's pilot cut through. "Roger." He looked again at Black. "ETA in ten."

"OK." Black nodded and then felt his eyes close. When he opened them again he was no longer on the helo.

"Black. Black!" Ibanescu clicked his fingers in front of the Delta operative's eyes.

Black sat up, a hammering in his head. The room started to spin and lose all colour. "I need...I need..."

Ibanescu held out a glass. "A drink."

"Blood!" Black grabbed Ibanescu's wrist. Shaking, he drew it towards his lips. Black's mouth widened and he sank his teeth into the vein. His eyes rolled back in his head as the warm coppery liquid gushed into his mouth.

"Black...Black...Black!" Ibanescu screamed.

Black opened his eyes. "What? What happened?"

"We're here." Ibanescu handed him a thermos. "You blacked-out on the way in."

Black took the flask but didn't drink, his eyes momentarily lingering on the Delta team leader's pulsating vein. "Where are we?"

"The ISAF FOB run by the Dutch, remember?" Ibanescu looked into Black's eyes. "You sure you're ok?"

"Just tired." Black sat up as the door was opened and a whirlwind of sand blew into the Helo.

"OK." Ibanescu shouted above the noise of the rotors. "Matthers wants to talk to us. We need to get to the comms shack."

"Just follow the guys in clogs." Hicks slapped Black on the back. Black shook his head. "Clogs…what?"

"The Dutch, wear clogs smoke weed." Hicks smiled. "I went there one time, fell in a canal."

The Delta team disgorged from the Helo. The base was on high alert following the attack on Python. Ibanescu and Black were escorted to the Comms shack whilst the rest hefted their equipment over to the mess area to get some chow and re-unite with the Delta team from the second Helo. The fresh faced communications officer, who looked too young to be in uniform handed a pair of headsets each to Black and Ibanescu before discreetly moving to the other end of the room.

"Look, we do not have much time." Matthers stated after greeting both Americans. "We have tracked the hostages to a new location. Is there anything you can tell me that may help in their rescue?"

Black had been thinking what to say and how. "The Taliban that have the hostages are wearing some sort of body armour. They only seem to be stopped by head shots."

"I can confirm that, sir." Ibanescu added. "But we could try using Raufoss rounds."

"High explosive incendiary rounds?" Matthers wanted clarification.

"Yes sir."

"Use whatever means necessary to get our people back." Matthers paused; he didn't have time to cross examine anything the Delta operative told him. "Black, who is the Russian that was at Python?"

"His name is Dratshev; he is a General in the GRU."

Unseen on the other end of the line Matthers' frowned. Nothing made sense. "What was he doing there?"

"He said he was making safe a chemical weapons cache we discovered in the cave complex. He is in-league with the Talibs sir. I think he is supplying them with weapons."

Matthers again wanted to cross examine but just said, "Ok Black. That's all. You will need to stay there until we can arrange a transport back to Leatherneck for you to be debriefed."

Black felt his anger rise. "With respect Colonel, if there is going to be a rescue mission I want in."

"I know you do but that is out of the question Black. You are to remain at the Dutch FOB. That is an order."

"Yes sir."

"Ok Black, stand-down. Go and get some food. Sargent Ibanescu I'm now going to send you over all the Intel we have on the location of the hostages. Work-up a rescue plan and get back to me. I want to get in there ASAP."

"Yes sir." Ibanescu stated.

Despondently Black handed his comms headset back to the Dutchman as he left the shack. The brilliant mid-morning sunlight felt as though it was tearing his skin as he followed his nose towards the 'mess hall'. He stopped and stared at his hands. No they were not starting to smoke, no he was not burning. Black looked up at the sun defiantly. He was a vampire, he was Ra-Hodok, he was a 'Sun-Walker' he was immortal and regardless of what anyone said or did he would rest until he had rescued his team and stopped Dratshev.

Hakim sat and ate in silence. The Delta Force operatives were brave men, the best soldiers he had ever seen but even they would be in the fight of their lives against the Hamada. He could not understand the spoken words making up the conversations around him but he recognised the tone. The

Americans were joking, releasing tension before the upcoming assault and washing away the horror of what they had seen at Firebase Python. Hakim wanted to be part of the attack on Ghulam Ali's base; he wanted to exact his own revenge on the man who had continuously in one way or another sold his country and its people to the highest bidder for the last thirty years. The man was nothing more than a dog and Hakim would kill him as one. He heard cheers and then some of the Delta members started to clap. Hakim looked up and could not believe his eyes. He recognised the American walking towards him as one of the Deltas from Firebase Python. He stood as several Americans greeted the newcomer.

Black froze as he saw the huge Afghan and then shook his head. If anyone could survive a vampire attack then it would be Hakim, the undisputed Afghan National Army 'arm wrestling champion'.

After shaking a couple of Delta hands he addressed the Afghan and extended his hand. "*Salaam.*" 'Hello'.

"*As-salaamu' alaykum.*" Hakim took the hand and shook it with a grip of iron. His face was quizzical. "*Ta sanga yee?*" 'How are you' he asked not expecting a long reply.

Black replied in Pashto. "I've had better days. How did you escape the attack?"

"I didn't. I fought the Hamada."

"The vampires."

Hakim's eyes widened "You know what they are? You have seen them?"

"Yes." Black said. "I have seen them, I have killed them."

"Sit." Hakim gestured to a seat at his table. "They murdered my family many years ago. Ghulam Ali was party to that then and he is party to this now."

"I know."

Hakim looked into Black's eyes and his nostrils flared. "What are you?"

"I am a vampire." It was the first time Black had said it aloud. Hakim's eyes narrowed as his hand moved for his blade.

"Stop." Black's hand was faster and grabbed the scabbard. "More importantly I am an American soldier. I am not one of Dratshev's men."

"Dratshev." The name filled Hakim's mouth with a bitter poison. He let go of the knife but kept his eyes fixed on Black's. "There were others."

Suddenly Black understood. "You are the one who helped Krasnov?"

Hakim relaxed a fraction. "You know of Krasnov?"

"It was Krasnov who rescued me when the Russians attacked us. He made me into a vampire." Black moved his hands away from the scabbard. "We share the same enemy."

Hakim slowly reached for a bottle of water and drank before wiping his hand across his mouth. "Tell me Hamada, why are you not burning in the daylight?"

"I am a Sun-Walker. Sunlight has no effect upon me."

"Such things exist?"

Black shrugged. "Apparently they do now."

Hakim drank some more. "I did not know that you spoke Pashto."

"Neither did I."

Hakim grunted. "That is proof then. All Hamada speak my language; they understand everything in all languages. Yet I cannot explain to the Americans what they will be fighting and if I could they would not believe me."

"How many of your men survived the attack?"

"One. And you are the only American survivor. If these Hamada are not stopped they will destroy all that is before them."

"Then we must stop them."

"We?"

"You and I."

106

Deh Rawod District, Uruzgan Province, Afghanistan

The Afghan warlord removed a bandage from his forehead and inspected the blood. His head still spun, if he had been a doctor he would have been able to diagnose a severe concussion. He was in fact lucky to be alive. He moved his eyes to meet the cold stare of the Russian and felt his wrath boil over. "You told me my men would be invincible! Yet many died at the base and many more were killed in the cave! We had to flee here for our lives! Perhaps you are not as powerful as you claim to be, comrade?"

Dratshev remained silent, the ranting of the Afghan had no meaning; all that mattered was that the tests continued. Summoning his own Black Hawk he had been spirited away by Vaha, to be with his own Vampires. As an after-thought he had collected Ghulam Ali. Now they were once again in his original test facility.

The Afghan stood and pointed at him, accusingly. "Whose side are you on Russian?"

"You are alive, the hostages are alive; many of your men are alive. If I had not been on your side you would all be dead already."

Ghulam Ali started to laugh and then coughed. "You really think that you are the one in charge here? You dare to threaten me, the mighty Ghulam Ali!"

"Let me crush him and then take his blood!" Petro snarled in Russian.

"That would be too easy." Dratshev replied.

"What are you talking about? You insult me by speaking in front of me in your foreign tongue!"

"You have over-estimated your importance." Dratshev stood and in a lightening quick action grabbed Ghulam Ali by the throat and lifted him into the air. The Afghan kicked and tore at Dratshev's hand as his face purpled. "Shall I let you live? What purpose would you serve? Any? Let us see how these savages

107

fight without a leader." Abruptly Dratshev dropped the warlord onto the dirt floor.

Ghulam Ali grabbed his neck and wheezed, fighting for air.

The Vampires looked on, as though the human were an ant. Kirill put his booted foot on the man's shoulder and pushed him further into the dirt.

Dratshev turned to his men. "The Americans will attack the compound. Are the cameras in place?"

"Da, Comrade General." Vaha replied. "Oleg and Victor are overseeing the preparations."

"Then we must make ready to move out. Petro, Kirill take the rest of our equipment and place it in the helicopter. Vaha send the second hostage video."

As the Vampires carried out their orders, Ghulam Ali scrabbled backwards to the wall and gradually pulled himself upright. His face was that of a beaten dog, but inside he was livid and ready to start a fight that the Russian would not win.

"The problem with your nation has always been one of self-importance." Dratshev stated calmly. "I stood with Alexander of Macedon when he conquered Herat and Kandahar. In the two millennia that have passed since, your people have progressed little more than rats. Then you slept with family members and donkeys, today the same. Do you have any idea who I am, or what I am Afghan? Yet it is you who call yourself mighty?"

The Afghan's voice was raspy. "Dratshev you are so mighty that you are afraid of the sun? You are so mighty that we Afghans defeated your army? We sent you scurrying back to Mother Russia, to your mother's skirts."

"Your wars, your fights are of no concern to me. They and you are insignificant." Dratshev turned his back on the Afghan. "Kirill, destroy the cave."

Ghulam Ali moved forward. "Wait...you can't leave me here to die! I am a Muslim, I am a warrior! I demand to die fighting!"

"Then you shall." Dratshev left the chamber.

Kirill opened his mouth as his fangs slowly extended and his top lip drew back. He now smelt the fear from the human and it made his thirst stronger.

Ghulam Ali raised his fists. "I shall die fighting! I shall die as a warrior!"

"Indeed you will." Kirill stated before he flew at the Afghan's neck and sliced open his jugular.

At the Dutch FOB the two Delta teams were crammed into a pre-fabricated briefing room away from the eyes and ears of the other ISAF personnel. The base was still on alert even though eyes in the sky had not reported any insurgent activity. ISAF command was being understandably cautious.

At the front Ibanescu stood and faced the rest of the Delta Force operatives. "Listen up. The hostages have been located and we are going in. Those of you who were with me in the caves have seen what we're up against and what effect our weapons had on them. Now is not the time for any of us to lose our nerve and start to talk about monsters, or super-humans or anything like that. We need to focus, suspend our disbelief if you will and just listen. Peter Pan and Hakim are the only two survivors of Python. Now hear what they have to say. Ok Peter Pan over to you."

Black stood. His throat was dry and he felt dizzy. In front of him the room swam in and out of focus. He tried to compose himself before he spoke. "Normal rounds have no effect on these Talibs, they'll knock them down but they won't keep em down. The only way to neutralise them is to sever their heads. A head-shot with a Raufoss will do it, if you don't have the ammo a standard .50 cal round will work. Either way these Talibs are highly dangerous, hard to kill." Black's voice trailed off as his vision blurred once more. He was brought back to the present by Hakim, who now stood and cleared his throat before speaking. Black translated a beat behind.

"These things murdered my family, my men and yours. They have the strength of many men. They are not human, they are animals. You must put them down. If you get near enough use your blade, cut the throat and then keep on cutting. Or even better make them eat a grenade. If all else fails get them into direct sunlight. "

"What are these friggin things vampires?" The remark caused some sniggers and came from Hank Albrecht, team leader of the second Delta team.

"Yes." Black stared back at the heckler.

"What? Ah, you ain't serious?"

Ibanescu took over again. "Yeah I know, this all sounds like junior high 'twilight' bullshit but believe me if you don't stop them they'll stop you. German if you'd seen these things you would not be questioning anything that Peter Pan is saying."

"Come on, vampires really?"

"Hey I pumped ten rounds into one of them Talibs and the mother just kept getting up." Bones stated. "He just wouldn't stay dead."

"So those bodies we saw in fire at Python were vampires?" Albrecht grimaced.

"Vampires kill your men." Hakim now spoke in heavily accented English. "Kill my men."

There was a silence. Ibanescu scanned the faces of his fellow warriors. Whatever they did or did not believe the fact was that Firebase Python had been destroyed, men had been KIA and hostages had been taken. "Now that is out of the way this is how we are going to proceed."

Ibanescu outlined the attack plan and after a Q&A the Deltas filed out of the hut to make their final preparations. Ibanescu put his hand on Black's arm. "Wait. Do you want in?"

"What?"

"Do you want in on the Op?"

"But Matthers said..."

Ibanescu held up his hand to stop Black from completing his sentence. "Since when do we care what Matthers says? He may be the current head of our SF Ops in the Sand Pit but my boss sits in an oval office. I'm pretty sure he'd want all available men in on this."

Hakim looked at Ibanescu and then said in English. "I want fight vampire."

"You must stay here. Delta only fight vampire, yes?" Ibanescu stated, trying not to sound patronising.

Hakim's face showed his true feeling; he swore in Pashto and walked away.

"What did he say?"

Black tried to keep a straight face. "Something about your mother, goats and a travelling rug salesman."

Ibanescu rolled his eyes. "Let's go."

The rotors of two Black Hawks kicked up dust clouds, momentarily engulfing them before they broke free into the vivid blue Afghan sky. The helos banked and headed towards the coordinates which were less than thirty minutes away. As they neared their target the modified Black Hawks would be running low, fast and almost silent. Team one in Black Hawk one, was again led by Ibanescu and included Black. The second team was led by Albrecht. The target compound had been under constant surveillance from a drone since the hostages had arrived. The imagery of the two hostages being herded into the compound had now been enhanced and Matthers was able with some certainty to identify the pair as Rockbridge and Gonzalez. Styles was still unaccounted for. To further confirm the presence of the hostages a second video had been uploaded to an Islamist website and was now playing on all the major news networks. The Taliban's demands were as ludicrous as before. A new deadline had been given, sunset. ISAF had no choice but to attack.

"I don't like it. It feels like we are being played." Ibanescu shouted across the helo. "The Talibs know we are watching and that we are coming. They just ain't afraid to die. Holy friggin warriors, we slot em they get to be molested by virgins. They slot us they become heroes. But what if they can't die?"

"They molest each other." Hicks joined in.

Ibanescu shook his head. "That is not a film I'll be watching, unlike Matthers."

"Gypsy, you know what we're up against and why we couldn't tell Matthers or anyone else."

"Yep. Blue sky is on our side? Shit man, it don't feel right assaulting in daylight."

At his control centre in Camp Bastion Matthers had been unexpectedly joined by a US General who'd suddenly appeared in country and commandeered an office at Camp Leatherneck, the American part of the base. An RQ-170 Sentinel was circling above the target compound. They watched the live feed from the drone based at the Aerial Vehicle Centre at Kandahar air field. As the afternoon sun burnt the scrub around the compound it was silent and looked deserted, but ISAF knew it wasn't. Destroying the complex would be an easy matter, a couple of Hellfire missiles launched from above, but with the world watching ISAF could ill afford to lose any more Americans hostages. Delta was going in and the drone would provide over-watch.

"Any idea what the glitch was?" Matthers asked the technician via a secure link who was monitoring the drone's systems.

"No sir. All systems are and were fully operational."

"What glitch?" General Hudson questioned.

Matthers answered. "The infrared sensors seemed to not be working. When the Taliban arrived with the hostages we could only make out two human heat signatures."

"Is that an issue?" Hudson asked curtly.

"Not in daylight sir, just strange that the Taliban should shield themselves."

"You said that they were wearing ballistic vests, well it looks like they are wise to our surveillance techniques too."

Matthers wasn't convinced but decided to keep quiet.

"Movement." The voice of the pilot, who remotely guided the drone from a glorified shipping container, was casual if slightly tinny. The high definition video feed showed a group of three men exit the main building. One was carrying an assault rifle whilst the other two manhandled a tripod mounted PKM. They climbed onto the roof and took up defensive positions.

"Give me the word and they vanish." The weapons officer added.

"Negative. 'Hot Blood' will engage." Matthers replied giving the call-sign of the USAF Apache providing fire support.

"What's the ETA on Deltas one and two?" Hudson grunted.

"They are Five minutes out, sir"

"Good."

The control room became focussed for the imminent attack. A USAF Apache attack helicopter popped up over the ridgeline then flared slightly as it fired 0.50cal Raufoss rounds into the Taliban crew manning the PKM. The Afghans disintegrated before they had time to react and then the roof of the compound's largest building collapsed. The threat from building #3 had been eliminated.

Black Hawk one swooped in, its doors slid open and high tensile lines fell away.

"Go...Go...Go..." The command signal hissed over the comms network.

Milliseconds later Black and the other members of Delta Force fast roped into position at building #1. The feed from the drone still said that the hut was empty save for the two Americans. Almost simultaneously Black Hawk two disgorged its team into the compound to form a perimeter and neutralise any incoming fire from building #2. Black was at the front of the snake of Deltas, who stood weapons ready in the dead-ground at the side of building #1. Black took a deep breath, turned the corner and then shoulder barged the door. It gave way under him and he crashed into the room. In less than a second his eyes had adjusted to the gloom and he saw Rockbridge and Gonzalez hog tied in the furthest corner. As he swung his HK in an arc to clear the room he was thrown sideways. Black sailed across the room and landed hard, dropping his HK 416. The air was knocked out of him but before he could register this fact a boot connected with his jaw lifting him clear off the ground and flinging him back against the wall. This time his head hit hard and even though he was wearing a helmet it jarred. Even with blurred vision he recognised the figure advancing towards him. Styles swung his right arm at Black's throat, his commando knife slashed deep into Black's skin. The unnatural speed with which Styles had attacked, took the Deltas by surprise and it was only now as Styles readied for another swing that Ibanescu and Hicks opened fire. Styles convulsed wildly as numerous rounds slammed into him. Black collapsed as blood surged from a severed vein. He and Styles both hit the floor at the same time, only to rise moments later. Black clamped his hand to his neck and could feel the hole in his throat close as he clambered to his feet.

"Peter Pan, you hit?" Ibanescu yelled but before he could move nearer a hidden trapdoor opened and vampires sprang into the room from an underground chamber. The unmistakable bark of their AK's sprayed rounds into the doorway.

Black saw Ibanescu fall and get dragged backwards into the daylight as the Delta team were forced to retreat. Black grabbed for the Makarov given to him by Krasnov and fired a double tap into the nearest vamp. The Talib-vamp fell with a look of confusion on its face as the home-made ammunition tore through it. Before Black could exchange any more rounds there was an explosion and then daylight blasted into the hut as an exterior wall gave way. Two flash-bangs sailed in through the opening further disorientating the vampires who momentarily cowered. The Deltas surged back into the hut, rounds spraying the vampires, grabbed the hostages and dragged them out. As the remaining vampires gave chase into the daylight one immediately burst into flames.

Outside a fire-fight raged. A concerto of gunfire as Talibs now also swarmed out of building #2 firing wildly. Like a plague of rats they advanced upon the American perimeter.

Inside in the half-darkness of the hut there was an unnatural silence.

Styles rose to his knees. "So you are one of us?"

"Why Marv?"

"Because I can!"

Styles lunged at Black with his blade, eyes red. Black lashed out with his foot, knocking Styles back and buying a couple of seconds as the knife caught his thigh a glancing blow. Black turned his Makarov on Styles and pulled the trigger. A silver jacketed round hit him in the chest. Styles shook as blood seeped from his mouth. He dropped the knife and stumbled. Styles put his hand on his chest and then looked at it. He scrabbled away and tried to steady himself.

"Blood...I don't understand...it's not healing."

"Silver jacketed rounds."

Styles locked eyes again with Black. For a moment both men seemed to sense their history, their friendship and the brotherly bond they had once shared and then Styles screamed and ran at Black. The second round opened up a hole in the middle of his forehead. This time Minute Man was dead before he hit the floor, permanently.

Black stumbled backwards. He had killed a man who yesterday had been his friend. If Minute Man had been turned how many of the other Deltas were now vampires? As he collected his HK he felt dizzy, his neck wound had caused him to lose blood and with it strength. He needed to feed, the blood-lust took over and any thoughts of remorse or pity vanished. Black crouched next to Styles' cadaver, sunk his teeth into his neck and fed. He felt his strength return and then he felt something else, he felt invincible. It had only been a matter of seconds but he had been renewed. Black exited the hut. The surreal panorama around him made him freeze. Team two's perimeter had just held, past this he could see Talibs burning and stumbling whilst others mindlessly charged headlong onto the incoming fire. The Deltas were keeping the vampires at bay but the lack of Raufoss rounds in anything but the .50 cal weapons meant that they continued to come. It looked like a scene from 'The Walking Dead' or his favourite game 'Resident Evil' only this was real and these were vampires. Snapping back into the present, Black immediately picked off two Talibs with silver rounds before he emptied his clip into a third.

Matthers continued to watch the feed from the drone as he saw team one hustle the hostages out of the compound to await Black Hawk one. He blinked as he saw what looked like figures on fire running around the compound as team two provided perimeter fire. Black Hawk one landed and then as soon as it was wheels up the pilot spoke over the net. "Hostages are secure. Repeat hostages are secure. Over."
"Understood. RTB. Repeat. RTB."

Team two exfiltrated the compound as Hot Blood now provided covering fire. When he was certain that the Americans were clear General Hudson calmly assumed command from Matthers. He spoke directly to the two-man crew of the USAF Apache and ordered them to deploy a pair of Hellfire missiles on the target. All evidence of the fire-fight would be destroyed.

He did not want any more trouble from Ghulam Ali's private army.

Nearer to the scene and watching his own feed, Dratshev was both irritated and perplexed. His serum had worked for mere minutes before wearing off. All the test subjects had been immolated but then something again had caught his eye. Could it be? Could it really be so? Was Ra blessing him? He watched the recording again. The footage inside the hostage hut showed both Styles and yes, it was Black, fighting to the death. But it showed not only Styles, but Black too rising once more. Dratshev slowed the tape and focussed his eyes. Black should be dead, he should have bled out but he hadn't. Black was immortal, Black could exist in sunlight. Black was Ra-Hodok…

SIX: Camp Leatherneck, Helmand Province, Afghanistan

It had been only a couple of hours since the end of the operation but Matthers was still livid that Hudson had taken command of his mission. He had now been summoned by Hudson to his temporary office in Camp Leatherneck to be debriefed. Matthers had sat and bitten his British stiff upper lip for five full minutes but could now control himself no longer.

"Classified? Are you telling me I am not cleared to know what the hell happened at that Taliban base?"

"Correct." Hudson folded his arms.

"How can that be? I am the UKSF liaison officer for ISAF!"

"Colonel Matthers, what we have here is something my President has deemed way above your pay scale. Even I am forced to be a messenger boy, and the message is: thank you for your great support but we shall take it from here."

"We General? This is an ISAF operation. WE are ISAF not the US, WE the International community. Where is any of this in the ISAF mandate?"

Hudson felt no annoyance; he knew the Brit would be angered. "Rest assured your Prime Minister and ISAF command is fully aware of the situation. Once again Colonel, your work has been greatly appreciated." Hudson stood, none too subtle a sign that the meeting was over and Matthers should leave.

"This is highly irregular."

Hudson extended his hand. "We are the goddam Special Forces Colonel, irregular is our regular."

Matthers shook Hudson's hand. "General."

"Colonel."

Matthers left the pre-fab office and stepped into his waiting Land Rover.

"Home sir?" His driver asked.

"Yes Palmer, unless you know of any good bars?"

Palmer smirked, 'Heroes' was the pub in Bastion but it was 'dry'. Both Bastion and Leatherneck were 'dry bases' which in a desert he though was outrageous. "If I knew of one I'd take you."

Matthers nodded. "I believe you would Palmer."

The Land Rover moved away from the pre-fabricated office buildings and back onto the main access road linking the US compound, Camp Leatherneck to the main British-run core of Camp Bastion. It was only when Matthers moved from one part of the base to another that he really appreciated the true enormity of ISAFs presence in Afghanistan. Camp Bastion in mileage was approximately the size of Matthers' hometown of Reading. Unlike Reading however Bastion housed thirty thousand international servicemen and women, one of the world's busiest airports with two runways handling over six hundred aircraft a day, a large helicopter base and the Afghan National Army's own Camp Shorabak. In short the drive was noisy with the roar of aircraft overhead and the grunting of diesel engines on the ground. Matthers used this to black out his anger over the meeting with Hudson. In all his years with the British Armed Forces he had never been brushed off in such a manner. He thought back to the initial Intel he had been given by the Americans on the cave complex and the specific orders that came with them. The Americans had been very insistent, Delta were to be tasked with the Op and no any other SF unit. It had seemed nothing more than the usual overbearing 'American demand' at the time, but now the more Matthers thought about it the stranger it became. There were many competent officers in his command within ISAF so why had he been 'asked' specifically to oversee the Op and why had the Deltas been requested? He had only been in post for eleven months and the Op had to go through him, officially but...but he was no fool and knew the Americans could and did often act autonomously. They owned the satellites, the drones, the Intel. Had they been pretending to abide by the rules, to play down the reason for the Op? He sat up straighter, would he now be held responsible for the loss of Firebase Python? Was he to blame for the loss of both US and Afghan lives? Matthers had never been one to panic, in fact he had never believed in the concept of a panic attack, but as he bumped back to his office in the Land Rover he felt his chest tighten. As another helo circled overhead he could feel the buzzards readying themselves to swoop down and feast on his lifeless carcass.

Turner watched Matthers arrive back at the entrance to the compound which housed the members of the UKSF. On the pretence of getting some more candid footage of the neighbouring logistics personnel and their views on everyday life at Camp Bastion, she had managed to get close enough to wait for him. Turner nodded at Raymond who continued to film a truck being laden with cooking oil, then crossed the service road and approached the guard in the small hut at the blast wall.

"I'm Paige Turner. I've got an appointment with Colonel Matthers. He is expecting me."

The British soldier studied the BBC journalist; he'd never seen her in the flesh before and had to stop himself from drooling like a schoolboy. "I can't let you in without his direct instruction Ms turner."

She smiled at him. "Then please could you call him? I would really appreciate your help."

Matthers' head rested on his desk, his forehead sticking to the metal surface. He heard a ringing in his ears, then realised it was the phone. "Yes. What is it?"

"There is a Ms Turner at the gate to see you, sir."

Matthers sat up. He wanted to be alone, in order to think but then again he also needed to vent his anger and putting the supercilious woman in her place would help. "Send her in."

Two minutes later there was an assertive knock at his door then it opened. "Colonel Matthers."

"Ms Turner. What can I do for you?"

"Colonel I've come for my story." She was brusque as usual.

"What story?" He gestured for her to sit.

"The exclusive you promised me after the rescue Op was over."

"Ah, that exclusive."

"Yes."

"So tell me what you would like to know."

Turner wrinkled her brow in frustration. "Everything but let's start with how the Taliban were able to wipe out a firebase and take its CO and several Deltas hostage."

"I don't know and if I did I couldn't tell you."

"But there must have been some indication that the base was going to be attacked, I mean ISAF must have had 'eyes on'?"

"I'm sorry I can't answer that either."

"What about the Russian?

"No comment and no clue."

"So what questions can you answer for me?"

"None Ms Turner, the operations I run here are classified."

Turner tried to control her rising resentment. "Is that it then?"

"Yes."

There was a silence as Turner stared at Matthers before she stood. "Thank you Colonel."

"The pleasure was all mine Ms Turner."

Turner left the office, went back through the security post at the blast wall and crossed the road. She found Raymond sitting on a crate looking into his camera.

"That was quick."

"The bastard clammed up on me."

"Oh?"

"He said that he can't tell me anything as what he does here is classified. The sod pumped me for Intel and now won't share any of his."

Raymond grimaced. "You let him 'pump' you?"

"Shut up. You know what I mean. Now what have I got?"

Raymond stood and hoisted his camera onto his shoulder. "You've got what we came to 'the Stan' for; you've got your documentary."

"But there is something else happening here, something big, I can feel it." She caught Raymond's eyes. "Stop it. Dirty bugger. It's always sex with you isn't it?"

"And that surprises you how? Come on, there's no use us being here let's get back to our tent – at least we can look at what footage we have."

Turner put her hands on her hips and sighed. "O.k."

The two Black Hawks shadowed by Hot Blood flew directly to Camp Bastion. The injured Deltas and recovered hostages were immediately taken to the US infirmary at Camp Leatherneck whilst the remaining Deltas were hurried away to their secure barracks to log in their equipment before being de-briefed.

As the ten remaining Deltas trooped into the briefing room, Black noticed that he was the only man in the room without even a scratch. No fingers had been pointed yet but Rockbridge, Gonzalez, Ibanescu and Hicks had seen him go down at the hand of Styles only to rise seemingly 'from the dead' moments later. The feed from their helmet cams would also show what had happened, including the fact that Styles had been immune to their rounds. Black swore silently. He had forgotten about the helmet cams, they were worn so much that they became just another item of kit. But he was a badged member of Delta Force and if he did possess 'super-human' abilities then he would use them to serve his President and his Nation. What he would have to explain however was Styles, why he had attacked. Black sat in silence and looked at the floor whilst the other Deltas yakked. The door opened and he prepared to have his ears chewed by Matthers. It was not Matthers however who entered the room but an officer that Black did not recognise. It was a General. His hair was a stark white and he carried a few extra pounds around his waist.

"Gentlemen and I use that term very loosely on you bunch of Delta reprobates; that was a job well done."

There were a few sly smiles around the room but no one spoke.

"You may be asking yourself 'who the heck I am' or using stronger words. I'm General Hudson, boys the President has sent me here to thank you personally. In seeking out those responsible for the American and Afghan lives lost when Firebase Python fell, you showed courage and tenacity. For that reason I am informing you of this personally; talk of what you think you may or may not have seen at the Taliban base or in the caves cannot leave this room. The Taliban insurgents had help from an outside state sponsored source; you have put a stop to this. What you have fought against today is a new type of enemy. Gentlemen I will not insult you by going further, but needless to say that this mission comes under Executive Order

13526 and has been rated as Top Secret. That is all for now, Gentlemen."

Black watched as Hudson left the briefing room. A moment later he and the remaining Deltas trailed out. Black didn't know what he could say or who he could say it to. Was he meant to act as though nothing had happened, was he meant to pretend that he was not a vampire? He had killed another Delta operative; he had murdered Minute-Man. He stopped, suddenly realising that he didn't know where he was meant to be heading. He was part of an Advanced Force Operations team whose operational base had been destroyed and he had yet to be reassigned. "Hey Nomad, am I with you guys now?"

"I guess, until we hear otherwise."

"That's a yes." Albrecht added. "So what the hell happened back there?"

"You heard what Hudson said? We're not meant to be talking about the mission."

Albrecht gave Black a sideways glance. "Who gives a shit what the brass say?"

The three Deltas headed towards the general area of the infirmary, away from the rest of the assaulters. The two members of Albrecht's team that had been hit by enemy fire were both receiving urgent but non-life threatening medical treatment. Ibanescu was in a more serious condition. Four rounds had hit him; two had not exited and had all but torn him apart inside. The medical staff had been frantically attempting to stabilise him.

Albrecht shook his head. "I've never seen anything like it; it was like shooting fish in a barrel. But the fish didn't friggin die."

"Peter Pan did tell you what to expect." Hicks said, putting his hand on Black's shoulder.

"Yeah but, c'mon no offence, I didn't believe you."

Hicks checked they were out of earshot of anyone else before he tightened his grip on Black's shoulder. "Tell me about Minute Man."

Black stopped and stared at the two men. "He was a vampire. He was attacked in the caves at the same time as me."

"I saw the way he fought you, I filled him full of rounds but then he got up and so did you. Peter Pan are you a vampire?"

Albrecht's chest started to heave as he attempted to control his laughter. "Is that what they were?"

"What else could they have been?" Hicks answered as he held Black's gaze.

"Come on, vampires?"

"German, you saw them, you shot them but now you don't believe in them?" Black said.

"I don't believe in the Muslim faith but I can sure kill Talibs. Were those Talibs vampires? No. Why? Because vampires do not exist. Were those Talibs as high as kites on Afghanistan's finest national export? Yep, that is what it was."

"So they were high - I'll buy that, but how do you account for them igniting?" Asked Hicks

"Hey, I didn't say I understood what I saw."

"So Black, you a vampire?"

"Are you three with Delta?" A voice asked before Black could reply.

Hicks turned and saw a Doctor who had emerged from the infirmary. "If you need to ask I can't tell you." He said flatly.

"The sergeant is not making much sense, he is asking for a Peter Pan?"

"Wendy is standing right here." Albrecht nodded at Hicks.

The doctor ignored the wise cracks and asked again. "Is there a Delta on base with the call-sign of Peter Pan? If so you need to get him here."

"I'm Peter Pan."

"Follow me. We are losing him." The Doctor marched back to his lair.

Uruzgan Province, Afghanistan

Outside the cave a vicious wind battered the mountain with a banshee's howl, whilst inside the real ghouls were addressed by their commander. "Black is the creature we have been trying to find for millennia, but the irony is that he was sired by the traitor Krasnov!"

"Then we must find Krasnov and test him, perhaps it is he who holds the answer?" Vaha the Chechen, questioned.

"An understandable observation, but the rest of us have seen Krasnov sire others, he is nothing special. The man is a traitor that is all. I have no doubt that it is Black's DNA which is the salient factor in this. And now Black is in the middle of one of the world's largest military bases. To attempt to take him from there would be suicide even for us."

"I do not agree with that." Kirill, the oldest after Dratshev stated. "They would not be expecting an attack; they believe their base to be impregnable."

"Never the less it would prove even too much for us."

"So what is your suggestion Comrade General?" Victor asked slowly.

"We know where he is now and we must wait until he is moved to a less secure location. Ghost, you have the best knowledge. What is your opinion?"

Miller thought for a moment. "Any wounded Americans would be flown back to the US via Germany."

"Where Specifically in Germany?"

"They would be flown into Ramstein Air Base and taken to the Landstuhl Regional Medical Centre."

"The infirmary at Leatherneck is well equipped but the centre at Landstuhl is the biggest Military hospital outside of the US. The two men you held hostage and any inured Deltas will be taken there to be assessed."

"And this will include Black?" Dratshev asked.

"Yes."

"But how can Black be injured?" Vaha asked.

Miller sneered. "We Americans have become soft. Black will be given counselling because he has been through a traumatic chain of events."

Dratshev let his lips form a thin smile. "Are you certain of this?"

"If I could place a bet on it I would."

"Then we shall snatch him in Germany." Dratshev had one more weapon and calculated that it would remain concealed until then. "We now are nearer the end of our quest than we have ever been. We shall secure Black and then we shall find a cure for our curse."

Vaha climbed up the slope to where their helo had been hidden next to the wreckage of a soviet era tank to disguise it from the 'unblinking eye' of ISAF. Mortal men could not have moved the rusting hulk, but he and his group were not mortal men. They were warriors who moved at night and gave away no heat signatures to be spotted by drone or satellite. They were invisible and invincible. They were The Vampires. Vaha assessed the wind, too strong no doubt for the women who flew the ISAF helos but not for him the 'vampire of Grozny'. He had earned his place with Dratshev for he had led countless missions against the Islamic militants who had taken over his homeland of Chechnya. He had flown into areas that others said were impossible to navigate in and he had personally pressed the switch to annihilate hundreds of insurgents and collaborators. Vaha was a Chechen yet whilst human he had despised with a passion how religion was twisted and used an agent of oblivion. Those who did not question had become like goats in the field. Chechens were a proud and noble race but they had been corrupted. In Grozny Vaha had been carrying out the wishes of Moscow, which mirrored his own when he had been brought down by a lucky shot from an RPG. Captured by militants he had been tortured for days by the 'Islamic International Brigade' until on the very edge of death a man he had not known had rescued him and given him a real chance at life, a chance to avenge, a chance to make a difference. Dratshev had made him vampire and he became one of The Vampires. Vaha was proud and had served Dratshev ever since. Now the squabbles of the humans meant nothing to him. Vaha reached the Black Hawk and opened the door to start pre-flight checks.

In the black of night a silent figure moved. Krasnov was a man who had nothing to lose, not even his own life. He could smell them; he had known that they would be here and had waited for them. He was going to finish The Vampires this night and then come the dawn he would sacrifice himself to the new day as an offering to god for the lives he had taken. He watched silently as the pilot approached the Black Hawk. The vampire would be easy 'prey'; his guard lowered as he was focussed on the helicopter. But no he would not take him now. Krasnov paused to listen to the sound of the wind and remembered the screams of those he and The Vampires had sacrificed on the very same spot all those years before. If he had not lost the ability to weep then he would do so now, but remorse would not stop Dratshev. What was needed was something else. Krasnov moved back into the caves, into the hiding place where he had waited for Dratshev to return. Krasnov knew the layout of the caves like no other living being for he had spent years mapping them. He had found the equipment that Dratshev had cached and had listened to their plans from a neighbouring chamber, part sealed by the fire-fight with the Americans. Krasnov had known that The Vampires would return here, a fact that he had cared not to share with Black or anyone else. It was his duty alone to stop them. Krasnov edged back along the passage that would bring him into another chamber directly above the one that his prey was in. There was a cavity in the ceiling caused by water erosion, shielded somewhat by stalactites it made for a perfect means of entry. As he neared the hole the roof lowered so that he had to fall to his haunches. He could hear his prey, above the sound of the distant wind and the running of water he could hear them, words mumbled but voices definite. He said a silent pray and spoke to his birth god for the first time since he had left Moscow and then he dropped two 'silver grenades' into the hole.

A movement caught Dratshev's eye as he turned his head to address Oleg, something falling. Then he saw a second object. Without hesitation Dratshev grabbed Oleg by the lapels of his greatcoat and used him as a shield. Two almost simultaneous explosions tore through the chamber, forcing air out and ripping eardrums. Dratshev's eyes were closed but he felt his hands being shredded, and then the fire-fight started.

Krasnov dropped through the hole into the chamber below, his folding stock AK47 seeking out targets. Directly in front of him Petro had been floored by thousands of pieces of silver ripping through him. Krasnov now saw five more figures ahead. One had its back towards him, a second was curled up and holding its head, another was crawling away but the other two were facing his way. One was American. The American open fired, sending a stream of rounds in the direction of Krasnov. The Ukrainian was too slow to avoid them all and was hit in the chest. Krasnov stumbled backwards. Now he saw Dratshev push aside the vampire whose body had protected him. Raising his AK again Krasnov depressed the trigger to send silver jacket rounds tearing towards the Russian. Dratshev fell, hit twice in the torso and once in the left arm. Oleg suddenly turned and sprang at Krasnov, his body a mass of blood, hands extended like claws. Krasnov tried to move aside but his rapidly regenerating wounds slowed him. Oleg's right hand grabbed Krasnov's face ripping through skin to bone. As both men fell back Krasnov kept his finger depressed on the trigger. The rounds tore through Oleg who now landed on top of him motionless. Kirill pulled Dratshev to his feet. Dratshev clamped his bloody hand over the larger of the two entrance wounds in his chest. It was the first time in his more than two thousand years of existence that he could not stop the bleeding. Ghost opened up again with his Delta issue HK 416, and kept Krasnov subdued whilst Kirill dragged Dratshev away. As Krasnov heaved himself up, Victor rolled to his feet and hurled a grenade. It sailed through the air and landed in front of Krasnov. The explosion sent the Ukrainian flying backwards against the sheer rock wall. Krasnov felt bones in his body smash and then the back of his head crumble against the rock. If he were human he would have died.

Dratshev swore in an ancient language. How could he have made such a naïve mistake as to go back to the cave? It had cost him two of his best men but more importantly could cost him his life and his quest. He could feel his life draining away with each step. The silver needed to be removed. As they neared the entrance Ghost took point and confirmed that there was no one waiting for them outside. He gestured for Dratshev to leave the cave. Supported by Kirill, the Russian staggered out of the mountain towards the helo.

Vaha was rotors hot and unaware of the fire-fight. As he saw the group approach he dropped out of the helo holding a side arm. "What has happened?"

"Krasnov attacked us whilst you were playing with your flying machine." Kirill's words carried an anger that Vaha had never felt before.

"Get...us...out...of...here." Dratshev was barely able to speak.

"Da Comrade General." Vaha saluted and then noticed the moonlight glinting off of the exposed bones of Dratshev's hands where the flesh had been torn away.

Vaha re-took his seat as Ghost and Kirill lifted Dratshev into the helo. Victor acted as tail-end Charlie and was the last to get in. As Kirill applied pressure to Krasnov's chest the helo pulled up into the shadowy Afghan sky.

Camp Leatherneck, Helmand Province, Afghanistan

Black followed the doctor into the hospital and was directed to a bed sectioned off by curtains. Black stepped inside to see Ibanescu horizontal with his torso bandaged. He was deathly white and his pupils were bloodshot. The two Deltas made eye contact as Black leaned over the bed.

"Peter Pan...I haven't got much time...I know what you are...I need your help."

"What do you want me to do?"

"Save me...make me like you...I don't want to die...not here...not like this."

"I don't know how, I don't know if I can."

Ibanescu grabbed Black's wrist and held it with all his strength. "What about never leaving a man behind? Don't leave me behind...don't let me die..." Ibanescu started to cough and blood seeped from his mouth.

Black's eye followed a tendril of blood as is slowly moved down Ibanescu's chin. "I can't, it's a curse. You'll be forever damned."

Ibanescu coughed again and his bloody spittle hit Black in the face. Unable to control his thirst anymore, Black's lips drew back; he then thrust his head forward and sank his teeth into Ibanescu's neck. Black felt the blood fill his mouth before he swallowed hungrily. Ibanescu started to shake as his blood began to drain. Using every last ounce of willpower Black unlatched himself.

"Thank you..." Was all Ibanescu managed to say before his body went limp. An alarm sounded as the soldier's monitors flat-lined.

Black stared intensely, but Ibanescu did not move. A flurry of medical personnel seemingly oblivious to what Black had done pushed around him and tried to resuscitate their patient. Black let himself get pushed back and away. He moved to the exit. What had he done? Had he just killed another Delta? The door in front of him abruptly opened and a man dressed in digital camo fatigues bearing no insignia shot him with a Taser X26. Black's body contorted as spasm gripped his muscles. He dropped to the floor and then a second man plunged a needle into his arm.

SEVEN: Camp Leatherneck, Helmand Province, Afghanistan

"Major I'm glad to see you back." Matthers shook the American's left hand as his right was in plaster.

"Not as much as I am. I'm surprised they let you in."

"The medical team didn't want to, I had to pull rank." Matthers sat. "How's the shoulder?"

"Busted. Can you tell me where my two missing men are?"

Matthers blinked. "Who is missing?"

"Black and Ibanescu."

"I'm confused; I didn't know they were missing."

"Well they are. Black vanished immediately after his de-brief. Ibanescu was admitted to the infirmary and never came out."

"That all sounds very odd Major, but I'm sorry General Hudson assumed command of the rescue mission from me. I have no idea as to the whereabouts of your men."

"I've never heard of a 'General Hudson'."

"He's not stationed in-country. I suggest you speak to JSOC."

"To do what, report two of my best operatives as AWOL?"

"I see no other alternative. Black disobeyed my direct order and went on the mission. Perhaps Hudson has decided to put him in the stockade?"

"Ok." Rockbridge was not convinced.

"So when are they shipping you off to Germany?"

"I'm not, if I have my say." Rockbridge held out his left hand again. "Thank you for coming. I appreciate it."

"My pleasure." Matthers nodded and left the room.

Rockbridge climbed off the cot and moved to the window. He watched Matthers climb into his jeep and head back to Bastion. As the jeep moved off a wave of tiredness hit Rockbridge and he yawned. The relentless Afghan sun felt as though it was bursting through the window and into his bones. He started to feel dizzy. Rockbridge shook his head but then he noticed that everything around him had changed colour. It was as though he was seeing the world through a crimson tinted lens. He stumbled backwards, unexpectedly giddy and then the redness turned to grey and then to black. As he slipped into unconsciousness he heard a medic calling his name.

Landstuhl Regional Medical Centre, Germany

Black started to make out shapes and then he felt blood rushing in his ears. His eyes snapped open then quickly closed again against the blinding light. His body pulled at the straps that he realised were securing him.

"How are you feeling soldier?" A voice spoke.

"Where am I?"

"You are at a medical facility in Germany."

"Where is Ibanescu?" Black slowly opened his eyes again.

"He's here too, after having made a miraculous recovery, by the way."

Black's eyes started to focus. He turned his head and he saw that the man he had been speaking to was not in the room with him but behind a viewing window. "General Hudson?"

"Correct. And you are Brad Black, call-sign 'Peter Pan' of Delta."

Black tried to sit up but the straps prevented him. "What am I doing here?"

"I think you know why. We can dance around the subject or you can just confess and we'll get along just fine. Are you a vampire?"

The frankness of the question stunned Black but he saw no reason to lie. "Yes sir. But I am also a Delta, sir."

"Did you have anything to do with the planning of the attack on Firebase Python?"

Anger surged through Black. Pulling his arms upwards the restraining straps ripped as the leather gave way. Black sat up. He raised his right hand and pointed a finger at Hudson. "Are you accusing me of what happened at the base?"

"I have to ask, son."

Black tore the bonds from his legs and strode over to the window. At eye level he glowered at the General through the toughened glass. "I had to fight my way out of there; I tried to stop those monsters that destroyed the base, Sir."

"Black I have a problem. You were the only American survivor of the attack but you are a vampire, like the creatures that destroyed the base. It was an inside job, you were on the inside. Putting it frankly Peter Pan, I don't know what you are or if I can trust you."

Black brought his fist up and slammed it against the glass. It groaned but did not break and Hudson on the other side did not flinch. "Sir. I did not attack my own base, sir."

"You killed a fellow Delta, didn't you son? You killed Marvin Styles, 'Minute Man'."

"He was a vampire sir, he attacked me."

"How did you become a vampire son? I want you to tell me everything, from the moment you went on the mission to just now when you woke up. Omit anything or lie to me and I'll know it."

As Black relayed what Krasnov had told him and what he had been through, he re-lived it. Black sat on the bed, drained. "Did you know about the cave? About the Russians?"

"Why would I share classified information with you?"

For a moment Black was speechless. "Because I have a right to know!"

"Ok, good answer. We had reason to believe that there was a cave that contained research carried out by the Soviets concerning vampirism. We didn't know about 'The Vampires' as your Ukrainian called them or indeed his presence."

"How long has the Pentagon known about the existence of vampires?"

"Long enough."

"So what's going to happen now?" Black asked.

"To you?"

"Yes."

"That is up to me. If I decide that I can use you then I will."

"If not?"

"You will have to answer for your actions son."

"Actions?"

"Crimes. You killed Styles and Ibanescu."

"Styles attacked me, it's on tape and Ibanescu is alive."

"Helmet cams are funny things. Sometimes they just cut out. Ibanescu was pronounced dead before my team took him from the camp. And there is that nagging doubt in my mind about the attack on your base."

Something inside Black snapped. He lost all respect for Hudson and the rank he represented. The fury, the anger that he had learned to manage and to focus to get into Delta was seeping out. He was going to be no one's scapegoat. He knew what he had done and he also knew what he was capable of. The question however was, were they? How much exactly did the Pentagon know about vampires? Surely he was too valuable for the US to ever get rid of or were there others like him who could survive in sunlight? Black took a deep breath. He couldn't let any of this show. He would play along until he could escape. "What is your suggestion, sir?"

Hudson was taken aback. "About what?"

"How do I show you that I can be trusted, that you can use me?"

"I'll let you know. Now you just hold tight in there."

Hudson pressed a button which made the glass in the viewing room opaque before leaving and entering an office two doors along. He closed the door and asked the man on the opposite side of the desk. "Your assessment?"

"What we are looking at is perhaps the most extraordinary individual the world has ever seen, and you Colin are just trying to 'piss' him off."

"Adam what I am trying to do is exactly that. I want to see his fangs; I want to see him bite." Hudson sat wearily in the office chair. "OK 'Professor', answer me this. How do we know that he is still one of us? How do we know that he's not going to kill us all as soon as we open his door?"

Professor Adam Thurlbeck popped a polo-mint into his mouth and sucked thoughtfully. "I've asked myself the same questions, of course I have but there comes a time in all scientific experiments when one has to take a leap of faith."

"Well what if he leaps on us?" Hudson folded his arms.

"We shall have the Taser ready. The qualities he possesses make him unique. Do you know how many times in recorded history there has been mention of a Ra-Hodok?"

"Nope. Enlighten me."

"Well it's twelve as a matter of fact, but do you know how many times the actual existence of one has been confirmed?"

"I'm guessing none?"

"A good guess."

"So this guy is unique and we just so happen to find him, here and now."

"Things happen for a reason, I know that is a very unscientific assertion to make, but finding Black now will speed up our research and our understanding no end. If we can complete the synthesization of the battle vaccine the number of lives lost will drop dramatically. The limiting factors have always been sunlight and the blood-lust. Perhaps Black can be the cure for at least one of these elements?"

"So your suggestion is that we keep him in the lab and use him as what Adam, a guinea pig?"

"We must use him to gather research."

Hudson shook his head. "I disagree. He is the most deadly combat soldier in history. He must be used as such."

"He's not Superman, Colin."

"Is he not Adam?"

"No. He can't fly."

Camp Leatherneck, Helmand Province. Afghanistan

"We don't know what caused you to black out and can't find nothing wrong with you now Major." The doctor held the rank of Captain and his scrubs were pristine. "However I feel that we should send you as quickly as possible to Landstuhl."

"Captain I'm fine. I think it must have been the heat or…"

The Captain cut him off. "Or stress or perhaps you have picked up a bug somewhere?"

"Yes."

"I agree with you, but due to the nature of where you have been and what you may or may not have been exposed to it is my medical opinion that you need to undergo further tests. Protocol stipulates that these are to be carried out at the Landstuhl

Regional Medical Centre. It has the best equipment this side of the Atlantic."

Rockbridge grunted. "So I guess I have no choice in this?"

"None."

"One question, were my two other men, Black and Ibanescu also sent there?"

"Yes Major. General Hudson informed me of that."

Rockbridge was silent. Again the name Hudson had been used. "Is there any chance that I have Ebola?"

The Doctor raised his eyebrows. "What? I mean what sir? Ebola?"

"Yes, Ebola the African disease. Could I have it?"

"Why would you ask?" The start of a smile began to crease the Captain's face.

"That's classified, Captain." Hudson used the Doctor's rank for emphasis.

"Anything is possible Major, which is why you are going to be prodded and poked in Germany."

Landstuhl Regional Medical Centre, Germany

The cell door opened and a middle aged man dressed in a tweed suit entered. He gestured at the table where Black sat and asked in a polished English accent. "Mind if I join you?"

"Be my guest." Who are you he thought?

The visitor sat and placed a shopping bag by the side of the table. As if reading Black's mind he spoke. "I am Professor Adam Thurlbeck of Detachment V."

Black smirked. "V as in vampire?"

"That's right. Would you care for a drink?" Without waiting for a reply Thurlbeck removed a thermos flask and two tin mugs from the bag, unscrewed the top and poured. He handed a mug to Black. "Best drink whilst it's warm, always tastes better."

Black noticed his visitor's hair was too dark for a man of his age. He peered into the mug; the content was a dark red. He didn't need to ask what it was.

"Cheers." Thurlbeck held up his mug in a mock salute before drinking. "Ah that's better."

Black cautiously followed suit. As the blood slipped down his throat he felt bolts of electricity course through his veins.

"Would you like some more?" Thurlbeck asked. "The flask holds three mugs, one is enough for me."

Black nodded and the Englishman poured. When Black had finished he met Thurlbeck's gaze and asked. "Vampire?"

"Yes I am but not like you; I'm not allowed to tan." Thurlbeck laughed at his own wit. "You really are something you know, somewhat of an anomaly. It's a bit like going for a swim and coming face to face with a mermaid."

"Are you saying I smell of fish?"

It took a second before Thurlbeck understood the joke. "You are funny. Yes, you could do with a wash."

"So who are you?"

"Well I'm a scientist, and a vampire."

"I seem to be meeting a lot of them."

"Really? Oh. My job is to attempt to understand what we are and how our abilities can be harnessed."

"For what? To kill people?"

"To help humanity dear boy, but this does inevitably involve 'killing' somewhere along the line."

"Wait, are you saying that I am not human?"

"Ah, I'm glad you asked that. We look and feel the same as a human but what sustains us is different. In that sense we could be classified as non-human."

"Because we eat differently?"

"Yes."

"So is a vegetarian considered a non-human then?"

"No, not in my book. Refusing to eat meat is just not natural."

Black licked his lips and tasted blood. "So you are not military then?"

"Not since my youth, and believe you and me that was a very long time ago. But I do work for your government."

"Look professor, I'm sure you are a great guy and a perfect party guest but can you tell me what you want from me? I've had enough of being cooped up."

"What I want from you Brad is for you to show me what you can do. I want to know what you are capable of. Then I want to see if I can duplicate it in a controlled environment with a test subject."

"You want me to be a lab-rat?"

"I wouldn't put it like that, but if we are being candid then yes."

"Hudson said that if I was useful I'd be working for him."

"Quite. After studying you we may be able to put you back in the field."

"Doing what exactly?"

The Englishman smiled. "Part of the job is hunting and eliminating terrorists."

Uruzgan Province, Afghanistan

The blood was tepid but the temperature did not matter. Krasnov felt as though he was falling from a great height as the rushing sound in his head intensified. Then there was a bolt of pain and he opened his eyes.

"It has been a long time, Hadama." Hakim thrust the flask into the Ukrainian's unsteady hands. "I knew I would find you here."

"You?"

"Who else would know of this place?"

"You have not aged."

"You have."

"If you live in this warzone; Hadama or not you will age!"

"What are you doing here?" Krasnov emptied the flask.

"I came to destroy them."

"As did I."

"Where is Dratshev?"

"I do not know exactly. He and four others escaped from this place."

Hakim helped Krasnov to his feet. "Then our work is not done."

"I believe it is."

Hakim scowled. "What are you talking about Krasnov?"

"Dratshev was injured; I shot him with silver rounds. He is in need of medical attention."

"Can it not just be dug out?"

"No. All the shards must be retrieved. He will also need new blood."

Hakim thought for a moment. "He has his helicopter?"

"Yes. He will make for a medical centre. The nearest one is the ISAF base at Tarin Kowt."

Hakim shook his head. "Even Dratshev would not dare enter another coalition base!"

"He is a wounded animal and as such has a heightened sense of self-preservation. He will go there and seek treatment."

"I know the location."

"But they will not arrive. Their helicopter is rigged to explode. I have placed a silver laden incendiary device in the cockpit and a second in the passenger area. They will be destroyed in the air and fall to the earth as dust." Krasnov imagined the scene in his head. First the IED in the cockpit would explode, joined a millisecond later by the second erupting in the passenger bay of the Black Hawk. Two white fireballs would then race towards the centre of the bird before meeting and incinerating everything.

There was a silence as the pair of soldiers stood, eye to eye. Their war was over. They had started as enemies, had then been forced to work together and now...

Krasnov decided to again clear the air. "I am sorry about your family."

Hakim's eyes narrowed. "You had no choice; I understand that more now than ever before."

Vaha had a smile on his face as he tugged at the collective and fought the ferocious Afghan wind. As the Black Hawk flew under radar level it shook like a giant's plaything. They skirted a compound and all but hit a roof as a tremendous gust attempted to ground them. Vaha knew that no one else had the ability to fly like him, not even America's famed 'Night Stalkers' of the 160th Special Operations Aviation Regiment. They had state of the art equipment, computers and NVGs but he had real night vision, reaction times quicker than any human and of course no fear of flying to his death. They were not far from Tarin Kowt and Vaha was enjoying the irony of their anticipated arrival at yet another ISAF base. In the back Dratshev was unconscious even though both Ghost and Kirill had bled for him. His wounds were seeping as the silver prevented any regeneration or clotting. The one thing on the face of the earth that elicited anything resembling an emotion in Kirill was Dratshev. The ancient vampire had saved Kirill over eight-hundred years before from the Mongol armies of Genghis Khan at the Battle of the Kalka River. The Mongols had defeated the Rus Army, forcing them to surrender. The Mongols then massacred every last man until only Kirill remained. As the Mongols encircled him a man stepped forward and spoke in Russian. The man was Dratshev. With a speed that none of the warriors could believe Dratshev disarmed Kirill before piercing his neck with razor sharp fangs. It was the last time Kirill had lost a fight and tonight he would not lose the fight to save Dratshev.

DELTA FORCE VAMPIRE: INSURGENCY

Helmand Province, Afghanistan

For the second time in her career Paige Turner was being made to leave Afghanistan. She and Raymond were passengers on a noisy RAF transport plane that would deposit them back in the UK. Around them servicemen chatted animatedly, eager to get home and see their loved ones and glad to be alive. They seemed immune to the rough-ride caused by the high winds and turbulence which sent the Hercules crashing up and down like a yacht in a stormy sea. As the plane lurched to the left Turner nudged Raymond, who had fallen asleep and was snoring.

"W…what?"

"You were snoring."

"For god's sake Paige. You woke me up to tell me I was snoring?"

"You don't deny it?"

"Paige, I don't care. Just let me sleep."

"I can't sleep like this, thinking that the plane is going to be shaken apart at any moment or fly into a mountain."

"The chances of us crashing are minimal Paige. Planes just don't fall out of the sky."

Turner grunted as Raymond closed his eyes. "This is bollocks."

Raymond rubbed his face and sighed wearily. "What is?"

She gestured around them "This. We're being sent home like naughty school kids."

"We've finished our assignment; we were due to fly back any day, anyway."

"No. This is Matthers' doing. He wanted us out of his way. He's hiding something Dave and I need to find out what it is."

"From up here? Come on; think about it, he's actually done us a favour. We were the last civvies to leave Firebase Python. Just think how much our stories are worth!"

"I'm not in this for the money."

"I am. I need a new car."

"Something happened back there, something that they are trying to cover up."

"Some secrets should stay secret."

"A-ha. So you agree; Matthers was keeping something from us?"

"It's Op-sec. If he tells us he breaks operational security. Whatever it is he may or may not be hiding, may or may not be harmful to ISAF if it gets into the hands of the Taliban."

"Bollocks, that's all I've got to say. Bollocks and bollocks to the lot of it."

Raymond put his hand on her knee. "When we get home I'll buy you a drink, a real drink and we can forget all about Matthers and his secrets. Agreed?"

Turner removed his hand. "As long as it is only a drink."

Raymond sighed. "How long can you continue to resist me?"

"For as long as you are married. Now shut your eyes and don't bloody snore."

Turner shut her own eyes but sleep would not come. There was a story and something inside her told her that she must not let it be covered up. How she would follow it or where it would lead she did not know.

Uruzgan Province, Afghanistan

The shaking in the Black Hawk intensified as the buffeting of the wind increased. Ghost was used to 'hairy' helo rides but this was something else. The weather and Vaha's skill as a pilot seemed to be bending the laws of physics. Ghost had no idea how they were still in the air. A sudden loss of height caused him to lose his grip and fall sideways. His back struck a black box which came loose from the fuselage. As Ghost pushed himself back into his position he froze. A thin wire was now protruding from the box. He moved towards it and his eyes widened.

"Jesus Christ!"

Kirill looked up. "What?"

As Ghost turned his head he heard an explosion from the cockpit and threw himself in the opposite direction at Dratshev and the door. A millisecond later a white fireball tore into the cabin. Flames engulfed every interior surface. The Black Hawk plummeted and smashed into ground. There was a moment of calm as the rotors came to a stop in the sand and then the fuel ignited followed by a much larger explosion from the cabin which all but tore the bird apart. Flames licked the ground and surrounding vegetation.

Landstuhl Regional Medical Centre, Germany

Hudson swallowed the strong coffee and pointed at the file on the desk in front of him. "That the report?"

"Yes."

"And?"

"Take a look for yourself, it's all very impressive."

Hudson rolled his eyes. "Just give me an overview Adam."

"As you wish." Thurlbeck opened the file and took out the top page. "Well, he is the fastest and the strongest subject we have ever tested. The attributes that got him into Delta have been vastly improved by his vampiric state. In short he makes an Olympic athlete look like a couch potato."

"Adam you are a funny man but that's a good analogy. Ok so we know that physically he is A+."

"I'd say AAA+."

"Whatever, he's physically fit etc." Hudson tapped the side of his head with his forefinger. "But how is he mentally? If we let this vampire loose how do I know he won't go on some kind of killing spree?"

Thurlbeck remained calm; he was used to Hudson's lack of tact. "When was the last time you saw me kill anyone?"

147

"You are different."

"In what way? I am a vampire; I must drink human blood in order to function."

"But you are not a trained killer."

Thurlbeck's eyes hardened. "I am six hundred years older than you, I may not have picked up a gun in a while, but I know how to use one."

"Adam, sometimes I also find you very irritating. You know what I mean. You are a 'good guy' ok? What about Black, is he?"

"In my opinion? Yes he is. When he was sired he seems to have not taken on any of the primordial vampiric tendencies, like some of the others we have seen. In fact he seems quite human, quite super-human."

"So he is good to go?"

"You mean into the field?"

"Yes."

"He is too valuable to our research, if he was to get killed or if he fell into the wrong hands it would be a disaster."

"Adam, if we followed that logic we'd never deploy drones or stealth fighters or I'd never get to take my 1955 Merc out for a burn."

"Colin, he is not a machine."

"Adam he is no longer a man. He's a weapon, and we have to deploy him."

Epilogue: Tarin Kowt, Uruzgan Province, Afghanistan

The wreckage was still smouldering as the Mounted Reconnaissance Troop of the US Army's 14th Cavalry Regiment arrived at the crash site in their Stryker armoured personnel carriers. The turret gunners on the 0.50 cals did a sweep with NVGs as the men in the first vehicle debussed and formed a perimeter whilst the group in the second made for the charred Black Hawk. The helo had come down almost on top of the highway leading south to the regional centre of Kandahar. It was Tarin Kowt's only road to the outside world and ISAF forces had been subjected frequently to Taliban attack on the exposed route. Lieutenant Jimmy Novak took his trained medic looked for signs of any survivors. In the pre-dawn light the air was still cold but even so he was sweating under his body armour as something inside him said that this was not a normal crash site. Using a flashlight they peered inside the carcass of the Black Hawk and saw only the charred remains of the pilot in the cockpit and one other in the back. Novak squinted, he could not be sure but in the torchlight he thought he saw a body a few meters away from the helo. It was not long before they discovered a total of three bodies which had miraculously been thrown clear on impact. One was wearing US fatigues.

"Bag em and put em in the Strykers. There's nothing else we can do here."

A private gave Novak a strange look. "You want us to travel back to the base with a body at our feet?"

"What is it Gaynor, you afraid of ghosts?"

The young private shook his head. "No, Lt."

"Good then get em in the back. We ain't leaving em here to become trophies for the Talibs. They are Americans and deserve to get a chance to be taken home. We'll put em in the morgue and let the doc look at em."

With the bodies loaded aboard, the two Strykers headed back to Camp Holland as the first fiery fingers of dawn appeared on the horizon.

***

DELTA FORCE VAMPIRE: INSURGENCY

ALEX SHAW

Also by Alex Shaw:

HETMAN
A Special Forces Thriller introducing a reluctant hero, former SAS Trooper Aidan Snow.

Attacked by an unknown adversary, **Framed** for two assassinations, **Hunted** by the Ukrainian Security Service, the life of former SAS Trooper Aidan Snow has been destroyed.

Teaching at an international school in Ukraine, former SAS Trooper Aidan Snow has laid the nightmares of his past to rest. But when after ten years Snow meets again the man who put a gun to his head and ended his military career his past becomes very real.

Told by the British Secret Intelligence Service (SIS) that his would be tormenter is dead Snow tries to forget...

Attacked by an unknown adversary, Framed for two high profile assassinations and Hunted by the Ukrainian Security Service, Snow is torn from the life he has worked so hard to build and must once again rely on his SAS training in an attempt to clear his name.

Discovering a mercenary brigade made up of former Soviet Spetsnaz soldiers Snow trusts only himself to stop them and save those he cares about.
Snow is left one step ahead of the authorities with no one to watch his back.

In a Fire Fight, Pray for SNOW....

COLD BLACK – Hetman 2

Abduction
Veteran SAS trooper, Paddy Fox has lost his job, his wife and his temper. Whilst bitterly job hunting, Fox witnesses a car crash and finds himself rescuing a kidnapped Saudi Royal. Persuaded by MI6 to accept a job as security adviser in Saudi Arabia, Fox travels to Riyadh.

Assassination
In Kyiv, a director of the Belorussian KGB is gunned down whilst trying to pass shocking intelligence to his counterpart in the Ukrainian SBU. Intelligence, which if verified, sets out plans to commit international acts of terror.

Al-Qaeda
In Saudi Arabia, an entire British Trade mission is taken hostage by a new, highly funded, group aligned to Al-Qaeda. But who is funding this new insurgency and why?

An International Conspiracy
Former SAS Trooper turned MI6 operative, Aidan Snow is caught in a maelstrom involving East, West and Middle East which endangers the world's supply of oil.

HETMAN: Donetsk Calling – an Aidan Snow short story

Former SAS Trooper turned MI6 Operative Aidan Snow returns in a short story preceding the release of the third Aidan Snow thriller.

As an ex-pat Brian Webb has a great life, a sexy wife and a perfect daughter. But all this is put in jeopardy when on his way home from a night of heavy drinking he is chased by a group of armed assailants. Who are his pursuers, what do they want from him and why are they shooting? Webb would rather not hang around to find out. Crashing a stolen car in an attempt to escape Webb is blooded, cornered and out of options…left with no other choice he calls the only person who would never let him down. He calls Aidan Snow.

Arriving in Kyiv, Snow takes the law into his own hands in an attempt to find and rescue one of his oldest friends. With the ghosts of the past on his shoulders Snow must again rely on his SAS training and will not stop until he discovers the truth.

***

Printed in Great Britain
by Amazon